Andy Grant

This is copy 51 of 200.

Steve [illegible]

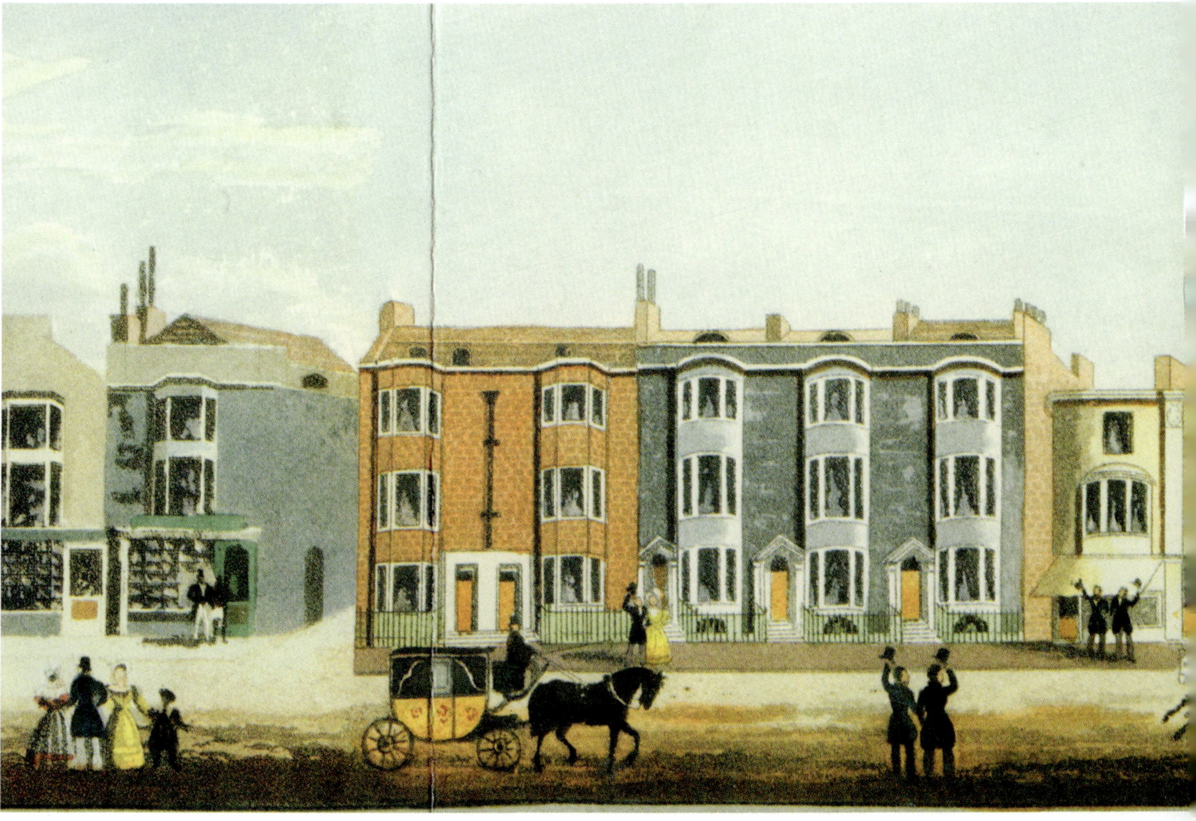

Victorian Chroniclers of Brighton

Andy Grant and Steve Myall

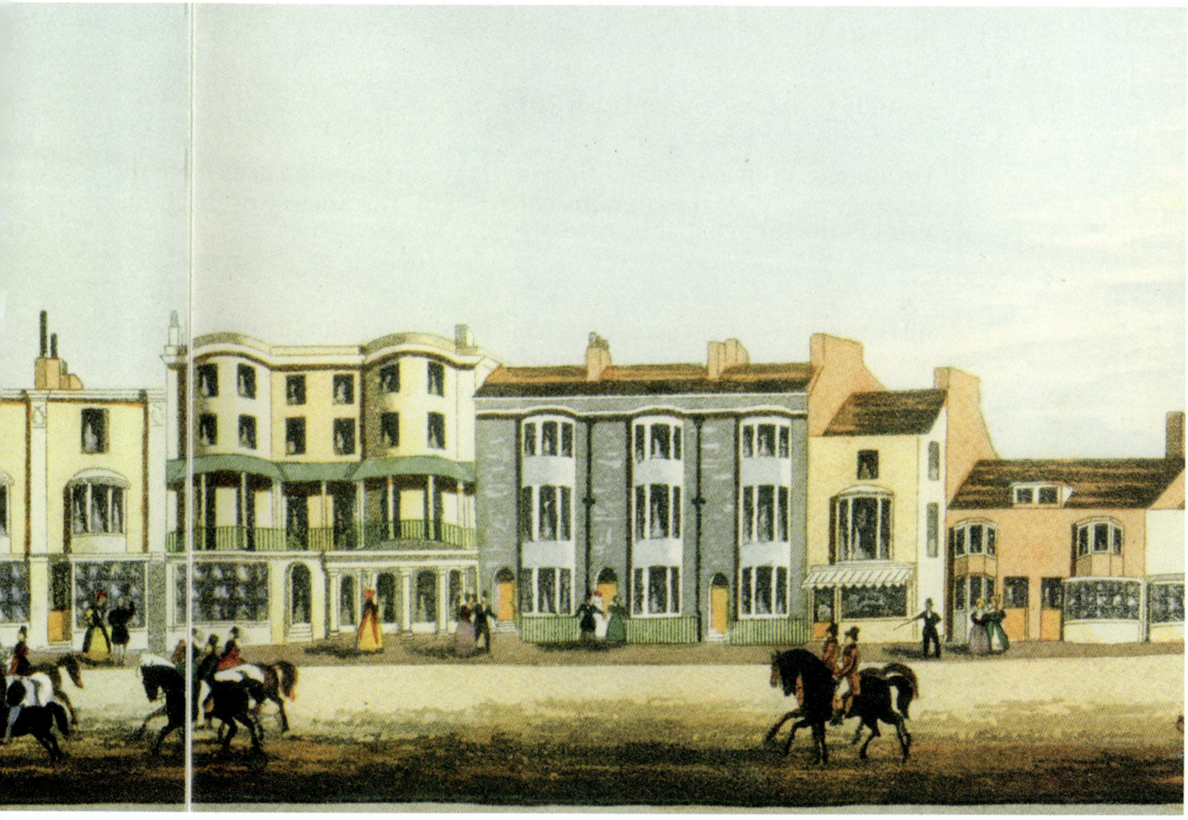

Regency Society of Brighton and Hove

Victorian Chroniclers of Brighton
by Andy Grant and Steve Myall

Published by
The Regency Society of Brighton and Hove
18 Bedford Place
Brighton BN1 2PT

www.regencysociety.org

The Regency Society of Brighton and Hove is a registered charity, no 210194

For images of Brighton and Hove and the surrounding area from the Regency and Victorian periods collected by The Society of Brighton Print Collectors visit sbpc.regencysociety.org/

Editing and design: David Fisher
Typeset in Cambria and News Gothic MT
Printed and bound in England by
Sussex Print Services Ltd, 01323 872466

ISBN 978-1-9998963-0-0

Contents

The authors

Andy Grant has been a lifelong collector of antiquarian books and ephemera centred upon Brighton, with one of the most comprehensive private collections of local directories spanning two centuries. He started his working life as an architectural illustrator for the Department of Ancient Monuments and Historic Buildings, but after six years changed careers to become a railway signal engineer. He has been a volunteer researcher for the MyBrightonandHove website for many years, writing occasional articles and assisting others with their queries on Brighton local history, including contributions to radio and TV programmes and the works of other authors. He is the great-great-grandson of the Brighton print publisher William Grant and has a modest collection of his topographical prints.

Steve Myall has been a collector of 18th and 19th century engravings of Brighton and Hove for over 40 years, and is the author of *The Victorian Development of the Clifton, Montpelier & Powis Estates of Brighton*. He spent the first 26 years of his working life with the Mayfair art gallery Arthur Ackermann & Son—the same business where, under its founder Rudolph Ackermann, W H Mason worked as a young apprentice before opening his own gallery in Brighton early in 1832.

Foreword

The transformation of the small fishing port of Brighthelmston, with its population of no more than 2,000, may be said to date from the late eighteenth century. It was then that Dr Russell's sea-cure and the Prince of Wales's residence first attracted fashionable visitors. By 1800 housing development along the sea front and to the north of old town houses between East and West Street accommodated a population of 7,000.

It was not until the second quarter of the 19th century, however, that the town of Brighton had begun to assume something of its later character and appearance. Only now did the signature architectural buildings of Nash's Pavilion, the Chain Pier, St Peter's Church, and the great housing developments of Kemp Town and Brunswick Town join old St Nicholas's Church, the Steyne and the Royal Crescent in the artists' and print publishers' images. The arrival of the railway from London in 1841 brought the day-trippers and new industrial developments further stimulated the growth in population to 65,000 by the mid-century. There were new subjects for the historian and for the print publisher.

This period of Brighton's growth has been well served by its historians. What more is there to be discovered? The answer is much more, and it is revealed in this deeply researched study by Grant and Myall. Their unique approach has been predominantly to examine the work and the personal lives of four of Brighton's contemporary chroniclers: two historians, Bishop and Erredge, and two print publishers, Mason and Grant. Much new light is thrown not only on their characters and influences but also on Brighton's civic, social and economic life in the Victorian age. Three of the four suffered bankruptcy and Mason endured a false charge of child molestation.

The greater section of the book relates to William Henry Mason and William Grant and here the authors fill in gaps in the record of Brighton images and, notably in the case of Mason, of the many non-Brighton prints which he published. Trained at the celebrated London firm of Ackermanns, Mason came to Brighton around 1830 and subsequently opened his own 'Repository of Art'. He continued the Ackermann tradition of publishing fine copper-plate aquatints and tinted and coloured lithographs. The prices, notably for his wonderful long panorama of the sea front and his celebrated Cricket Match, were expensive and his market was found amongst rich residents and visitors.

Grant, a local newsagent, published the majority of his Brighton views as cheaper and small steel-plate engravings and found a successful market among the day-trippers who could buy six small uncoloured views of the town for sixpence. But Grant also published some fine lithographs—every collector desires his pair of views looking to the West and the North-East from the tower of St Nicholas.

We are reminded once again that cultural, economic and social history cannot be confined to metropolitan London. Grant and Myall's assiduously researched and well-illustrated book is a worthy addition to the work of their predecessors as chroniclers of Brighton's history.

John & Jill Ford
Authors of *Images of Brighton*, St Helena Press (1981)

Introduction

A great number of books have been written about the history and development of Brighton, with some of the earliest surviving copies of published works dating back to the 18th century. Any modern scholar contemplating publication of their own work on this subject will invariably draw upon these earlier accounts. Similarly, those with merely a keen interest in local history will also have encountered references to the contributions made by these earlier generations of chroniclers. The availability of source material generally diminishes as we look further back in time, so it is inevitable that what early records do survive are heavily drawn upon by successive generations of historical writers.

Our view of history is influenced to a very large extent by the manner in which the information has been passed down to us. There is often a political or social aspect applied to events which is commensurate with the social norms at the time of writing. Similarly, an author compiling source information will convey their own personal biases, beliefs and prejudices to it, which may heavily influence the published history. Subsequent historians are left to interpret whatever data remains, but more often than not, the key details are drawn directly from previous reportage.

As we go back further in time, the lack of diverse source information compounds this problem. Given the propensity for newspapers and other media forms to distort the coverage of news items in line with their own agendas, contributions by the likes of Parry, Erredge and Bishop—all intimately connected with the press—might need to be closely scrutinised for signs of partiality. In order to better understand the context of the historical source material, the subject matter of this book focuses largely on the individuals who have made such a significant contribution to our understanding of Brighton in bygone eras. Both the authors share a common inquisitive interest in those earlier contributors, all of whom feature extensively in later works by successive writers and who will no doubt continue to do so in the future.

The chroniclers that have been included need not necessarily have put pen to paper when making their contribution, indeed they may not have even consciously been making an effort to document Brighton's historical development. A chronicle is a chronological record of events and as such, this may not necessarily be in written form. It is often said that 'a picture paints a thousand words' and in this context, the variety of topographical engravings published for public consumption constitute an equally important visual record of how a place has changed over the course of time. More often than not these images convey far more detail about a place than a description by a writer can.

In choosing who to include within this book, the publishers of prints were also considered to have been chroniclers. Individual artists may have produced one or many illustrations of the town, but it was generally the publishers who commissioned a whole series of prints that later formed a historical record. A single series of published prints might not individually be considered to constitute a chronicle, but collectively they often provide a wonderfully comprehensive record of a particular place over a period of time. Detailed biographies have been given for John Ackerson Erredge, John George Bishop, William Grant and William Henry Mason, as some of the most significant chroniclers of Brighton.

Of course, it is always possible to find others who significantly contributed to Brighton's historical development and who have not been included in this book. It is not intended or implied that omission should in any way diminish the contribution made by them. Inclusion has been determined principally upon the availability of information about the lives of the chosen individuals and this tends to be concentrated to those who lived during the 19th century.

The objective of this book is not to analyse or re-interpret the actual historical contributions made by the chroniclers but to establish in detail their respective life stories in order for others to evaluate how this might have influenced their output. In order to fully appreciate the context, relevance and accuracy of the individual contributions of these chroniclers, it is of great benefit to understand their own backgrounds and life experience.

John George Bishop was reputed to have had an extraordinarily retentive memory, which, coupled with his experiences in his early life, enabled him to relate a detailed and authoritative account of the town as it was in the early 19th century. This was supplemented in later years with his ability to access the archives of the *Brighton Herald*. Similarly, John Ackerson Erredge was evidently able to draw extensively from the recollections of his elderly aunt and the experiences related to the civic connections within his family. His later involvement as a journalist and newspaper editor supplemented his considerable personal knowledge of Brighton's history.

William Mason and William Grant were by far the most prolific publishers of Brighton prints, between them producing in excess of 150 prints depicting scenic views of Brighton. 'The prints were published for immediate sale or distribution and were not designed to be a historical record. But they reveal much of the life and character of the times and they provide the principal graphic source of Brighton's history'[1]. However, their approach to print publication was very different. Mason had been a protégé of Rudolph Ackermann and took over his mantle with the Repository of Arts at Brighton specifically to sell expensive prints to a predominantly discerning clientele as works of art. Grant had opened the first newsagent's shop in Brighton and subsequently diversified into the publishing and selling of cheap mass-produced prints to the hoi polloi, much akin to modern day postcards. Mason's prints covered topographical scenes, pastiches of Brighton's social activities, portraits, caricatures and sporting prints. Grant solely offered local topographical views, produced in mass quantities, which Jill and John Ford aptly describe as 'pot-boilers'[2]. Despite these differences, both rendered a significant contribution to Brighton's visual history.

It would be interesting to fully understand whether there was any personal relationship between any of the chroniclers. Suffice to say that Erredge and Mason were of similar age and must have had some contact with each other. Robert Ackerson was landlord of 81, King's Road, the property occupied by Mason. As executor and beneficiary of Ackerson's will, Erredge must have had some dealings with him. Similarly, there was an age difference of seven years between Bishop and Grant but it would be highly unlikely that their paths did not cross at various times. As the leading newsagent in Brighton, the older Grant must have had regular dealings with the nearby offices of the *Brighton Herald*. It is clear from comments in his books, *A Peep into the Past* and *Strolls in the Extra Mural Cemetery* that Bishop had some personal knowledge of Grant and his family.

Although there was also a seven-year age difference between Mason and Grant, as competitors in the print publishing business, it would be most unlikely that they were unaware of each other. There must have been some sort of business relationship between the two as Grant acquired four of Mason's prints around 1850 and republished them under his own name. Bishop certainly used the writings of Erredge as source material for his own books. Both were journalists and later editors but this has to be set against a 14-year age difference between them and the fact that Erredge died two years before Bishop was promoted to editor.

Unfortunately, as much as one could speculate about the relationships between any or all of them, there is no substantive evidence available that could be used to support the notion that one might have had any significant personal influence upon the output of another.

[1] Jill and John Ford: *Images of Brighton*. Richmond-upon-Thames: St Helena Press, 1981, p15

[2] *Ibid*

Acknowledgements

This book could never have been written without the help and active support of our many friends and colleagues and the unending patience of our families whilst tolerating the process of its production.

We would like to thank all of those who have helped, guided and offered valuable advice, in particular the late Henry Smith, Ian Warrell, John and Jill Ford, Geoffrey Mead, John Lyne, Jennifer and Tony Drury of the mybrightonandhove website, the archivists at the Keep, staff at Brighton Museum, Brighton Public Reference Library and the National Archives.

We would also like to thank Tony Mould of the mybrightonandhove website for undertaking photography upon demand and to the Regency Society for use of pictures in the James Gray Collection.

Nearly all of the engravings are from the authors' own collections or in a few cases by permission of those who have kindly contributed them specifically for this publication.

All reasonable steps have been taken to trace copyright holders of any remaining illustrations not otherwise mentioned. If any unintentional infringements to copyright or other omissions have occurred we unreservedly apologise.

Image sources

References are to image numbers

Erredge Collection, Brighton Reference Library: 37

Fitzwilliam Museum, Cambridge: 41

James Gray Collection, the Photographic Archive of the Regency Society: 11, 12, 13, 17, 31, 35, 51, 56, 57

Royal Collection Trust. © Her Majesty Queen Elizabeth II, 2015: 53

My Brighton & Hove website, ©Tony Mould: 14, 28

List of illustrations

1 Early histories and historians

The earliest published histories of Brighton might be said to have been a product of the 18th century as a response to the town having become a fashionable place to 'take the waters'. In 1750 Dr Richard Russell offered his dissertation about the medicinal properties of sea water and advocated the benefits of bathing at Brighton. Taking up his mantle, in 1761 Anthony Relhan produced *A Short History of Brighthelmston*, a guide and historical account, which was later re-issued in 1829.

The influx of wealthy visitors arriving into the rapidly expanding town resulted in a similar increase in the number of published guide-books, together with some of the earliest scenic depictions. Some of these guide-books were attributable to unknown authors, but although the printers, publishers and distributors changed over the years, the guide-books remained largely the same.

By the early 1760s, Edward Baker, a bookseller of Tunbridge Wells had opened a library on the eastern side of the Steyne. The establishment may have been called a library, but effectively it served during 'the season' as a sort of 'high class' social club—a venue for the well-to-do to exchange pleasantries, listen to music from a band playing on the rotunda, play billiards or partake in card games. Following the format previously used by Relhan, Baker offered *The Brighthelmston Directory: or Guide for that Place*, initially printed and sold by I Taylor of Holborn, London, circa 1769. Upon the death of Baker in 1774 a later edition was sold by his successor, R Thomas, printed by R Baldwin of Paternoster Row, London.

A few years after Baker's Library was established, Mr Woodgate opened his own Library to the south of the Steyne. Around 1784 Andrew Crawford took over the premises and published his own guide, written by an anonymous author and entitled *A Description of Brighthelmston, etc.* (1794). The preface in the guide espoused the benefits of Brighton as a watering place but also underlined to visiting clientele its purpose as a description of 'whatever is worthy of observation, either in the town or its vicinity'.

Whilst all of these guide-books and their successors form a chronicle of the town's development, there are few reliable records that can be drawn upon to substantively illustrate the biographical details of their authors. Inasmuch, a single guide-book may provide an excellent snapshot of Brighton as it existed at the time of writing, but it would require a substantial number, over a considerable time frame, to provide a chronicle of the town's development.

Some important chroniclers are not included in this book simply because of the lack of sufficient biographical information, so the few known facts about the four most important omissions, Relhan, Dunvan, Parry and Horsfield, are briefly looked at here.

Anthony Relhan

Anthony Relhan was born around 1715 and was of Irish descent. He was educated at Trinity College, Dublin between 1734 and his graduation as MD on 12 July 1743. He was accepted as a fellow of the King and Queen's College of Physicians of Ireland in October 1747 and elected president of the college in 1755.

In 1759, upon the death of Dr Richard Russell, Relhan took over his mantle as a physician in Brighton. He continued to promote the drinking of mineral waters and sea bathing for the treatment of glandular diseases, becoming the principal authority on the subject. In 1761 he produced *A Short History of Brighthelmston, with remarks on its Air, and an analysis of its Waters*[1], a guide and historical account, which was later re-edited by James Charles Michell and re-issued by the Philanthropic Society, St George's Fields, London in July 1829.

A scan through the bibliographic sources relating to the history of Brighton will usually reveal this to have been the earliest published history of the town. However, it is worth noting that the most significant proportion of this guide is devoted to the 'analysis of the sea water', espousing the value of Brighton as a spa town. The purported history is confined to the first 20 pages, of which a significant proportion consists of a contemporaneous description of the town. It might readily be adduced that the main purpose of the book was to promote the benefits of Relhan's treatment and of Brighton as a health resort.

Relhan practised at Brighton during the bathing season, returning to his office in Southampton Street, London during the remainder of the year. He was admitted as a Fellow of the College of Physicians, London on 25 June 1763. He was married twice, having a son, Richard, and a daughter by his first wife. He died in October 1776 and was buried in the Marylebone graveyard, Paddington Street, London.

Paul Dunvan

The first published historical account, methodically researched by a writer with access to documents penned in earlier times, was written by Paul Dunvan. He was the unattributed author of a book commonly known as 'Lee's History', originally edited, published and printed as a part-work by William Lee, the *Ancient and Modern History of Lewes and Brighthelmston* [**1**]. The first two of 12 parts were announced in June 1792 and the series finished with the three final sections covering Brighton by 25th March 1795. The completed work could be obtained through Messrs Rivington, St Paul's Church-Yard, London.

Dunvan would have been an ideal candidate for inclusion as a chronicler of Brighton, were it not for the paucity of facts about him. Virtually all that is known of him is that he was of a resident of Lewes of French extraction and that he was an usher at the Grammar School in Lewes[2]. Perhaps his anonymity may be explained by an account of him being singled out as a riotous Radical Whig at a town meeting to launch

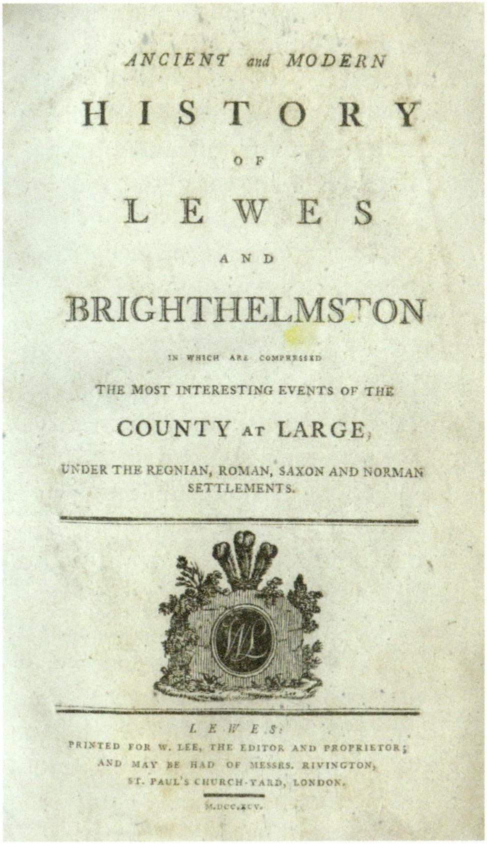
ANCIENT and MODERN
HISTORY
OF
LEWES
AND
BRIGHTHELMSTON
IN WHICH ARE COMPRESSED
THE MOST INTERESTING EVENTS OF THE
COUNTY AT LARGE,
UNDER THE REGNIAN, ROMAN, SAXON AND NORMAN SETTLEMENTS.

LEWES:
PRINTED FOR W. LEE, THE EDITOR AND PROPRIETOR;
AND MAY BE HAD OF MESSRS. RIVINGTON,
ST. PAUL'S CHURCH-YARD, LONDON.
M.DCC.XCV.

1
Paul Dunvan's *Ancient and Modern History of Lewes and* Brighthelmston (1792-95)

a Loyalist Association against Republicanism and Levellers in December 1792, a time where national fears had been aroused by the French revolution.

'A Lewes branch was formed of the Association for preserving Liberty and Property against Republicans and Levellers. A keen member, George Shiffner of Coombe Place, immediately noted down two riotous Radicals, Drowley and Dunvan, who publicly opposed it, and seemingly they became marked men.'[3]

Although a progressive thinker, his views attacking Catholic priests as blasphemous jugglers could hardly have made him many friends in the town. In view of the sensibilities of the 128 subscribers to the work, many of them being pillars of the establishment, it may have proved to have been a prudent move by Lee to conceal the true identity of its author.

There were other candidates who may also have been worthy of closer attention, such as Thomas Attree, the founder of the *Brighton Herald*. Similarly, where the tradition of guides had continued into the nineteenth century, a number of those whose names are borne upon the works might have been included. John Baxter, Richard Sickelmore, John Bruce, Charles Wright, James Taylor, William Saunders, William Pearce and Hannah Wallis are a few of these, but when viewed as the publishers of individual guide-books, rather than history books, they do not warrant biographical attention.

Guides of the early 1830s

Many of the published guide-books did include illustrations of local landmarks within the town that have allowed later generations of local historians to visualise the development of a particular place through a period of time. By the 1830s, the choice and subject matter of such illustrations had burgeoned. They subsequently were sold singly, as writing paper, discrete views or in album form, the forerunner to the scenic post-card.

As the 19th century progressed, the increase in the number of newspapers, supplemented by the large number of previously published sources and plethora of civic records would enable those with access to them to have a detailed view of the town and its development that had hitherto been impossible for a single individual to achieve.

During the first half of the 1830s, four books dealing with Brighton's history were published in quick succession. Although none was exclusively about Brighton, they are all worthy of consideration. Unfortunately the first two had unacknowledged authors, whilst the other two were written or edited by academics with only a tenuous connection to Brighton. Nonetheless, all provided a ready source of reference for later authors.

The first of these was *The Watering Places of Great Britain*, by an unknown author, published in 1831 by Isaac Taylor Hinton of 17 Warwick Square, London. This was released between 1831 and 1833 as a monthly part-work of 20 pages, plus three steel plate engravings and four further pages of advertisements, each part costing three shillings by subscription. The volumes were originally published in two sizes: octavo and quarto. Each 20-page volume covered a specific sector of the country and the first four parts, released between May and August 1831 covered Brighton.

The publisher appeared to be having difficulties by this time, with a review stating that the illustrations 'fall far short in merit' to those in Hinton's previous publications and that 'accident may have occasioned the falling off in the present number'[4]. Although volumes five and six were published by October 1832, the series was subsequently taken over by Joseph Robins, but it would appear that it was never completed by either publisher.

2
Fry's *Fashionable Guide and Directory* (1840-42)

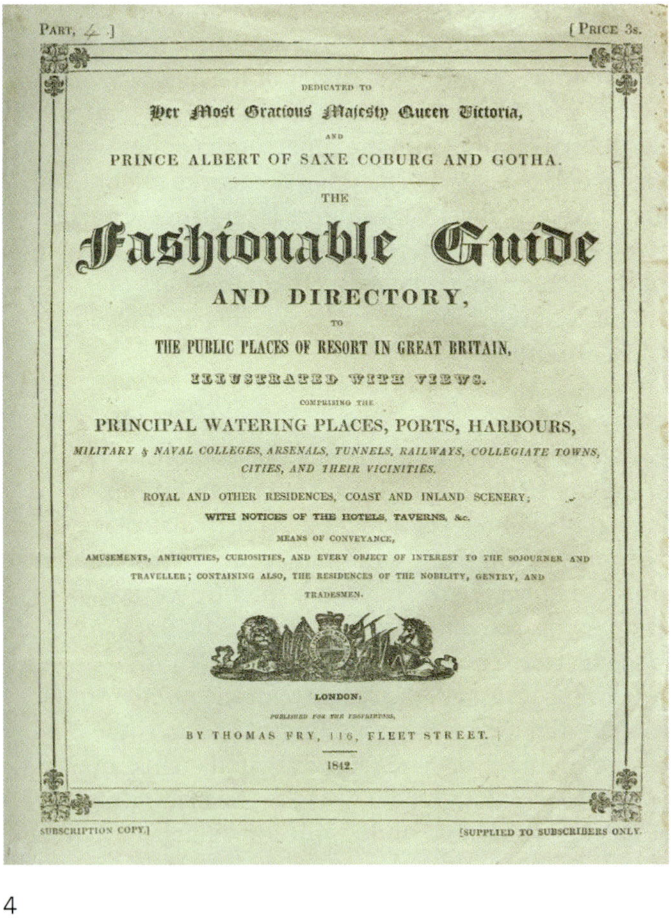
PART, 4.] [PRICE 3s.

DEDICATED TO
Her Most Gracious Majesty Queen Victoria,
AND
PRINCE ALBERT OF SAXE COBURG AND GOTHA.

THE
Fashionable Guide
AND DIRECTORY,
TO
THE PUBLIC PLACES OF RESORT IN GREAT BRITAIN,
ILLUSTRATED WITH VIEWS.
COMPRISING THE
PRINCIPAL WATERING PLACES, PORTS, HARBOURS,
MILITARY & NAVAL COLLEGES, ARSENALS, TUNNELS, RAILWAYS, COLLEGIATE TOWNS, CITIES, AND THEIR VICINITIES.
ROYAL AND OTHER RESIDENCES, COAST AND INLAND SCENERY;
WITH NOTICES OF THE HOTELS, TAVERNS, &c.
MEANS OF CONVEYANCE,
AMUSEMENTS, ANTIQUITIES, CURIOSITIES, AND EVERY OBJECT OF INTEREST TO THE SOJOURNER AND TRAVELLER; CONTAINING ALSO, THE RESIDENCES OF THE NOBILITY, GENTRY, AND TRADESMEN.

LONDON:
PUBLISHED FOR THE PROPRIETORS,
BY THOMAS FRY, 116, FLEET STREET.
1842.

SUBSCRIPTION COPY.] [SUPPLIED TO SUBSCRIBERS ONLY.

Between 1840 and 1842, 17 volumes of the series were published by Thomas Fry of 116 Fleet Street, London in the quarto version only and later again by The Fashionable Guide Office at 116, Stamford Street, London [**2**]. One of the major disadvantages of releasing such a work by subscription was that subscribers may cease to want parts beyond their own locale and this may account for the frequent changes of publisher and inability to complete the project.

In a similar vein, the London publisher, William Kidd, released *Kidd's Picturesque Pocket Companion to Brighton, Worthing, Bognor, etc* [**3**] starting from around 1831, with a volume dedicated to the area around

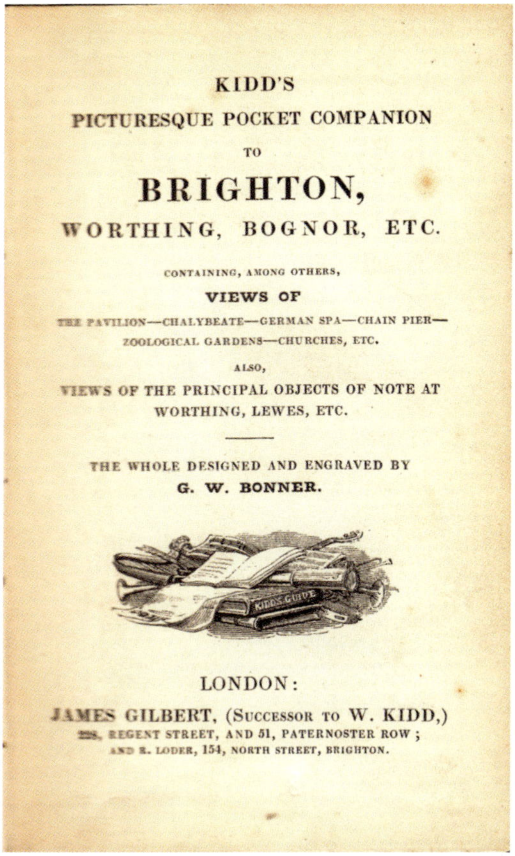
KIDD'S
PICTURESQUE POCKET COMPANION
TO
BRIGHTON,
WORTHING, BOGNOR, ETC.
CONTAINING, AMONG OTHERS,
VIEWS OF
THE PAVILION—CHALYBEATE—GERMAN SPA—CHAIN PIER—
ZOOLOGICAL GARDENS—CHURCHES, ETC.
ALSO,
VIEWS OF THE PRINCIPAL OBJECTS OF NOTE AT
WORTHING, LEWES, ETC.
THE WHOLE DESIGNED AND ENGRAVED BY
G. W. BONNER.

LONDON:
JAMES GILBERT, (SUCCESSOR TO W. KIDD,)
228, REGENT STREET, AND 51, PATERNOSTER ROW;
AND R. LODER, 154, NORTH STREET, BRIGHTON.

3
Kidd's *Picturesque Pocket Companion* (1833)

Brighton being published in 1833. Essentially a pocket-sized guide-book, it was the first to contain numerous small wood engravings by G W Bonner, interspersed between the text. The same engravings and format were later also used in successive other guides.

John Docwra Parry

In January 1833 John Docwra Parry published his *Historical and Descriptive Account of the Coast of Sussex*. He was born in Woburn, Bedfordshire on 13 July 1800, the only son of the Rev. John and Mary Parry. A bright student, at the age of 18 he was admitted into Peterhouse, Cambridge, and graduated with a Bachelor of Arts degree in April 1823 and Master in 1827. In the same year he had followed in his father's footsteps and attained the position of curate at Aspley Guise, Bedfordshire, subsequently becoming the incumbent there and also the domestic chaplain to the Duke of Bedford. He later took deacon's orders, but due to a deficiency in his voice he was ultimately unsuccessful in the further pursuit of a career in the clergy.

Although his first book, *Select Illustrations, Historical and Topographical, of Bedfordshire*, was published by Longman and Co, London in 1827, under the name of the Rev. I D Parry (sic), it is worthy of note that he claims on the title page to have been author of 'The History of Woburn, etc.', a work generally considered to have been published later in 1831. He had originally written and published this work at the age of 18 but did not finish the more comprehensive final version of the book until 1831. Unfortunately, his first book had to be discontinued, owing to the subscription unexpectedly and totally failing.

Further works were subsequently published with a greater degree of success. It was his fifth book, the *Historical and Descriptive Account of the Coast of Sussex* [**4**], published for the author by Charles Wright & Son, Brighton, that appears to have come about with his moving to Brighton, having researched the subject matter over a period of six months. In his preface he readily acknowledges that, in writing his book, 'it is not easy in practice, however it be recommended in theory, to speak with perfect impartiality and good temper'. He adds: 'the author can respectfully, but boldly, assert, that he has not merely attempted this, but knows that he has succeeded.'

Although this scholarly work deals with the whole of Sussex, there is nonetheless a very comprehensive chapter covering Brighton. The first

4
Parry's *Historical and Descriptive Account of the Coast of Sussex*

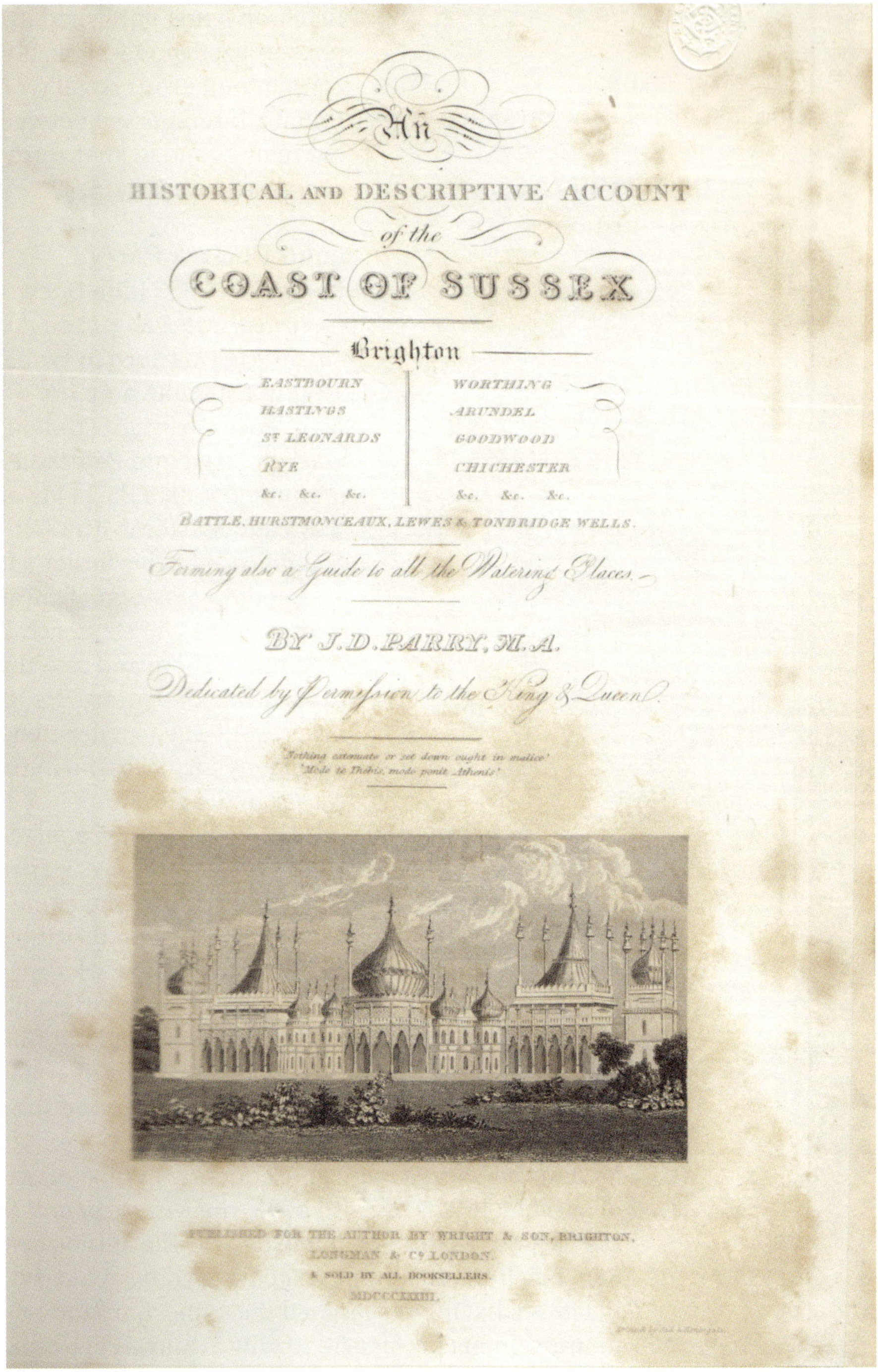
An
HISTORICAL AND DESCRIPTIVE ACCOUNT
of the
COAST OF SUSSEX

Brighton

EASTBOURN	WORTHING
HASTINGS	ARUNDEL
S^T LEONARDS	GOODWOOD
RYE	CHICHESTER
&c. &c. &c.	&c. &c. &c.

BATTLE, HURSTMONCEAUX, LEWES & TONBRIDGE WELLS.

Forming also a Guide to all the Watering Places.

BY J. D. PARRY, M.A.

Dedicated by Permission to the King & Queen.

'Nothing extenuate or set down ought in malice'
'Modo te Thebis, modo ponit Athenis'

PUBLISHED FOR THE AUTHOR BY WRIGHT & SON, BRIGHTON,
LONGMAN & Co LONDON.
& SOLD BY ALL BOOKSELLERS.
MDCCCXXXIII.

96 pages deal with the history of Brighton, whereas the remaining 79 pages form a guide-book to the town. The framework for reference uses manuscripts from the collection of Sir William Burrell in the British Museum, extracts from newspapers from 1761 until 1810 and information derived from Lee's *History*.

Sadly, Parry later recounted that the expense of publishing the book cost him £700, 'by which I have been ruined. ... Through this I have been compelled to relinquish the *Portsmouth Herald*, a paper which at my own risk I turned from a neutral or semi-Whig to an efficacious Conservative one'[5]. In consequence, on 11 November 1834, the execution of an indenture made between Parry of Surrey Street, The Strand, London, and Wholesale Stationers, James Barry and George Hayward, resulted in all of his property and possessions being assigned to the latter. Parry's health suffered as a result of his financial misfortune and he never really fully recovered, remaining embittered by his experience throughout the rest of his life. He continued to write articles over the next 40 years, supported by generous grants from a charitable organisation called the Royal Literary Fund and an allowance of £2 per month from a subscription raised in his home town, Woburn.

He next emerges in the 1851 census as a 'Contributor to Newspapers', living in Old Street, London. He was said to be a long-standing correspondent of the *Northampton Mercury*. By the time of the 1871 census he was living in casual lodgings at 3 Albermarle Street, Finsbury, eking a living as a seller of literary publications and was recorded at that time as being deaf. He died on 29th December 1876 at 107 St John's Street, Clerkenwell, London.

5
Horsfield's *The History, Antiquities and Topography of the County of* Sussex (1834)

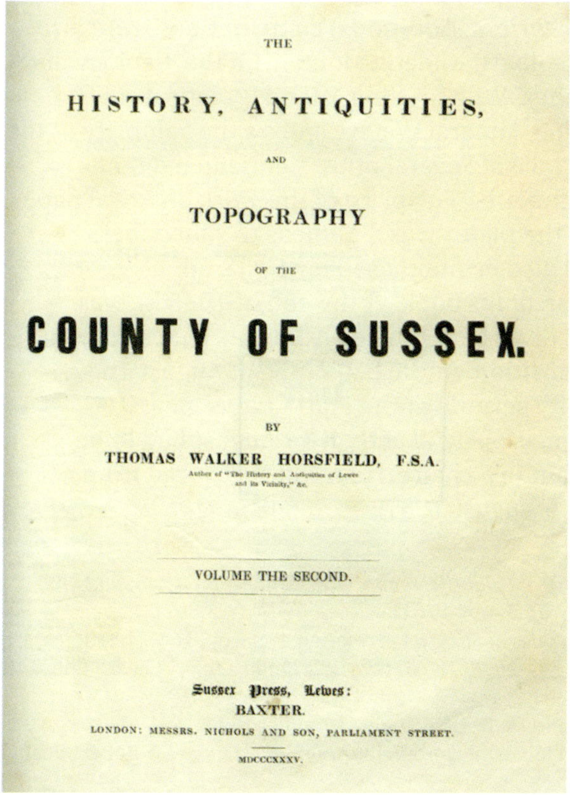
THE

HISTORY, ANTIQUITIES,

AND

TOPOGRAPHY

OF THE

COUNTY OF SUSSEX.

BY

THOMAS WALKER HORSFIELD, F.S.A.

Author of "The History and Antiquities of Lewes and its Vicinity," &c.

VOLUME THE SECOND.

Sussex Press, Lewes:
BAXTER.
LONDON: MESSRS. NICHOLS AND SON, PARLIAMENT STREET.
MDCCCXXXV.

Thomas Walker Horsfield

Following hot on Parry's heels at the end of 1834, John Baxter published a definitive work entitled *The History, Antiquities and Topography of the County of Sussex* [**5**]. This monumental two-volume work included 52 pages covering Brighton. The author was Thomas Walker Horsfield, the son of James and Ann Horsfield (née Hewett), being born in Sheffield on 6 November 1792.

As a youth he had become acquainted with and greatly influenced by a well-known poet, James Montgomery. In 1814 he moved to Hackney to study under the guidance of the Rev. Robert Apsland, with Dr Morrell and Jeremiah Joyce as his tutors. Having completed his academic course-work, he became the minister of the dissenting Presbyterian congregation at the Westgate Chapel, Lewes. On 8 June 1818 he revisited Sheffield to marry Hannah Waterhouse at St Peter's Cathedral. Returning with his new wife to Lewes, he set up a private boarding school, which gained much acclaim within the town.

With a number of other liberal townsmen, he was instrumental in setting up a Mechanics' Institute in 1825. On 5 April 1824 he had published *The History and Antiquities of Lewes and its Vicinity*, with an appendix on the natural history of the district by Gideon Mantell. As a result of this work, he was accepted as a Fellow of the Society of Antiquaries of London (FSA) in 1826.

With the deaths of some of the wealthiest members of his Lewes congregation, his ministry began to decline. This, coupled with a degree of enmity shown to him in the town because of his liberal views, resulted in his decision to quit the town. In December 1827 he was invited to preach by the Society of Unitarian Christians at Taunton, Somerset. While there he became an accomplished amateur oil painter.

Following on from his earlier work he had been amassing information, with a view to another book entitled *History of Brighton and the South Coast*. However, at the request of his publisher, John Baxter of Lewes, he had extended his history to embrace the entire county and revised the name to *The History and Antiquities of the County of Sussex*. It is evident from the preface of the book that much of the information had been collected and compiled by agents of the publisher and that Horsfield readily described himself as being the editor of the work, rather than as its author. The first volume of the set (containing the section on Brighton) was partly written by William Durrant Cooper and the second volume drew heavily on previous histories by James Dallaway and Edmund Cartwright. Additional contributions were also included by the eminent geologist, Gideon Mantell, on the 'Geology and Natural History of the County', William King MD on 'Practical Observations on Sea Bathing, Mineral Waters and on the Salubrity of the Coast' and 'with the assistance of Several other Gentlemen distinguished for scientific attainments'. The price of the work on Royal paper with proof impressions of the plates was 4 guineas to subscribers. A demi-quarto edition could also be purchased for £2 12 6d.

Shortly after publication of his book, at the end of 1835 he was appointed as the Pastor at Chowbent Chapel, Atherton, Lancashire and left Sussex to take up the position. At the beginning of August 1837, whilst preaching at a charity sermon at the Platt Chapel, near Manchester, he became dangerously ill and on 14 August had to be conveyed home to Chowbent in a chaise. He never recovered from his illness and died there on 26 August 1837.

[1] Anthony Relhan: *A Short History of Brighthelmston, with remarks on its Air, and an analysis of its Waters*. London: W Johnston, 1761

[2] Mark Anthony Lower: *The Worthies of Sussex*. Lewes: Geo. P. Bacon, 1865, p333

[3] Colin Brent: *Georgian Lewes, 1714-1830, The Heyday of a County Town*. Lewes: Colin Brent Books, p189

[4] A review in the *Public Ledger and Daily Advertiser*, 31 August 1831

[5] The 'Peel papers' in the British Museum contain letters from Parry to Sir Robert Peel in 1845

2 John Ackerson Erredge
(c1811-1862)

Of all the historical books written about Brighton, perhaps the most often referenced source is *The History of Brighthelmston, or Brighton as I View It and Others Knew It* by John Ackerson Erredge, first published in 1862.

Ancestry and family background

The exact date of birth of John Ackerson Erredge could not be established but according to the various accounts of his sudden death on 5 November 1862, he was stated to be 51 years of age when he died, implying the year he was born was 1811.

At the time of his birth, the Erredge family were living in a tenement that his father had purchased from a Mr Kent[1] in what was known as Kent Street, at the bottom of West Street. This little enclave came into existence in the 1770s, when Thomas Kent began to develop the cliff-top area behind West Street, extending the urban spread of Brighton beyond its previous westernmost limit. At the time it was built, Kent Street had formed the coastal access from the west into West Street as a continuation of the cliff-top road and the new houses of Kent's development. By 1787 it was known as Kent's Court[2], although it was also often referred to as Kent's Rents[3]. This should not be confused with the contemporaneous development of Kent's Buildings, which stood in Upper Russell Street and the later Kent's Court off the east side of Russell Street.

With the construction of a new coastal road, accompanied by a continuous row of new seafront buildings lining it, the earlier development became sealed off at its western end and the resultant cul-de-sac was later simply known as Kent Street, consisting of a total of 16 dwellings by 1826[4]. As the 'old town' evolved into a fashionable resort towards the turn of the 18th century, the displaced fishing community started to cluster around the newly developed housing to the west of the town. A key factor in the choice of this location was that it lay directly opposite the West Street Gap, with its ramp down to the beach affording easy access to their boats and fishing huts.

It has often been contended that John was born into a long-established family of Brighton fishermen. Indeed, newspapers reporting his death state 'deceased was a member of a very old Brighton family, and his father, Samuel Erredge, his grandfather, and we believe his great grandfather, carried on extensive fishing businesses here; when the vocation of fishermen—in the time of the Tattersells, Erredges and Gunns—was very different from what it is now'[5]. It is indisputable that his father, Samuel Cynic Erredge[6] (1756-1816), was a fisherman. This is evident from his will, but there are also various other references to him connecting him with maritime activities[7].

However, connecting the Erredges with the Tattersells and Gunns as another of the old Brighton fishing families is nothing more than a fanciful notion. Samuel's father, also named Samuel Sinnock Erredge[8] (1733-) came to Brighton around 1755 from Willingdon, near Eastbourne, in order to marry Mary Greenwood. There is little doubt that the Erredge family had been residents of Willingdon for many generations; in all probability they had not been fishermen at that time. The village of Willingdon stands some three miles from the sea and although the parish has a small coastal section at Langney Point, this was not really suitable at that time as a base for a fishing fleet. A very large marshy area separated the village from the coast and the beach itself was described in a Victorian guide-book as being 'too exposed' to make it a suitable haven in bad weather. The parish derived almost all of its income from agriculture, making it most likely that the Erredges either worked upon, or farmed, the land.

An interesting aside was that Frederick Fisher's *Description of Brighthelmstone and the Adjacent Country* and Cobby's *Directory*, both published in 1800, record that there was a carrier named Erridge offering a regular cart service to Eastbourne, leaving from the Gun Inn on Brighton's East Cliff on Tuesdays at about 08:00 and returning on Monday about 19:00. Sickelmore's 1809 guide details that a cart service was still operating then, but it does not record the name of the carrier.

In all likelihood, Samuel Cynic Erredge's first wife was Elizabeth Spicer[9] and there were evidently four offspring born to the couple[10]. An Elizabeth Erredge was subsequently recorded in the St Nicholas burials on 16 November 1807, almost certainly being the first wife of Samuel, as he was described as a widower when he married Hannah Ackerson[11] on 21 June 1808. The first child of this second marriage, Ackerson, was born around a year later[12] and John Ackerson followed around 1811 but was not christened until 1815[13]. It would seem that Hannah, who was 39 at the time of John's birth, suffered post-natal complications which resulted in her death on 3 March 1811[14] and burial six days later[15]. At this time Samuel was in his late fifties and would have found it very difficult to raise two children as he tried to earn a living as a fisherman.

While they were still babies, John and Ackerson were taken in and brought up by Hannah's brother Robert Ackerson and his wife Jane. It is entirely conceivable that Jane had taken John into her care immediately after his birth, which might explain the close bond that existed between them, as opposed to his brother Ackerson, who would have been around two years old at that time. With the death of Samuel in 1816[16], the grandparents became the de facto guardians of the two infants.

In his will[17], Samuel Erredge named Robert Ackerson as his sole executor and the trustee of his estate on behalf of his children. This estate consisted of Samuel's house in Kent Street, together with a herring deese[18] and tan house and another house, occupied by his son, Richard, all of which were to be held in trust until his son Ackerson attained the age of 21. The trust was to provide maintenance support for

Ackerson and his step-sister Elizabeth, by way of the residue from rents received on the properties, after deduction of mortgage payments. Upon Ackerson coming of age, the money and equities held in trust were to be shared equally between his five surviving offspring, namely Samuel, Richard, Elizabeth, Ackerson and John.

Robert Ackerson was born in Brighton around 1763, the son of John Ackerson, a builder, and his wife Mary. Robert followed in his father's footsteps, being variously recorded as a bricklayer and builder, residing at 17 Duke Street from the turn of the century until the 1820s. On 30 September 1798 he married Jane (née Marchant), the survivor of twins born in Pyecombe on Boxing Day 1758. Her brother Richard had died a few hours after birth. As Jane married Robert quite late in life, she had no children of her own but she was to have a very significant influence throughout the life of John Ackerson Erredge. There is little doubt that her personal recollection of the couple's involvement with civic affairs and attendance at social functions formed a primary source for much of the content of Erredge's historical gleanings. It might be contended that, with his father being a fisherman and a landsman acting as his guardian, Erredge had a first-hand insight of the dichotomous relationship between these two disparate groups in Brighton.

During the first quarter of the 19th century, Robert Ackerson had undertaken numerous important civic duties, acting as a Director and Guardian of the Poor, church warden (until he resigned in 1826), treasurer to Grimmett's Charity School, Town Surveyor and also as Assessor for the Parish Rates. At the Easter session of the Court Leet, William Williams was chosen to serve as the High Constable of the town throughout 1814. However, his term of office was postponed until 1815 and Robert Ackerson served as High Constable in his place[19].

His role as a builder in the town included work on municipal structures, such as the boy's school in Warwick Street. On 30 May 1822, Ackerson and George Sawyer, another builder, paid £300 for a plot of land in the home furlong of the West Laine. This was the remainder of a parcel of land consisting of eight paul-pieces (approximately one acre or one tenantry measure) abutting land, already held by Ackerson and Richard Bodle, to the west[20]. The plot measured 162ft long north to south by 52ft, narrowing to 48ft 6ins wide at the south end, being situated on the southern corner of Clarence Place and Clarence Street. It was on this plot that he built his new residence, which subsequently became the family home for Robert, his wife Jane and their two Erredge charges from 1824 onwards.

Education, business and financial life

Some sources contend that John was tutored by Dr Henry Stewart Byron but this is almost certainly an exaggerated claim, as John was already 16 or 17 by the time of Byron's arrival in Brighton. Byron had qualified as a Doctor in Law in Glasgow in 1828. In the previous year he had married

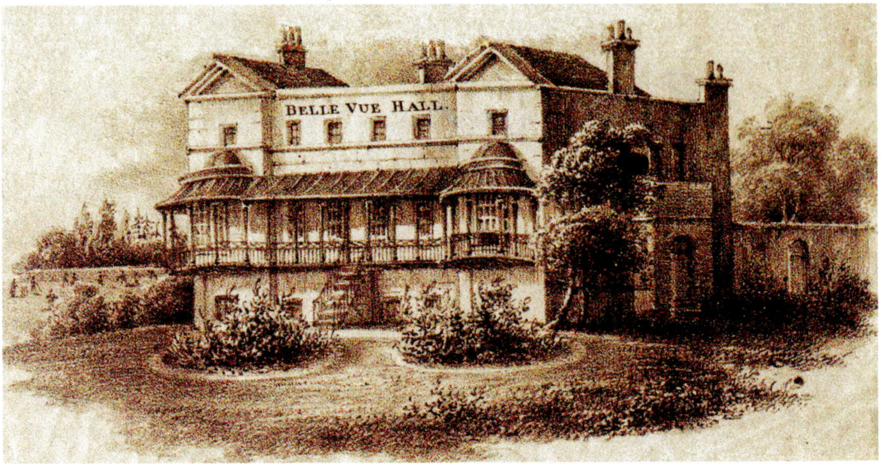

6
Belle Vue Hall, the premises where from 1829 Byron and later from 1844 Grix set up their schools. The building was demolished around 1968

Ann Stocker, the widow of Thomas Stocker[21], who was likely to have been the real tutor of the young Erredge. Thomas Stocker had opened a classical and commercial school on the East Cliff of Brighton around the time of his marriage in 1814. Later the establishment was listed at 71 East Street and it was while he was at the school that he tragically collapsed and died on 28 August 1825. His widow, Ann Stocker, continued to run the school 'assisted by a gentleman of the University of Cambridge of approved talents and long experience of tuition'[22].

After her marriage to Henry Byron in 1827[23], the partnership of Stocker and Byron was formed and is shown listed in the 1828 directory, offering a syllabus of classical and mathematical studies from the same premises. With Ann becoming pregnant, the partnership proved to be short-lived and in January 1829, Byron announced that he was relocating the school to Belle-Vue Hall in the Marine Parade [**6**]. By 2 May of that year, Byron's wife gave birth to their son. Thus, the bulk of Erredge's tuition had been undertaken by the Stockers and he most likely became acquainted with Byron following his marriage to Ann Stocker. Subsequently Erredge became an assistant to Byron at Belle Vue, before moving on to a teaching post with William Grix.

Grix had come to Brighton from the east end of London shortly after his marriage to Elizabeth Mary Bevern[24] and by 1826 the couple had settled at Crescent Street[25]. At the end of that year he announced that he had taken over the Crescent Street establishment of Mr Fisher and that he would be continuing to operate a school there, commencing on Monday 15 January 1827. By 1831 Grix was operating a Boarding School for Young Gentlemen from 12 Marlborough Place. It was at one of these establishments that Erredge began his career as a teacher. Within a short period of time Erredge began courting Mary Ann Bevern, Grix's sister-in-law, who he subsequently married by licence at St Anne's, Lewes on 29 June 1832. Three months later his brother, Ackerson, married Catherine Butcher, daughter of Edward Butcher and Catherine (née Marchant)[26].

In accordance with the stipulations set out in Samuel Erredge's will,

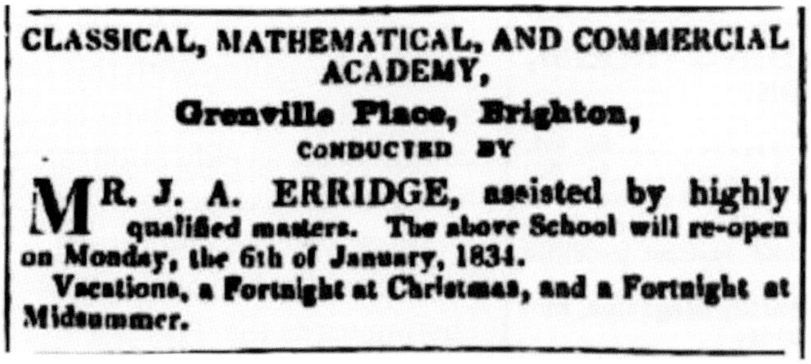
CLASSICAL, MATHEMATICAL, AND COMMERCIAL ACADEMY,
Grenville Place, Brighton,
CONDUCTED BY
MR. J. A. ERRIDGE, assisted by highly qualified masters. The above School will re-open on Monday, the 6th of January, 1834.
Vacations, a Fortnight at Christmas, and a Fortnight at Midsummer.

7
Advert for Erredge's Academy from the *Brighton Gazette*, 26 December 1833

by 1830 his son Ackerson had attained the age of 21 and by 1832 John had also reached this age, making it likely that John would have been in receipt of his inheritance from the trust set up in the will of his father. This would have given him the wherewithal to pursue the setting up of his own 'classical, mathematical and commercial academy', which he evidently did by 1833[27], utilising one of his uncle's properties in Grenville Place [**7**].

By 1835 he was recorded as teaching languages at his Academy at 28 West Street and employing William Barnard as a teaching assistant. The unfortunate Barnard was learning to swim in the sea at the bottom of East Street on 26 June 26 1835, when he got out of his depth and drowned. Miraculously his body was recovered and taken to Brill's baths, where he was resuscitated, but he subsequently succumbed to complications and died five days later.

The method of teaching used by Erredge may be determined by reference to the first book that he wrote, a catechetical volume entitled *The Student's Handbook of General Information* [**8**][28], intended as a sequel to Blair's *Why and Because*. First published at the end of 1839 as a 110 page, octodecimo (around four inches by six-and-a-half inches page size), half-bound volume containing several hundred questions and answers on inventions, origins, institutions, causes, derivations, definitions and subjects of general interest, interspersed with explanatory notes and observations. These were evidently intended to be learned by the students by way of recital. In the book's preface, Erredge claims that 'the works produced for youths are generally too abstruse or too dry'[29] and that he had done much to simplify the subject matter.

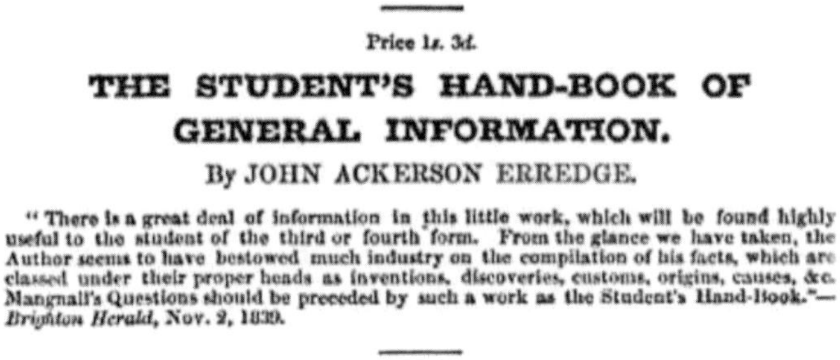
Price 1s. 3d.
THE STUDENT'S HAND-BOOK OF GENERAL INFORMATION.
By JOHN ACKERSON ERREDGE.
"There is a great deal of information in this little work, which will be found highly useful to the student of the third or fourth form. From the glance we have taken, the Author seems to have bestowed much industry on the compilation of his facts, which are classed under their proper heads as inventions, discoveries, customs, origins, causes, &c. Mangnall's Questions should be preceded by such a work as the Student's Hand-Book."—*Brighton Herald*, Nov. 2, 1839.

8
Advert for Erredge's *Student's Handbook* (1839)

A contemporary advertisement claimed that 'there is a great deal of information in this little work, which will be found highly useful to a student in the third or fourth form'[30]. The book was initially offered at 1s 3d at the time of release but by February 1840 the price had increased to 1s 6d. Although well received, it would appear around a year later that Erredge was still indebted to the publishers, Relfe and Fletcher, to the tune of £142 2s 3d.

By the 1840s, Erredge had diversified into various other fields, also conducting business as a Newsagent, Bookseller, and Stationer from his

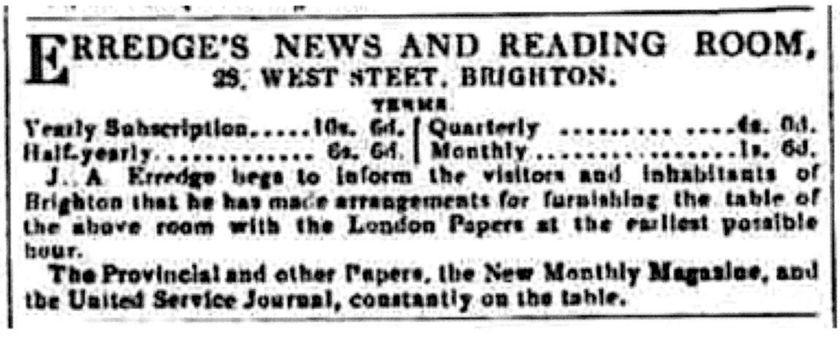
ERREDGE'S NEWS AND READING ROOM,
28, WEST STEET, BRIGHTON.
TERMS
Yearly Subscription.....10s. 6d. | Quarterly ....4s. 0d.
Half-yearly............. 6s. 6d. | Monthly.......................1s. 6d.
J. A. Erredge begs to inform the visitors and inhabitants of Brighton that he has made arrangements for furnishing the table of the above room with the London Papers at the earliest possible hour.
The Provincial and other Papers, the New Monthly Magazine, and the United Service Journal, constantly on the table.

9
Advert for Erredge's Reading Room from the *Brighton Gazette*, 2 April 1840

premises at 28 West Street [**9**]. Shortly thereafter, with the advent of the 'penny post' he commenced weekly publication of advertisements printed on the envelopes containing letters, which he sold to customers as the 'Postage Advertiser'. This subsequently brought him into conflict with the Office of Stamps and Taxes.

On 11 August 1840 Charles Pressly, Secretary to the Commissioners of Stamps and Taxes, wrote to him from Somerset House, advising that the publication was deemed to be a newspaper and was thus liable to Stamp Duty. The individual advertisements were similarly liable to duty. Erredge was duly instructed to either register the newspaper for duty or discontinue publication. He queried this by submitting the correspondence between himself and the tax authority to the London and provincial newspapers but Pressly wrote again on 26 August to restate that Erredge must comply with the ruling or face the consequences. It is not known whether he complied with this instruction, but it is on record that by October 1840, the Stamp Office authorities had acted to prevent the publication of numerous similar advertising sheets and that their publishers were pursued and subsequently forced to discontinue production.

On 29 January 1841, Robert Ackerson petitioned for the issue of a fiat from the Court of Bankruptcy in respect of debts owed by his nephew. On 9 February 1841, the appointed Commissioners determined that John Ackerson Erredge was eligible for bankruptcy proceedings and issued a notice requiring him to surrender at the Town Hall for a meeting of the Commissioners on the 13th. At this time there were two courts dealing with debt: the Court for the Relief of Insolvent Debtors and the Court of Bankruptcy. The distinction between the two may be better appreciated by a short explanation. The status of being bankrupt at that time applied only to traders owing in excess of £100. A trader was defined as one who made a living by buying and selling. Those individuals who did not meet the criteria were deemed to be insolvent debtors. Such unfortunate individuals, who could not pay their debts, could be subject to indefinite imprisonment. Those that qualified to become bankrupt could discharge their debts by equitable and independent redistribution of their remaining assets, effectively wiping out the outstanding debt. Described in the proceedings as a 'Bookseller, Stationer, Dealer and Chapman', Erredge was deemed to be a trader and was consequently declared bankrupt with debts totalling £1,133 14s 1d[31].

Unfortunately there is no direct evidence to show what precipitated Erredge's bankruptcy but there are clues within the surviving court papers. In the list of losses and expenses, there is a breakdown of

Erredge's expenditure from 1833 until 1840. This reveals that after acquiring the school, his expenditure on rent and 'house expenses' increased threefold during the years 1834 to 1836. In the following three years it had increased fivefold. It is highly unlikely that Erredge had the income to support this additional expenditure. His average annual expenditure over the course of 1833-1840 was £338 a year, but this increased to over £432 if his loans are taken into account. The number of pupils required to generate an equivalent income almost certainly exceeded the practicable size of an average class.

It is most revealing that in the evidence he submitted to the Commissioners his uncle cites loans made by him to Erredge dating back to 1837. It is also significant that a sizeable proportion of the debt (excluding loans made by his uncle) was owed to builders. As the debts started to mount and Erredge chose to avoid the demands of his creditors[32], matters came to a head. Having earlier effectively underwritten many of Erredge's debts by loaning money to meet his increased expenditure, it might be conjectured that Robert Ackerson and William Grix were approached by Erredge's other creditors and that they subsequently sought to distance themselves from any further liabilities incurred by their spendthrift relative.

All of his assets and estate were vested in the assignees and the process of selling these commenced. In the meantime, Erredge was granted an allowance of £2 0s 0d a week to maintain his family during the course of the proceedings. By 24 February 1841, over a period of three days, his stock-in-trade, the contents of his home in West Street and his personal effects were auctioned off[33]. The list of contents included 'four-post, French and tent bedsteads, goose-feather beds, hair mattresses, mahogany chests of drawers, . . . occasional tables, sofa, mahogany dining, Pembroke and other tables, . . . window carpets, . . . Brussels carpets, sitting room and chamber chairs, . . . china, glass plate, linen' and many other household items. The stock-in-trade included '300 volumes of circulating books, . . . a quantity of new books, . . . school desks, shop and school fittings, fixtures and numerous other effects'. The proceeds of the sale came to a total of £138 4s 3d, which, when added to the recovered total of the debts owed to Erredge plus any funds held in his bank accounts, amounted to a grand total of £184 18s 0d.

By 19 June 1841 the Commissioners had audited the accounts of the assignee and after the deduction of all expenses agreed to a first and final dividend of around 8.75 per cent to each of the certified creditors, totalling £90 17s 9d. The largest proportion of the debt was owed to family members (Robert Ackerson, his uncle; William Grix, his brother-in-law, and Ackerson Erredge, his brother) who had collectively loaned Erredge around £510 and received just under £43 in dividends. The largest creditor outside of the family group was the publisher Relfe & Fletcher, owed £142 2s 3d and who received around £12 in dividends. The publishers also either obtained by equitable agreement or by

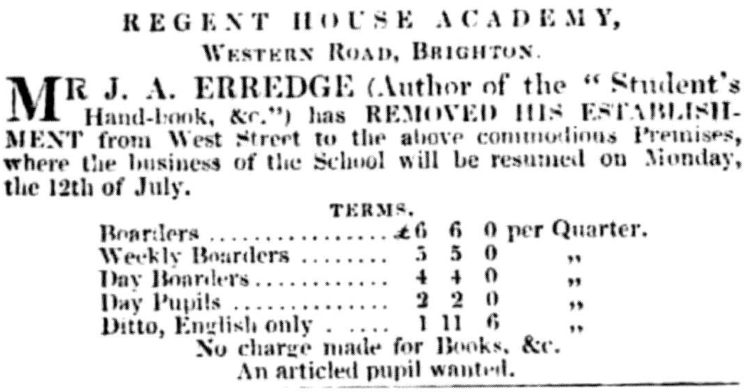

REGENT HOUSE ACADEMY,
WESTERN ROAD, BRIGHTON.

MR J. A. ERREDGE (Author of the "Student's Hand-book, &c.") has REMOVED HIS ESTABLISHMENT from West Street to the above commodious Premises, where the business of the School will be resumed on Monday, the 12th of July.

TERMS.

Boarders	£6	6	0	per Quarter.
Weekly Boarders	5	5	0	"
Day Boarders	4	4	0	"
Day Pupils	2	2	0	"
Ditto, English only	1	11	6	"

No charge made for Books, &c.
An articled pupil wanted.

10
Advert for the Regent House Academy from the *Brighton Gazette*, 1 July 1841

purchase the copyright of *The Student's Handbook* and continued to sell it thereafter, using an editor named John Quested to revise the work for a new edition in 1859.

After the settlement of his bankruptcy case, Erredge took up residence at another of his uncle's premises, 175 Western Road [**10**]. It was here that he opened his Regent House Academy on 12 July 1841 as a 'School for Young Gentlemen'[34]. Evidently by the following year Erredge must have considered the venture successful enough to warrant taking on additional staff, as an advertisement was placed for a young assistant to teach French and Latin at a salary of £25 a year[35]. In March 1844 the Chief Constable of Brighton, Henry Solomon, was murdered by John Lawrence. By the end of the month, the Town Commissioners had convened a meeting in order to raise subscription to support Solomon's widow and nine children. The sum collected from the townsfolk exceeded £1,000 and Erredge magnanimously offered to educate one of Solomon's children at his academy for free[36].

During the course of 1842, Erredge had a brief dalliance as a cricketer, playing for the fledgling West Brighton Cricket Club. In June[37] the West Brighton side played the Clarence Cricket Club on Harvey's grounds with Erredge as the opening bowler. The match was decided in favour of West Brighton. Further matches were played throughout August against the Gentlemen of Cuckfield and Lindfield at Haywards Heath, Alfriston Club on Lillywhite's ground and Cuckfield Club, also on Lillywhite's ground.

Erredge moved into his uncle's house at 43 Clarence Place around 1845, possibly because of his elderly uncle's deteriorating health, advertising that his 'Academy' was operating from that address in 1845 and 1846. On 6 June 1846, Robert Ackerson died at the age of 83. His will had been drafted on 21 May 1843[38], stipulating that he bequeathed the freehold, copyhold and leasehold estates to his wife Jane for the remainder of her life. Provision was also made in equal share for his nephew and Mary Marchant (Jane's sister) by way of 'all of his household furniture and implements of household'.

The will also devised that, following the death of his wife, certain properties were to be apportioned between several other beneficiaries. He bequeathed 44 Clarence Place (subject to a mortgage of £250) and 52 London Road, with a parcel of land adjoining (subject to a mortgage of £600), to John Ackerson Erredge. Robert Ackerson's former residence at 43 Clarence Place [**11**], which had been occupied by Jane after his demise, was devised to his other nephew, Ackerson Erredge.

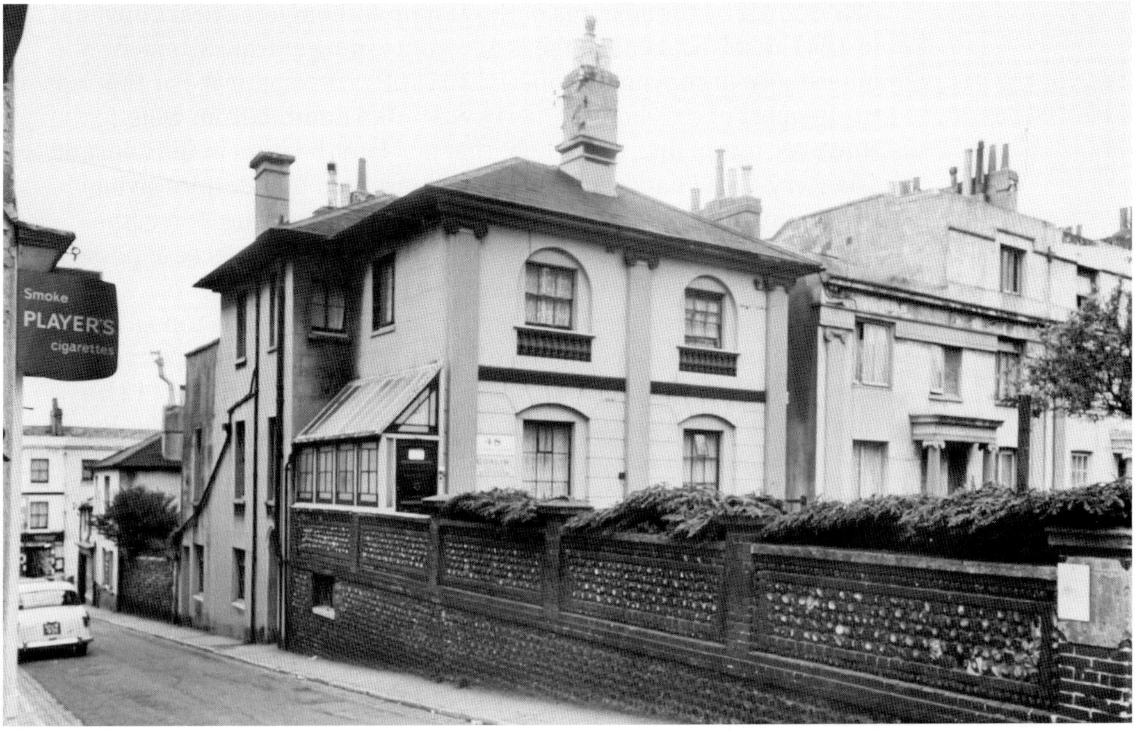

11
43/44 Clarence Place. 44 (left) was bequeathed to John Ackerson Erredge and 43 (right) to his brother Ackerson

The content of the will belies the actual size of Robert Ackerson's property portfolio. The named properties bequeathed in the will were 81 King's Road to Henry Verrall; 43 Clarence Place to Ackerson Erredge; 44 Clarence Place and 87 London Road to John Ackerson Erredge; 23 Cambridge Street to Abraham Hobbs; 24 Cambridge Street to Richard Pelling; 15 Grenville Place to the daughter of James Marchant and 27 Grenville Place to be sold to pay off a mortgage to W John Blaker of Lewes. Some of these properties were devised to the beneficiaries on the basis that when they (and their wives in some cases) died, the property would be sold for the benefit of the surviving children of Henry Verrall and the two Erredge brothers.

Aside from those properties specifically named in the will, there were a considerable number of houses that were not named, situated in West Street, North Street, Gardner Street, William Street[39] and Pavilion Street[40]. Ackerson instructed that John Ackerson Erredge and Henry Verrall would act as executors of his will and were to become trustees for the houses not otherwise devised within the portfolio of property. It was further stipulated that the residual estate should be disposed of within two years of Jane's demise and the monies realised distributed amongst certain named beneficiaries. However, Verrall died within a year of proving the will, leaving Erredge as the sole executor and trustee.

There was also a further problem with the inclusion of copyhold properties contained within Ackerson's estate. Copyhold titles could not necessarily be devised in a will, as inheritance of such a title was usually determined by the customs of the Manor. Although the first Copyhold Act in 1841 resolved some of the issues concerning enfranchisement, the inheritance of copyhold property was still problematical. For this reason the bequest of copyhold property was often omitted from wills. However, it is of interest to note that at a later hearing in the Court of Chancery, Vice Chancellor Kindersley observed that despite giving explicit instructions for the disposal of his copyhold property, 'the testator (Robert Ackerson) was not at the time of his decease possessed or entitled of or to any copyhold estate'[41].

At this juncture, it is worth further exploration of the topography and the relationship between some of the properties Robert Ackerson left in his will. From 1824 Ackerson had lived at 43 Clarence Place [**12**], a property probably designed by Amon Henry Wilds and Charles Busby and built by Ackerson on the plot he had acquired in 1822. The house certainly had the hallmarks of being designed by the partnership but it was also strikingly similar to Erredge's later school premises, Cambridge Lodge in London Road, also designed by Wilds and Busby. Not long afterwards a section of the plot to the west had been used to build the end property of a row of terraced houses. It is evident from Pigot's 1824 map that his own house in Clarence Place may have originally been built as a detached villa on the corner of Clarence Street but by 1840 it had been divided into a pair of semi-detached houses, numbered as 43 and 44. A portion of land at the end of the original garden had been used to erect another structure, probably originally as an outbuilding for the use

12
10 Clarence Street, the premises of Erredge's school from around 1848 until 1853

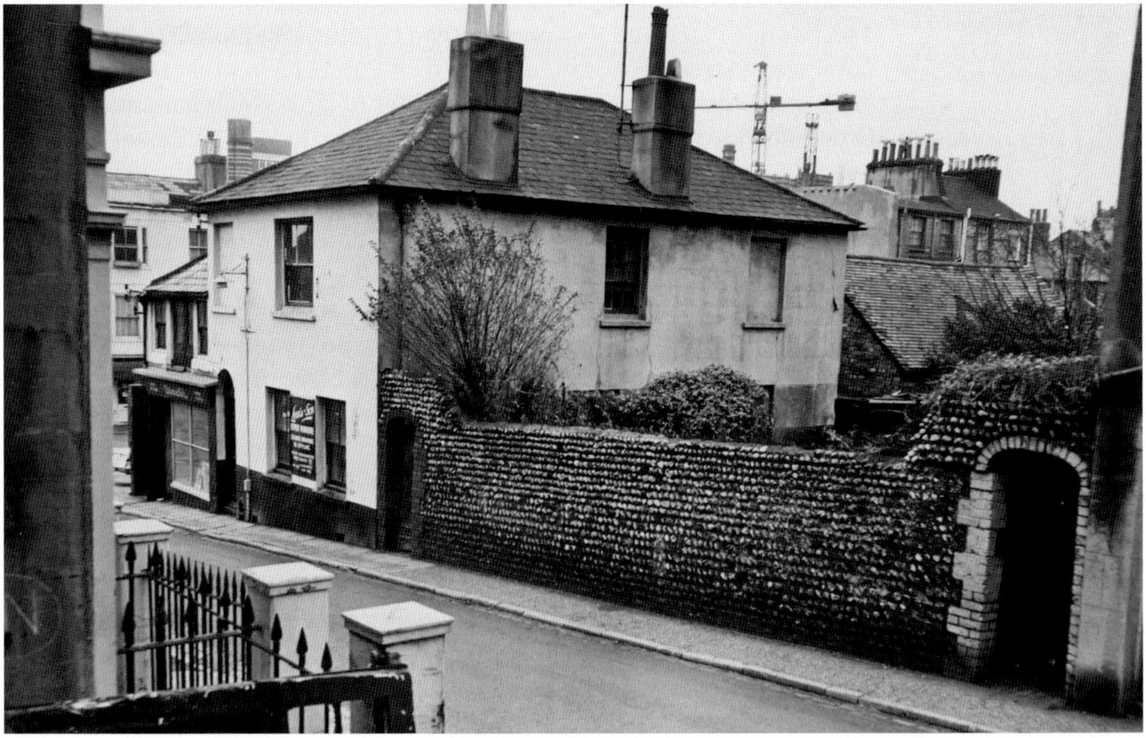

of Ackerson Erredge's carpentry business. This building was initially incorporated into the L-shaped plot of 43 Clarence Place but later separately numbered 10 Clarence Street[42].

After Robert's death John had lived with his aunt for a short period, utilising this building at the rear as his school. However, by 1848 it would seem that Jane had permitted her nephew to move into the property adjacent to her own (which he was due to inherit upon her death) whilst still retaining the property at the rear as a school. Clarence Place was subsequently renumbered into Clarence Square although the numbering scheme confusingly ran in the opposite direction (43 and 44 Clarence Place respectively became 49 and 48 Clarence Square). All of the properties mentioned were cleared in 1964 as part of a redevelopment scheme for Churchill Square.

The other property devised to Erredge was Cambridge Lodge, which still stands in London Road. The title deeds for Cambridge Lodge make it clear that this property had been jointly acquired by Robert Ackerson and Nathaniel Cooke on 21 September 1826. A mortgage on the property had been transferred to William Catt during the course of 1843 and this was ultimately to be voided upon the payment of £600. It is obvious from this and other court records that it was the same property Ackerson had bequeathed to his nephew in his will, described in that document as 52 London Road.

With the death on 7 September 1847 of Henry Verrall, the other trustee to Ackerson's will, it would appear that his restraining influence on Erredge's profligacy was lifted. Without Verrall there to fetter his capitalisation of the properties held in trust, he was virtually free to do as he saw fit with the estate in trust. By February 1848 Jane Erredge had evidently been persuaded to dispose prematurely of certain properties that had been bequeathed to her by her late husband. In later years, with her demise, this action would lead to problems for other family members, including his brother, to pursue redress from Erredge through the courts. The copyhold properties offered for sale at an auction dated 16 February 1848 included 18, 19 and 20 Duke Street (17 Duke had been the home of Robert Ackerson prior to 1824, but by the time of the sale it had been renumbered to 18. It was again renumbered to 24 in 1855/56); 54 West Street (on the corner with Duke Street and abutting number 18, the home of Ackerson Erredge); 2 Pavilion Street and 175 Western Road, on the corner with Regent Hill (premises previously used by her nephew as the Regent House Academy until around 1845, after which it was subdivided into two properties. Thereafter the ground floor shop was being used by Bishop and Strange, china and glass merchants, whilst the upper floor was used by an auctioneer, Charles Verrall. It was renumbered to 188/9 Western Road in 1851/52).

As has already been mentioned, the transfer of copyhold property was still subject to feudal law and as such, a Court Baron was convened on 27 March 1848 to deal with the case. A Court Baron consisted of an assembly of freehold tenants of the manor, known as the homage, presided over by a steward appointed by the lord of the manor. In essence, the purpose of convening the court was to allow transfer of copyhold property, through the acceptance of a new tenant into the homage. It may seem rather odd but these particular properties fell under the auspices of the Lord of the Manor of Old Shoreham (Rusper), Harry Colvill Bridger. He had appointed Somers Clarke as his steward to preside over the court, with John Knapp and Richard Patching forming the homage and Beadle Bridger Woolgar as the appraiser[43].

The reasons for disposal of the properties are now lost in time but it might be speculated that it could be either borne of necessity from managing Robert Ackerson's estate or possibly in order to address Erredge's mounting debts. Most, if not all of the properties in Ackerson's portfolio were subject to mortgages, typically at a rate of five per cent a year, interest only, until the principal sum was repaid in full. Ackerson may easily have covered the repayments from the rents paid to him by the tenants in his properties but with a significant number of the properties having been bequeathed to relatives, it may have become necessary to dispose of others in order to pay off outstanding mortgages and bequests.

Less than a month after the Court Baron, Rev. Henry Michell Wagner, acting as the executor of his wife's will, wrote to Erredge calling in a mortgage that had been made between her and Robert Ackerson in 1837. Erredge was required to pay the principal sum of £300 plus the interest due. On 16 May 1849 he entered into an indenture with John Butcher[44], a builder of Ditchling, for a conveyance in trust by way of mortgage of the two properties bequeathed to him, 44 Clarence Place and Cambridge Lodge, London Road. This was undertaken in order to satisfy three promissory notes, made by Erredge shortly after the death of Henry Verrall, of £50 each to members of the Verrall family and which now fell due for payment. It might be considered that this was a prudent move by Erredge, recognising that insolvency would divest him of whatever property he had. By vesting the properties in such a way, it ensured that the bequests to Robert Ackerson's grandchildren could be satisfied whilst he still had beneficial use of them during his lifetime.

That same year Erredge suffered a burglary at his school premises, when Thomas Holmes broke in through a window and stole a pistol, a curb chain and some cash from Erredge's desk.

In August 1851, by his own petition, Erredge's brother-in-law William Grix was declared an insolvent debtor and subsequently imprisoned in Lewes gaol. A month later his creditors had requested an examination of his schedule, due to 'insufficient schedule concealment of property, improvident and extravagant expenditure and undue preference'[45]. The cross examination by the creditor's solicitor, Mr Sharood, had reduced Grix to tears, who pleaded the case that an outbreak of scarlet fever had not only decimated his school but also claimed one of his own children. He had been forced from Belle Vue Hall into lodgings in Little East Street and declared out of business. Furthermore, Grix had appointed Erredge (who was one of his creditors) and another person as assignees.

In summing up the judge concluded that 'there was no doubt that the insolvent had given a fraudulent preference to some of his creditors. Although that assignment was an illegal one, he exonerated the insolvent on the grounds of his having been advised by a professional man, and he might not be aware that he was acting illegally when he signed the deed.' Grix was discharged and Richard Tuppen and Joseph Ames were appointed by the court as assignees. The final dividend of just over three per cent was not settled until 1853.

On 29 September 1851 Jane agreed to convey the properties in Clarence Place to her two nephews, as bequeathed in her late husband's will. Shortly thereafter Erredge leased 44 Clarence Place as a day school to a Mrs Barker, moving his wife, children and Jane into Cambridge Lodge at 87 London Road. From this time until 1853 he was still recorded as having a school-house in Clarence Street.

Public life

On the civic scene, there were 18 vacancies for the town's 112 Commissioners in August 1852. Erredge was nominated by one of the existing Commissioners, Mr Good. He was successful in securing 655 votes, sufficient to become one of those elected to fill the vacancies. During the course of 1853, the Brighton and Hove Regatta[**13**][46] was instituted and a committee was formed to oversee the event. H Tamplin, the High Constable, became the chairman and Erredge the honorary secretary.

The inaugural meeting raised £148 in funds, including a donation of 50 guineas from the London Brighton & South Coast Railway Company, with an equal amount from the residents and proprietors of Cliftonville. Unfortunately the weather prevented the eagerly awaited three-day

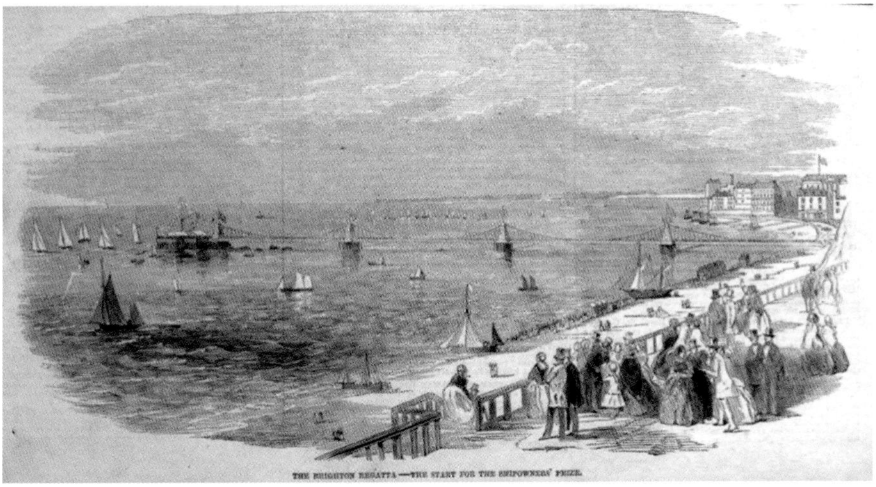

13
A print of the Brighton and Hove Regatta from the *Illustrated London News*, 30 July 1853

event from taking place until Thursday 21 July. The first day was marred by poor visibility and Friday's events had to be moved to the following day. Nevertheless the regatta was deemed to have been a huge success. A dinner was subsequently arranged to present Erredge with an inscribed silver mounted portemonnaie (wallet), in commemoration of the gratitude of the committee for his valuable services as their honorary secretary. Such was their confidence in him that he was elected to continue in this role for subsequent events.

When Erredge had acquired property he also became eligible to vote in the elections for the town's members of parliament. The poll returns for 1841 indicate that he supported Dalrymple (Conservative) and Pechell (Whig), whilst the poll returns for 1847 and 1852 show that he supported Pechell (Whig) and Coningham (Liberal) in the former and Pechell (Whig) and Hervey (Conservative) in the latter.

Unfortunately, in September 1853 he again found himself financially embarrassed and by his own submission, petitioned as an insolvent debtor. He was duly summonsed to attend the County Court on 22 October to examine his debts, estate and effects. In consequence, a vesting order was made by the court, whereby all of Erredge's real and personal estate and effects were vested in his assignees, James Aukett and John Jones Rogers. A further hearing was arranged for 17 December to make a final order. However, as the insolvency laws also took into account 'all the future estate to which he might become entitled until his final discharge', the case became complicated, partly due to the beneficiaries of the trust that had been mentioned in Ackerson's will. This consisted of property in trust that had been bequeathed to Erredge's children, as well as instructions on the disposal of the residual estate, which was to provide an inheritance for other family members after Jane's death. As a result, Ackerson Erredge, representing the beneficiaries[47], petitioned the Court of Chancery in order to safeguard their own interests.

On 24 March 1854, the Vice Chancellor, Sir Richard Torin Kindersley, ordered that John Ackerson Erredge 'should convey and assign the lands and premises subject to the trusts of the said will' to a new trust, with the trustees comprised of John Ackerson Erredge, George Shelley and Edward Bodle.

It should be borne in mind that at this stage Jane Ackerson was still the beneficiary of most of the properties left by her late husband and, although she had permitted her nephew to utilise some of them, many did not belong to him. Where he had been given or obtained property that he now owned, it was subject to immediate assignment by order of the court. Whilst still advertising his academy in Cambridge Lodge [**14**], it is evident that he moved his school into alternative premises at 21 Middle Street in 1854[48] and set up his twenty-year-old daughter, Ada Mary, as a schoolmistress at the same address [**15**]. It is not known whether Erredge was actually imprisoned during his period of

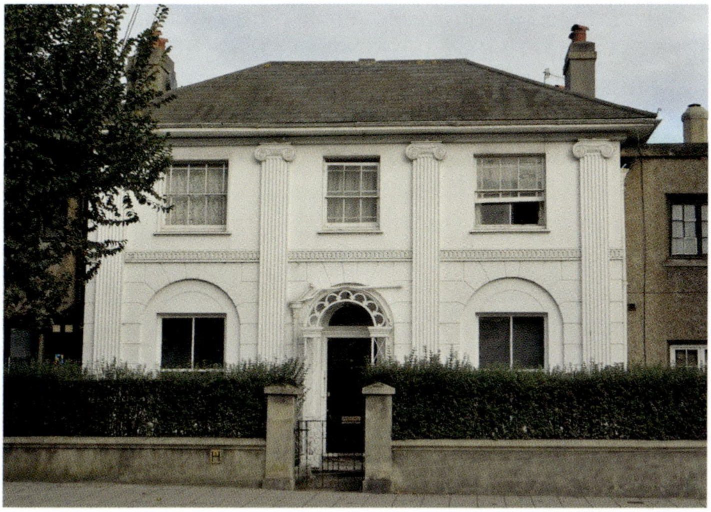

14
Cambridge Lodge, 87 London Road, the premises of Erredge's Academy from 1853 until 1856

insolvency but it seems unlikely that his aunt would permit this to happen. In all probability, she staved off his debts, as by the summer of 1854 the issue of his insolvency seems to have largely subsided. Undaunted by his financial misfortunes, he again stood for election as a Town Commissioner, but was ultimately unsuccessful.

Whether Erredge's egregious financial affairs resulted from his own omissions or purely arose through force of circumstance is now difficult to discern but the death of Jane Ackerson on 2 February 1855 was an ominous portent to Erredge's ultimate financial downfall. Almost as soon as his aunt had been interred, Erredge's brother, representing the family members with a beneficial interest in Robert Ackerson's will, again filed a complaint at the Court of Chancery[49]. At the hearing, on 14 February, Vice Chancellor Kindersley observed that Erredge had not conveyed any lands or premises pursuant to his previous order. Erredge might rightly have been excused of not complying while Jane was still alive and was the beneficial owner but with her demise there was nothing to impede execution of the will. The plaintiffs requested 'that the trusts of the [Robert Ackerson's] will . . . be performed and carried into execution by and under the order of the court'.

To further compound his financial problems, with Jane dead, his other creditors also now sought to recover outstanding monies from Erredge's own inheritance. By 21 September 1855 he had been summoned to court to explain why he had still not satisfied the ruling by the Court of Chancery. It was disclosed that he had contracted debts of £230 since his last insolvency. Although he still had property that could be used to meet the debts, Erredge claimed that 'he had no access to it'—presumably because it was held in trust. The following day he was again forced by his circumstances to petition as an insolvent debtor. An interim order for protection from process was granted on 16 October and at Sussex County Court a final order was made on 18 November. Worse still, it was ruled by the court that Erredge should be divested of his school

15
Advert for Cambridge Lodge from Taylor's *Directory of Brighton*, 1854

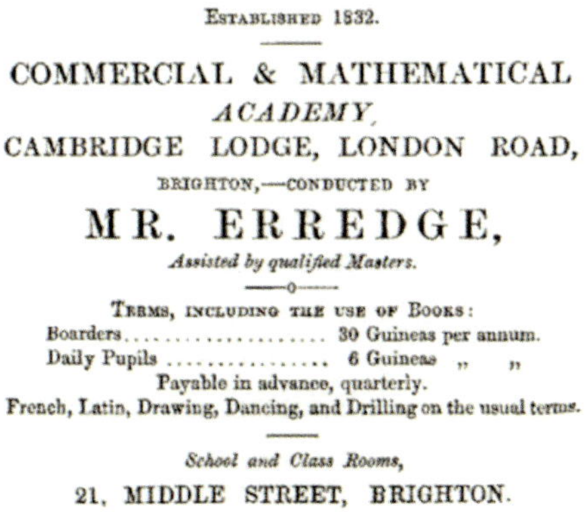

ESTABLISHED 1832.

COMMERCIAL & MATHEMATICAL
ACADEMY,
CAMBRIDGE LODGE, LONDON ROAD,
BRIGHTON,—CONDUCTED BY

MR. ERREDGE,
Assisted by qualified Masters.

TERMS, INCLUDING THE USE OF BOOKS:
Boarders.................... 30 Guineas per annum.
Daily Pupils .... 6 Guineas " "
Payable in advance, quarterly.
French, Latin, Drawing, Dancing, and Drilling on the usual terms.

School and Class Rooms,
21, MIDDLE STREET, BRIGHTON.

premises, Cambridge Lodge, which was advertised on 2 October 1856 'to be sold, pursuant to an order of the High Court of Chancery'[50], together with a row of four houses, 63 to 66 North Street, also held in trust.

During this turbulent period of his life, Erredge had continued to run a school, for day pupils only, from 55 West Street, although his financial worries were still far from settled. On 5 June 1857, Hannah Swift[51] and Arthur Joseph Head filed a complaint at the Court of Chancery to order the trustees to perform and execute the provisions contained within the will, regarding their own inheritance. All of the properties held in trust had by now been duly disposed of and presumably the proceeds were subsequently distributed in compliance with the court order. With the matter of the will having been resolved, his insolvency could also be finally settled and by October the court had distributed a dividend of 37 per cent amongst his creditors. After settlement of all of his debts, Erredge was left penniless and thereafter reduced to renting accommodation.

It is likely that whilst residing at 55 West Street during the course of 1856, he became closely acquainted with his neighbour, Ebenezer Lewis. As a boy Lewis had been an assistant printer to the well-known Lewes printer and publisher, John Baxter. Lewis had arrived in Brighton around 1850 after his marriage to Caroline Emma Chapman and the newlyweds took up residence at 17 Duke Street, where he was described as a 'reporter and printer'[52]. Lewis later founded the *Brighton Observer*, publishing the first edition on 28 November 1856 from his address at 54 West Street. As has already been noted, both of these properties abutted each other and were previously owned by Robert Ackerson, being more recently occupied by Ackerson Erredge. It is very probable that John played a major role in this[53], although his circumstances could not have allowed him to have any financial stake in the business.

After Lewis moved from West Street, both he and Erredge later took up residence in West Hill Street. Without the wherewithal to run a school, Erredge could no longer teach and subsequently took employment as a journalist. By 1858 he was listed as living at 35 West Hill Street and had also fleetingly turned his attention to the manufacturing of 'Erredge's Brighton Relish' [**16**]. The following year Ebenezer Lewis was living at Elmore Cottage, West Hill Street. However, Erredge's condiment appears to have had a very short and inauspicious existence and by 1859 directories no longer contain any listings at all for him.

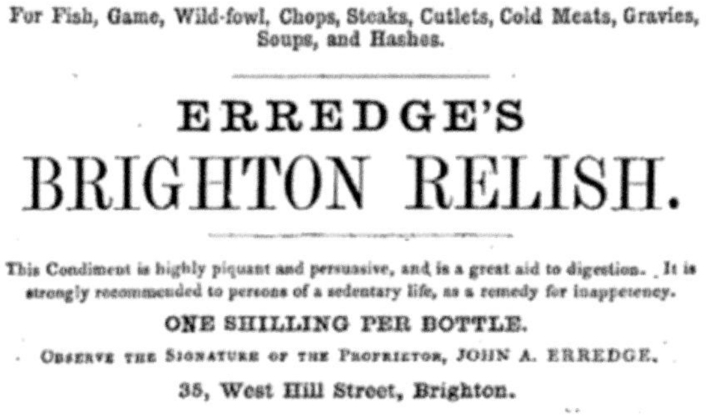

16
Advert for Erredge's Brighton Relish from Melville & Co's *Directory & Gazetteer of Sussex*, 1858

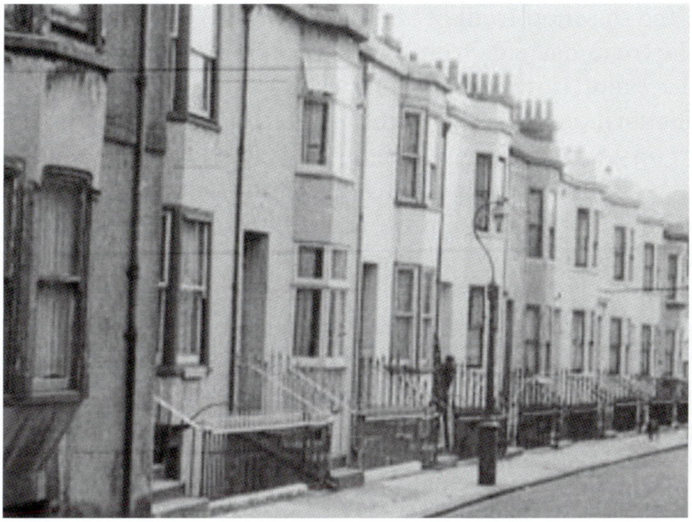

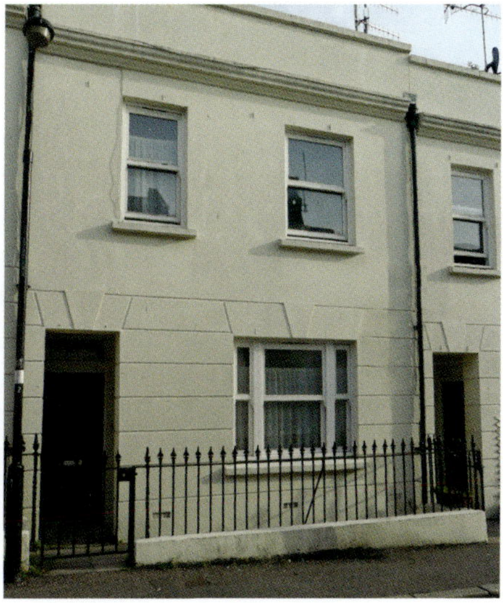

17
left
Erredge's house in Sydney Terrace/ Gloucester Street (behind lamp-post) as it was and
18
right
as it is now, the façade having been rebuilt in the 1970s

Within another couple of years, Erredge and his family were renting a small terraced house at 16 Sydney Terrace [**17**]. These houses, lining either side of the western end of Gloucester Street, numbered 1 to 11 on the south side and 12 to 21 on the north side, had been developed from around 1852. In common with most of the north side properties, number 16 consisted of a two-up, two-down tenement, basement rooms, area and a reasonable size garden, with a rear gate into Pelham Square. After 1861 the houses of Sydney Terrace were incorporated into the numbering scheme of Gloucester Street, with Erredge's house being renumbered to 33 Gloucester Street. The house still exists but the whole terrace was remodelled around 1972 [**18**]. The original canted bay windows were removed and the whole façade now presents a flat facing. Between the time when Erredge lived there and today, later housing in Pelham Square has been also been built in the rear garden.

At some stage in his life, Erredge suffered from a condition affecting the use of his leg, such that surgeons recommended that it should be amputated[54]. However, he sought treatment from Mr Henry Harrap, a well-known local surgical practitioner of great repute. To his eternal gratitude, the leg responded to treatment and was saved. Harrap had been a shoemaker with no medical qualifications and was largely uneducated. During the 1830s he had made frequent visits to Sake Deen Mahomed's shampooing baths, where he learned the art of professional rubbing, and also to the house of a neighbour, Mrs Williams, where he learned about the medicinal application of poultices and unguents. By his own endeavours, he acquired a detailed knowledge of anatomy which astonished established surgeons and other members of the medical profession. Such was his ability, that by 1850, the leading surgeons of the town acknowledged him as an irregular fellow practitioner and accepted him into the profession.

Having converted the shop-front of his premises at 28 Grand Parade into his surgery, he treated clients from all over the country, to considerable personal acclaim. However, his abilities might be considered questionable in modern times, as was demonstrated by a case, heard in Oxford Civil Court on 14 June 1860, where he was sued 'to recover damages for negligent and unskilful practice as a surgeon in treating the plaintiff for a bad knee'[55]. The case illustrates the type of treatment that Erredge might have had, consisting of continued painful applications to the affected leg, of a very strong lotion smelling of ammonia and then wrapping the leg in wet plasters from above the knee to the ankle. In the case of the plaintiff, 117 sessions, of between 30 minutes and two hours, were undertaken. The treatment caused severe reactions and gave no relief to the plaintiff's affected knee.

When complications set in, Harrap proved to be out of his depth, ultimately contending that his patient had 'softening of the brain' and was trying to avoid paying fees for his treatment. The medical profession in Oxford were scathing in their condemnation of his treatment. In support of Harrap, another Brighton doctor, George Hilbers, took the stand and gave evidence that in his opinion 'the defendant's treatment was very skilful and generally successful'. Taking into account that 'there appeared to be no doubt that the defendant enjoyed a considerable reputation, and had a great number of patients', the jury ultimately decided in favour of Harrap. The judge ordered the plaintiff to pay compensation of £300 to Harrap. However, as regards his own treatment, Erredge was far more fortunate in that a complete cure was effected.

John George Bishop said of him that 'in business Mr Erredge was very precise and methodical, none more so; but out of it he was the most pleasant of companions, his conversation being full of wit and humour. It is but just to add, that, while a schoolmaster, Mr Erredge received many flattering marks of his pupil's esteem'[56].

Family life

Erredge had a total of eight children, the first being Ada Mary, born in 1834. Ada had served as a governess from the beginning of the 1850s and by 1854 her father had set her up as a school mistress. However, this appears to have been a short-lived enterprise, as by 1861 she had returned to being a governess. On 1 May 1866 she married Frederick Michael Cosgrave and subsequently moved to Portsea, Hampshire.

The second child was Ileen Jane, born in 1836 and who married Charles Leake in 1883. The third child, Robert Ackerson was born in 1838 and was educated by William Grix. He married Wilhelmina Sloan and became a coal merchant.

The fourth child was Helen Rose, born in 1840, who sadly died in 1861. The fifth child was Herbert Edward, born in 1843, who was taken on by Ebenezer Lewis as an apprentice and then as a journalist for the

Brighton Observer. Herbert played a major part in the completion of his father's unfinished part-work, ultimately becoming a newspaper editor and the writer of *The History of Bramber Castle*.

The sixth child was Marian Constance, born in 1848, who never married and was a companion to her aunt, Mary Hewett, for many years. The seventh child was Walter James, born in 1850, who became the manager of a paper staining company. The eighth and final child was Frank Bevern, born in 1854, who moved to the West Country to study music and theology, before becoming a bank manager.

Erredge's brother, Ackerson, died on 9 January 1860 at his home in Russell Square leaving his estate to his widow, Catherine. She remarried Henry Coward in 1864, but ironically, with her death on 17 February 1879, under the terms of Robert Ackerson's will, John Ackerson Erredge and Henry Verrall's surviving children received their inheritance of £82 6s 7d each from the sale of 49 Clarence Square (formerly 43 Clarence Place).

During the second half of 1862, Erredge had started to feel unwell. By October 1862, he had complained to his son Herbert about a pain on the left side of his chest and a slight difficulty in breathing. Believing he had a digestive problem, he visited a chemist in Ship Street and explained that he had a pain in the chest and distension of the stomach. The chemist, Mr A H Cox, a personal friend of Erredge, gave him cardamoms with soda and ammonia but warned him that, because the pain was continuous, he should consult a medical man. However, Erredge considered that this was unnecessary. His condition worsened, such that he complained to his daughter Ada about having giddiness in his head accompanied by a pain in his chest through to his back.

During the week commencing Monday 27 October, he was absent from his office for four days, due to illness, although he did attend a theatrical performance entitled *The Seven Ages of Woman* by Miss Emma Stanley at the Pavilion on the Tuesday evening. He remained in his bed on Friday 31 October and Saturday 1 November and said to Ada that he thought he had a diseased heart, but by the following day he felt much improved. On the morning of Wednesday 5 November he ate his breakfast with Ada and was in good spirits. He left for work shortly after 9:00 and upon his arrival was called by Mr Lewis to come into his back room. Lewis was sat at his desk with Erredge stood opposite, leaning over the desk with both hands placed upon it. The two men had spoken cordially about business matters for less than a couple of minutes, when Erredge suddenly reeled over, hitting his head on the sideboard as he fell. Lewis lifted him onto his knee and called out for assistance, upon which a foreman and Erredge's son Herbert came into the room to attend his father. Mr Rugg the surgeon was sent for and arrived within 10 minutes but during this time Erredge had suffered a violent spasmodic action, followed by a gurgling sound in his throat. By the time the surgeon

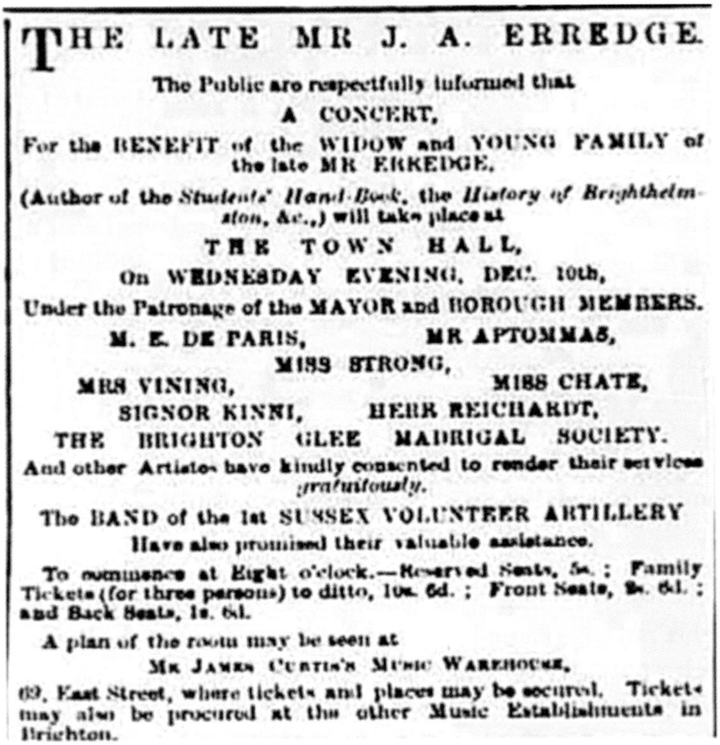

THE LATE MR J. A. ERREDGE.

The Public are respectfully informed that

A CONCERT,

For the BENEFIT of the WIDOW and YOUNG FAMILY of the late MR ERREDGE,

(Author of the *Students' Hand-Book*, the *History of Brighthelmston*, &c.,) will take place at

THE TOWN HALL,

On WEDNESDAY EVENING, DEC. 10th,

Under the Patronage of the MAYOR and BOROUGH MEMBERS.

M. E. DE PARIS, MR APTOMMAS,

MISS STRONG,

MRS VINING, MISS CHATE,

SIGNOR KINNI, HERR REICHARDT,

THE BRIGHTON GLEE MADRIGAL SOCIETY.

And other Artistes have kindly consented to render their services *gratuitously*.

The BAND of the 1st SUSSEX VOLUNTEER ARTILLERY Have also promised their valuable assistance.

To commence at Eight o'clock.—Reserved Seats, 5s.; Family Tickets (for three persons) to ditto, 10s. 6d.; Front Seats, 2s. 6d.; and Back Seats, 1s. 6d.

A plan of the room may be seen at

MR JAMES CURTIS'S MUSIC WAREHOUSE,

69, East Street, where tickets and places may be secured. Tickets may also be procured at the other Music Establishments in Brighton.

19
Advert for the benefit concert for John Ackerson Erredge from the *Brighton Gazette*, 4 December 1862

arrived, Erredge was dead[57]. An inquest before the Borough Coroner, Mr David Black, was convened the same afternoon at the Blacksmith's Arms in North Street. Upon his direction, the jury immediately returned a verdict that 'the deceased had died from disease of the heart'.

The funeral took place at the Extra-Mural Cemetery on the afternoon of Monday 10 November 1862 and he was interred in the re-opened grave of his daughter, Helen. It was reported that 'a large number of the tradesmen of the town and personal friends of the deceased manifested their respect by meeting at the gate of the cemetery, where they formed a double line for the mournful cortege to pass through, and then followed on to the chapel and the grave'[58].

On the evening of Wednesday that week, a concert was given at the Town Hall for the benefit of Erredge's widow and young family [**19**], under the patronage of the Mayor, borough members and other distinguished persons[59]. Over 500 people attended the event, with popular artistes of the day, the Brighton Glee Madrigal Society and the 1st Sussex Volunteer Artillery Band all rendering their services gratuitously. There is no record to show how much was raised but the family subsequently posted an advertisement in the local papers returning their grateful acknowledgement [**20**].

The flat, weather-worn tombstone can still be found on the northern slopes of the Extra-Mural Cemetery.

Contribution to Brighton's history

Although Erredge had previously written *The Student's Handbook*, *To Dieppe and Back* and *The Nomenclature of Trades and Tradespersons*, he will be primarily remembered for his book *History of Brighthelmston (or, Brighton as I View It and Others Knew It)*. The alternative title of his book is probably a reference to the contribution made to Erredge's knowledge of the town, as related to him by his aunt, Jane Ackerson.

In 1853, Samuel Shergold had commenced his *Recollections of Brighton in the Olden Times*[60], which was offered as a part-work by a competitor newspaper office. It is considered that both Erredge and John

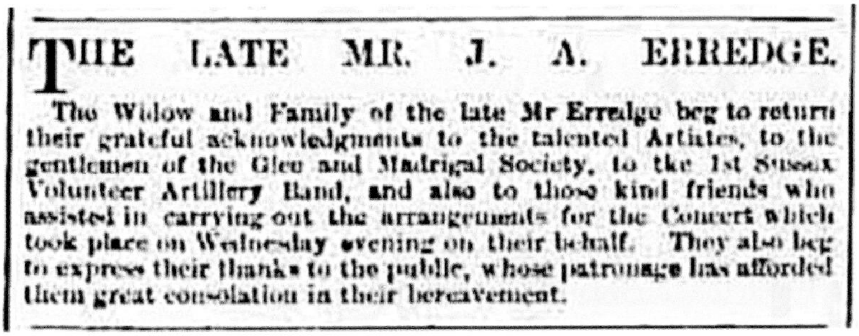
THE LATE MR. J. A. ERREDGE.

The Widow and Family of the late Mr Erredge beg to return their grateful acknowledgments to the talented Artistes, to the gentlemen of the Glee and Madrigal Society, to the 1st Sussex Volunteer Artillery Band, and also to those kind friends who assisted in carrying out the arrangements for the Concert which took place on Wednesday evening on their behalf. They also beg to express their thanks to the public, whose patronage has afforded them great consolation in their bereavement.

20
Response from the Erredge family to the Benefit Concert from the *Brighton Gazette*, 18 December 1862

George Bishop used this as a model for their own historical offerings. By the early 1860s Erredge had collected sufficient material to put pen to paper. From December 1861, the *Brighton Observer* started advertising the part-work, with further sections offered at roughly monthly intervals. Some of the pieces had been contributions by other parties: for example, Mr George Davies (1834-92), a botanist of 72 Springfield Road, contributed a paper on the wild flowers and mosses of Brighton[61]. The final parts were published in November and December 1862, after the death of Erredge. These last two parts were compiled from materials left by the author and completed by his sons.

Each of the part-works carried a coded letter in the bottom right-hand corner of the first and 17th pages; such that part one was coded B and C and so on (there was no letter J used). This helps to identify each of the original individual parts. The completed part-work could be case-bound by a local bookbinder, W Swane at 51 Market Street. Ebenezer Lewis of the *Brighton Observer* office continued to offer the book until 1867, when it was offered using a different title page, by another publisher, W J Smith of 41-43 North Street.

The source materials for the history that are acknowledged by Erredge include passages from Paul Dunvan's *Lee's History of Lewes and Brighton*, Dr Anthony Relhan's *A Short History of Brighthelmston*, a source he describes as written by Dr Coe and extracted from the February 1766 edition of *The Gentleman's Magazine*, Rev. William Gilpin's *Observations on the Coasts of Hampshire, Sussex and Kent* and sundry other books. There are also numerous references to documents in Sir William Burrell's collection of manuscripts, snippets from the *Morning Herald* and extracts taken from two diaries, purportedly held by the author. Erredge does not reveal who the author of one of the diaries is but the other he attributes to 'Mr Bew, who afterwards lived in East Street, was dentist to George IV and, in conjunction with Mr Frederick Vining, lessee of the Theatre Royal, Brighton'[62].

Upon investigation it will be seen that the quotations have in fact been derived from *A Sentimental Diary kept in an excursion to Littlehampton, near Arundel, and to Brighthelmston in Sussex*, author unattributed in the book but known to have been written by Peregrine Phillips in 1778 (Volume one) and 1779 (Volume two). A further edition, combining the two volumes, was published in 1780 and it seems to be from this later edition that Erredge derives most of his quotations.

The most plausible explanation for Erredge believing that the diary was written by Charles Bew, an inhabitant of Brighton during the early

19th century, was a reference on the title page of the second volume of the diary referring to J Bew of Paternoster Row, London, as an agent for the sale of the book. John Bew (1743-1793), a bookseller of 28 Patternoster Row was the father of Charles Bew (1773-1855), who came to Brighton around 1814 after becoming the dentist to George IV. Prior to this he had been an actor of some repute, appearing at theatres up and down the country and later becoming a lessee of the Theatre Royal in Brighton. Given that he was not a resident of Brighton prior to the early 1800s and with his father's name on the book, it is perhaps easy to see how Erredge may have mistaken Bew as a visitor to the town in 1778-79 and the author of the diary. It is also entirely plausible the Charles Bew may have given the diary to Erredge, who then thought it had been written by Bew. As has been mentioned, there is no attribution to Peregrine Phillips in either diary, but it is known from his other works that he was the author of the book.

He also makes a reference to himself, while discussing a Sussex newspaper with a Mr Cooper, as being the 'Peregrine' who had written a letter contained in it[63]. Phillips (1729-1801) was of Welsh extraction, being born to a father of the same name and a French mother named Mlle Cordé. He spent the early part of his life in America as a scholar of Dr Franklin, later returning to England and becoming a lawyer and official of the Wine Licence Office. His marriage in 1751 to Mary Gascoigne (Gaskin) was to result in the birth of the famous actress Anna Maria Crouch (née Phillips) in 1762.

Erredge had aspired to become Brighton's local historian and accumulated a very large collection of cuttings, flyers, trade cards and other ephemera[64], which is now held in Brighton Library Rare Books Department. In later years, Crawford Pocock, assisted by Frank Holford, took two volumes of Erredge's book and pasted the contiguous pages onto one side of 30-inch long strips of stout cartridge paper[65]. Additional materials were added to the other side (mainly topical prints, but also some of Erredges' original source materials) and the work was contained in a dust-proof portfolio. This process is known as grangerisation and it is thought that the Erredge collection in the Brighton Library in its present form is probably this grangerised collection of materials.

[1] The Keep (East Sussex Records Office) W/A 72.800; W/O 1817/34: Will of Samuel Erredge

[2] Budgen's Map of 1788 and Yeakell & Gardner's map of 1779

[3] Cobby map of 1799/1800

[4] The Keep (East Sussex Records Office) DB/B/65/1; Brighton Town Rates Book, 1826

[5] *Brighton Herald*, 5 November 1862

[6] The names in the Parish Registers of Brighton, Willingdon and Eastbourne that were recorded over successive generations are variously given as Cynic / Sinnock / Sennock / Sennoak / Sevenoke / Sevenoak / Synnack / Sannich for the middle name and Erredge / Erridge / Eridge for the surname. The middle name appears to have descended from

Katherine Stretton (née Sinnock, baptised Eastbourne 7 February 1696), who married George Erridge (1700-1784) upon the death of her first husband, Thomas Stretton

[7] Jennifer Killick: *Sea Fencibles Index, volume 2, Sussex coast, 1805*. PRO (ADM28/49&50). There are two Samuel Erredges recorded, probably John's father and his half-brother. His grandfather, if still living, would have been exempted by his age.

[8] Willingdon Parish Register, baptisms (15 September 1733) recorded Samuel Sannich Erredg, son of George Erredg and Katherine

[9] Brighton St Nicholas Parish Register—marriage took place 3 March 1782

[10] Brighton St Nicholas Parish Register, baptisms—namely Samuel Sennock (27 January 1786), Mary (13 April 1788), Richard (25 December 1790) and Elizabeth (25 December 1792)

[11] Hannah was born around 1772, the daughter of John and Mary Ackerson.

[12] The entry in Brighton St Nicholas Parish Register for the baptism on 3 December 1809 actually reads Erredge Ackerson, giving Samuel Ackerson as the father and Hannah as the mother. This is an obvious mistake by the recording cleric

[13] Brighton St Nicholas Parish Register, baptisms—17 February 1815

[14] Monumental Inscription recorded in Brighton churchyard, #294, (the grave of the Ackerson family): 'Hannah, wife of Samuel Erridge, Daughter of John and Mary ACKERSON, died 3rd March 1811, aged 39 years.'

[15] Brighton St Nicholas Parish Register, burials—9 March 1811

[16] Brighton St Nicholas Parish Register, burials—25 November 1816

[17] The Keep (East Sussex Records Office) ,W/A 72.800; W/O 1817/34: Will of Samuel Erredge

[18] A deese-house was used for smoking herrings, of Dutch origin [W. Durrant Cooper: A Glossary of Provincialisms (1853)]

[19] J A Erredge: History of Brighthelmston, p25

[20] The Keep (East Sussex Records Office), BH/G/2/4564 Deeds to 48 & 49, Clarence Square

[21] Brighton St Nicholas Parish Register—marriage between Thomas Stocker and Ann Turner, 3 January 1814

[22] *Brighton Gazette*, 8 September 1825

[23] Brighton St Nicholas Parish Register—marriage between Henry Byron and Ann Turner, 5 January 1827

[24] Stratford, Bow St Mary Parish Register—William Grix married Elizabeth Mary Bevern 28 December 1826

[25] Later renamed Upper St James's Street

[26] Catherine Marchant was the sister of Jane Ackerson (née Marchant)

[27] National Archives B3/1642—List E, Schedule of expenses. This shows that Erredge had expended £29 on the 'Goodwill of School' in 1833 and advertisements in the *Brighton Gazette* in December 1833 and January 1834

[28] Published in 1839 by Relfe & Fletcher of 17 Cornhill Street, London, School Booksellers & Stationers

[29] Review in the Literature section of the *Brighton Herald*, 2 November 1839

[30] Advert in the *Morning Chronicle*,15 February 1840

[31] National Archives B3/1642: List C—Schedule of debts due by the bankrupt

[32] National Archives B3/1642: Evidence of Ann Lake, servant to J A Erredge. She deposed that when Edward Andre called on 29 January 1841 to collect a debt from Erredge, she was told to say he was not at home.

[33] Advert in the *Brighton Herald*, 20 February 1841

[34] *The Stranger's Guide in Brighton for 1845*, W Saunders, St James's Street, p104 and Leppard's Directory for 1843.

[35] Advert in *The Times*, 20 August 1842

[36] *Sussex Advertiser*, 26 March 1844

[37] Cricket match reported in the *Brighton Herald*, 9 June 1842

[38] The Keep (East Sussex Records Office) ,W/A 82.143; W/O 1846/43: Will of Robert Ackerson

[39] Three of these properties were advertised in the *Brighton Gazette* on 19 August 1847 and sold at auction on 28 September 1847, namely 36 and 37 Gardner Street and 56 William Street

[40] 2 Pavilion Street (formerly Prince's Street) was offered as one of four lots on sale, the Brighton Herald, 3 February 1848

[41] National Archives C15/188/C90 1855 Cockburn v Aukett

[42] The Keep (East Sussex Records Office), BH/G/2/3412 Deeds to 10 Clarence Street

[43] The Keep (East Sussex Records Office) HOW/122/3/27: Draft notes of Court Baron, Manor of Old Shoreham, 27. March 1848.

[44] The Keep (East Sussex Records Office), BH/G/2/4564: Deeds to 48 & 49 Clarence Square. John Butcher was the brother-in-law of Ackerson Erredge and another beneficiary of Robert Ackerson's will.

[45] *Sussex Advertiser*, 15 September 1851

[46] *The Era*, 17 April 1853 and J A Erredge: *A History of Brighthelmston*, p321

[47] The surviving beneficiaries, specifically mentioned in Robert Ackerson's will, were Ackerson Erredge (John Ackerson Erredge's brother), Catherine his wife, Mary Hewitt (daughter of Mary Marchant, sister of Jane Ackerson), Robert Pelling (son of Mary Pelling, Robert Ackerson's sister), Abraham Hobbs (son of Susannah Hobbs, Robert Ackerson's sister) and James Stevens (son of Mary Stevens, Jane Ackerson's Sister) were the plaintiffs. *The Weekly Reporter*, 1854/5, vol 3, p641. Chancery: Cockburn v Aukett and National Archives C15/188/C90 1855. Cockburn v Aukett covers the case

[48] *Taylor's Directory of Brighton* 1854, advertisement on p18 and listing for Miss Ada Mary Erridge on p102

[49] National Archives, Chancery Records, C15/194/E8 1855, Erredge v Erredge

[50] *Sussex Advertiser*, 9 September 1856

[51] Hannah Swift was the daughter of Mary Stevens (Jane Ackerson's sister) and had a beneficial interest in the Robert Ackerson's will. National Archives, Chancery Records, C15/423/S124 1857, Swift v Erredge

[52] 1851 census HO107/1646/97

[53] Erredge's obituary in the *Brighton Herald* (5 November 1862) states that 'on the establishment of the *Brighton Observer* in 1856, he became the editor of that paper and remained so until his death'

[54] J A Erredge: *A History of Brighthelmston*, p343

[55] *The Lancet (Medical Trials)*, 21 July 1860, p73

[56] John George Bishop: *Strolls in the Brighton Extra-Mural Cemetery*. Fleet & Co. Brighton Herald Office, 1867

[57] *Brighton Herald*, 8 November 1862 contains a report of the Coroner's Inquest

[58] *Brighton Herald*, 15 November 1862

[59] The Era, 14 November 1862

[60] *Recollections of Brighton in the Olden Times*, written anonymously by 'A Native Thereof', printed by Fleet & Son, Brighton Herald Office

[61] Obituary of George Davies (died 6 April 1892)

[62] J A Erredge: History of Brighthelmston, p200fn

[63] *A Diary kept in an excursion to Little-Hampton and Brighthelmston, in Sussex in 1778 and also to the latter place in 1779*, Volume 2 of 2, p110 (chapter entitled 'In the Alcove')

[64] Although the 'Erredge Collection' was probably originally compiled by J A Erredge, others still continued to supplement it long after his death until the early 20th century

[65] From cuttings contained in the Erredge Collection volume 9, entitled 'A Unique Book of Brighton—Mr Pocock's Edition of Erredge' and 'Old Brighton in Pictures—the Late Mr Pocock's Collection'. Pocock died in early 1890

3 John George Bishop
(1825-1919)

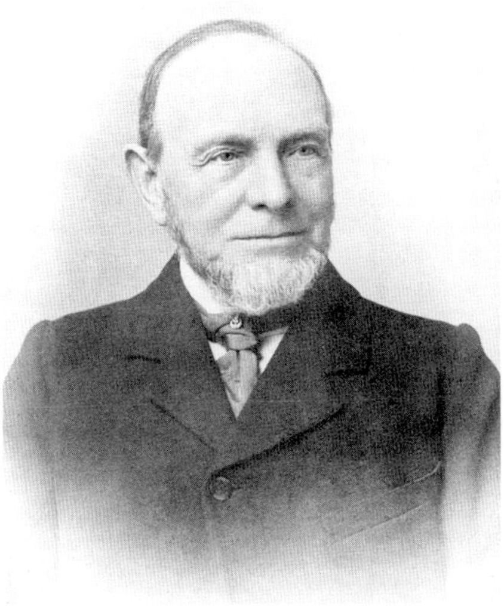

21
John George Bishop

Of all of the chroniclers of Brighton, perhaps the accolade 'Historian of Brighton', devised by an august collection of Brighton townspeople and conferred upon John George Bishop after celebrating 62 years at the *Brighton Herald*, is most justly deserved.

Ancestry and family background

John George Bishop was born on 1 January 1825 at 37 North Street[1]. This tenement was later simply described by Bishop himself as 'a cottage in North Street enclosed with a dwarf wall and wooden palings. Opposite was a house, the frontage of which was covered with a grape vine.'[2] The property was probably one of a small row of cottages, situated on the south side of North Street, between Ship Street and West Street, although there is reason to doubt the number of the house being 37. John Bishop senior was recorded as having lived at 46 North Street[3] immediately prior to a Mr Gardner taking over its occupancy in 1826. As a baby, it is unlikely that Bishop would have any personal memories of the time he lived in the house.

His father, John, was a tailor, born in Hove in 1800. His mother, Sarah (nee Baker), was born in Wickwar, Gloucestershire c1794. The couple had married at St Nicholas Church on 15 February 1824[4] and John George was their first child. He was christened at St Nicholas' on 9 February 1825[5]. Three further offspring followed: Sarah Jane (born 1828), George Baker (born 1830) and Charles (born 1834), all in Brighton. By 1828 the family were living 15 Portland Street, where they continued to reside until the mid 1840s.

As a young boy Bishop had witnessed the building of the town hall during 1830-31 but his memories were much more vividly impressed by the exhibition of John Holloway's semi-nude corpse, displayed upon a table in one of the upper rooms of the new town hall on Saturday 17 December 1831. Holloway had been hanged at Horsham jail on 10 December for the murder of his wife, Celia. He and his lover, Ann Kennet, had dismembered her corpse. The limbs were thrown into a common privy, whilst the torso was taken by wheelbarrow to Lover's Lane in Preston and dumped. The event became known as Brighton's first trunk murder. After Holloway's body had been publicly displayed to thousands of visitors to the town hall, it was removed to the County Hospital for dissection.

Bishop had also been in attendance at the Anthaeum, at that time the largest domed structure ever built, a few hours prior to its dramatic collapse on 30 August 1833. This had been the brainchild of a well-

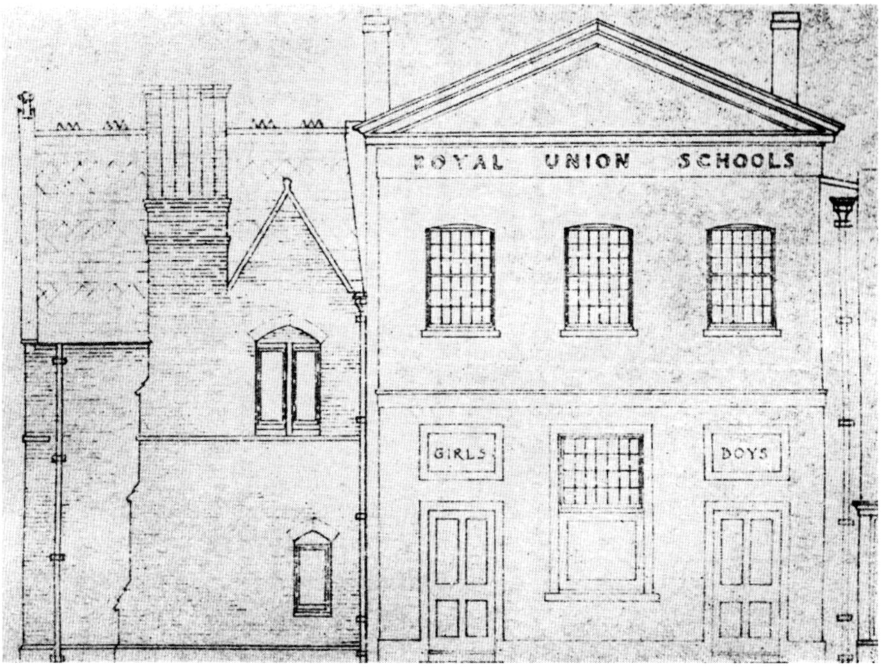

22
Drawing of Union Charity School as it was when Bishop attended

known botanist, Henry Phillips, who had commissioned an engineer named English to design the structure. It briefly stood at the top of what is now Palmeira Square. However, the design of the structure was flawed and Phillips sought the opinion of the celebrated civil engineer, John Rennie, as to whether the central scaffold should be removed. Without awaiting Rennie's opinion, the foreman had incautiously removed the scaffolding, causing structural failure of the supporting beams and a complete collapse of the building.

Another significant event that had made an impression upon his childhood memories was the death of Maria Fitzherbert, the unacknowledged wife of the Prince of Wales (later George IV), on 27 March 1837. He had been permitted to attend the splendid drawing room of her house in the Old Steyne, the walls heavily draped in black, where he stood beside her crimson Genoa velvet draped coffin. He later wrote that 'the remains of Mrs Fitzherbert were borne, "with all the trappings and suits of woe", to their last resting place, the Roman Catholic Chapel of St John the Baptist in Bristol Road'[6].

Education, business and financial life

In 1830, at the age of five, Bishop entered the Union Charity School in Middle Street [**22**]. There he became very attached to the master, James Ward, who had come from the school of the British and Foreign Society in Borough Road, London to run Middle Street School on 29 September 1817. The curriculum during Bishop's time at the school was based on the three 'r's—reading, 'riting and 'rithmetic'. Writing lessons entailed giving each boy a slate and a pencil to record a list of words dictated by

23
The Union Charity School layout as it was when Bishop attended

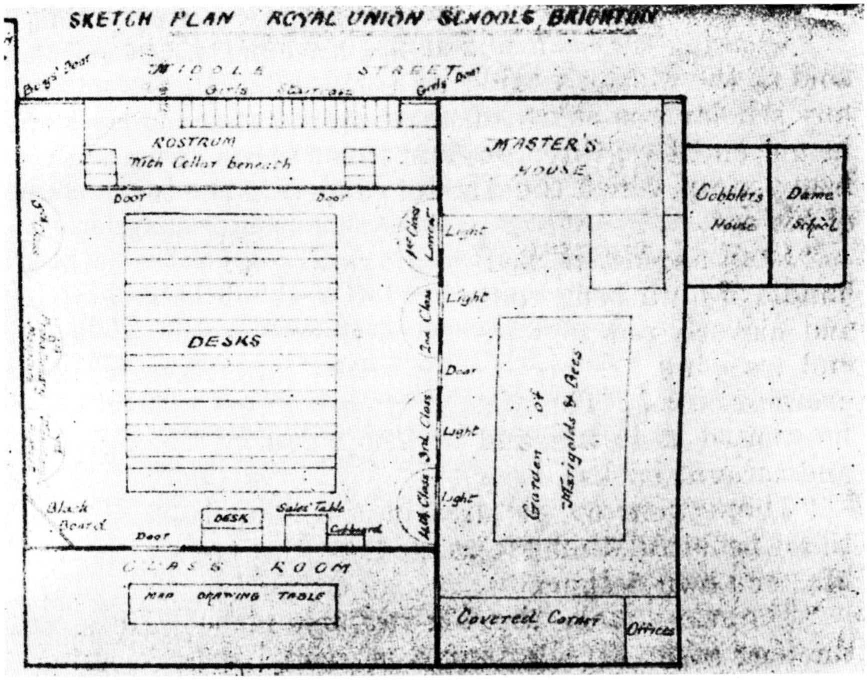

an appointed monitor. Upon completion, each slate would be checked for inaccuracies, corrected and the process repeated.

After having spent some time on this process, the pupils would be taught reading. Sentences from the scriptures were hung on boards around the classroom [**23**] and a monitor of reading and spelling would point out the words and sentences to be read. Each class was divided into companies of eight boys, which were formed into semi-circles that sat opposite to the lesson suited to their proficiency, each company being supervised by a monitor. A badge of merit was hung around the neck of the first boy, who would retain it so long as he was able to maintain his proficiency in reading and spelling. On making a mistake the badge was passed on to the next boy and so on, until whoever had the badge at the end of the lesson would receive a reward. Arithmetic was taught upon a similar principle, initially by reciting tables and then by summation of the columns of a series of three-figure numbers the boys had transcribed onto slates. It was considered that once a boy was competent in reading and writing, that they would be able to teach the elements of arithmetic to any number of other children in the same class.

When Ward left the school on 10 February 1836 to open the new British National School in North Lane (now North Road), Bishop followed him there and was appointed as one of the monitors. Although Ward was a strict disciplinarian, he was immensely respected by his pupils and his peers. Bishop later maintained that '. . . being a "Ward's boy" and armed with his recommendation, served as a passport to many who, on leaving school, sought to obtain an apprenticeship or a start in life.'[7] Bishop kept up his association with his former tutor and in 1852 gave an address at a testimonial commemorating Ward's 35th year of service. Presenting him with a silver inkstand, pen and pencil, together with a framed ornamental address, it was stated 'that Ward had educated over 10,000 boys in Brighton'[8].

Leaving school at the age of 14 in May 1839, he secured a place as an apprentice compositor in the printing department of the *Brighton Herald* in Prince's Place. The newspaper had been founded in 1806 by Henry Robinson Attree and brothers Matthew and Henry Phillips, with Robert Sickelmore as its editor. In 1807 William Fleet became the manager of the newspaper but by May 1808 the partnership of Attree and Phillips had been dissolved, leaving Attree as the sole proprietor. In January 1810 Attree took William Fleet as his partner but by April Attree had decided to leave the business. Another brief partnership was formed, Messrs Fleet and Bray, but this too was dissolved in 1811, leaving Fleet as the sole proprietor until 1843.

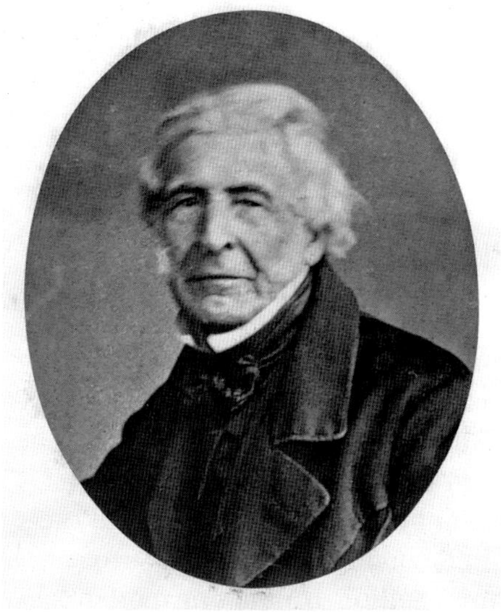

24
William Fleet

When Bishop joined the *Herald*, it was William Fleet [**24**] to whom he was apprenticed. For a fourteen-year-old boy this must have been an extremely arduous vocation, working 13-hour weekdays, starting at 07:00 until 20:00 and a 17-hour hour Saturday, starting at 03:00. On the Friday night he would sleep at Mr Fleet's private residence at 11 Grand Parade and would be awakened at 03:00 to go round and rouse the men for work. This successfully achieved, his next duty entailed awaiting the arrival of the mail coach from London at the post office in New Road. Here he collected the latest copy of the Globe and hurriedly conveyed it to the newspaper offices, in order that extracts could be incorporated into the *Brighton Herald* before going to press. After the papers were printed he would hastily snatch something to eat before setting out on a delivery round stretching as far as Kemp Town. So large was his round that it often required two deliveries and the assistance of his younger brother. Upon his return he was allowed an hour for breakfast before resuming his duties in the office.

It had also been a matter of importance for him to visit the local hotels and finish the round by contacting the Master of Ceremonies at each establishment in order to copy the latest list of visitors to the town entered in their respective reception books. These lists were rushed back to the newspaper offices and subsequently published in the next edition in the 'fashionable arrivals' column.

He had joined the newspaper at a time of great changes to the town; where trade and house-building had been stagnating there was now a new era of prosperity, brought about by the coming of the railway. However, he later opined that the whistle of the railway engine had sounded the death knell to the office of Master of Ceremonies.

Bishop served his apprenticeship with another aspiring youngster, William Woods Mitchell, the son of the founder of *Mitchell's Monthly Advertiser*. In his reminiscences, Bishop relates that he had 'the desire later on to become an actor instead of the proprietor of the Herald. At that time of the day we used to print the playbills for the theatre; and the printing was an early morning job commencing at five o'clock all the season through, which I had to execute with my fellow apprentice Mitchell'. He continues:

> 'Each evening Mitchell and I used to take the proof of the playbill round to the theatre stage, and as they were in no hurry to find the lessees, we made a pretty extensive acquaintance with the drama, and had the best of opportunities of seeing all the leading actors of the age that ever came to Brighton. Mitchell and I and other of the apprentices had already done a little reciting, and the office "Shakespeare" was often in secret requisition. By-and-by Mitchell and myself thought it folly to go on with such a prosaic a calling as printing, when the Muses had clearly destined us for great actors. So, summoning up courage one fine morning, we decided to interview Mr Fleet on the subject, and I was to be the spokesman. With beating hearts we knocked on the office door. Mr Fleet bade us to come in. "What did we want?" "Please Sir, we want our indentures cancelled, we want to go on the stage!" For a moment Mr Fleet looked at us with amazement. Then seizing each of us by the collar, he initiated us into one part of the actor's art—how to make an "exit", putting us outside the door without saying a word. And thus, summarily consigned to the oblivion of a printing office, two budding Macreadys were lost to the stage forever! We were then about sixteen years of age'[9].

The young Mitchell later went on to establish the *West Sussex Gazette* and became one of the foremost campaigners against stamp duty on newspapers, calling it 'a tax upon knowledge'. The two were to remain lifelong friends.

In 1846 the industrious young Bishop had been made overseer of the printing office and in recognition of his love of the stage he was entrusted to write the dramatic notices in the newspaper. Charles Bishop, John's youngest brother, was also taken on by the *Herald* as an apprentice printer in 1848.

By the early 1860s Bishop had been promoted to foreman at the print works. He had also written his first publication, a 'laborious' work on printing. After a full 12-hour days' work, he had been beavering away into the small hours of the morning, taking seven years to compile a series of statistical tables, collated from thousands of calculations that would be of use to printers and compositors. The publication consisted of a series of cards divided into three different headings of 'Book Work' (nine tables), 'News Work' (five tables) and 'Job Work' (12 tables). In February 1862, the original tables were published as a series of cards by Messrs H W Caslon and Co. of Chiswell Street, London and sold for 1s 6d. A few months later at the International Exhibition, running between

1 May and 1 November of that year, the publishers exhibited two framed sets of the cards on their stand, at their own expense. Newspaper articles of the time stated that they were 'so comprehensive in their contents, and of such general utility, as will probably in the trade lead to their general use'[10]. The publication received a degree of critical acclaim from reviews in *The Times* and *Daily Telegraph* and copies sold both at home and abroad, with the tables being adopted 'in most of the large offices in London, Liverpool, Manchester, Dublin and Edinburgh'[11].

In 1843 William Fleet had taken his son, Charles, into partnership. Charles had served his time with the *Brighton Herald* from an early age and had developed uncanny skills as a compositor. He also had an extremely good memory, such that he could memorise a speech or lecture and without recourse to notes, could set up the type ready for printing an article. Charles Fleet had a keen interest in the history of Brighton and Sussex, which he wrote about in *The Handbook of Brighton*[12] and *The Brighton Fishery*[13] during the 1850s. From 1875 onwards he wrote a series of articles entitled 'Glimpses of Our Sussex Ancestors' in the *Brighton Herald*. These were later compiled into a book of the same name, originally released in 1878 and published by W J Smith (Brighton). It was later expanded into two volumes[14].

Charles Fleet and Bishop had worked alongside each other for some years at the *Herald* news office and were like-minded colleagues. On 6 September 1856, the 50th Jubilee of the founding of the *Brighton Herald*, Bishop presented a handsomely-framed, illuminated address of congratulations, on behalf of the employees to William and Charles Fleet. On the retirement of William Fleet in November 1864, his son Charles showed no hesitation in taking Bishop as his partner. The first edition of the *Brighton Herald* bearing his name with that of Charles Fleet as the joint proprietors was issued on 19 November 1864.

Both Fleet and Bishop had a common interest in antiquarian matters and during the period of their tenure, the *Herald* office became a regular meeting place for those with similar interests. 'Amongst those who many a time and oft coming to discuss matters of early local history, and to bring the most recently discovered print or map or record, were such men as Crawford J Pocock, whose collection of local prints now finds a home in the Pavilion; Mr John Haines, a lifelong collector; and the late Mr F E Sawyer, who, with access to the old deeds of Brighton, was continually unearthing some new chapter of early history. All this was regularly communicated to Mr Bishop, through whom they were duly chronicled in the pages of the "Herald". In this and other ways Mr Bishop was gradually amassing material for his two chief works on local history.'[15]

June 1880 saw Charles Fleet retire from the *Brighton Herald* and with the official dissolution of the partnership on 2 July 1880, Bishop became the sole proprietor. The year also saw the release of what was probably Bishop's most important work, *A Peep into the Past —Brighton in the Olden Time*. He had also printed and published a number of significant Shakespearian volumes by J O Halliwell-Phillipps during the course of that year. However, 1880 also brought great tragedy to his life with the loss of his beloved Litty, who died on 9 October at the age of 60.

From around 1851 Bishop had been a member of the Brighton and Sussex Mutual Provident Society and had always taken an active interest in its works. In 1882 he was elected as a director of the society, a post that he held until 1903. He was also recognised for his philanthropy, having rendered valuable service to the charitable institutions of the town, personally raising nearly £1,400, including large sums of money for local individuals who had suffered misfortune.

Over the years Bishop was presented with numerous public and private testimonials. In 1889, in recognition of 50 years' service with the *Herald*, his employees presented him with a framed illuminated address, written by Mr James W Nias, the editor of the *Brighton Herald* and a leading member of the Institute of Journalists. In the address, it is stated that it was appropriate that the *Brighton Herald*, then in its 83rd year, 'should have for its proprietor the senior member of the Brighton press, who, in successive capacities has won his way by his own ability, prudence, integrity and industry. Whilst your career has thus afforded a bright example to others, we gladly welcome the unique opportunity of recording our recognition of the helpful and healthful influence you have brought to bear on those with whom you are daily in contact by your generous and kindly spirit as an employer, and the sterling worth of your character as a man.'[16]

25
Sir Joseph Ewart, Mayor of Brighton 1891-94. and his sister, Miss Grace Ewart, Mayoress

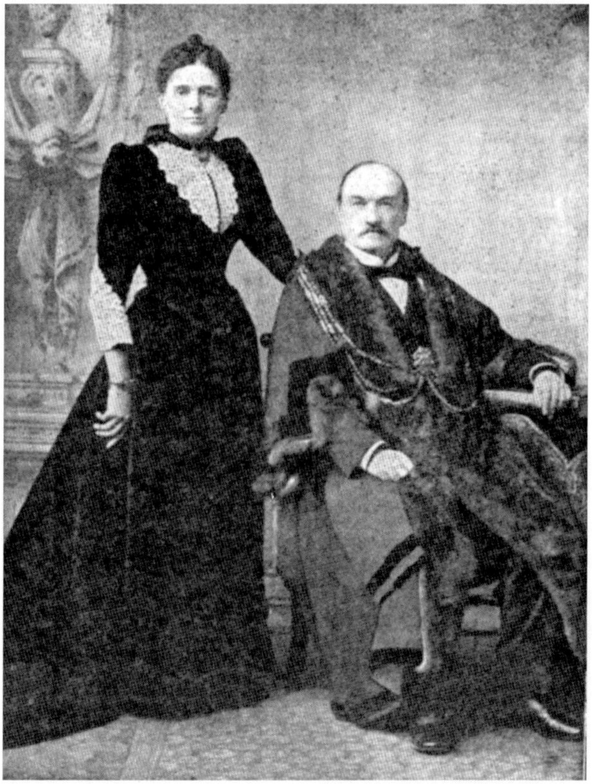

On 9 July 1894 Bishop visited Antwerp as one of the Sussex representatives to the first International Conference of Journalists. After the conclusion of the conference, on 12 July, the delegation visited Brussels, where they were received by the King and Queen of Belgium in the Royal Palace at Lacken. After being presented to King Leopold II and Queen Marie Henriette, Bishop conversed freely with their majesties and was later joined by Princess Clementine, who related how much she had admired Brighton on her visits there. Bishop subsequently sent them handsomely bound copies of his histories.

On the occasion of his 70th birthday on

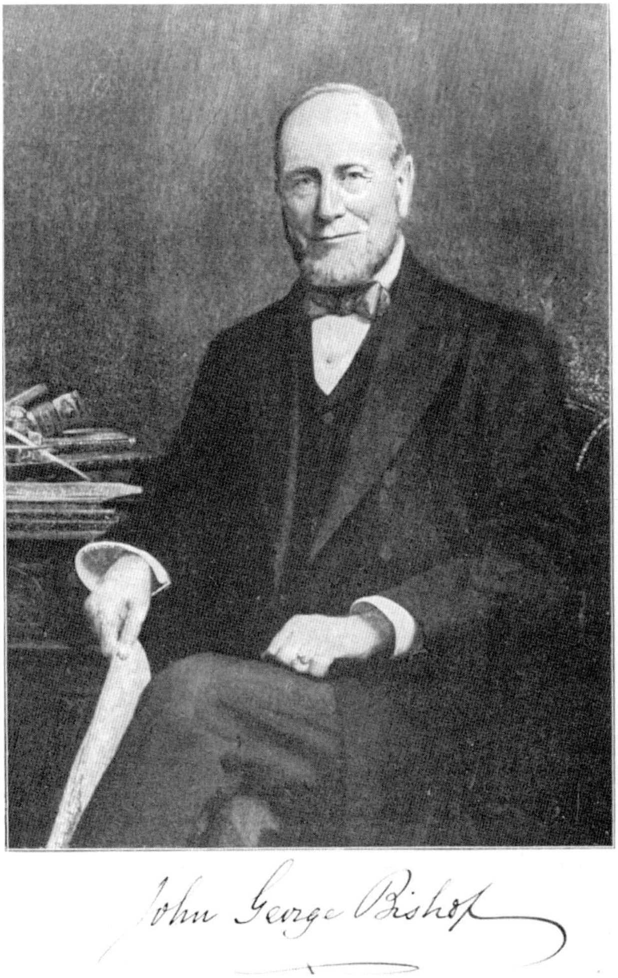

26
Photographic copy of the portrait of Bishop painted in oils by Frederick Brueton (1859-1916). This copy was autographed by Bishop for George Beal, one of the subscribers.

1 January 1895, in the Music Room at the Pavilion, some 250 of his fellow townsmen presided over by the former mayor, Sir Joseph Ewart JP MD MRCS FRCP [**25**], presented Bishop with a cheque for £300 and an illuminated address acknowledging his labours as a 'journalist, historian and philanthropist'. A month later, at a dinner in his honour at Booth's restaurant, the Institute of Journalists presented him with a framed life-size, half body portrait and an illuminated album containing the names and portraits of the subscribers.

With Bishop attaining 60 years of service to the *Brighton Herald* in May 1899, he joined his staff for a dinner at the Chinese Gardens in Hurst and in commemoration of the event he was presented with a gold ring. In return he gave each of them a mounted souvenir photograph of himself, with his autograph and the inscription 'This for Remembrance'. On 11 July 1899 a meeting was held at the town hall and a committee was formed, chaired by Mr John G Blaker JP. It was resolved 'that, as a permanent recognition of Mr John George Bishop's historical services to the Town of Brighton, it is desirable that his portrait should be painted, with the view of it being presented to the Town, and, with the sanction of the Corporation, placed in the Public Gallery'[17]. There were 78 subscribers to the 'Portrait Fund' and the biggest problem was not in raising subscriptions but in limiting the number of those subscribing. Frederick Brueton, a well-known portrait and figure artist, who at that time was living in Preston, employed as an art master at Brighton School of Art, was commissioned to paint the three-quarter length portrait in oils. The portrait, mounted in a Watt's frame with a plate at the foot bearing the inscription 'To the Corporation of Brighton. John George Bishop, Historian and Journalist, Brighton Herald, 1839-1899, from admiring Townsmen' [**26**], was presented by Sir John G Blaker on behalf of the Corporation to the Mayor, Alfred J Hawkes, in the presence of the subscribers at the Royal Pavilion on Monday 16 October 1899. At the same time Bishop was presented with a handsome commemorative set of solid silver plate. [**27**]

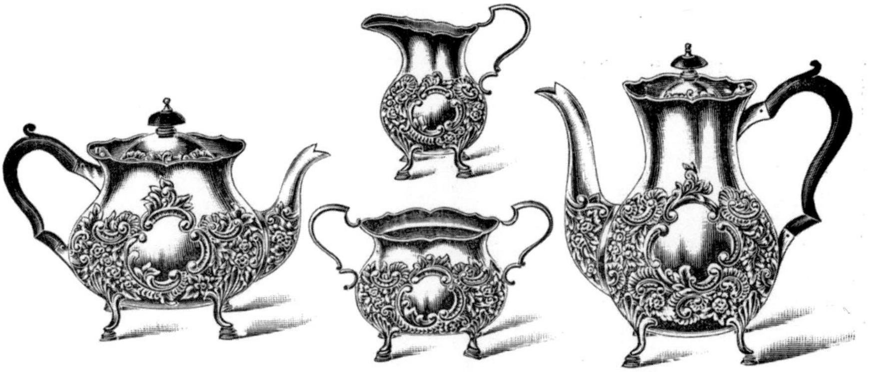

27
Silver Tea and Coffee Service presented to Bishop by the committee of the 'Portrait Fund'. Each of the pieces was engraved with the Brighton coat of arms and a salver, upon which was inscribed the message 'To John George Bishop, Brighton, Historian and Journalist, from many admiring friends, October 1899'

In his address to the gathering at the presentation of the portrait, Sir John Blaker, a staunch conservative, said of Bishop's political views that he had 'never hesitated to strike out for the side he thinks right—though I am bound to confess I think he is sometimes wrong! Mr Bishop has always expressed his views in the newspaper, as it were, straight from the shoulder, and his blows have always been above the belt, and I dare say I should not be wrong if I said he could probably claim as many friends, if not more, on the opposite political side, even than his own radical friends.'[18] The newspaper had started in 1806 with a Whig leaning but during Attree's tenure it had become a supporter of the Liberals[19]. This closely accorded with Bishop's own political views as the newspaper retained the same political allegiances throughout his tenure.

At the age of 75, in May 1901, Bishop announced that he was retiring from the *Brighton Herald* after completing 62 years of service. In 1903 he retired as a director of the Brighton and Sussex Mutual Provident Society, which passed a resolution 'conveying the sincere regret of the directors on his severing his connection with the board and tendering him their best thanks on behalf of the society for his long and valuable services'[20].

Family life

On 8 September 1849 Bishop married Felicia, the daughter of John and Mary Ann Hills, whom he affectionately referred to as 'Litty'. Their first child, Felicia Sarah, was born in December 1850 and by this time the family were living at 16 Tidy Street. In 1856 their first son was born and christened John Hampden but sadly the child died at the age of three on 28 April 1859. A second daughter, Mary Ann, was born in 1856. A third daughter, Kate Eliza, was born in 1858 and their fourth daughter, Ada Mary on 27 December 1867. Another son, John George, was born in 1870 but died very shortly after birth. The eldest daughter, Felicia, never married and died on 21 September 1868. Mary Ann married George Hobbs in 1887 and died in Birmingham on 8 August 1896. Kate married Edward Harry Cuddington on 14 December 1889 at Clermont Congregational Church in Preston and their first child was born a year later.

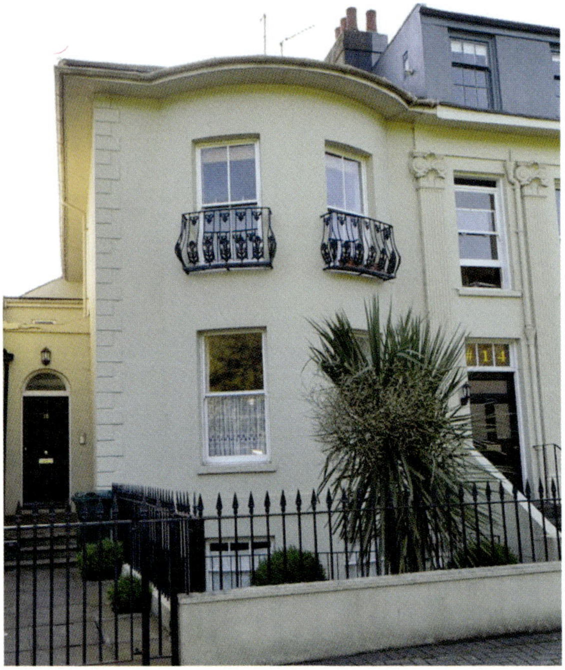

28
15 Hanover Crescent. Bishop's home from 1868 to 1878 and 1896 until his death in 1919. The road was built as a crescent of Palladian villas by Amon Wilds and Amon Henry Wilds around 1814 to 1823

The Bishop family moved frequently during the 1850s and 1860s, being listed at 10 Victoria Road from 1859 until 1861 and in the spring of the same year at 9 Hampden Road. By 1864 they had moved to 5 Rose Hill Terrace and in July 1868 Bishop acquired a Palladian villa overlooking the Level at 15 Hanover Crescent [**28**], where he remained until 1878. Thereafter he appears to have moved to Shoreham, where he was recorded as living at 12 Southdown Road[21]. By 1889 he had returned to Brighton, living at 11 Ditchling Road, a semi-detached villa overlooking Round Hill House, until 1891. Thereafter he moved to 3 Ditchling Terrace [**29**], overlooking the Level. His final move was around 1896, back into 15 Hanover Crescent, where he remained for the remainder of his life.

Bishop had enjoyed remarkably good health throughout most of his life but unsurprisingly with advancing age came a general deterioration in his health. In a letter to a Mrs Thorpe in 1908 he wrote, 'I am glad to add that I continue fairly well except for that everlasting complaint, "old age".'[22] A year after the outbreak of the Great War, when he was approaching his 90th year, he still retained his mental faculties, although some minor physical

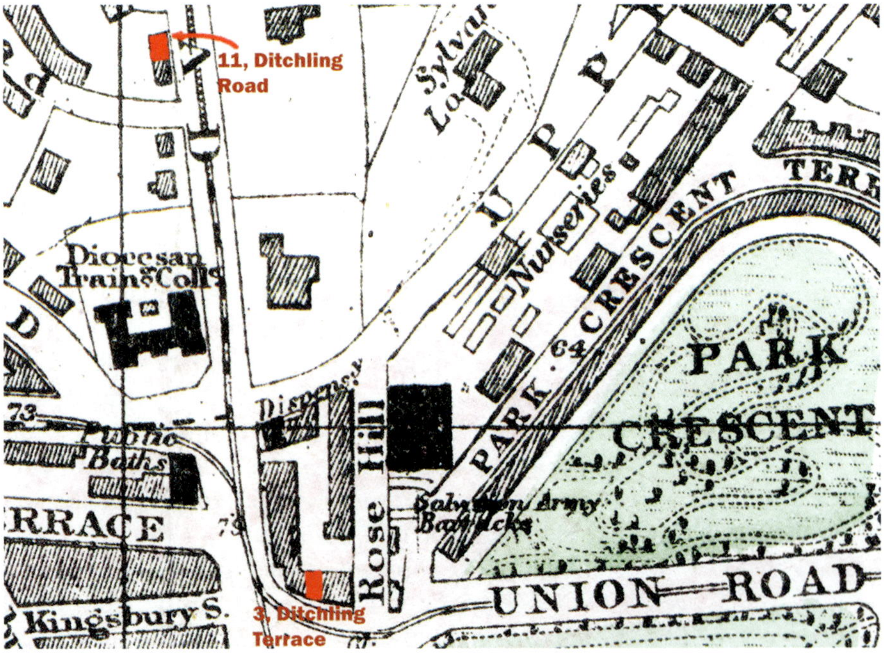

29
Contemporary map with the location of two of Bishop's houses in the 1890s. Ditchling Terrace was subsequently absorbed and renumbered into Ditchling Road c1900; 11 Ditchling Road was also renumbered and is now 107 Ditchling Road

infirmities began to assert themselves, ultimately making writing very difficult for him.

On 15 October 1915 he contacted his solicitor, Henry Cane and made out his last will and testament, appointing John Harry Gilkes and William Peckham Mundy as his joint executors and bequeathing them £10 each for their troubles. He stated a desire that his funeral 'may be plain and inexpensive and that not more than 20 guineas may be expended upon it '. For some considerable years his daughter, Ada, who never married, remained with him as his closest and constant companion, nursing and caring for him throughout his declining years. During the course of 1916 he suffered a paralytic seizure and was thereafter bedridden, with his memory becoming increasingly blurred and confused.

By 29 August 1916 Bishop found it necessary to add a codicil to the will 'in order to meet the expenses of my prolonged illness', which he did by cashing in part of his holding of bonds of the Corporation of Hove to the nominal value of £200, originally intended as a bequest to his daughter Kate Eliza Cuddington. Less than a month later, on 25 September. another codicil was added revoking bequests made to his son-in-law, Edward Harry Cuddington. In a third and final codicil, dated 19 March 1917, he revoked a bequest to his daughter Kate of a third part of his holding of bonds and shares and of an interest in his freehold property.

Whether some kind of rift had developed in the family that precipitated these changes to his will is not known but it is evident that his daughter Ada was ultimately the principal beneficiary of the will. By the spring of 1919 Bishop had become extremely weak and in the early hours of Monday 31 March he passed peacefully away, with his devoted daughter Ada at his side, holding his hand.

The arrangements for the funeral were carried out by Hanningtons Ltd, as requested by Bishop in his will. The funeral took place on Thursday 3 April, commencing with a procession to St Peter's Church, the coffin being covered with spring flowers, followed by the mourners, his two daughters (Mrs Kate Cuddington and Miss Ada Bishop), his executors (Mr J Harry Gilkes and Mr W P Mundy) and his solicitor, Councillor Henry Cane. The service was attended by a very large gathering of Brighton worthies, representatives from the press, Friendly Societies and all those who thought highly of him.

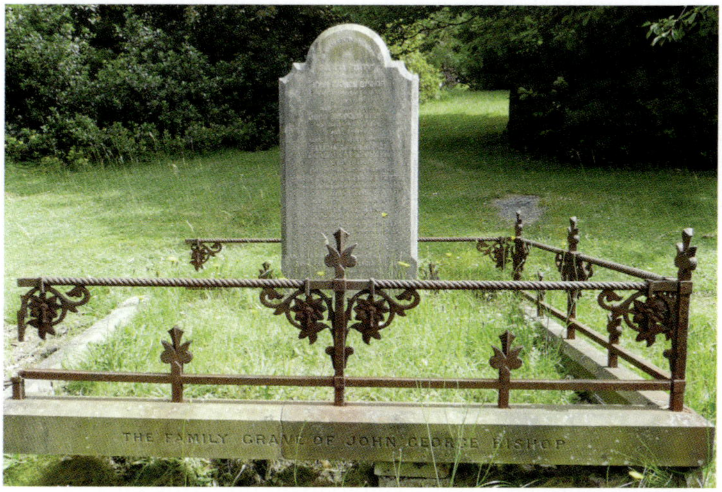

30
The family grave of John George Bishop in Brighton Extra-Mural Cemetery

After the service, the sound of Chopin's Funeral March vibrated through the church as the coffin, followed by the funeral cortège, departed on its final journey along the Lewes Road to the family grave in the Extra-Mural Cemetery [**30**].

In his will, Bishop bequeathed his properties, consisting of his principal abode at 15 Hanover Crescent and 1 North Road (a four-storey commercial building on the corner with Marlborough Place, in the occupation of Gates & Co., builders, decorators and shop fitters, which had been left to him in 1908 in the will of his brother, George Baker Bishop) to his daughter Ada. Similarly his considerable portfolio of bonds, shares and assurance policies was also largely devised to her, with the token exception of the sum of £30, plus an additional £7 10s 0d for mourning clothes and any additional nominal expenses incurred prior to execution of the will, for the benefit of his other daughter, Kate.

The silver tea and coffee service was bequeathed to his two daughters, to be divided such that Kate received the inscribed silver salver, the coffee pot and three of each sort of the souvenir spoons, whilst Ada was to receive the tea-tray, tea-pot, sugar basin, milk jug, hot water jug, three of each sort of the souvenir spoons and tongs with the case.

The copyright to some of his books had already been sold in 1912, although the sale was considered void as it had breached section 5(2) of the Copyright Act, 1911. To redress the situation Bishop effectuated the contract to sell them by bequeathing any reversionary interest in those works absolutely to the buyer, Walter Harrison. The copyright of the remainder of his works was devised to Ada. The will was proved at the District Probate Registry at Lewes on 29 May 1919, the gross value of the estate being £3,368 13s 0d.

Bishop's youngest daughter, Ada Mary, remained a spinster and continued to live in the house that her father had bequeathed to her until around 1925. In 1928 she moved to a property overlooking Blaker's Park at 27 Cleveland Road. Ada died at the Sussex Counties Nursing Home at 11 Cornwall Gardens on 10 May 1937. She was interred with her father in the family grave.

Edward Harry Cuddington was a civil servant, a statistician working for the Customs and Excise Department. He had become familiar with the Bishop family while they were living in New Shoreham, which is how he met Kate. However, not long after their marriage in 1889, Edward's work took him away from New Shoreham to work in London. This probably precipitated Bishop's return to Brighton.

In the meantime, Kate and her baby son continued to live with her father and sister until a suitable house could be found. The couple had five children, three boys and two girls. Edward predeceased Bishop, passing away on 23 October 1918. At this time the family were living at 33 Montholme Road in Wandsworth, where Kate continued to live after his death. Kate died at 75 Heath Street, Hampstead on 7 August 1945.

Contribution to Brighton's history

Bishop's main contribution to Brighton's history endures in the numerous books he wrote, but it should also be remembered that he also wrote countless articles during his long career at the *Brighton Herald*.

At the time that Bishop was the proprietor of the newspaper, *Friend's Brighton Almanack*[23] gave the following description: 'It contains accurate reports of all public proceedings and events; special attention is paid to fashionable and local intelligence, concerts and entertainments generally, and the journal is conducted in all its departments (particularly those concerned with literature and fine arts, and local intelligence) with great ability.'

Bishop's books

Strolls in the Brighton Extra-Mural Cemetery 1864-1867 (First & Second Series).
Brighton: Herald Office, 1867.

During the course of 1864, Bishop had written a three-part article entitled 'Strolls in the Brighton Cemeteries—the Extra-Mural Cemetery'. The first part appeared in the *Brighton Herald* of Saturday 28 May 1864, with part two and part three appearing in the following weeks' newspapers. The articles concluded with the final words: 'and here we must close our series of "Strolls in the Brighton Cemeteries", reserving for a future period some account of the parochial cemetery which adjoins it'.

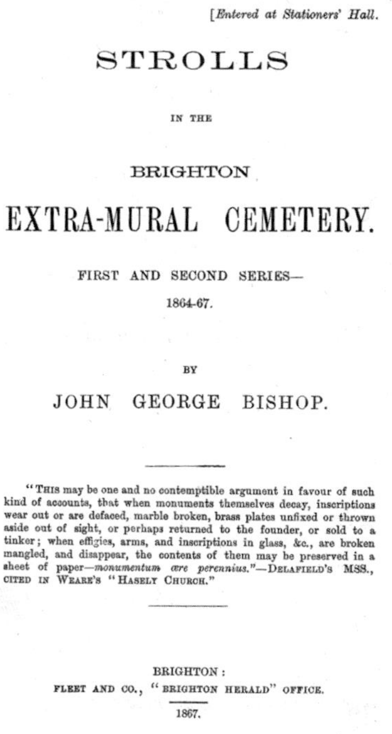

[*Entered at Stationers' Hall.*

STROLLS

IN THE

BRIGHTON

EXTRA-MURAL CEMETERY.

FIRST AND SECOND SERIES—
1864-67.

BY

JOHN GEORGE BISHOP.

"THIS may be one and no contemptible argument in favour of such kind of accounts, that when monuments themselves decay, inscriptions wear out or are defaced, marble broken, brass plates unfixed or thrown aside out of sight, or perhaps returned to the founder, or sold to a tinker; when effigies, arms, and inscriptions in glass, &c., are broken mangled, and disappear, the contents of them may be preserved in a sheet of paper—*monumentum ære perennius.*"—DELAFIELD'S MSS., CITED IN WEARE'S "HASELY CHURCH."

BRIGHTON:
FLEET AND CO., "BRIGHTON HERALD" OFFICE.
1867.

However, the next series of 'strolls' did not appear until June 1867, which he called the second series and comprised four parts. During the summer of 1867, Bishop collated the articles and expanded the text with additional material into a book entitled *Strolls in the Brighton Extra-Mural Cemetery* [**31**]. A particularly useful feature was added to the original work by way of an index to the names mentioned in the strolls.

A contemporary review remarked that 'Mr Bishop writes simply, fairly, not over-indulging in rhapsodies, or moralising more than the circumstances require. His work must have involved considerable labour, for he has evidently spared no pains. His work is one that commends itself, as we have said, to the great mass of our townsmen and townswomen, by whom it will doubtless be appreciated.'[24] The print-run for the book was relatively small and at 6d a copy, it sold out very quickly. Within a few years the book had become a collectors' item, changing hands at greatly inflated prices.

It is particularly interesting to note that Bishop's concluding paragraph in his original article details an 'ornamentation fund', set up at the suggestion of a Mr Yarrow, whereby the directors set aside an accumulating fund of £100 a year, which was added to benevolent bequests granted for the purpose. With the accrued interest, this was considered sufficient for the employment of 'gardeners to protect and keep in good order the whole grounds in perpetuity'.

A Peep into the Past—Brighton in 1800.
Brighton: Herald Office, unknown date.

In January 1865 the *Brighton Herald* had received a specimen sheet of *The Worthies of Sussex* by Mark Anthony Lower, which was reviewed in most favourable terms by Bishop. This series of biographical portraits had been compiled by Lower over the previous two years and was published at the end of August in that year. In December 1865 Bishop went on to write a review of Page's *Brighton Directory* for 1866, entitled 'Brighton Anatomised'[25], in which can be detected the catalyst for his later work *A Peep into the Past—Brighton in 1800*[26]. The likelihood is that it appeared as a newspaper article, similar to 'Brighton Anatomised', and may subsequently have been published as a small booklet. There is a clue to the content of the work in the later preface to *A Peep into the Past—Brighton in the Olden Time* of 1880.

The first chapter of the book, 'The Brighthelmston Directory for 1800', makes it clear that it was written around 1875, as Bishop states 'contemporaneous descriptions of a town, so long back as three quarters of a century, do not often come to light'. Cobby's Directory was included in the 1880 book, but in reading through Bishop's description, it seems as if he was conveying the information to the reader without the benefit of providing a copy of the directory. It is therefore considered likely that this chapter was probably the earlier work *A Peep into the Past—Brighton in 1800*, which was subsequently incorporated into his 1880 book, together with addition of the directory.

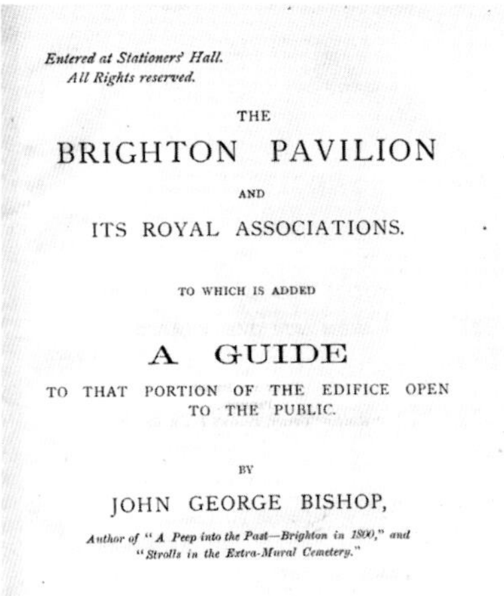
Entered at Stationers' Hall.
All Rights reserved.

THE
BRIGHTON PAVILION
AND
ITS ROYAL ASSOCIATIONS.

TO WHICH IS ADDED
A GUIDE
TO THAT PORTION OF THE EDIFICE OPEN TO THE PUBLIC.

BY
JOHN GEORGE BISHOP,
Author of "A Peep into the Past—Brighton in 1800," and "Strolls in the Extra-Mural Cemetery."

PRICE ONE SHILLING.

BRIGHTON:
FLEET AND BISHOP, "HERALD" OFFICE,
1875.

The Brighton Pavilion and its Royal Associations.
Brighton: Fleet & Bishop, Herald Office, 1875.

As previously mentioned, with the combined historical writings of Fleet and Bishop in the *Brighton Herald*, their offices became a regular forum for those with a historical interest. Collectors and historians, such as Crawford J Pocock, John Haines and Frederick E Sawyer regularly visited the offices of the newspaper and shared their own materials and new discoveries. In 1873, at the instigation of the mayor, James Ireland, Bishop used the materials he had accumulated to write *The Brighton Pavilion and its Royal Associations*. The work was completed by May 1875 and the first edition was released that same year.

This was, for many years, to become the *de facto* guide-

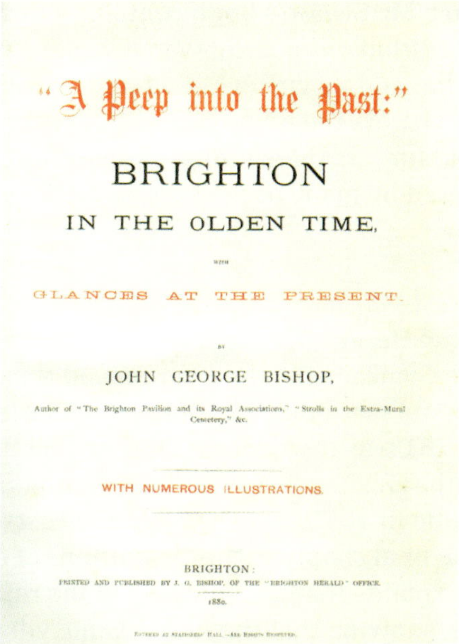

"A Peep into the Past:"

BRIGHTON

IN THE OLDEN TIME,

WITH

GLANCES AT THE PRESENT.

BY

JOHN GEORGE BISHOP,

Author of "The Brighton Pavilion and its Royal Associations," "Strolls in the Extra-Mural Cemetery," &c.

WITH NUMEROUS ILLUSTRATIONS.

BRIGHTON:

PRINTED AND PUBLISHED BY J. G. BISHOP, OF THE "BRIGHTON HERALD" OFFICE.

1880.

Entered at Stationers' Hall.—All Rights Reserved.

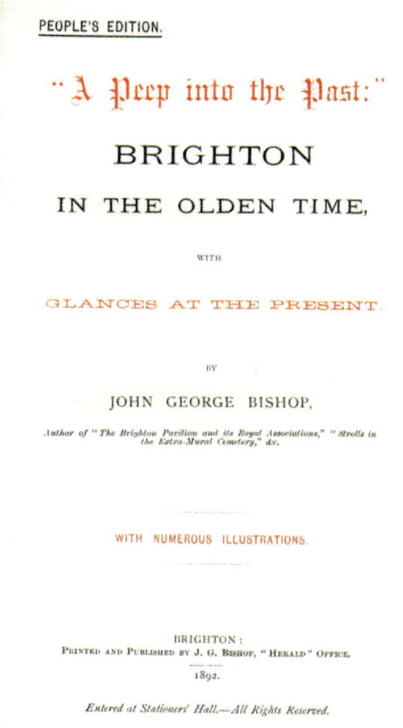

PEOPLE'S EDITION.

"A Peep into the Past:"

BRIGHTON

IN THE OLDEN TIME,

WITH

GLANCES AT THE PRESENT.

BY

JOHN GEORGE BISHOP,

Author of "The Brighton Pavilion and its Royal Associations," "Strolls in the Extra-Mural Cemetery," &c.

WITH NUMEROUS ILLUSTRATIONS.

BRIGHTON:

PRINTED AND PUBLISHED BY J. G. BISHOP, "HERALD" OFFICE.

1892.

Entered at Stationers' Hall.—All Rights Reserved.

book for the pavilion, being periodically reissued as revised editions. There were at least 13 editions of this book up to 1910. Around 1892 Bishop had taken on George Aitchison[27] as an apprentice and protégé. In 1910 they had jointly issued *The Brighton Pavilion: historical outlines, guide & catalogue of the Old Brighton Museum, an illustrated guide* which was extracted from the above work.

A Peep into the Past—Brighton in the Olden Time.
Brighton: Brighton Herald Office, 1880.

The first edition was published in November 1880 in quarto form, with portraits and numerous prints. Selling at 25s 0d, it was a comparatively expensive book, but nevertheless considerable numbers were sold.

An unusual feature for the time was the use of two colours, black and red, for the type on the title page, a feature that he continued to use in most of his subsequent works.

A Peep into the Past—Brighton in the Olden Time with Glances at the Present, People's Edition.
Brighton: Brighton Herald Office, 1892.

At the request of friends, Bishop was induced to publish a cheaper 'people's edition' of *A Peep into the Past — Brighton in the Olden Time* in the summer of 1892, being a virtual reprint of his earlier book to which was added supplementary information.

Literary reviews in the press were positive, describing Bishop as 'a beguiling writer, for he leads on from one to another of these memories in so pleasant a style that it is difficult to turn away from the book'[28].

Another adds that 'Mr Bishop's book contains a number of very quaint and curious illustrations, which show in a striking manner how very unlike the Brighton and its visitors of a hundred years ago are to the Brighton and its visitors today'[29].

The book sold for less than a third of the price of the original volume and was considered by many at the time to be the standard local history of Brighton.

A Peep into the Past—Brighton in 1744-61.
Brighton: Brighton Herald Office, 1895.

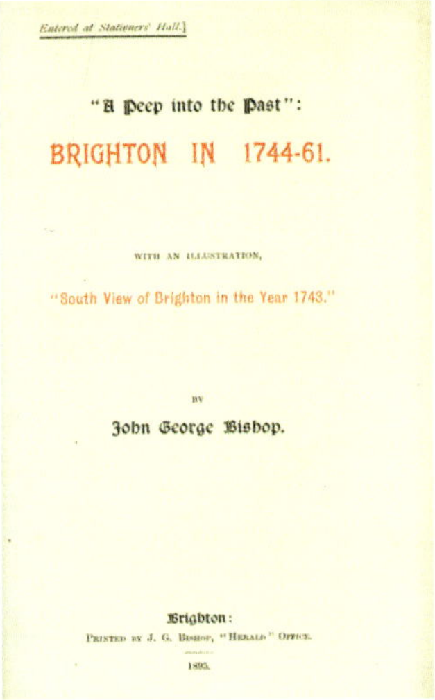

Entered at Stationers' Hall.]

"A Peep into the Past":

BRIGHTON IN 1744-61.

WITH AN ILLUSTRATION,

"South View of Brighton in the Year 1743."

BY

John George Bishop.

Brighton:

PRINTED BY J. G. BISHOP, "HERALD" OFFICE.

1895.

After the Guardians of the Poor moved their offices to Prince's Place, an old rate book containing entries from April 1744 to March 1761 was discovered. This formed the basis of a series of articles that Bishop wrote in the *Brighton Herald* and led to the publication in 1895 of *A Peep into the Past—Brighton in 1744-61*. In the final chapter, 'The "Evolution" of early Brighton', Bishop explains that the contents of the rate book came as a surprise, showing that the little fishing village had risen in a few brief years from the direst poverty to become a notable fashionable marine resort.

This particular premise is the one which has endured over the years and features in most historical descriptions concerning the development of Brighton. Like his previous works, the title page was printed in red and black.

The Brighton Chain Pier: In Memoriam.
Brighton: Brighton Herald Office, 1896.

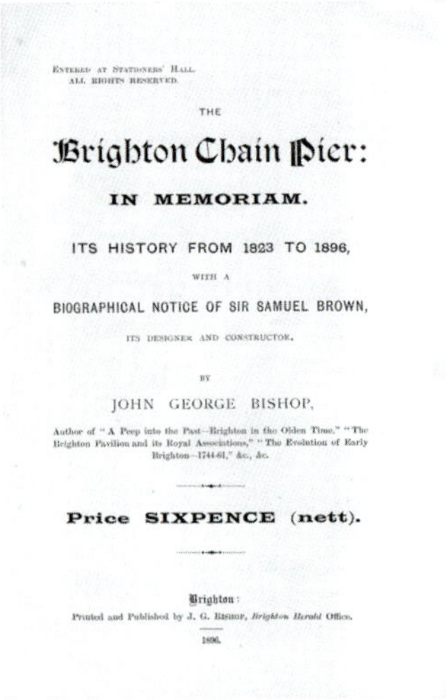

ENTERED AT STATIONERS' HALL.
ALL RIGHTS RESERVED.

THE

Brighton Chain Pier:

IN MEMORIAM.

ITS HISTORY FROM 1823 TO 1896,

WITH A

BIOGRAPHICAL NOTICE OF SIR SAMUEL BROWN,

ITS DESIGNER AND CONSTRUCTOR.

BY

JOHN GEORGE BISHOP,

Author of "A Peep into the Past—Brighton in the Olden Time," "The Brighton Pavilion and its Royal Associations," "The Evolution of Early Brighton—1744-61," &c., &c.

Price SIXPENCE (nett).

Brighton:

Printed and Published by J. G. BISHOP, *Brighton Herald* Office.

1896.

A cataclysmic event for Brighton—the destruction of the chain pier during a terrific storm that occurred at 22:30 on the night of 4 December 1896—led to the publication of *The Brighton Chain Pier: In Memoriam*. Although the pier had been purchased by the new Marine Palace and Pier Company and was already due to be removed after the Palace Pier had been constructed, there was great shock and sadness evident among the inhabitants of the town following its destruction in such a manner.

To show his appreciation for this historic volume, Mr Frederick Crunden, a well-known cabinet-maker of New Road, presented Bishop with a handsome, highly polished walking stick carved from the wood of the Chain Pier, embellished with a silver end cap and bands engraved with his name and a commemorative inscription.

Miscellaneous Subjects, Historical & Literary.
Brighton: Brighton Herald Office, 1899.
Bishop's final book was released in October 1899 as a dedication to the

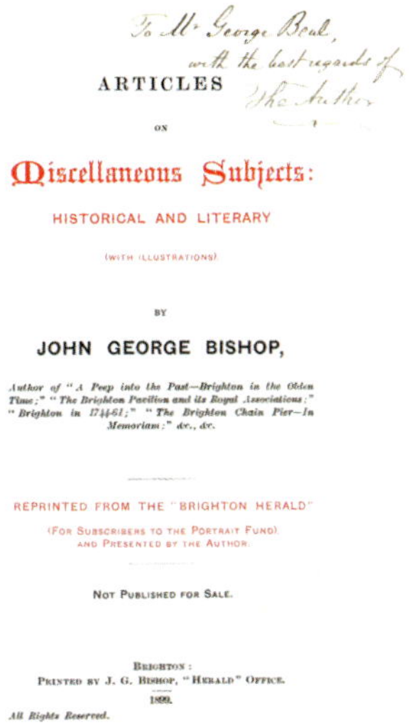

To Mr George Beal,
with the best regards of
The Author

ARTICLES

ON

Miscellaneous Subjects:

HISTORICAL AND LITERARY

(WITH ILLUSTRATIONS)

BY

JOHN GEORGE BISHOP,

Author of "A Peep into the Past—Brighton in the Olden Time;" "The Brighton Pavilion and its Royal Associations;" "Brighton in 1744-61;" "The Brighton Chain Pier—In Memoriam;" &c., &c.

REPRINTED FROM THE "BRIGHTON HERALD"

(FOR SUBSCRIBERS TO THE PORTRAIT FUND)
AND PRESENTED BY THE AUTHOR.

NOT PUBLISHED FOR SALE.

BRIGHTON:
PRINTED BY J. G. BISHOP, "HERALD" OFFICE.
1899.

All Rights Reserved.

subscribers of the portrait fund. A portrait of John George Bishop had been commissioned, funded by the subscribers and presented to the town (see page 40). In response, Bishop had compiled a collection of previous articles from the *Brighton Herald* and his own books, including 'The "Evolution" of early Brighton' from *A Peep into the Past—Brighton in 1744-61*, which he gave as souvenirs for each of the subscribers. The book was not released on sale to the public.

On 11 July 1912 Bishop sold the copyrights of a number of his books to a local dentist, Walter Harrison, DMD, LDS, for the sum of £62 10s 0d[30]. The copyrights were assigned to Harrison for the duration of Bishop's life and for a further 25 years after his death. The following works were sold:

A Peep into the Past—Brighton in the Olden Time. Brighton: Brighton Herald Office, 1880.

A Peep into the Past—Brighton in the Olden Time with Glances at the Present, 'People's Edition'. Brighton: Brighton Herald Office, 1892.

A Peep into the Past—Brighton in 1744-61. Brighton: Brighton Herald Office, 1895.

A Peece of Ye Olde Shippe. Brighton: Brighton Herald Office, 1912[31].

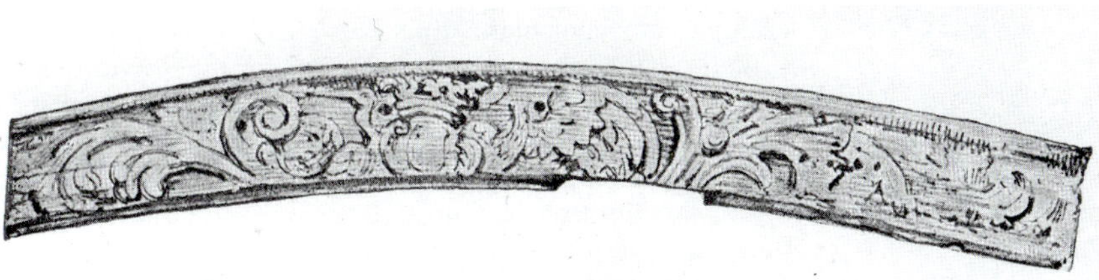

PEECE OF YE OLDE SHIPPE.

[1] *Who's Who in Kent, Surrey & Sussex, 1911*, p303 gives this date and address

[2] *Brighton Herald & Hove Chronicle*, 5 April 1919, article entitled 'Death of Mr Bishop—62 Years with the Herald'

[3] Brighton Town Rate Book 1826, BH/B4/16/1 (formerly DB/B 65/1)

[4] Brighton St Nicholas Parish Register: Marriages

[5] Brighton St Nicholas Parish Register: Baptisms

[6] J G Bishop: *Miscellaneous Subjects, Historical & Literary*, Herald Office, Brighton 1899, p148

[7] George Haffenden: *Brighton Middle Street School 1805-1905*. Brighton: J Beal & Son, p55

[8] *Brighton Gazette*, 23 September 1852, article entitled 'Testimonial to Mr Ward'

[9] Extract from cuttings in the Erredge collection, volume 10, ('Sixty Two Years at the Herald'). Brighton Library Rare Books Department

[10] *Falkirk Herald*, 20 February 1862 and *Elgin Courier and Morayshire Advertiser*, 21 February 1862

[11] *Brighton Gazette*, 19 June 1862

[12] *Handbook of Brighton*, Fleet & Son, Herald Office, Prince's Place, Brighton, 1854

[13] *The Brighton Fishery and Handbook of Brighton* (3rd edition) were advertised in the *Brighton Herald* during 1858

[14] *Glimpses of Our Sussex Ancestors*. A subsequent edition of Volume I was published in 1882 and volume II in 1883, both by Farncombe & Co, East Sussex News Office, Lewes

[15] Extract from cuttings in the Erredge collection, volume 10 ('The Brothers Fleet' p122). Brighton Library, Rare Books Department

[16] Extract from cuttings in the Erredge collection, volume 10 ('Employees Jubilee Presentation' p122). Brighton Library, Rare Books Department

[17] *Miscellaneous Subjects Historical & Literary*, Brighton: Brighton Herald Office, 1899. Preface

[18] *Brighton Heral*d, 21 October 1899

[19] The Liberals had arisen from an alliance of Whigs, free trade Peelites and Radicals in the 1850s

[20] Extract from cuttings in the Erredge collection ('Death of Mr J G Bishop'). Brighton Library, Rare Books Department

[21] The 1881 census records Bishop and his family at 12 South Down Road, New Shoreham

[22] The Keep (East Sussex Record Office) AMS6944/2/1: 'Letters from John George Bishop', letter to Mrs Thorpe dated 24 October 1908

[23] Daniel Burchell Friend: *D B Friend's Brighton Almanack*, 1888. Brighton: December 1887, p204

[24] *Brighton Gazette*, 25 July 1867. Column entitled 'Literature'

[25] Article in the *Brighton Herald*, 16 December 1865

[26] The frontispiece of the 1875 edition of *The Brighton Pavilion and its Royal Associations* states this was another work by the author. Although it is known that Bishop wrote such a newspaper article in the Brighton Herald, there are no known examples of a book of this title

[27] George Aitcheson continued working for the *Brighton Herald* and became the hon. secretary of the Sussex District of the Institute of Journalists. He wrote numerous books and pamphlets including *Unknown Brighton* (1926) and *Sussex* (1936).

[28] *Bristol Mercury*, 9 September 1892. Article entitled 'Our Library Table'

[29] *Pall Mall Gazette*, 13 August 1892. Article entitled 'Brighton in the days of the Georges'

[30] The Keep (East Sussex Record Office) ACC4299/1/49/1: 11 July 1912. Deed of assignment of literary copyright

[31] *A Peece of Ye Olde Shippe* was a typed account by Bishop that appeared in the *Brighton Herald* on 30 March 1912

4 William Grant
(1818-1860)

William Grant had a brief but auspicious career during the middle of the 19th century, primarily as a newsagent, but he is more commonly remembered among collectors as the publisher of a large number of Brighton prints. Pick up almost any reference book on the history of Brighton and it will invariably contain a print once published by him.

Ancestry and family background

William Grant was born in Brighton in 1818 at the family home in Cumberland Street[1], the sixth of 10 children. William's father, John Grant, was considerably older than his bride, Sarah (née Spicer), when they married at St Nicholas' Church on 11 July 1808, but there is scant information on the origins of the family before that date.

By the early 19th century Brighton had grown into a thriving, fashionable resort. One of the consequences of this growth was a boom in house building, leading to a commensurate requirement for artisans to build and service the new developments. Capitalising on this surge in demand, John had built up a successful business as a painter and glazier. By the mid-1820s, John was in his fifties and the older sons were starting to assist with the business, a career that William was originally destined to follow. However, 1827 was a disastrous year that was to blight the family. The two youngest children died during the spring of that year, but far worse for the family, so did their father. The Brighton Herald reported on Saturday 12 May 1827 that 'a poor man named Grant, a Painter, was returning from his work in this town, he was attacked with apoplexy and expired soon after'[2]. Although initially the eldest son, Robert, may have tried to support the remaining family, as a 17 year old he could not realistically be expected to provide for himself, his mother and four of his siblings.

It was about this time that John Jones, the former book-keeper for William Genn's coaching business, took the young William Grant under his wing[3] . Despite his humble position, Jones was an immensely respected individual within the town. Following a serious financial misfortune during the course of 1825, the Countess of Winterton had organised a collection to assist Jones recover from his plight[4]. The fund was very much over-subscribed from her endeavours, more than covering his financial misfortune, but Jones insisted on returning the excess amount and declined any further charitable appeal.

William Genn had operated the 'Royal Sussex', 'New Dart' and 'Royal George' coaches, running from London to Brighton throughout the 1820s, from the Union offices at 135 North Street and premises in Castle Square. Jones would have been a familiar sight to any of those departing from the Brighton coach office or those arriving there from London and the provinces. By the end of the decade, he had identified an opportunity to sell newspapers to both travellers and townsfolk from the coach office. By utilising the daily deliveries carried by the coaches arriving from London, he could offer them for sale from a stall at Genn's 'New Dart Coach Office'. By the 1830s Genn's coach office had ceased to operate but Jones continued to sell newspapers at the corner of Prince's Place and North Street from a stall within the premises of James Taylor's Bookshop and Library and later from the Globe Coach Office in Castle Square. Thus he effectively became Brighton's first newsagent[5].

Education, business and financial life

From the outset, the young William Grant had assisted Jones, although he still occasionally resorted to casual work with his brother Robert, as a painter. Jones was already of advanced years at the time he had set up as a newsagent and it is evident that within a few years he was barely eking a living. As the decade had progressed, others also commenced offering newspapers from bookselling premises and the well-frequented libraries had a supply of their own, available for perusal by their clientele. By 1836 Jones's plight was such that a group of Brighton townspeople staged a benefit concert[6] for him, recognising that he was 'living in reduced circumstances'. Due to his financial distress, it seems likely that Jones could no longer continue to support Grant, who instead had reverted to assisting his brother Robert as a painter.

While living with his brother in a small tenement in Apollo Terrace, Grant met, and on 2 July 1837, married Elizabeth Anderson. The couple set up home in Nelson Street, where their first child, a daughter named after her mother, was born in April 1838. In the meantime, Jones had gratefully accepted the charitable gesture and continued to run the business with his wife, until his death from 'inflammation' on 20 March 1839, aged 79. Ten days later, his widow placed a boxed advertisement[7] in the newspapers stating that 'William Grant, for ten years the confidential assistant to Mr Jones, will continue to conduct the newspaper business at The London Daily & Sunday Newspaper Office, 11 Castle Square, on her behalf'. In reality this was a shared section of the Globe Coach Office, then being operated by William Vaughan. It was from this modest start that Grant began to develop what would become the principal news office in Brighton.

Grant had been running the newspaper office for barely six months when he became embroiled in a significant legal battle, unknowingly becoming implicated in a libel case. In July 1839, a fire had occurred at the St James's Street shop of bookseller and stationer Charles Andrews, destroying all of the stock and severely damaging the premises. A satirical paper, by the title of Paul Pry, had published a series of defamatory articles in their editions #71, #73 and #80, which alleged that Andrews had started the fire himself to claim the £2,600 insurance value for the damage occasioned. In one article the paper referred to 'Swill-tub Andrews, the St James fire eater' and added that 'firing, although expensive in the winter, was a devilish good way . . . to gull the insurance people'.[8] An association of traders and Brighton's 'most respectable inhabitants' were outraged by the libellous remarks and appointed local solicitor, George Dempster, to pursue all of those involved, 'at whatever cost'.

On Tuesday 15 October 1839, a warrant was issued, charging that William Grant on the previous day 'unlawfully and maliciously published, or caused to be published, in a certain paper called the "Paul Pry", certain defamatory libels of and concerning Charles Andrews, to his great damage'. Grant was not the only person who faced these serious charges. A number of other individuals, who had by then started selling newspapers in Brighton, were similarly indicted. Grant was held in custody until a court hearing on 19 October decided on bail conditions. In response to the presiding magistrate, Mr W Seymour's question 'Are you prepared to give bail?' Grant stated that 'friends had promised to attend, but had not yet come', to which the Magistrate retorted that he would have to be returned to the cells. Fortunately, Grant's friends did subsequently turn up to post two sureties of £25 each, while Grant also had to post £50 himself, thus securing his release from custody.

At that time the law of libel was far more wide-ranging than it is nowadays. By the following week, Dempster had circulated a handbill around the town on behalf of 'the Association for the Suppression of the 'Paul Pry' Publication', in order to warn other likely offenders about the consequence of offending. On the handbill, he quoted Starkie's Law of Libel & Slander, detailing that anyone doing the following was guilty of the misdemeanour:

- Writing the libel
- Printing the paper wherein the libel is contained
- Selling the paper or giving it away
- Letting it out to hire
- Lending it to read, even without reward
- Merely handing it over to another person
- Reading the libellous matter aloud to a third party, knowing beforehand the contents

Much was made of the case at the time. The 'Association', fronted by Dempster, fomented emotions of outrage within the town and fiercely denounced the perpetrators. The Sussex Advertiser gives a good indication of the feverish emotions manifested in the town in an editorial entitled 'The Paul Pry Libel' in its edition of 28 October 1839. It states: 'This publication has so grossly slandered many inhabitants of this place of both sexes, and of all ranks and ages that as Mr Seymour said the other day on the bench in allusion to the band of assassins who forge slanders to wound their neighbours' fames through its columns, "Good men should associate when bad men conspire", and an Association for the suppression of this vile abortion of the press has been formed here, which comprises some of the worthiest characters in our borough'.

Letters to the editor were published in the Brighton Guardian and the Sussex Advertiser from indignant inhabitants, almost bordering on hysterical ranting. One reads: 'It is impossible but that one feeling should exist—that of universal abhorrence—towards this vile and mischievous publication.' It continues: 'Do the heartless and malignant publishers of this infamous and contemptible print, or their still more base and detestable abettors . . . they are proving themselves to be among the vilest of the vile. The slanderous tongue is bad enough and (let them remember and tremble) is dreadfully offensive in the sight of God: but the slanderous pen of the anonymous libeller exhibits tenfold more malignity, and can only be compared to a poisonous weapon in the hands of a cowardly miscreant who dares not openly attack his victim, but stabs in the darkness, and then with the malignity of a demon gloats over the mischief he has done.' Such was the baying for blood among the local populace.

However, some of the local newspapers took a far more measured view of the situation and published editorials that stopped just short of providing support for those charged with the offence. The Brighton Herald on 26 October 1839 carried an editorial response to George Dempster's handbill:

> 'Now, although this may be very well as far as the miserable publication in question is concerned, and the public may plume themselves on having such a stringent law to guard their reputations, it ought not to be forgotten that what is sauce for the "Paul Pry" is sauce for every other publication, and that it is under this very libel law that the greatest tyranny has been exercised against the press of this country, till its usefulness and independence has been threatened. Under Tory Governments, the most infamous persecution was carried out against the press by this very law, and even now it stands as an instrument to be wielded to the annoyance of every independent journalist by any unscrupulous unmasked knave. We have no objection to its rigorous provisions being employed against the "Paul Pry", although we think even this a matter the public have the remedy in their own hands if they would not have the good sense to employ it; but, when we see the law of libel paraded forth as something for which the public ought to be deeply grateful to the Legislature, we cannot forget what we, with every other honest journalist, have suffered, nor let pass an opportunity of once more appealing against a law which is as foreign to the spirit of this country, as it is opposed to common sense and justice'.

Having been released on bail of £100, Grant appeared before the Lewes Quarter Sessions on 30 December 1839, before Mr Sergeant D'Oyley, with Mr Roupel prosecuting. It is obvious from the court transcripts that Charles Andrews had reconsidered his own position within the case. Perhaps mindful of the editorial in the Brighton Herald and of his own position as a fellow bookseller, far from being railroaded by the association purportedly acting on his behalf, Andrews declared that he did not wish to press for punishment of the offenders. In accordance with his wishes, Mr Roupel submitted that if Grant were to plead guilty and sign in court a declaration that the publications were false and malicious libels, the prosecution would not press for punishment. At a further session for sentencing , Grant agreed to the prosecution's demand, was fined £20 and required to be of good behaviour for one year, but the Chairman was also at pains to point out how much more serious it would have been, had the prosecution pressed for a judgement of the case[9].

With hindsight it might well be speculated that both Andrews and the editors of the Brighton newspapers had recognised that it was nigh on impossible for a bookseller or newspaper vendor to have vetted every publication that they had, prior to offering them for sale. Grant had been an unwitting participant in the libel and here was a pitfall that might entrap any one of them in the future. At the behest of the association, Dempster had zealously pursued the Brighton vendors that had been involved with selling the Paul Pry. However, it was not until over a year later that the real perpetrators[10], the elusive writers and publishers of the notorious Paul Pry paper, were brought before the Queen's Bench on that charge, with a further 42 counts of libel and of trying to extort money.

By 1840 William and Elizabeth had moved into a house at 34 George Street Gardens, behind its eastern corner with Edward Street [**31**]. Sometime between late 1841 and early 1842 he took over the adjacent shop that had been the premises of William Hill, a clothes salesman. Situated in Edward Street at the eastern corner of its junction with George Street Gardens (then numbered 27 Edward Street), he refurbished the premises and opened as a newsagent's shop, the first

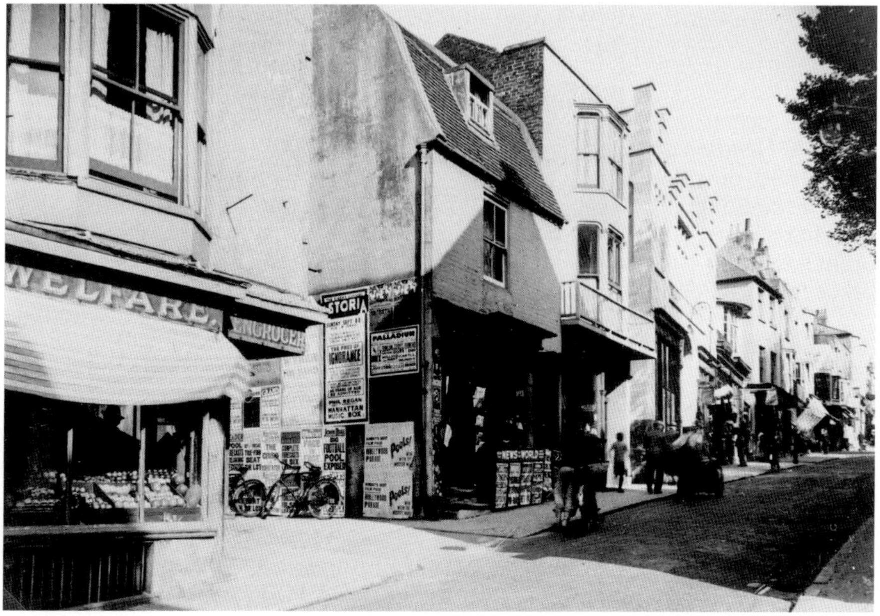

31
27 Edward Street. Grant opened Brighton's first newsagent's shop here

premises in Brighton solely and specifically dedicated to selling newspapers. During the early 1840s Brighton underwent some momentous changes and Grant was able to capitalise on a number of favourable circumstances.

Until 1840 the epicentre of the coaching industry within Brighton had been Castle Square, with most coaches terminating here and almost every other building being used as a coach office. With the advent of the railway, the coaching industry spiralled into an almost overnight collapse. Whereas Jones had naturally affiliated his business to the coaching industry, his successor recognised that the coaches were no longer the best or fastest means of obtaining bulk deliveries of the London newspapers. Very early on, he started procuring newspapers through the London wholesalers, collecting them twice each day from the railway terminus.

Another unrelated event was also to play a major part in assisting Grant with his business. The collapse of Wigney's bank in 1842 ruined many Brighton businesses and one such that suffered was Thomas Ward Capps' The Age Coach Office [**32**]. Capps had £1,249 6s 3d on deposit at Wigney's Bank and as a creditor he ultimately received barely five per cent of the total sum owed to him.

With this financial setback and the decline in the coaching business, Capps moved out of his coach office at 5 Castle Square to share premises with another coach operator. Grant had already been using these premises to sell newspapers from as early as February 1841 but as a consequence of Capps's misfortune by March 1842 Grant had taken over Capps's former premises.

Situated in a prime location opposite the Pavilion's south gate, this was to become Grant's News Office, the 'oldest established general newspaper and periodical office' and the centre of news in Brighton [**33**, **34**]. A further service offered by Grant from the outset was to deliver the

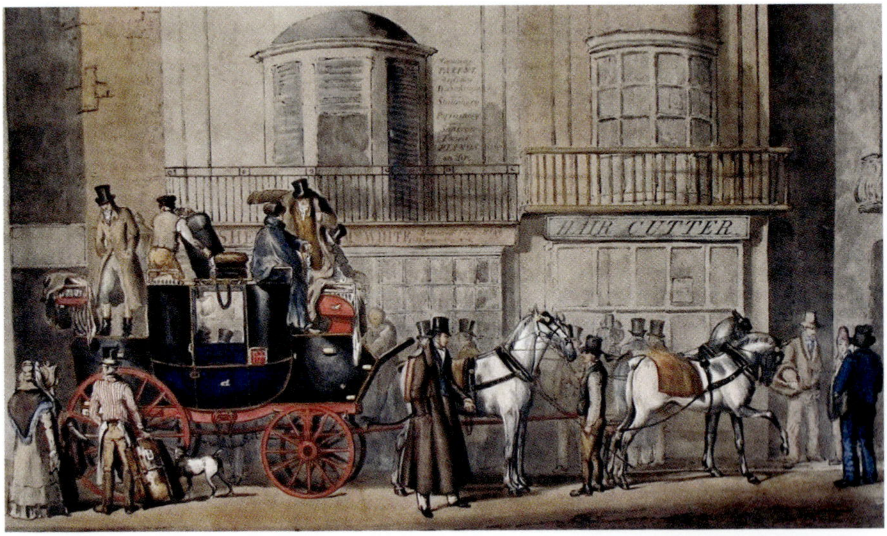

32
'The Age' coach after C C Henderson, c1830, outside 5&6 Castle Square, later to become Grant's News Office. From *A Peep into the Past—Brighton in the Olden Time*, 1892, p258

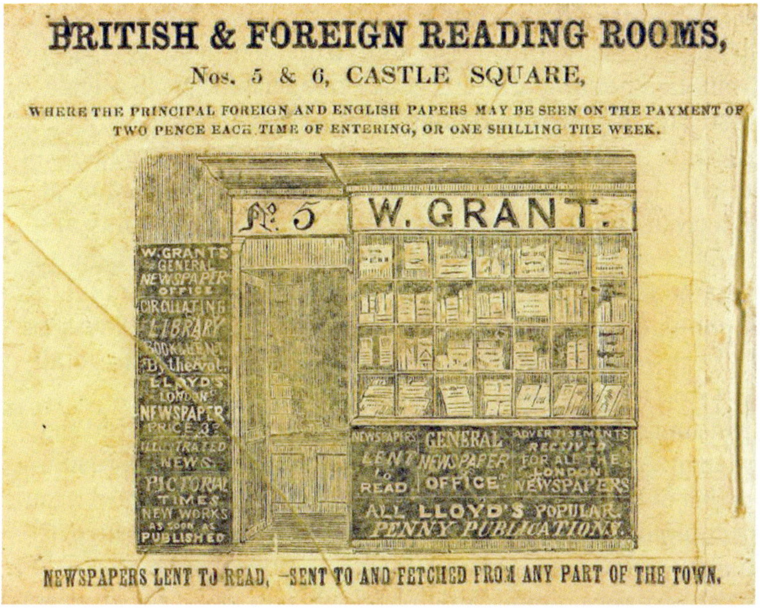

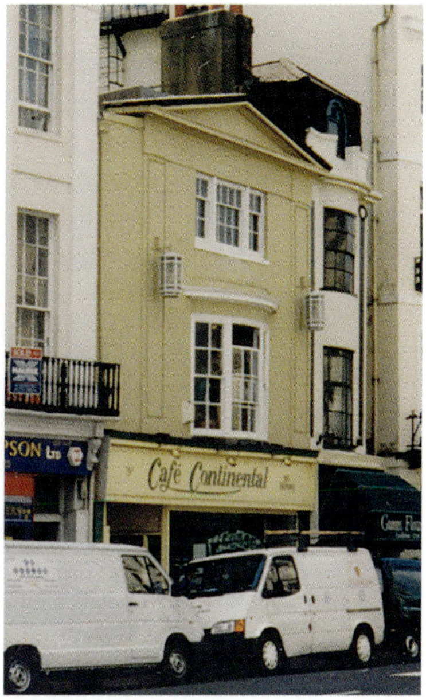

33
above left
Shop front of Grant's premises at 5&6 Castle Square, c1852

34
above right
5&6 Castle Square in 1996

daily newspapers anywhere in town. In 1842 the newspapers usually arrived at Brighton station at 10:15 and delivery to any part of the town was assured within half-an-hour of the arrival of the train. After their round of deliveries, the 'newsboys' would continue to sell the latest editions from hand-barrows stationed at strategic junctions around the town. A similar arrangement took place later in the day from 18:30, when copies of the evening papers would arrive at the station. Newspapers from the continent probably arrived on the packet-steamers that plied between Dieppe and Boulogne to Brighton, arriving at the Chain Pier or at Newhaven, in the case of bad weather. From the early 1840s onwards, Grant was to dominate as the leading newsagent in Brighton.

It would appear that he had little regard for authority, or for some of the laws in force at that time, as in 1844 he again found himself back in court at the behest of the High Constable and the churchwardens. Major Allen, the chairman of the Brighton Bench of Magistrates, had previously stated 'that numerous complaints had been made about the desecration of the Sabbath by persons carrying on their usual pursuits on Sundays' [11]. As a result, the High Constable and churchwardens had issued notices warning that the law for preventing Sunday trading would be strictly enforced. The law pertaining to this had been drafted during the reign of Charles II and the penalties had not been amended over the course of time, which had led to a diminution in adherence to the act by some tradespersons.

Whilst the notice had the desired effect on many shop-keepers, who thenceforth ceased opening on the sabbath, others had openly proclaimed their determination to disregard the notices and continue trading. In the words of Major Allen 'the person who had made himself most obnoxious, Mr William Grant, the principal newsvendor in

Brighton, was summoned before the bench on Thursday, for carrying on his trade on the Lord's-day'. During the course of the hearing, it transpired that Grant had not only kept his shop open on Sunday 25 August, but he had also used placards to attract the attention of passers-by. Such was the magistrate's outrage that he refused to allow Grant's request for an adjournment due to his solicitor being unable to attend the court at that time. As a result, he had little option other than to plead guilty and was duly fined five shillings, with 10 shillings in costs. In summing up Major Allen stated that 'not only your office, but a great number of tradesmen's shops, have been kept open, and it is now become so crying an evil that it is absolutely necessary, for the sake of decency and good order, to put a stop to it'.

During the course of the following week it must have appeared that Grant had been utterly contemptuous of the court's stance. As a result, Mr Isaacson, one of the churchwardens, appeared before the court again, requesting a summons be made against Grant for a further instance of Sunday trading. However, this time the request was refused by the magistrates because the churchwarden had only witnessed the shop was open, not that any sales had taken place.

Although Grant was becoming quite a regular attendee at the courts, any future appearances were not to be as a transgressor but as either a victim or as a witness to a case. During the 1840s, the Castle Square shop had the dominant role in the provision of newspapers and periodicals to the town. By 1845, Grant had not only strengthened this position, but had also diversified into book lending and sales, stationery, sheet-music sales, as a publisher of prints and by acting as an advertising agent for all national and international publications. There was also a very short dalliance with the property market[12], with the acquisition of 93 King's Road, at which Grant was briefly recorded as a lodging house keeper. The circumstances surrounding this are unclear but perhaps he found that he

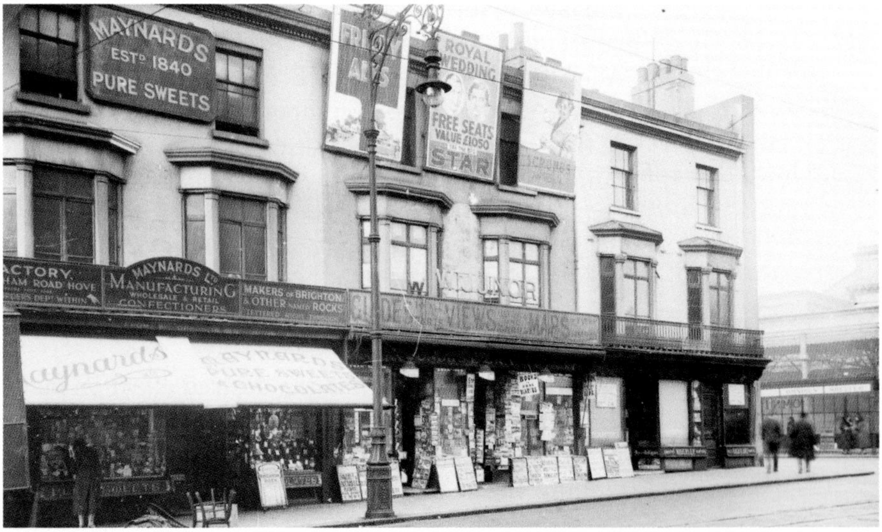

35
The third of Grant's premises at 72 Queen's Road, Brighton

had over-extended himself and that the lodging house was a distraction from his main business. From around March 1845 he had been heavily promoting his business by advertising in the local newspapers[13]. What is most notable from these adverts is the advent of the use of the premises as a library but there is no mention at this juncture of the sale of prints.

As the railway terminus became more important, both for commercial traffic and as a gateway for travellers to and from Brighton, so Queen's Road was being developed into the principal thoroughfare between the terminus and the town. Grant recognised the potential of having premises near to the terminus and wasted no time in securing an additional copyhold property. Originally numbered 19, but later renumbered to 40 and then to 72 Queen's Road [**35**], this became the third shop in the chain. From here he sold 'a larger assortment of sheet music than at any one shop in or out of London'.

The staffing of three branches required the employment of a number of persons in order to maintain the business effectively. Predominating in the principal roles were other family members: his mother-in-law Sarah Anderson managed the shop in Edward Street, sometimes assisted by his wife's sister, Christiana Triphook (née Anderson). William and his immediate family ran the premises in Castle Square, whilst his younger brother, Henry, probably managed the shop in Queen's Road and acted as an erstwhile travelling salesman.

In the more menial roles a number of boys were employed to collect and deliver newspapers, selling them on the street from hand-carts [**36**], carrying placards advertising the News Office and also acting as errand-boys. These often became troublesome for him, as on a number of occasions petty pilfering and embezzling would occur, necessitating action through the courts. At Lewes Quarter Sessions[14] on 8 April 1844, Henry Hawks, an errand boy, aged 14, pleaded guilty to three counts of embezzlement amounting to a total of 11s 6d. The punishment for such

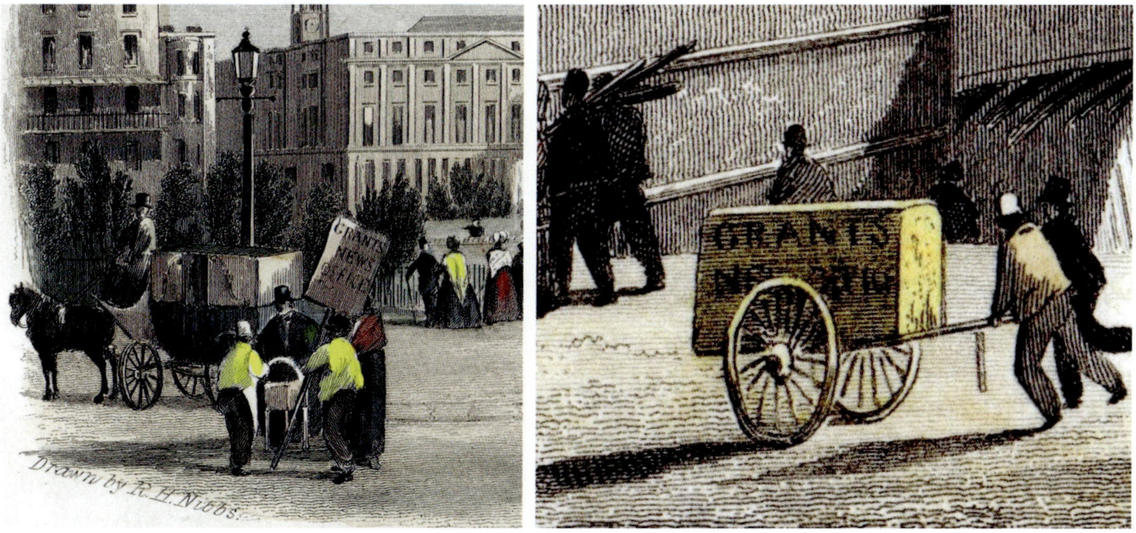

36
Details from two of Grant's prints, showing errand boys selling and delivering newspapers. Note Grant's use of advertising

an offence was harsh at that time, particularly for such a young boy. He was duly sentenced to two months hard labour, the final 10 days to be served in solitary confinement.

A little over a year later[15] on 30 August 1845, a second 14-year-old boy, George Barton, who had been employed by Grant for the three to four previous months, was similarly charged at Lewes. The boy had pleaded not guilty to three counts of embezzlement but a jury found him guilty and he was duly sentenced to 10 days in solitary confinement and to be privately whipped. On the evening of Monday 7 January 1848, it was noticed that a window pane at the front of the shop in Edward Street had been removed and that some theatre tickets and bundles of books had been stolen[16]. A 16-year-old local lad named Abraham Offen was charged with the offence and appeared at Lewes Crown Court on 11 February. Sarah Anderson, as the manager of the shop, gave evidence on Grant's behalf but in this instance it was insufficient to gain a conviction. The boy was subsequently discharged by proclamation.

A similar incident occurred in November 1849, when Sarah Anderson was locking up the Edward Street premises at between 23:00 and midnight. She discovered a lad of 16, Edward Feldwicke, hiding under the counter. At his trial, it was revealed that he had recently served one month in prison for an almost identical crime at Petworth. The judge

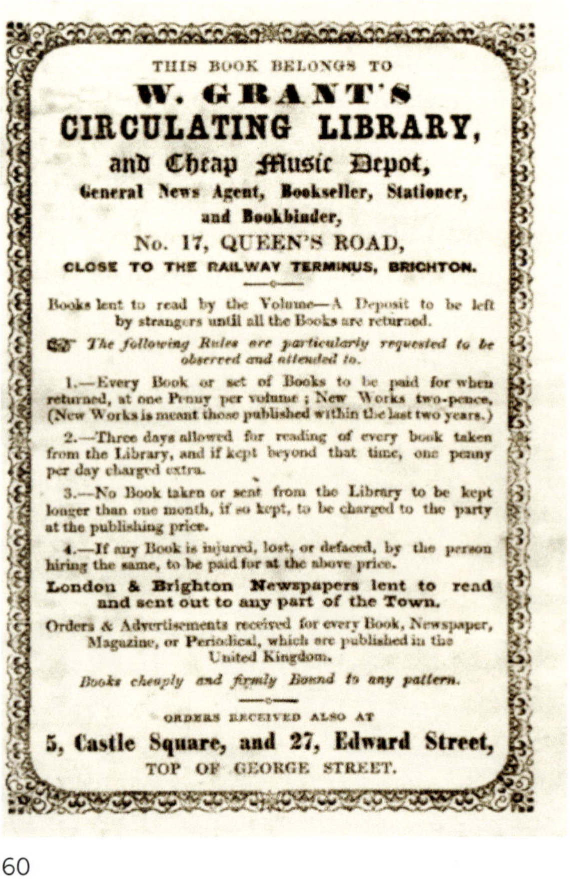
THIS BOOK BELONGS TO
W. GRANT'S
CIRCULATING LIBRARY,
and Cheap Music Depot,
General News Agent, Bookseller, Stationer, and Bookbinder,
No. 17, QUEEN'S ROAD,
CLOSE TO THE RAILWAY TERMINUS, BRIGHTON.

Books lent to read by the Volume—A Deposit to be left by strangers until all the Books are returned.

The following Rules are particularly requested to be observed and attended to.

1.—Every Book or set of Books to be paid for when returned, at one Penny per volume ; New Works two-pence, (New Works is meant those published within the last two years.)

2.—Three days allowed for reading of every book taken from the Library, and if kept beyond that time, one penny per day charged extra.

3.—No Book taken or sent from the Library to be kept longer than one month, if so kept, to be charged to the party at the publishing price.

4.—If any Book is injured, lost, or defaced, by the person hiring the same, to be paid for at the above price.

London & Brighton Newspapers lent to read and sent out to any part of the Town.

Orders & Advertisements received for every Book, Newspaper, Magazine, or Periodical, which are published in the United Kingdom.

Books cheaply and firmly Bound to any pattern.

ORDERS RECEIVED ALSO AT
5, Castle Square, and 27, Edward Street,
TOP OF GEORGE STREET.

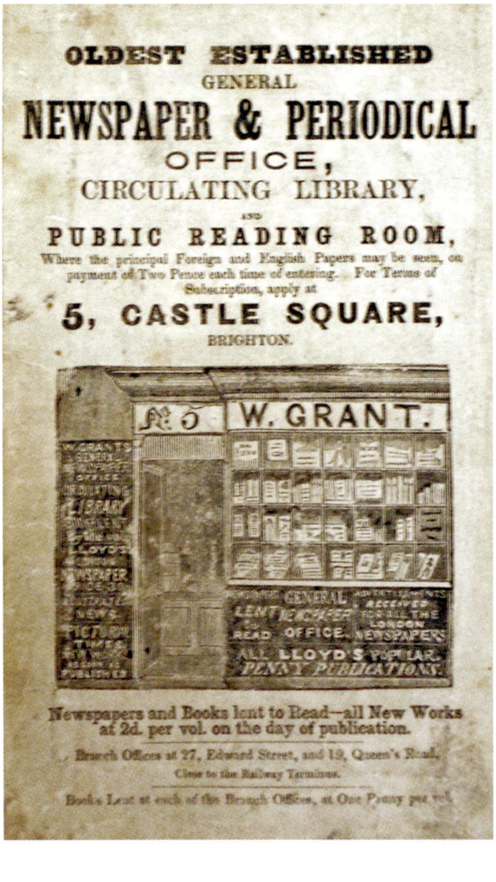
OLDEST ESTABLISHED
GENERAL
NEWSPAPER & PERIODICAL
OFFICE,
CIRCULATING LIBRARY,
AND
PUBLIC READING ROOM,
Where the principal Foreign and English Papers may be seen, on payment of Two Pence each time of entering. For Terms of Subscription, apply at
5, CASTLE SQUARE,
BRIGHTON.

Newspapers and Books lent to Read—all New Works at 2d. per vol. on the day of publication.

Branch Offices at 27, Edward Street, and 19, Queen's Road, Close to the Railway Terminus.

Books Lent at each of the Branch Offices, at One Penny per vol.

37
Book insert detailing library rules, and handbill, both 1845-6

had no hesitation in awarding him the most severe punishment permitted: three months' hard labour at Lewes Prison.

As the business expanded, demanding additional skills that were not possessed by family members, it became necessary to contract work out or have live-in employees. Such an example was George Rotherham, a print colourer, who lived with his wife above the Edward Street premises. For around 10 years Rotherham hand-coloured each of the prints published by his employer, probably assisting in the shop at other times.

When Grant had originally taken over his principal premises in Castle Square, he did not have the exclusive use of the building; the upper floors were occupied by tenants. Having later secured sole occupancy, he moved his family into the upper floors of the building and started fitting out the first floor for retail purposes. Upon completion of the enlargement and refurbishment of his premises, on 13 December 1847, Grant proclaimed with front-page advertising[17] that he was opening a 'Circulating Library on a system which has never yet been attempted by any provincial town in the kingdom' [**37a**]. He offered the principal foreign and English newspapers in addition to the London daily, evening and provincial newspapers [**37b**]. From 09:00 until 22:00, subscribers paying 2d for entry or 1s.0d weekly could read the latest editions of over 50 different newspapers, including the following:

Bombay Times	*Paris Journal des Débats*	*Risorgimento Turin*
Brussels Herald	*Paris Galignani*	*Roman Advertiser*
Boulogne Gazette	*Paris La Presse*	
Malta Mail	*Paris La Semaine*	*Algemeine Zeitung*
New York Herald	*Paris Journal pour Rire*	*Frankfurter Journal*
Birmingham Advertiser	*Dublin Nation*	*Manchester Courier*
Birmingham Journal	*Edinburgh Advertiser*	*Plymouth Journal*
Bristol Gazette	*Hampshire Advertiser*	*Sunderland Herald*
Bath Herald	*Liverpool Mercantile Gazette*	*Woolwich Journal*
Belfast Mercantile Register	*Liverpool Albion*	*Yorkshire Gazette*
Belfast News Letter	*Leeds Mercury*	
Cheltenham Chronicle	*Maidstone Gazette*	

Virtually any paper and journal could also be made available, upon request, together with a complete set of back issues of *The Times* from August 1813, the *Weekly Despatch* from January 1837, the *Illustrated London News*, *Pictorial Times* and *Punch* from their commencement.

On 1st May 1849 he had been initiated as a freemason into the Royal York Lodge, No. 394, which met on the first Tuesday in every month at the Old Ship Inn. He remained a member until 1859, probably failing to attend thereafter due to ill health. At the Odd Fellows' dinner held at the Globe Inn on 5 October 1853, to celebrate the 31st anniversary of the Loyal Brunswick Lodge, it was noted 'that the vice-chair was ably filled by Mr Grant'[18].

In January 1850 the *Sussex Advertiser* ran an article entitled 'Brighton Journal', which served as a guide for visitors to the town. In it, the principal libraries were extolled, but it is a testament to Grant's business that the article concludes 'last though not least is the reading room and library of Mr Grant, Newsagent, Castle Square. In the former may be found supplies of the daily London journals, the principal provincial, Brighton, French and other foreign papers, access to which may be gained at all times for a trifling charge, or by a small annual subscription. Mr Grant richly deserves the countenance and support he receives'[19].

Grant may have upset other members of the community in Brighton from time to time but he was not without influential friends in the town. On 8 and 9 February 1853 William Wood, a footman for the Peel family of Sussex Square, fraudulently obtained sums of money from Lawrence Coppard, a carver and gilder of North Street and also from Grant, claiming he had not come out with enough money and requesting that he may borrow money to pay her Ladyship's bills. As Wood was dressed in the appropriate livery and Grant knew Laurence and Lady Jane Peel[20], he readily complied with the request. After hearing evidence in court from Lady Jane Peel and Grant, Wood was found guilty of defrauding Coppard and sentenced to four months' hard labour. However, the second count of defrauding Grant was not proceeded with. Presumably Grant's losses had already been reimbursed to him by Lady Peel.

38
Advertisement from the *Brighton Gazette*, 8 April 1845

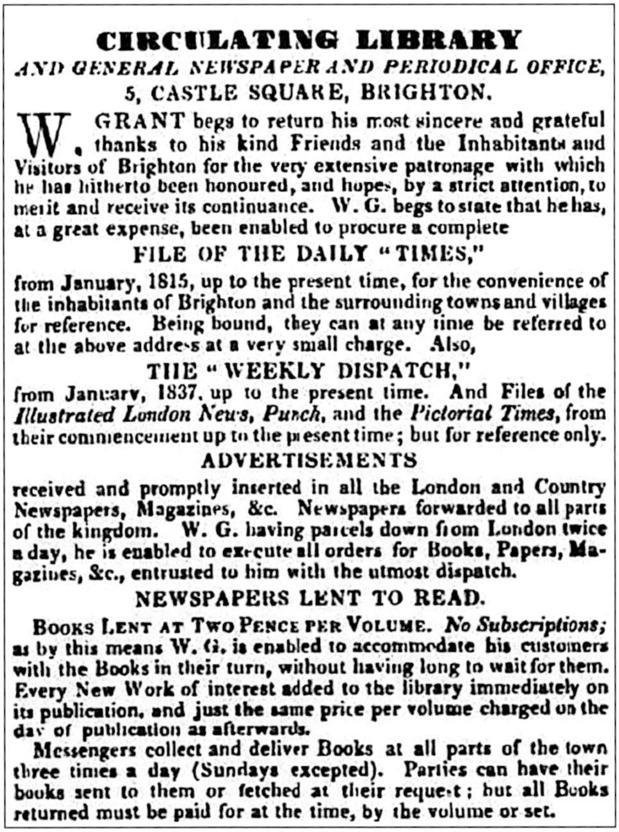
CIRCULATING LIBRARY
AND GENERAL NEWSPAPER AND PERIODICAL OFFICE,
5, CASTLE SQUARE, BRIGHTON.

W. GRANT begs to return his most sincere and grateful thanks to his kind Friends and the Inhabitants and Visitors of Brighton for the very extensive patronage with which he has hitherto been honoured, and hopes, by a strict attention, to merit and receive its continuance. W. G. begs to state that he has, at a great expense, been enabled to procure a complete

FILE OF THE DAILY "TIMES,"

from January, 1815, up to the present time, for the convenience of the inhabitants of Brighton and the surrounding towns and villages for reference. Being bound, they can at any time be referred to at the above address at a very small charge. Also,

THE "WEEKLY DISPATCH,"

from January, 1837, up to the present time. And Files of the *Illustrated London News, Punch,* and the *Pictorial Times,* from their commencement up to the present time; but for reference only.

ADVERTISEMENTS

received and promptly inserted in all the London and Country Newspapers, Magazines, &c. Newspapers forwarded to all parts of the kingdom. W. G. having parcels down from London twice a day, he is enabled to execute all orders for Books, Papers, Magazines, &c., entrusted to him with the utmost dispatch.

NEWSPAPERS LENT TO READ.

BOOKS LENT AT TWO PENCE PER VOLUME. *No Subscriptions;* as by this means W. G. is enabled to accommodate his customers with the Books in their turn, without having long to wait for them. Every New Work of interest added to the library immediately on its publication, and just the same price per volume charged on the day of publication as afterwards.

Messengers collect and deliver Books at all parts of the town three times a day (Sundays excepted). Parties can have their books sent to them or fetched at their request; but all Books returned must be paid for at the time, by the volume or set.

Grant's business had reached its apogee between 1845 and 1854, during which he tried to change from being a big fish in a little pond (as a newsagent and print publisher) to a little fish in a big pond (as a circulating library) [**38**]. Having spent as much as £5,000 to stock his library with approximately 8,000 books, it was still unlikely to offer serious competition to the likes of Robert Folthorp's Royal Library (formerly Loder's Library), which possessed over 40,000 books at that time. The timing of the change was also inopportune, as a number of similar concerns in Brighton were going to the wall during the 1850s. Even Folthorp's library later became a victim of these changed circumstances. A glut of books from bankrupt booksellers had resulted in very rapid depreciation in the value of the stock held by the remaining libraries.

Although Grant's business was still

returning an annual profit of between £200 and £300 a year, by January 1855 Grant owed a number of sums to various creditors. This problem was compounded by numerous defaulted subscription payments owed to Grant, totalling around £450. Because many of the defaulting customers were only occasional visitors to Brighton, there was little hope of easily recovering the outstanding sums. Because he owed £700 to his principal supplier, W H & E Dawson, they refused to supply any further newspapers unless a security was offered. Despite mortgaging to them some insurance policies and his two properties, by May matters had come to a head. A demand of £20 for taxes and the execution of a debt of £23 7s 6d, owed to printers and publishers Bradbury and Evans led to an appeal by Grant to Messrs Dawson for an advance to settle the debt and to facilitate the continued provision of newspapers for a fortnight. In return, he was required to sign over part of his stock to the value of £155 7s 6d.

By 7 June, Grant had no other option than to enter into a deed that would allow all of his stock-in-trade to be assigned to them as a security on the outstanding debt, for the continued supply of newspapers and other publications and for further advances which would enable him to carry on his business[21]. Shortly thereafter Messrs Dawson put the deed into effect and placed the entire stock up for sale. As a result of this action, the other creditors sought to recover their own debts and Grant was consequently summonsed to a bankruptcy hearing[22]. The arrangement that had been made whereby Grant assigned all of his stock and re-mortgaged his properties to Dawson in order to fully discharge the debt was considered by the solicitors acting on behalf of the other plaintiffs as 'an attempt to defeat and delay the creditors'. It had been proposed that Dawson's would settle the outstanding debts totalling £1,120 15s 8d with the remaining creditors from the mortgaging of two of Grant's properties for £700, the cashing in of a life assurance policy of £270 and from the sale of his stock-in-trade (which raised only £278 7s 9d, after rent and expenses were deducted). It was further proposed that Grant would be retained to manage the business for and on their behalf.

However, the other creditors refused to accept this agreement and a protracted landmark legal battle ensued at the Court of Common Pleas in London between Pennell (and another assignee of William Grant) and Dawson. Although the court found for the plaintiffs, the judgement was appealed against on the basis that the judge had misdirected the jury. The appeal was granted and at a retrial on Monday 30 June 1856 the original verdict was overturned. Thus Grant retained his business, although his premises were now mortgaged to Dawson.

Once again he would need to confine himself predominantly to the sale of newspapers. The repeal of the Newspaper Tax in 1855 had led to a boom in the sale of newspapers but it was a double-edged sword for Grant. Whilst it led to an increase in the volume of newspapers sold, it also encouraged large numbers of newcomers into that market sector. In

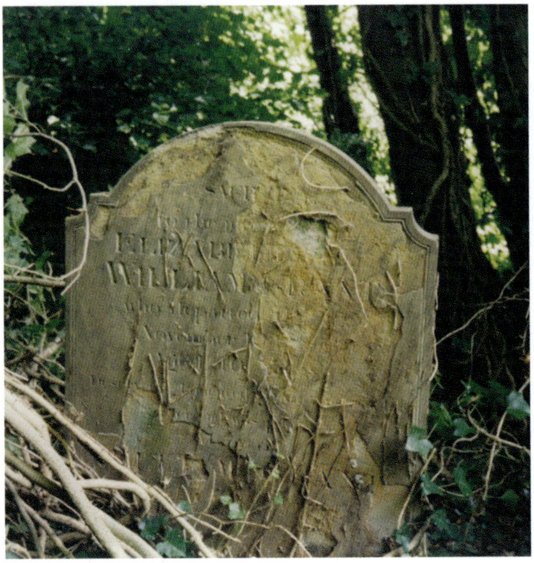

39
William Grant's grave in Brighton Extra Mural Cemetery

an attempt to keep ahead of the field, Grant adopted another innovation and had an electric telegraph installed at his Castle Square premises, announcing in the local press that 'Electric Telegraph News may be read throughout the day at Mr Grant's Newsroom'[23]. Despite the stiff competition, Grant's News Office remained the dominant newsagent in Brighton, although the business never succeeded in matching its earlier diversity.

During the course of 1857, Grant was to lose his wife, Elizabeth, at the age of 40, to consumption. She was interred in the Brighton Extra Mural Cemetery, in a grave situated on the slope behind the gothic chapel. As the decade drew to a close, assisted by his daughters, his brother and a full-time assistant, Henry Hyde, at his Castle Square premises, the business had once again picked up. However, by the start of 1860 Grant had been diagnosed with TB, which he finally succumbed to on 25 July 1860, aged 42, and he was interred with his wife in the same plot in the Extra Mural Cemetery [**39**]. John George Bishop mentions the grave 'of William Grant (and his wife), a well-known news-agent, of Castle Square, a few years ago'[24]. Located high on the slopes, immediately behind the chapel of rest, the grave is now shrouded in ivy and undergrowth. The tall headstone is badly eroded but the inscription is still discernible: 'Sacred to the memory of Elizabeth, the wife of William Grant, who departed this life November 10th 1857, age 40 years. Deservedly lamented by all who knew her, her end was peace. Also . . . William Grant . . . (eroded away)'. A small, well-preserved footstone also records 'E.G. 1857; W.G. 1860'.

For a couple of years after his death, his eldest daughter Elizabeth, assisted by her sister Mary continued to run the business from 5 Castle Square, managed by Henry Hyde and employing three other men and four boys, having been divested of the premises in Queen's Road. This must have been extremely arduous for her. At the end of 1860 she had begun a dalliance with Bartholomew Parker Bidder, the nephew of the famous brothers, George Parker Bidder[25] and Bartholomew Parker Bidder[26]. By late 1861 she had had an illegitimate child by him that died in the following year. In 1862 she had to vacate the Castle Square premises and move to 1 Pavilion Buildings. Shortly thereafter she married Bidder and subsequently he was listed as running the business. By the middle of 1863 he had been adjudged as bankrupt but had succeeded in discharging his debts by 20 June. The timing of all of this could not have been worse. Elizabeth gave birth to their second child eight days later. The couple finally decided to cease trading and in the summer of 1864 they left Brighton for good.

Contribution to Brighton's history

The legacy of William Grant is now largely forgotten, all but for the local historians and collectors of 19th century Brighton prints that invariably come across his name borne upon the quantity of diverse scenes that he published.

Throughout the 19th century the publication of prints of Brighton had grown steadily as an increasing number of booksellers, printers and stationers sought to satisfy the demands of the fashionable visitors to the town. As Ford observes, in the 1840s 'the opening of the London railway brought a positive avalanche of day-trippers and created a new market for prints'[27]. He continues that 'the established Brighton publishers, Mason, Bruce, Sickelmore and Cordwell did not enter the market but new local publishers stepped in. William Grant of Castle Square, Andrews and his successor Willmott of St James's Street, and William Leppard (later Taylor's) of East Street competed with the London publishers, Richard Rock of Blackheath, Newman and Co. and JS & Co.' However, this greatly understates the true situation and the role that Grant had in the changing circumstances.

'The publication of prints involved the work of a number of specialists: the artist, the engraver, the printer, the colourist and not least the publisher . . . but the production, and of course the distribution and sale of a print, required the services of an integrated team'[28]. One aspect of the change in demand was the number of visitors to Brighton but a more significant factor was the type of visitor buying prints. The established publishers of prints had traditionally sold them either as works of art in their own right or as plates accompanying a guide-book. Prior to the coming of the railway, this type of business lent itself to either the publisher having a small press and his own plates (literally 'print-on-demand') or alternatively carrying a small stock of a limited number of prints. Perhaps the most sizeable numbers of prints offered were those that were appended in guide-books.

Shortly before the arrival of the railway, new processes, particularly the increasing use of steel plates, had enabled the mass production of prints. Unlike copper plates, which would show signs of deterioration of print quality after a run of around 100 imprints, steel plates would allow almost indefinite runs without a deterioration of quality.

A new breed of publishers capitalised on this just as demand was exploding, with Grant taking a dominant role in the revolution from the outset. Where others tried to cater for the increased demand, most failed. Charles Andrews was succeeded around 1848 by Charles Willmott but he had ceased trading by around 1853 and was succeeded by Henry Hatchard Sugg. Similarly, William Leppard was succeeded from 1850 onwards by William John Taylor, who had himself ceased trading by 1855.

Grant subsequently acquired the rights to many, if not all, of his prints. Virtually from the outset he had invested in a stock of large quantities of each of his prints[29] and released new scenic depictions on a grand scale (17 new prints were issued simultaneously at the end of 1847). Of his three shops offering prints for sale, the one at 72 Queen's Road was the closest premises to the station. Any visitor to Brighton could not fail to pass the shop or to notice the sizeable range of prints on offer. His main premises at 5 & 6 Castle Square were in a similarly commanding position, opposite the Pavilion gates, at the commercial hub of the old town.

The publishing of prints by Grant spanned only a very brief period, possibly commencing as early as 1844 until the autumn of 1855, with most of the prints bearing his trademark titling: 'Pubd by W. Grant, Newsagent, 5 Castle Sq., Brighton' beneath or surrounding the bottom of the scene. Many of his prints came in variant sizes, allowing him to service different market niches or be used for other purposes. For example, many were produced in a large size for framing (typically around 100mm x 160mm), which can often be found either plain or coloured, and a smaller size (typically around 60mm x 90mm), which were used for greetings cards or headed notepaper.

Grant commissioned some of the finest local artists to provide the original artworks for the prints, including Richard Henry Nibbs, William Delamotte, George Atwick, Frederick Forde and George Ruff. The range of views, subject matter and the level of detail depicted in his best prints surpassed many of his contemporaries and predecessors. Nowadays many of these are an invaluable aid to understanding the topography of Brighton as it was then. The work of engraving was undertaken by a number of different London engravers and lithographers, among whom were Thomas Jeavons, William John Alais, Charles Graf, James Vizetelly, William Day (Day & Haghe became Day & Son after 1845, lithographers to the Queen) and John Newman & Son (also its later successor, John Newman & Co), prior to being printed by either an intaglio process using a steel plate or by lithographic means. Colouring was generally added afterwards by a hand-colourist employed specifically for the purpose but there were also a few tinted lithographs.

It is worth mentioning the process and representative cost that Grant would have used for producing some of his later prints. The example given is for a single lithographic print, around 1850, although by far the greatest quantities of prints published by Grant were cheaper steel engravings. After commissioning an artist to produce a drawing of a particular scene or subject, the drawing would have been taken to a lithographer to produce a stone plate. The lithographer would have transferred the drawing onto the stone and once approved by Grant, the final work on preparing the stone for printing would be executed. Typically, 100 proof impressions would be made onto India paper by the lithographer at a cost of around £9 10s 0d., including the cost of his drawing and making the plate.

Grant would have been given the option of either purchasing the stone or renting it, typically at around £1 a year. Further print runs would have cost around £2 15s 0d per 100 prints, discounted for larger runs. It is not known whether Grant purchased or rented the stones but the lack of any mention of them (or any steel plates) in his stock-in-trade sale indicates that the printer retained them at their premises and ran off quantities of prints as and when required. It is considered likely that some plates were probably owned by Grant (ie, that he had purchased them), whilst others were rented. In the case of his bankruptcy, those that were rented could easily have been altered to allow a new publisher to take over.

Grant also embraced another innovation during the late 1840s. Although greetings cards had been exchanged for centuries beforehand, it was not until 1843 that the first Christmas card was published in the UK and the commercial publication and mass-production of Valentines cards followed shortly afterwards. By the late 1840s Grant was offering 'the largest and best variety of Valentines ever yet seen in or out of London, from one penny upwards'[30]. These could be discretely viewed by prospective lady customers in a private room at the back of the shop, from 14:00 onwards, after 29 January until 21 February. He was also producing his own greetings cards as embossed variants of the prints he had to offer.

The earliest known adverts for Grant's prints do not appear until the end of 1847, when he published 17 'Views in Brighton' by R H Nibbs and G Attwick, all of these engraved by Jeavons. However, it is probable that a number of his other prints were published before that date. It is known that a number of prints were acquisitions by Grant from other publishers and verifiable copies of such prints have emerged from time-to-time. One example is the 'Chain Pier, Brighton' (Cat no 290) by an unnamed artist, engraved by J Newman. This was first published by bookseller and stationer Samuel Ballard of 99 St James's Street around the end of 1845 and probably acquired by Grant in 1847 when Ballard ceased trading, thereafter being published by Grant under his own name. It is possible that the same also applies to the only other known print by Ballard, 'View in the Queen's Park, Brighton' (Cat no. 1122)[31], although no copies of this bearing Grant's name have yet been found.

Another series of prints, first published by William John Taylor of 16-17 East Street, was also acquired during the 1850s. Four known copies published by Grant exist, being 'Brighton from Race Hill' (Cat no. 29), 'West Cliff and Esplanade' (Cat no. 1008), 'The Marine Parade, Brighton' (Cat no. 1071) and 'The East Cliff, Brighton' (Cat no. 1179). There are also a few other prints by Taylor that were probably acquired at the same time, but where examples of the Grant versions have not been found. These are 'The Old Steine' (Cat no. 379), 'The Parish Church' (Cat no. 691) and 'Brunswick Terrace and Esplanade' (Cat no. 1015).

Only one of the prints, 'West Cliff and Esplanade' (Cat no. 1008), can be positively associated with an artist, although it is likely that the others were also drawn by him. John Baker Pyne was a very eminent artist and it is known that he painted the scene in 1848, simply titling it 'Brighton'.

William John Taylor and William Henry Tabberer formed a partnership in October 1850 and took over the Brighton printing and stationery business of William Leppard at 16-17 East Street. The print by the partnership of 'The Old Steine' (Cat no. 369) must have been published between October 1850 and 31 January 1851, as the partnership was dissolved on that latter date. Other prints followed, some described as published by W J Taylor and others by J W Taylor, until the business was ultimately disposed of by Taylor in April 1855 to Robert S Holmes of Oxford Street, London and then Henry Trussell. It is thought likely that the publication of a directory[32] by Taylor in July 1854 may have resulted in a severe financial setback for him, which precipitated the cessation of his business in Brighton. The acquisition by Grant of the rights to publish the prints, using new lithographic stones, probably occurred as a direct consequence of Taylor's misfortune and took place a short time before he ceased to trade.

It is worth mentioning at this juncture that there had been a revival of an 'old and very disreputable trick in the art-trade'[33], whereby comparatively worn plates were purchased by 'certain parties from London', the lettering removed and new prints made on India paper without letters. These were then offered in auction houses all over the country as genuine proof copies. These 'mock proofs' were considered to be injurious to publishers, print-sellers and their customers and were described as 'not worth the paper they are printed on'. It should be borne in mind that publishers such as Mason derived their income from selling collectable prints and would be detrimentally affected by the trade of 'mock proofs', whereas Grant sold prints in volume and was probably not affected to any real extent. This does not pejoratively intimate that Grant was in any way involved in such a trade, particularly as he nearly always added 'Published by W. Grant, News Agent, 5 Castle Square' on his prints, but it does demonstrate the comparative market for used plates and of their use for fraudulent purposes.

During the early 1850s a series of prints was published by Grant depicting scenes at the Swiss Gardens, Shoreham. This may have come about by virtue of Grant's association with the Odd Fellows, who held fêtes and functions at that place around that time. Three examples of this series have been noted: 'The Pavilion and Observatory', 'The Lake and Temple' and 'View from the Castle of Falkenstein', all engraved by Newman & Co.

One print of particular note is 'The Gloucester Hotel, Railway Terminus and St Peter's Church, Brighton', drawn by George Ruff and engraved by William John Alais, probably around 1852. Aside from the size of the steel engraving, there is a glaring anomaly with the scene. Looking at the right hand side of the hill-top, All Saints' Church in what is now Compton Avenue can be seen, standing in virtual isolation. However, the artist must have drawn the church conjecturally, before it was completed, as the depiction is wholly at odds with the actual building that was erected there. The artist may have seen the proposed plans for All Saints' Church, which was projected in 1847 by the Rev. H M Wagner, using a design by Richard Cromwell Carpenter. The original design was to have incorporated a tower at the north-west corner but this was never completed and it thus never had the spire that the artist shows. The building was not completed until 1852.

When Grant's own bankruptcy occurred in 1855, his stock-in-trade of 'books and single views of Brighton' and '20 reams of paper illustrated with views of Brighton in 37 varieties'[34] were among the items put up for auction. This gives some idea of the huge volume of prints that were published by him, particularly when it is considered that these 37 varieties formed over half the sum total of scenes that were ultimately released. To put this into context: in under a decade, Grant had gone from being just a newsagent to being probably the most prolific publisher, by volume, of Brighton prints. Divested of any copies of the prints, the original plates and the rights to reproduce any further copies, it is most unlikely that Grant published any further prints after August 1855, although it is most likely that he continued to act as an agent for the new publisher, selling the remaining stock of prints still bearing his name.

Following his bankruptcy, it is evident that the rights to many of Grant's prints were acquired by others, most notably Newman and Co, who obtained the lion's share and subsequently republished variants of them under their own name. William Saunders, a local printer and stationer, acquired the ex-Taylor prints and republished them in subsequent editions of his guide-book, The Stranger's Guide in Brighton (1855 & 1856). A couple of other local traders also successively acquired the rights to a pair of Grant's most well-known lithographic views, depicted from the top of the Old Church (catalogue nos. 48 & 49). Samuel George Cox, a bookseller and stationer of 55-56 Queen's Road, obtained the rights after the bankruptcy sale in 1855 and had W T Harris engrave new steel plates but a year later ceded them to a hairdresser and stationer Henry Holden of 98 St George's Road.

[1] The address at Cumberland Street was later renumbered as 22 Cavendish Street. St Nicholas Parish Register, Baptisms, 1813-37 and contemporary trade directories.
[2] *Brighton Herald*, 19 May 1827. Most likely to have been a stroke in modern terms.
[3] Bishop alludes to William Grant being the nephew of John Jones (*A Peep into the Past*, p302) but this term is probably euphemistically used, there being no tangible evidence to indicate any sort of blood relationship between them.

[4] In *Brighton and Its Coaches* (p131), William C A Blew states that John Jones returned thanks 'to Countess Winterton and those Ladies and Gentlemen who had kindly assisted him in the hour of misfortune'

[5] Bishop (*A Peep into the Past*, p302) states that 'Old Jones started at the same shop a bookstall, and turned news-vendor—the first in Brighton'

[6] The concert was advertised in the *Brighton Patriot* of 19 April 1836 and the following edition of 26 April states that the proceeds were £70

[7] *Brighton Herald*, 30 March 1839

[8] Transcribed from court records, East Sussex Quarter Sessions 1839/866

[9] For example, on 21 April 1840 another vendor of the *Paul Pry* on the Isle of Wight was sentenced to three months' hard labour and agreed to be of good behaviour for two years (*Bristol Journal*)

[10] The *Paul Pry* magazine was published from premises at 4 Wellington Street, Strand, London and printed at premises in Bow Street. The proprietors of the magazine were Christopher Hawdon, James Archdeacon Richardson, Henry Richardson, Henry Watson, James Lewis (aka Pople) and John Sprawle. After a series of protracted court battles, Hawdon and Richardson received lengthy jail sentences for conspiracy and libel

[11] *Brighton Herald*, 31 August 1844

[12] *Post Office Directory* 1846

[13] Similar adverts in *Sussex Advertiser*, 25 March 1845, *Brighton Herald*, 5 April 1845, etc

[14] The Keep (East Sussex Records Office) QR/E 899 1844

[15] The Keep (East Sussex Records Office), QR/E 910 1845

[16] The Keep (East Sussex Records Office), QR/E 930 1848

[17] *Brighton Herald*, 8 January 1848

[18] *Sussex Advertiser*, 13 October 1853, 'Odd Fellows' Dinner'

[19] *Sussex Advertiser*, 8 January 1850

[20] *Sussex Advertiser*, 22 March 1853, 'Sussex Spring Assizes'

[21] *Common Bench Reports. Cases argued and determined at the Court of Common Pleas*, 1856. Pennell v Dawson, pp354-370

[22] *Brighton Gazette*, 13 July 1855, #2720. By 11 July, Joseph Clayton, a newsagent of Strand, London had petitioned for a bankruptcy hearing after Grant had failed to pay debts to the amount of £105 11s 2d. A second creditor, William Holmes, a printer of Putney had also submitted proof of debt for £114 16s 0d

[23] Advertisement in the *Brighton Gazette*, 10 May 1855

[24] John George Bishop: *Strolls in the Brighton Extra Mural Cemetery: First and Second Series, 1864-67*. Brighton: Herald Office, Fleet & Co, 1867, p14

[25] George Parker Bidder (1806–1878) was a child prodigy known as the 'calculating boy', who could astonish others with his amazing mathematical abilities. He went on to become a famous civil engineer.

[26] Bartholomew Parker Bidder (1809–1849) was an actuary at the Royal Exchange Assurance Company. When the firm's records were destroyed by fire, he was able to reconstruct them from memory in six months.

[27] John & Jill Ford: *Images of Brighton*. Richmond-upon-Thames: St Helena Press, 1980, p139

[28] *Ibid*, p129

[29] It is estimated that he carried an average stock in excess of 250-300 copies of each print at any one time, based upon the sale of his stock-in-trade in 1855

[30] *Brighton Herald*, 3 February 1849

[31] The catalogue numbers referred to henceforth are as conferred in Ford: *op cit*

[32] *The Original Brighton and Hove Directory, including Cliftonville*, 4th issue. Brighton (16-17 East Street): W J Taylor (late Leppard), July 1854

[33] *Brighton Gazette*, 21 June 1855, article entitled 'Mock Proofs'

[34] *Brighton Gazette*, 9 August 1855

5 William Henry Goodburn Mason
(1810-1879)

William Henry Goodburn Mason was the only nineteenth century Brighton publisher known to serve his apprenticeship with an important London publishing house, namely Rudolph Ackermann's gallery at 96 Strand. This pedigree enabled Mason to produce some of the finest aquatint engravings and lithographs of Brighton and views as far afield as India and China. He also presented novel and inventive exhibitions, until his passion for the game of cricket finally brought him to bankruptcy.

Ancestry and family background

Henry Mason of St Bride's, East London, married Mary Braysher at the Church of The Sepulchre, Cambridge in 1781. The witnesses were Stephen Dew and William Jones, although the 1754 Marriage Act did not require a record of occupations or parents. Their first child was a son, Henry Martin Mason, born in 1782, who became an excise officer in Cambridge. Their second son, William Mason, was born on 26 June 1786 in Yaxley, Cambridgeshire. He became a watercolourist, (examples are in the Fitzwilliam Museum) silhouette artist and print publisher, and was the father of our William Henry Goodburn Mason.

William Mason senior married Elizabeth Goodburn on 28 January 1810 at St George-in-the-East Congregational Church, Cannon Street Road, Stepney, East London. Elizabeth was 20 years old, having been born in London on 5 August 1789. Their marriage certificate reads: 'Bachelor William Mason and Elizabeth Goodburn (spinster and minor) of this same parish (Stepney) were married in the presence of Robert Goodburn and Elizabeth Scott'. Elizabeth Goodburn is noted as 'married with the consent of Robert Goodburn, her natural and lawful father'.

W H G Mason was William and Elizabeth's first child, shown in the parish baptismal records for Shoreditch as being born on 13 October 1810 in London, when the family lived in Moffatt Street. He was baptised on 25 November 1810 at St Leonard's Church, Shoreditch. The earlier church had been rebuilt by 1740 but the original 17th century font is still in place, and the bells of the earlier church are those in the 'Oranges and Lemons' nursery rhyme—'when I grow rich, say the bells of Shoreditch'.

Shoreditch was a poor and industrialised area. Its population had grown faster than any other London parish in the first half of the 19th century, almost doubling between 1800 and 1830, causing great housing difficulties. The line 'when I grow rich' might have been sung with some desperation. With the difficulty in finding birth certificates at this time, the parish baptism register showing his birth date of 13 October is contradicted by the illustrations below.

The detail on the tomb in this nineteenth century print of St

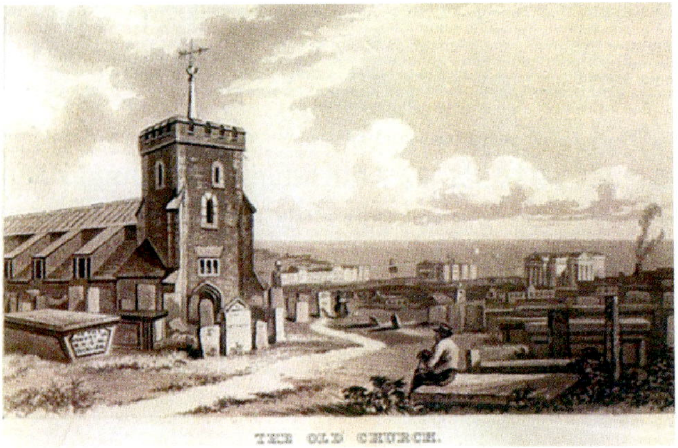

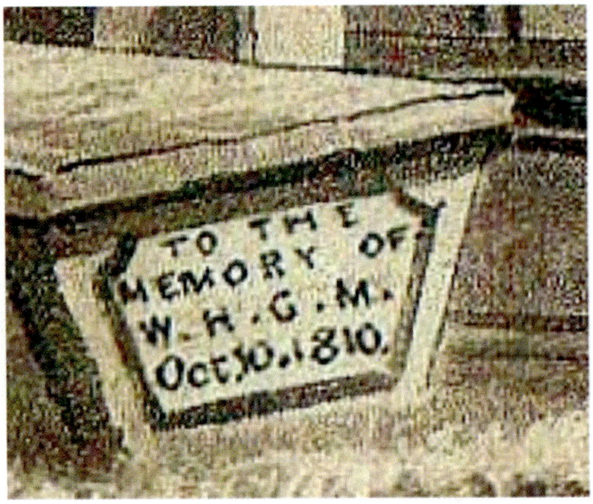

40
'The Old Church'. Aquatint engraving by Charles Hunt, published by W H Mason, 1 Ship Street, Brighton c1835. The right-hand illustration is a detail of the large tomb to the left of the tower

Nicholas Church, Brighton [**40**] clearly states 'W.H.G.M. Oct 30. 1810'. Assuming that Mason is recording the date of his birth on one of his own publications, it is possible that the baptism clerk taking the date of birth misheard 30th for 13th and incorrectly recorded the latter in the baptism register. In the absence of other evidence for his actual birth date, this engraving seems the most reliable witness. For the publisher to put the date of birth so prominently in a print is unusual; possibly Mason had become aware of the mistake and felt the need to make this public correction, with the wry comment 'To the memory of' on the side of the tomb, indicating that he thought the church had buried his true birthday long ago.

William and Elizabeth's second child, Elizabeth Sarah, was born on 13 November 1811, also in Shoreditch. Bearing in mind that Mason senior's earliest Cambridge watercolour view in the Fitzwilliam Museum is dated 1810 and that he married Elizabeth in the January of that year in Stepney, it seems that his time was divided between Cambridge and Shoreditch for a while.

So the family was living in Shoreditch for the births of their first two children, W H G and his sister Elizabeth Sarah, but according to an advertisement in the *Cambridge Independent Press* they had moved back to their family origins in Cambridge by 1813, where William and Elizabeth established their artists' supplies and print publishing business. Their first address was 'near the hospital' or 'near Addenbrooke's', in Trumpington Street, but in another advertisement in the *Cambridge Independent* on 19 October 1821, he 'begs to inform his friends and the public that he has removed from near the Hospital and Christ College to the House late in occupation of Tollworthy and Calver, in St Mary's Passage'. In this same advertisement he advises his public that he has on sale 'a variety of Ancient and Modern Paintings and Drawings, and Prints, by and from the best Masters, also miniature frames, Drawing Papers, Sketch Books, Camel Hair and Black Lead Pencils, Water Colours, Gold Borders, and a great variety of Fancy Paper and Ornaments'.

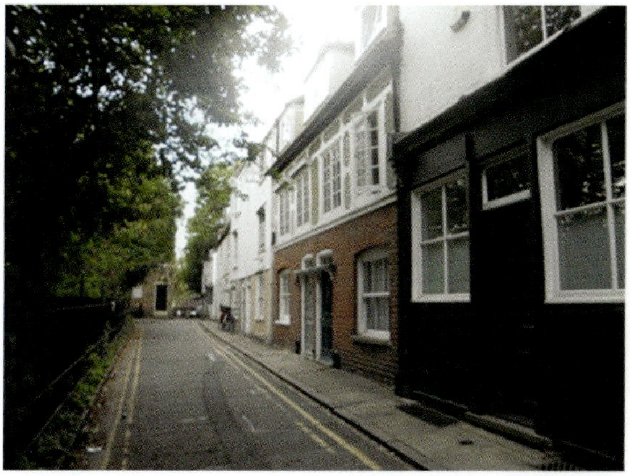

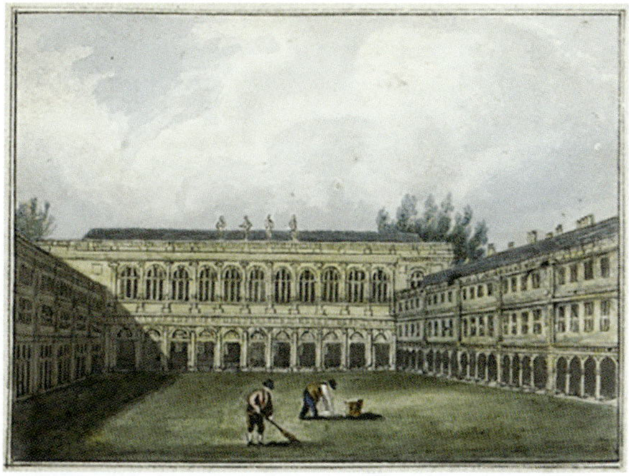

41
a *Left* The black painted frontage is William Mason Sr's premises, as it is today in Little St Mary's Lane. Their eldest son, W H G Mason, was 11 years old when the family moved to this shop. The railings of Little St Mary's Church are on the left
b *Right* Watercolour of Trinity College, Cambridge, by William Mason 1810

This new address of St Mary's Passage, to which Mason senior moved his business, is now known as Little St Mary's Lane and his shop and family home can still be seen [**41a**] in the narrow street running along the north side of Little St Mary's Church. On the other side of the church is Peterhouse College. In the middle of a terrace of small two-storey houses in the re-named Little St Mary's Lane, Mason senior's premises is a four storey plus basement building, converted into a private home from its past life as various shops, and lastly as the Crescent Moon public house.

Sue McKechnie[1] records Mason senior's trade card that advertised: 'Stationery, Paintings, Drawings etc. copied, Frames of all descriptions, Looking Glasses and Mirrors Re-silvered'. These last phrases give a clue to his employment in Shoreditch. Within a few years of the family leaving the East End, furniture manufacturing had increased to the point where 30 per cent of London's furniture makers were based there. So apart from his topographical painting, Mason senior obviously moved from Shoreditch to Cambridge with established skills in picture, print and mirror framing.

From the Fitzwilliam Museum archive[2] we know that he was the original artist on many of his own prints, often describing himself on his publication line as 'Profile Painter & Printseller'. He painted a range of watercolour views of Cambridge, there are 18 in the Fitzwilliam Museum, one of which, a view of Jesus College, is monogrammed and dated 1810. These are all small images done with water-colour, pencil and sometimes graphite [**41b**].

In the National Portrait Gallery[3] there is a John Swaine engraving of a profile by William Mason of Herbert Marsh, Bishop of Peterborough, which bears the inscription 'Drawn and Publd, with permission, by W. Mason, near the Hospital, Cambridge, also 27 views of the above university'. There are a number of his engravings in the Royal Collection at Windsor and the Victoria & Albert Museum has his profile study of the eighteenth century Italian explorer Giovani Baptista Belzoni, dated February 1821.

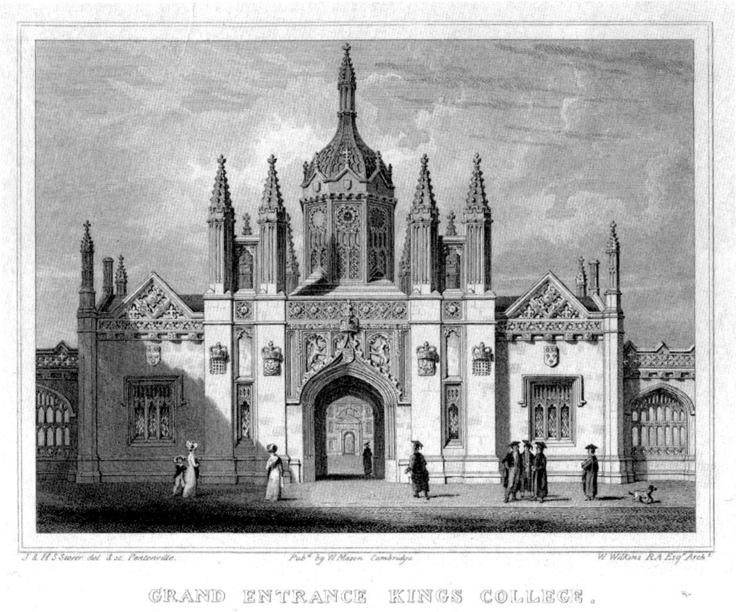

42
'Grand Entrance, Kings College'. An example of Mason Sr's fine quality publishing, printed on India paper. Steel plate line engraving by and after J & H S Storer. Published by W Mason, Cambridge 1827.On the publication line Mason also credits the architect W Wilkins RA. One of many Cambridge views Mason Sr published for the Storers

Mason senior also published prints for James and Henry Storer, father and son, who lived in Cambridge for a short while [**42**]. The Storers were artists of topography and ancient architecture, distinguished and esteemed in their day. Pugin pronounced their publication *The Cathedrals of Great Britain* to be the most accurate views of those buildings in existence[4].

Through the 1820s and 1830s Mason senior published several prints by and after the portraitist Henry Dawe, who co-published with Ackermann's Repository of Arts in London several of his own prints during the early 1830s. This was a few years prior to Mason's son (our W H G Mason) marrying Henry Dawe's daughter Mary in 1838. One of Henry Dawe's engravings for Mason senior was a print of 'The late Gilbert Ives of Cambridge', a fellow bookseller in the city. He died in June 1825 and the print was issued six months later.

Ives was one of a number of colourful local characters whom Mason portrayed. He had started his career as a barber but turned to bookselling, amassing considerable wealth selling old prints, with which he endowed four local almshouses[5]. Two other prints which Mason senior published from his own hand were of 'Dr Barnes, Master of St Peter's College' and 'Prince Leberecht von Blucher', Field Marshall of the Prussian Armies at Waterloo, which Mason dedicated to the Duke of Gloucester, Chancellor of Cambridge University.

Sue McKechnie writes: 'Mason (senior) was a versatile artist who passed his career in Cambridge, his extant works date from 1810–1830 and known addresses were near the Hospital and St Mary's Passage'. This original Addenbrooke's hospital building was just a few steps along Trumpington Street from his second premises in St Mary's Passage. The hospital's old front entrance is now a restaurant, with the stone inscription 'Outpatients' above its front portico. McKechnie illustrates two other works by William Mason, one being a watercolour illustrating St Catharine's College, Cambridge, from his series in the Fitzwilliam Museum. The other is a silhouette, painted on card, of the Duke of Sussex, dated verso 'August 1826'. On his trade card, Mason senior advertised that he was 'Patronised by HRH the Duke of Sussex'—Augustus Frederick, the sixth son of George III.

William Henry Goodburn Mason grew up in the family culture of topographical painting, engraving, framing and publishing, and was surrounded by the supplies needed to create fine pictorial art. But later, having been established in Brighton for some years, during 1849 W H G Mason was involved in a trial where his defence counsel stated that: 'He resided in Brighton, but had previously carried on business in Windsor'. In this trial at Lewes (see p113) one of the character witnesses for Mason was W F Taylor of Windsor, who said he had known Mason since 1842. Taylor's father owned a bookshop; in Hunt's 1846 *Windsor Street Directory* he is described as 'librarian, printer, stationer, book and music seller and binder', of 13 High Street, Windsor. At a later date Mason co-published a lithograph with W F Taylor showing 'Eton from the North Terrace'. Taking his defence counsel's statement as a fact that must have been given by W H G Mason himself, it seems that William Mason senior sent his teenage son to work as an apprentice with Taylor in Windsor.

On 11 November 1825 the *Cambridge Independent Press* carried an advertisement by William Mason senior of St Mary's Passage, for Rudolph Ackermann's successful Christmas literary annual Forget Me Not, stating that he also had in stock No 34 from the third series of Ackermann's *Repository of Arts Magazine*. This date of 1825 is the first instance found of William Mason selling Rudolph Ackermann's publications, and this new business association between the two publishers probably indicates the move of the young 15-year-old Mason directly from Mr Taylor's shop in Windsor to gain experience working in Ackermann's Repository of Arts at 101 Strand. The portraitist Henry Dawe (1790–1848), who became W H G Mason's father-in-law, was probably instrumental in the introduction of the Mason and Ackermann businesses—Dawe had his prints issued by both companies at this time.

Later, it appears Mason returned temporarily to his father's shop and was listed in the 1832 electoral roll book for the Hundred of Cambridge. He is still on the Cambridge roll book in 1835 but by this date is noted as 'living in Brighton'. The supposition is that he went back to the family home for his 21st birthday on 30 October 1831, at which point his father transferred the freehold of the St Mary's Passage premises to him, thus giving him voting rights and the possibility of bank finance. Mason senior, not listed on the electoral roll, continued in these premises until an advertisement in the local press on 11 June 1842 announced that John B Mason (William Mason's third son) had succeeded his father in the business. An earlier notice in the *Cambridge Independent Press* of 23 September 1825 announced the death, by the tragic accident of a coach passing over him, of William Mason's second son, Robert Clark Mason, aged 12. William Mason himself died in retirement at his home in Cambridge on 20 January 1855, and on 26 February that year his fourth son, Goodburn Mason, died of fever whilst serving with the 30th Regiment during the Crimean war.

Having briefly returned to Cambridge in 1831 for his 21st birthday,

W H G Mason was certainly with Ackermann's in their Strand gallery in January 1830 when Rudolph Ackermann suffered his first stroke. The initial hope in London might have been that Ackermann would still be actively involved in the business, but this was not to be and he had a second stroke in 1832. As explained in detail later, by 1830 Ackermann's had appointed an agent in Brighton and were advertising their London business in the local papers. This could have been the precursor to a planned Ackermann presence in the town but with Rudolph's stroke these plans were changed and the decision was made to help their employee, the 21-year-old Mason, still a bachelor at this stage, to open his own business instead.

The temporary return to Cambridge at the end of October 1831 for his birthday was probably quite short. It was most likely to discuss the move to Brighton and arrange for the transfer of the Cambridge premises and the rights that came with property ownership, from father to eldest son. He then rejoined Ackermann's at 96 Strand, by then their new address, with less than five months left for the final preparations to open his own Repository in Ship Street, Brighton at the end of March 1832. Since the Mason family had no connection with the south coast, it must have been Ackermann's suggestion that he should move to Brighton. Also, Mason himself may well have seen the sales that advertising in Brighton brought in to the London Repository and possibly he delivered some of the purchases to their Brighton clients.

Being supported by Ackermann stock, business contacts and the co-publishing of prints, the prospect of a career on the south coast must have been appealing. In the spring of 1832, on his new gallery at the seafront corner of 1 Ship Street and King's Road [**43**[6]], Mason introduced himself to Brighton as 'W H Mason from Ackermann's Repository of Arts'. The Ackermann company that Mason came from at 96 Strand was the successor to their father's business, run by the three younger sons, George, Ferdinand and Adolphus Ackermann. The youngest of the three, Adolphus, was the same age as Mason. The eldest Ackermann son, Rudolph Jr, had his own sporting gallery at 191 Regent Street.

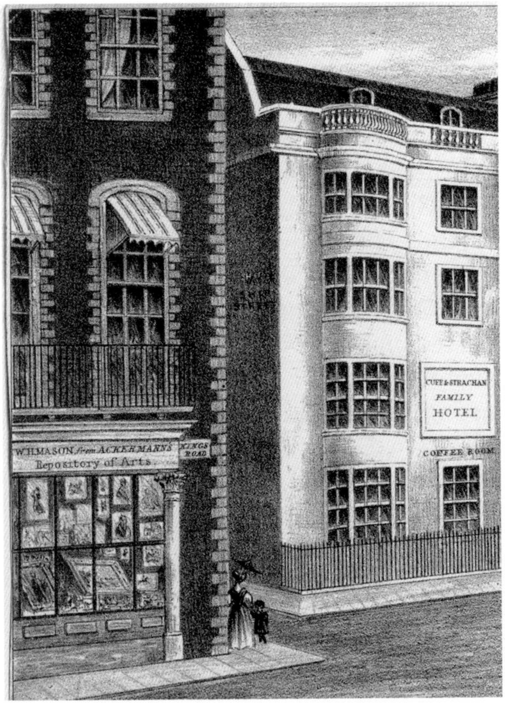

43
Detail from a rare lithograph printed by L M Lefevre entitled 'Cuff & Strachan, Old Ship Hotel, Brighton', c1837. It shows Mason's Repository of Arts on the corner of Ship Street and King's Road, Brighton, and on the shop front can be seen 'W.H. MASON from ACKERMANN'S Repository of Arts'

Moving on a few years, Mason is listed on Brighton's 1837 electoral register, and in the column noting the qualification to vote, he had 'two houses in succession—Preston Street and Ship Street'. He could have been on the voting register as a tenant occupying a property with a rental value of more than £10 a year and as a property owner in Cambridge. It seems likely that he became a co-tenant in Preston Street on his arrival in Brighton in the autumn of 1831, while arranging the lease on Ship Street, and this first co-tenancy would have been by introduction from Ackermann's again. The *Brighton Gazette* of 15 November 1832 carried an advertisement for parts 1 and 2 of a series of topographical views of 'The Banks of the Loire' by the landscape and portrait artist Louis Parez. The series was published by Parez in Brighton and Ackermann in London, and 'the work may be seen at the Repository of Arts, 32 Preston Street'.

So the electoral register puts Mason in Preston Street, we know it must have been before he took over the Ship Street premises in March 1832, and the advertisement also puts an Ackermann artist in Preston Street that year. This Repository of Arts did not have the name of Parez or Ackermann attached to it, but in a later *Brighton Gazette* advertisement, on 3 October 1833, Parez announced that he had moved his Classical Drawing Academy from 6 Regency Square, presumably his home, to the Repository of Arts, with its number changed to 58 Preston Street, 'where his works may be seen daily' and where his Drawing Academy 'will be run on Tuesdays and Fridays at 12 o'clock'.

It looks as if Ackermann's sent Mason to be a temporary co-tenant with Parez of the Preston Street Repository of Arts (it being Parez's own establishment and not Ackermann's) while arrangements to open the Ship Street gallery were being made. We could wonder how Mason and Parez got on together. Parez seemed to have a gruesome interest in the notorious local murder of Celia Bashford in 1831, producing six prints of the subject, including portraits of the two murderers[7]. Mason's preferred portrait subjects were clergymen.

44
Wood engraving from Bishop's *A Peep into the Past*, included in the second edition of 1892

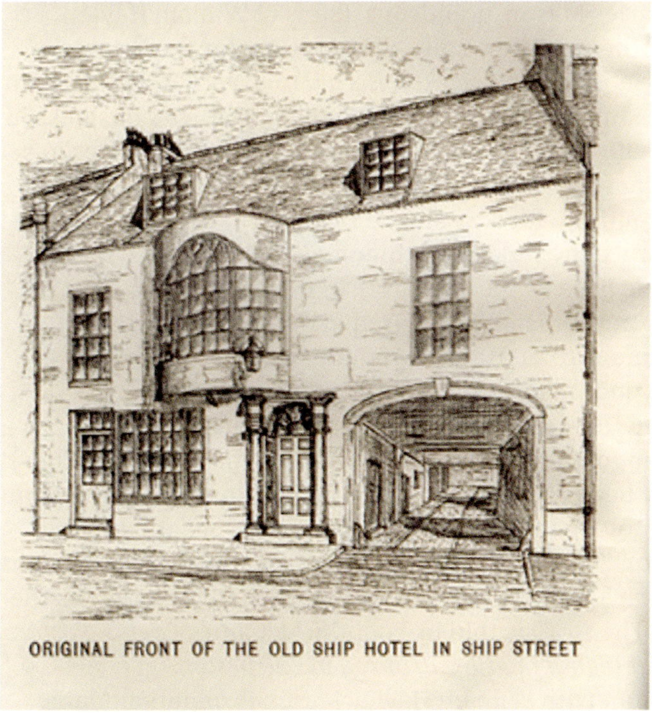
ORIGINAL FRONT OF THE OLD SHIP HOTEL IN SHIP STREET

To get an appreciation of Mason's chosen location of Ship Street at this time, H M Walbrook in *One Hundred Years of the Royal York Brighton* (1919) enthusiastically describes four of the houses in 'this old thoroughfare', numbers 67 to 70, as 'charming, pretty, picturesque and quite beautiful'. William Attree, solicitor to the Prince Regent for the Pavilion purchase, had also built his own home and business premises at number 8 in 1773; it is still there today. Just opposite Mason's shop windows in Ship Street was the original front door and carriage entrance to the Old Ship Hotel [**44**[8]].

The Chichester confusion

Our subject, William Henry Mason of Brighton, has sometimes been confused with William Hayley Mason of Chichester, but to date no family connection has been found. The confusion is understandable as William Hayley was in the same line of business—book and print publishing—and he was born within a year of William Henry Mason. Furthermore, William Hayley had family connections with Brighton, in both families the fathers were William, and they both had sons named William Henry.

William Hayley Mason's connection with Brighton was through William Fleet (1787-1874), who was for many years the proprietor and editor of the *Brighton Herald*. Fleet's sister, Mary Ann, married a Mr William Mason by licence at St Andrew's Church, Chichester, on 21 June 1810. Several years earlier, in 1806, this William Mason had produced the first edition of the *Brighton Herald* for the then owners, Robinson Attree and Matthew Phillips. By 1808 he had left the *Brighton Herald*, moved to Chichester, carried on the business of bookseller, printer and publisher, and married Fleet's sister, Miss Mary Ann (or Marianna) Fleet. He became the printer for Jacques' *Guidebook of Goodwood House*, together with a *Guidebook to Bognor* in 1822. They had a son, William Hayley Mason, who was christened in St Andrew's, Chichester, on 18 April 1811. William Hayley married his cousin, William Fleet's daughter, Marianne, on 25 March 1837 and they had two sons, William Henry Mason (not our man) and Charles Mason.

On William Fleet's death, J G Bishop[9] wrote regarding the funeral: 'the body was followed by the only surviving son, Charles Fleet, and by W H Mason and Charles Mason, grandsons' (sons of William Hayley Mason). Here is another possible cause of confusion: for the Brighton funeral of the proprietor of the *Brighton Herald* to have a 'W H Mason' in the procession. William Hayley Mason continued his father's business in Chichester. James Peill, Curator of the Goodwood Collection, writes in a private letter: 'William Hayley Mason was the author of Goodwood, its House, Park and Grounds with a catalogue raisonné of the Pictures in the Gallery of His Grace the Duke of Richmond KG'. William Hayley is described on the title page as the 'Librarian of Goodwood'.

In a letter to the authors in 2007, Rosemary Baird, Curator at Goodwood at the time, wrote: 'Hayley Mason's catalogue of the collection at Goodwood was based on the earlier guidebook by the Goodwood Librarian Dennett Jacques, although Mason added far more paintings'. The letter goes on: 'William Mason, (William Hayley's father) who had previously been apprenticed to the printer Joseph Seagrave in Chichester, before moving to Brighton, had succeeded Seagrave as the Chichester Printer on Seagrave's death in 1808. William Hayley Mason (the poet William Hayley was his godfather) succeeded his father as the Chichester Printer. The story is told in Timothy McCann's *Poems, Posters and Poll Books—Eighteenth Century Printing in Chichester*'.

Thus the confusion with William Hayley Mason is understandable.

Business and financial life

Having established himself as the virtual representative of Ackermann's, for the next 25 years W H G Mason was the most prolific Brighton publisher of fine quality aquatints and lithographs and produced 78 known views of the town and beach (counting the many pairs and sets as one unit publication). This included a very limited number of steel engravings.

The publisher Rudolph Ackermann, with his well-known business in London's Strand, had a strong connection with Brighton due to his publication of the Pavilion aquatints from the drawings by John Nash, resulting in the superb 1826 colour plate book *The Royal Pavilion at Brighton*. From his involvement with this publication Ackermann undoubtedly saw Brighton as an important market-place for his goods. He was advertising in the local papers there in the early 1830s; the *Brighton Gazette* of 3 November 1831 advertised a range of fashionable and humorous publications available in their London gallery, and in the local press of the autumn of 1830 he had named Joseph Cordwell as his Brighton agent.

It has been suggested that Rudolph Ackermann opened a shop there in 1830[10] but this is not borne out by the Brighton guides and trade directories, and the earlier Repository of Arts in Preston Street did not bear his name, although the sons did briefly open a shop in King's Road in the mid-1850s. Rudolph Ackermann may have had intentions to open in Brighton but these would have been abandoned when he had his first stroke in January 1830 and there was the opportunity for their young employee.

Mason had ample resources at his disposal, being able to sell Ackermann stock and fancy goods, he was introduced to various established Ackermann artists and engravers and had the co-operation of the Ackermann sons on his first and many subsequent Brighton and non-Brighton publications. So, in the *Brighton Guardian* on 28 March 1832, the 21-year old Mason advertised that he had opened his 'Repository of Arts' at 1 Ship Street. On his subsequent shop fronts, and in newspaper advertisements, he kept to this introduction of 'W H Mason from Ackermanns', a name with which so many of the London visitors to Brighton would be familiar.

Without having to open their own premises, Ackermann's at last had much of their available merchandise in the market-place of Brighton. Mason opened his gallery after a decade of great improvements to the mail and stage coach connections with London. Charles Fleet[11] wrote: 'The Progress of improvement was never greater in Brighton than between 1820 and 1830. Travelling had now arrived at such perfection that, instead of being a day's journey from the Metropolis, Brighton was within a five, and even four hours' ride of London'.

The financing of Mason's move to the south coast could have been by a short leasehold mortgage or loan based on his being a property owner in Cambridge, and particularly by Ackermann's providing the opening stock. Possibly with Ackermann's advice, Mason had chosen an ideal position for his Brighton venture. Just a decade earlier that part of the seafront—where Ship Street entered what was to become King's Road—had no access to carriages, it being the site of the original sea-port for the fishing fleet, and for the colliers to unload. But some roadway improvements on the seafront had been completed before Mason took over his new premises and these brought great advantages to the seafront businesses.

There had been two blockages that stopped through traffic between West Street and Russell House, situated at the southern end of the Steine, and on to Marine Parade. The first section of the seafront between West Street and East Street was changed from a pathway 'only passable in fair weather'[12] to a road, by public subscription, giving carriage access to the sea-end of Ship Street. It was officially opened by George IV in January 1822. Attwick[13] described how 'the footpath between Ship Street and West Street had been widened out into a narrow carriage road'. Then the Albion Hotel had replaced Russell House in 1826 and by 1829 King's Road to the west was linked to the Marine Parade in the east by the newly arranged Grand Junction Road, which Bruce described as 'the most important alteration that has taken place at Brighton for some years'[14]. In addition to the Albion Hotel, the Royal York had opened in September 1819. So with these road improvements, guests would be able to walk or ride along the seafront from both hotels and those in Marine Parade, and view Mason's gallery windows.

The other municipal improvements that made it such an opportune time to open a business on this part of the sea-front were the two sea-wall constructions. The first was from Ship Street east to Mahomed's Baths (where the Queen's Hotel is today) which was started in 1825, and the second wall, started in 1846, secured the sea-defences from the Battery (where the Grand Hotel now is) eastwards to West Street, and then on to Ship Street. Fleet[15] wrote about 'the Sea Wall, by which the Marine drive and promenade of Brighton will be made of a width and extent to compete with the finest streets of any European capital'. It was on this 'finest street' that Mason spent his entire business career.

His new gallery was part of the Manor of Atlingworth, which came to Thomas Attree on 31 March 1818[16], inherited from his father William Attree by his will, proved in London on 12 February 1811. In these 1818 deeds 1 Ship Street, together with 46 West Cliff, were described as 'lodging houses'. In Mason's 'Panorama of Brighton' publication of 1833 his gallery, together with the house next door, certainly look to have been rebuilt from this original 1818 description and, moving along his panorama to the next street corner of Middle Street, the Sea House Hotel was an identical building to Mason's shop. This hotel at 13 King's Road, previously the Ship in Distress inn, was rebuilt in 1825 and renamed the Sea House Hotel shortly after the part of King's Road between West

Street and East Street was opened up for carriage traffic. It seems likely that the premises making up the corner of 1 Ship Street were rebuilt at much the same time and obviously to the same design.

In September 1818 Thomas Attree, as the new freeholder and Lord of the Manor of Atlingworth, sold a lifetime lease to Charles Scrase Dickins the elder and the younger—for whoever lived the longer—for £1,030. The Dickins family held the Lordship of the Manor of Brighthelmstone Michelham. Charles Scrase Dickins the elder was married to Lady Frances-Elizabeth Compton, whose family owned Compton Place in Eastbourne, and he was the cousin of William Attree's mother. Attree, with Scrase Dickins, obviously took on existing tenants and the surgeon Mr T B Pitt was the sub-lease holder of 1 Ship Street and 46 West Cliff. He in turn sub-let 1 Ship Street to another surgeon, Mr J N Janes, and it was this lease that Mason took over in March 1832. Mr Pitt then moved his practice to Cannon Place and offered his remaining sub-leases on the two premises for sale on 25 March 1833 in the auction room of Mr Creasy, advertised in the *Brighton Gazette* on 28 February.

This must have put Mason in a slightly urgent position but he obviously managed to bid successfully for the lease of 1 Ship Street and traded from there until his move along King's Road in 1839. Thus the Scrase Dickins family were Mason's immediate landlords by 1833, with Thomas Attree as the freeholder. It was under Scrase Dickins' stewardship that this corner block was probably rebuilt, a few years before Mason took it over, with a new professional/commercial frontage to make the most of the opportunities offered by the passing trade of this new section of King's Road. In Pigot & Co's *Sussex Directory* for 1832-34, included under 'Print-sellers' is the entry 'Mason – Wm (publisher), 1 Ship st'. In this directory there was just one of the other five contemporary print publishers listed: Rudolph Ackermann's previous agent, Joseph Cordwell of 4 St James's Street. Another ex-Ackermann employee, W Arundale, advertised himself as 'from Ackermann's' when he set up as a carver and gilder in Hastings in 1837[17].

The detail overleaf from Mason's first publication in Brighton, the 1833 aquatint engraving of the 'Panorama of Brighton' [**45**], shows his new premises, Mason's Repository of Arts, at 1 Ship Street, from where he published 10 views of Brighton before moving to 81 King's Road.

Mason's gallery is the green-fronted window that goes around the corner into Ship Street and includes the next light-orange-coloured window. On the wall above the Ship Street window is the title 'Mason's Repository of Arts', no doubt with the lithographic printing presses at the rear of the shop and the upper floors used for colouring rooms, storage and accommodation.

On the last line of the title page for this 'Panorama of Brighton' is the credit 'Drawn by H. Wilds, Architect, Brighton'. His father, Amon Wilds, had died the year of this publication and the son, Amon Henry, is here identifying himself by the initial of his middle name. The engraver is

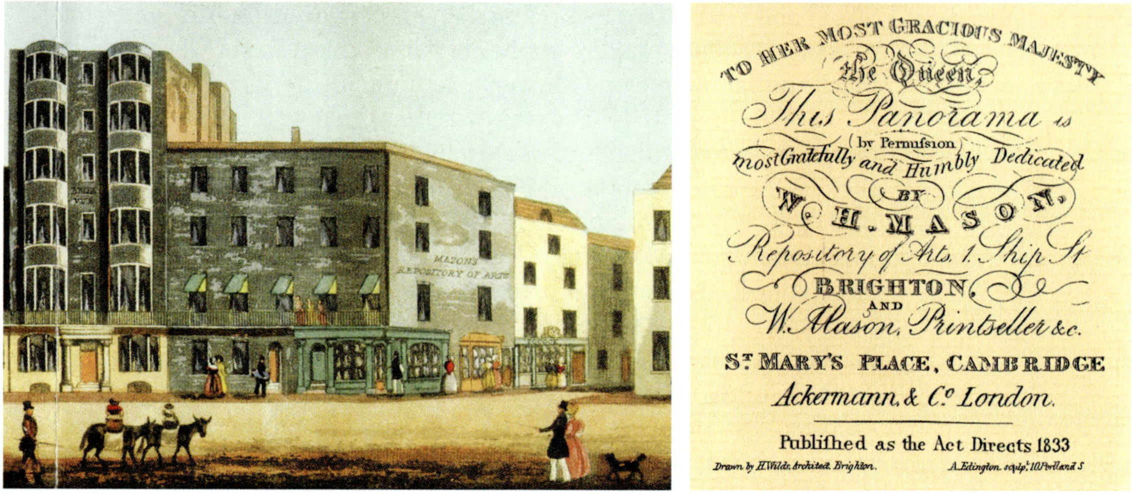

45
The right-hand edge and opening scene of the 'Panorama of Brighton', an aquatint engraving by A Edington after A H Wilds, published by W H Mason, Brighton, William Mason of Cambridge, and Ackermann & Co, London, 1833. Throughout his career in Brighton, Mason was the only local publisher who worked closely with a London publishing house on so many prints

identified as A Edington of 10 Portland Street, London. This was Adolphus Frederick Edington, son of John Edington, jeweller of that address. Adolphus was in his early twenties when he engraved the panorama. He was doubtless introduced to Mason by the Ackermann sons and his work shows an immature hand, most of his walking horses are drawn to just one format and, with one exception, all windows are dark with no variation of blinds or curtains being drawn, details which Wilds as the artist/architect would have left to the engraver. The exception is West Field Lodge, between Russell Street and Regency Square, which has coloured blinds to all its windows.

The scene portrayed a mile of seafront development. Mason chose to start at the beginning of the West Cliff, which of course put his new gallery, on the corner with Ship Street, as the opening image when the panorama was unwound. The view extended to just beyond Adelaide Terrace, that stretch of seafront then referred to as West Brighton. The combined process of Wilds creating the drawing, then the London-based engraver Edington preparing the copper plates in sections—in total nearly 15 feet long—together with a number of colourists who would have been used, must have taken several months. This panorama was a remarkably ambitious undertaking for Mason's first publication—a proud and confident statement that there was a new publisher in Brighton, and that Ackermann's of London was behind him.

There were other established book and print sellers already in the town when Mason opened his Repository. Joseph Cordwell of St James's Street was publishing by 1819, C & R Sickelmore of the King's Road by 1824, Robert Paine of St James's Street had produced several aquatints in the 1790s, and J Taylor and W Saunders had both published illustrated guides before Mason arrived. Mason could have conceived the idea of a panorama from seeing Robert Havell's 'A Coasting View of Brighton' published in 1824. In his publishing output Mason was something of a copyist, certainly in his early years, but occasionally it might be said that

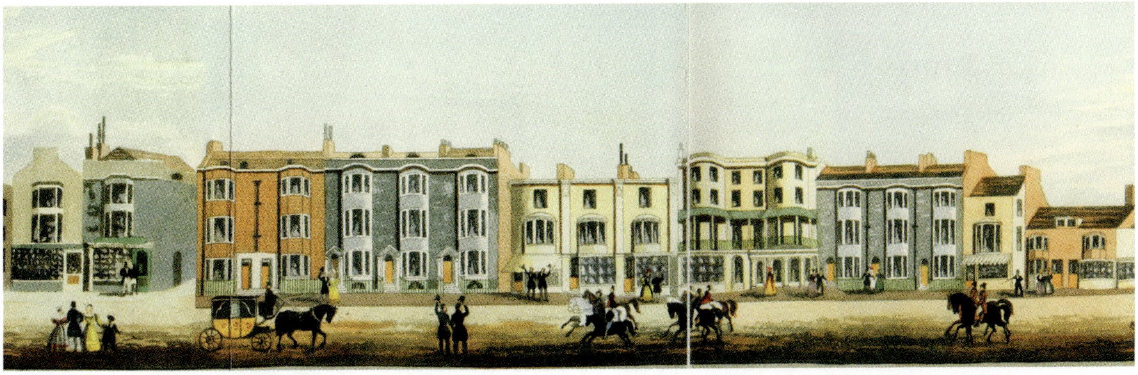

46
A detail of Mason's 'Panorama of Brighton' showing buildings between Russell Street and West Street, the part of the King's Road that Mason moved to in 1839

his version was an improvement. The lower half of the Havell image was taken up by the sea, and because he included the East and West cliff views, in a narrower format, the details of the seafront buildings are not easy to discern. Mason's view was just of the West Cliff, without any portrayal of sea, and as such it was a far more definitive and impressive account of the west side of Brighton's seafront architecture and must have created quite a stir among the established local publishers [**46**].

Some 20 years later William Grant published his 'Panoramic View of Brighton from the Sea', but this copied the format and composition of the Havell scene, so leaving Mason's strictly architectural 1833 image unique among the various Brighton panoramas. By his 1841 *Fashionable Hand-Book* Mason was describing it as 'The Royal Panorama of Brighton—nearly twenty feet long'.

Several years before the Grant publication, in 1839 Mason produced his second panorama, after the work of C Derby [**47**] with sales in aid of the Sussex County Hospital. It was a much more picturesque scene, three times the depth of the Wilds production, but just under a third of its length and included the sea and beach.

Mason collaborated with A H Wilds on one other publication, Wilds' proposed development of 'Roe Park, Withdean, Near Brighton' [**48**], published by Mason from 81 King's Road, which dates it between 1839

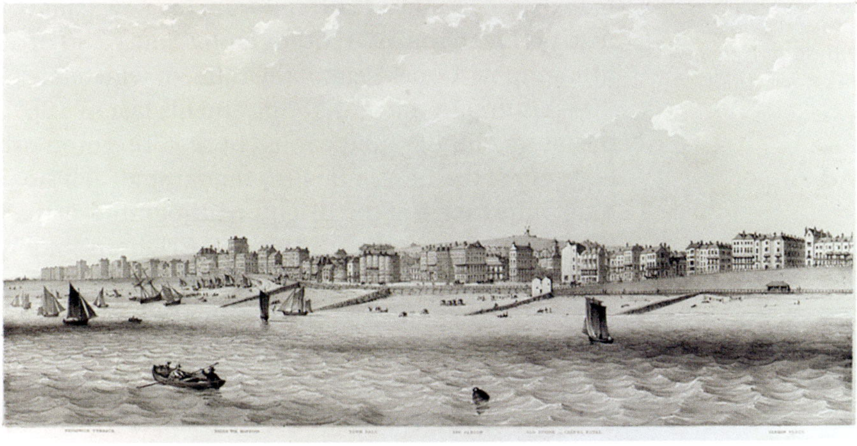

47
The left-hand part of 'Brighton 1839', a lithograph by Day & Haghe after C Derby, Published in three sections by Mason from 81 King's Road. Also issued with the title 'Panoramic View of Brighton'

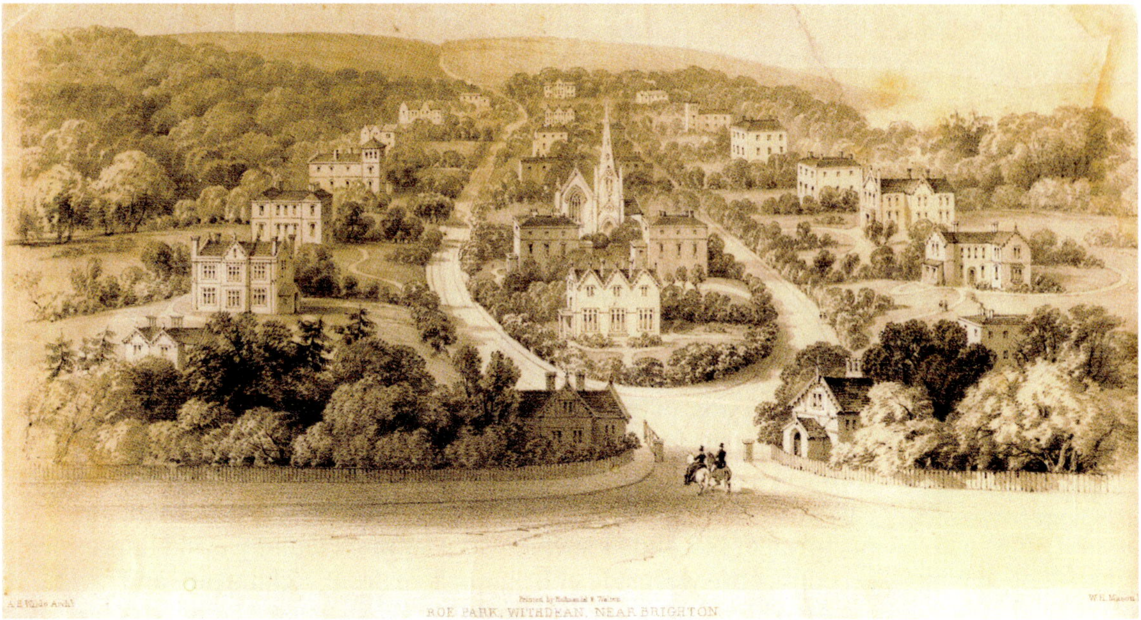

48
'Roe Park, Withdean, Near Brighton' (detail). Drawn on stone by W H Mason after A H Wilds, published by W H Mason, 81 King's Road, Brighton. The lower half of this engraving is a plan of the estate, probably for what is now the site of Withdean Stadium. Wilds' proposed design, although quite similar to parts of Withdean today, was never built

and 1848, when the Withdean Estate was owned by William Thomas Roe's heiress, Eliza Ogle. The lettering on the print reads: 'A.H.Wilds, Archt.—Printed by Hullmandel and Walton—W.H.Mason litho'. This credits Mason as the artist of the lithographic stone from the drawing by Wilds, and it is an accomplished piece of landscape/architectural drawing by Mason, albeit copied from Wilds' original, showing the proficiency of drawing on stone that he had no doubt attained during his time with Ackermann. There is a further known example of Mason drawing the lithographic stone, on a set of four prints of 'Arundel Castle', published in 1846 after drawings by members of the Earp family.

Rudolph Ackermann had played an important part in establishing lithography, the new German printing process, as a commercial success in England. His *Repository of Arts Magazine* in 1817 had carried one of the earliest lithographs printed in an English publication and one of the many services Mason offered from his new gallery in Brighton was instruction in the art of lithography. Some 230 of all Brighton prints are lithographs, 17 per cent of the total, of which Mason was responsible for 30—his first in the mid-1830s and his last in 1867. John & Jill Ford[18], in discussing lithography, comment that 'Brighton prints provide the epitome of the best in English topographical lithography'. Among the most impressive of the Brighton lithographs is the pair, published by William Grant, 'North East View of Brighton' and 'West View of Brighton from the top of the Old Church', of which the original watercolours by J Newman are in the British Museum collection.

Mason continued trading from his first premises in Ship Street until 1839, when he moved westwards to 81 King's Road. He took on the lease of number 81 from John Foakes on 15 May 1839 but by the wording of the lease document Mason had already occupied the premises from 12 April[19]. The lease included full repair except in the case of fire, and in the event of fire making the premises uninhabitable, Mason could 'deduct out of the rent any sum which would be payable to Robert Ackerson'.

John Foakes was the head leaseholder of 81 King's Road, which interest he purchased from the freeholder Robert Ackerson on 19 January 1839. John Foakes granted a 21-year lease (less seven days) to Mason, at a rent of £100 a year. There were options for Mason to surrender his interest on seven years and 14 years. This new shop was between West Street and Great Russell Street, where the Brighton Centre now stands. The modern remains of Great Russell Street is a very short piece of north/south tarmac presently called Russell Place, at the back of Churchill Square.

One feature of his second gallery that has caused some confusion is that just as Mason moved from Ship Street, the numbering of King's Road was changed, so one reference to Mason at 39 King's Road has been found, before that shop was changed to 81. In the lease agreement the premises is referred to as 'lately No: 39 but now No: 81'. As in Ship Street, this new location had Mason's living accommodation above, and the lease also mentions a garden at the rear. Mason had married in February 1838, having spent most of his time in Ship Street as a bachelor, so a reason for the move in the spring of the following year might have been the need for better accommodation and a garden. The couple obviously hoped for children: they had eight in the end.

From this new address Mason embarked on a particularly productive period, with many publications including his *Fashionable Hand-Book for Visitors*, the *New Drawing Book of Sketches from Brighton Beach* and C Derby's *Panoramic View of Brighton for the benefit of the Sussex County Hospital.* His new gallery was close to Mutton's establishment, which Edmund Gilbert[20] describes as 'that great institution . . . the chief confectioner's shop in the King's Road, a place which dealt in wines and spirits, had no end of eating rooms, and kept an hotel' [**49**].

Harold Clunn[21] wrote that 'the King's Road replaced the Steine as the favourite rendezvous of fashionable society' by the mid-nineteenth century. The *Brighton Herald* described King's Road as 'so thronged with company these fine days that it is almost impossible to get along the pavement, and the road is equally crowded with carriages'[22]. In such a busy thoroughfare the Repository itself was equally busy. The 1841 census, looked at in detail later, names five staff employed by Mason, aged from 14 to 45.

Unfortunately, this flourish of publishing activity from his new gallery on the King's Road came to a temporary halt in August 1844. The businessman Thomas Wisden, a successful local builder and property owner[23] (with much in the Montpelier area) brought a high court judgement against Mason on 17 August 1844, claiming a debt of £450, plus £6 7s 0d damages[24], the equivalent of nearly £30,000 today. Just a

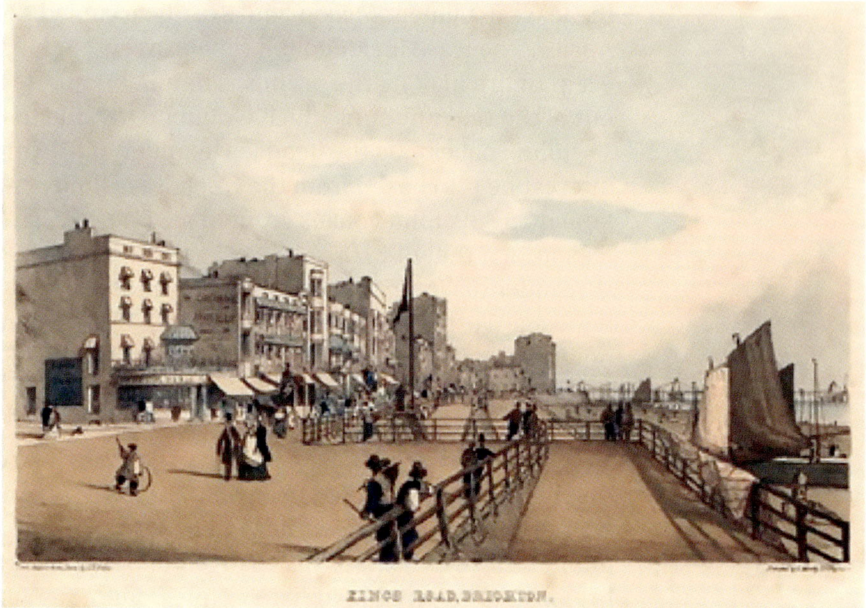

49
'King's Road, Brighton', lithograph after R H Nibbs, 1846. This is the King's Road as Mason knew it. The building on the left, Booty's Library, was at 66 on the corner of West Street, so the artist's viewpoint was almost level with Mason's gallery at number 81. This print was published by William Lane, Mason's apprentice, who was living at the Repository in the 1841 census, but by 1846 was publishing good quality lithographs from his own business at 3 Market Street, Brighton

few years earlier, in April 1837, both Wisden and Mason were among seven men sworn in as headboroughs for that year. As a result of this claim, the Sheriff of Sussex, Edward Hussey, confiscated Mason's lease on 20 August and by deed poll (changing the name of the leaseholder to himself as Sheriff) sold the lease on to Thomas Wisden for £35. The *Brighton Herald* carried an auction announcement by Mr Parsons of Marine Parade: 'Consequent upon an execution from the Sheriff of Sussex, costly engravings, stock-in-trade of a Publisher, artists' materials, fancy goods and effects of 81 King's Road—to be sold by auction this day, August 31st 1844, at 12 o'clock precisely'. The notice continued: 'This attractive stock, which is quite fresh, abounds with novelties and articles of taste, a large collection of fine engravings (many proofs before letters) from the pencils of eminent artists, oil paintings and water-colour drawings of great merit, portfolios of valuable prints, books of sketches by Atkinson, Stanfield, Sir David Wilkie, scrap books, sketch books and blocks, drawing paper, music books, bibles, prayers and lessons, elegantly bound in velvet and morocco, albums, writing, travelling, and envelope cases, Russia goods, fancy stationary etc. etc.'

The next advertisement below this stated that 'for 81 King's Road, Thursday 5th September 1844, is fixed for the sale of the Household Furniture by Mr. Parsons, on the premises at 12 o'Clock punctually'. The auctioneer's list of the Repository's stock on offer shows a high-class range of everything to do with the pictorial arts, and the following description of the domestic items for sale gives us an insight into Mason's home. According to the advertisement the sitting room included rosewood and mahogany card, dining, Pembroke and café tables, double scroll Grecian sofas, Bengal easy chair, Trafalgar chairs, chimney glasses, brass fenders and fire brasses, Brussels carpet, rugs, time-piece in rosewood case and window curtains in suits of moreen dimity. The bedrooms had a mahogany and japanned four-post, French press and other bedsteads, bordered hair and wool mattresses, goose feather beds, blankets and Marseilles quilts, chamber carpets, fenders and chairs, chests of drawers, toilet tables and glasses, washing stands and appendages, towel horses, etc. etc. The notice ended by advertising that 'A subsequent day will be announced for the sale of the valuable lease, shop and house fixtures'. This auctioneer was Mr Joseph Parsons, the founder of the present Parsons, Son & Basley and his premises was on the western corner of Camelford Street with Marine Parade.

With the size of Wisden's claim, no wonder all his stock, home contents and lease was on the line. However, no lasting damage came from this crisis. Mason had published the print of 'Capt. Warner's Experiment' the month before Wisden served his writ in 1844, and after the high court judgement he remained at number 81 for another four years. His eventual move was in mid-1848, when he went next door to 80. The record of what happened to Parson's auction has not been found. Presumably the stock was not dispersed, and it seems from the transactions detailed below that it was the intention of William Drummond, the artist who resided with the Mason family, to enable his friend and business companion to continue trading at number 81. Drummond bought the lease and presumably came to some arrangement with Thomas Wisden over the stock and the debt, which must have been greatly reduced by the court, in order to keep the Repository open.

After this advertised auction crisis of Mason's stock and home contents, in the end Wisden did not offer the actual lease for auction, but rather on 26 September 1844 he sold it to Francis Gladding, jeweller of Brighton, for £135. The following day Gladding sold three years of this lease, at £115 a year, to William Drummond, who also had the option to buy the remaining years of the original 21-year lease. He did not take this up. Instead, at the expiry of his three years, the lease reverted to Gladding, and on 28 September 1847 (the day after Drummond's three-year lease expired) Mason repurchased the remainder of his original 21 years from Gladding for £180. So during these three years Mason continued to run the Repository of Arts just as a retail outlet rather than a publishing house, with the artist Drummond as his immediate landlord.

As will be seen in the section on bankruptcy, this William Drummond, a successful portraitist from London, was one of Mason's artists involved in the publication of 'The Cricket Match between Sussex and Kent' and was clearly the saviour of the Repository of Arts business during the September of 1844. Francis Gladding was a local jeweller, silversmith and watchmaker of 46-47 King's Road, and by 1848 was a Town Commissioner. Helping Mason may have made good sense to

Gladding. Apart from his main trade he advertised himself as an engraver and importer of fancy goods and Mason could have been one of his outlets. For some reason Wisden, the original plaintiff, did not sell the lease direct to Mason's business partner William Drummond but rather to Gladding, and it was this local businessman who eventually provided Mason with the route back into the leasehold of his premises at number 81.

By May 1846, still with Drummond as his landlord, Mason was publishing again from 81 King's Road. In fact, having produced nothing for over 20 months from August 1844, he published more prints in May 1846 than in any other single month during his career. This surge of activity included prints of 'The Pavilion' and 'St. Nicholas Church', both after George Earp Jr, 'The Dyke House', 'The Victoria Fountain', 'The Chain Pier', the set of four lithographs 'Views on the Downs' after Frederick Earp, and a republished edition of his *Fashionable Hand-Book*. This Handbook had two seaside aquatint illustrations, catalogue numbers 128 and 131 in *Images of Brighton*. In addition, the watercolour of the proposed 'Cricket Match' engraving was sent on exhibition to Cambridge and then on to Bristol.

In all four of his premises Mason kept the title 'Repository of Arts', and remained close to Rudolph Ackermann's younger sons, continuing to publish prints with them until 1844, and they later briefly opened their own gallery in Brighton, Ackermann's Repository of Arts at 59 King's Road, during 1854. Taylor's directory for that year reads '59 King's Road: R. Ackermann, printseller, stationer and repository of arts', but in 1855 the premises belonged to Tapsell & Baker's lace, ribbon and glove warehouse.

In Brighton, Mason was not alone in using the Repository of Arts title. Before the Mason/Ackermann enterprise opened in 1832, the artist Joseph Cordwell, who had acted as agent for Ackermanns, was using the same title for his drawing academy and publishing business, first at 19 East Street, then at 4 St James's Street. There was a Repository of Arts in Preston Street in the 1830s run by the local artist Louis Parez, and later Mr Shelley's at 69 Western Road used this title, advertising drawing lessons by the local artist F Forde in the *Brighton Gazette* of 28 November 1850. Ford was a Brighton artist who Mason used for his large 1850 lithograph of the great storm which inundated Pool Valley [**50**].

Mason's stock listed in Parson's auction was typical Ackermann merchandise direct from the Strand Repository. He offered the work of some first-class artists, including G B Campion, who worked for Ackermann's in London, together with three members of the local Earp family. In his *Fashionable Hand-Book* he advertised that 'Mr George Earp gives lessons in oils and watercolours. Specimens at his Repository'. He also had two permanent company artists, William Drummond, already mentioned, and Charles Basebe—both of whom worked on Mason's print of 'The Cricket Match between Sussex and Kent'. Drummond

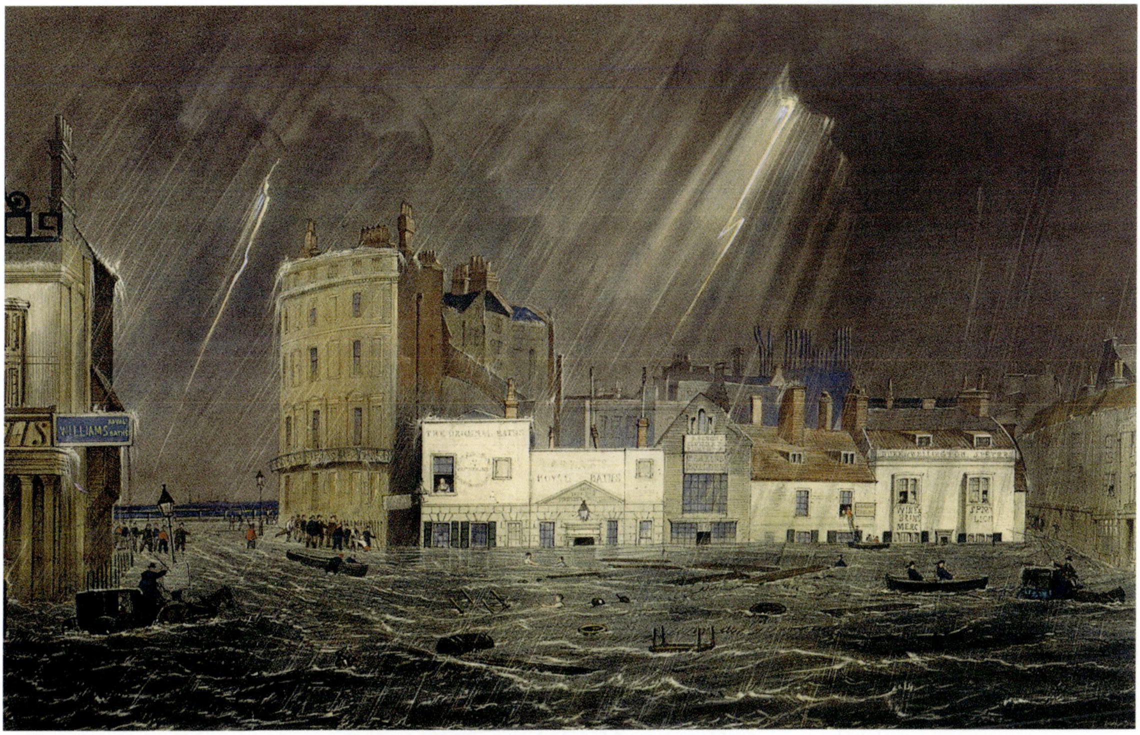

50
'Pool Valley, during the storm at Brighton. July 17th 1850'. Lithograph by Day & Son after F Ford, published by Mason 19 August 1850. The text beneath the publication line reads: 'On Wednesday evening July 17th 1850 between 6 and 7 o'clock a most terrific and destructive Thunder storm, accompanied with a complete deluge of rain burst over the Town raging above an hour and occasioning much injury and loss of property, inundating Pool Valley and other parts of the Town to a depth of several feet'

exhibited portraits in London during the 1830s. The fact of him living in Mason's household is mentioned in his 1846 *Hand-Book*; he had been there since the 1841 census. Drummond was originally from Huntingdon and was much the same age as Mason, born in 1811. There are 19 of his prints in the National Portrait Gallery, which describes him as a draughtsman, portraitist and lithographer.

C J Basebe exhibited 34 paintings at the Royal Academy in London between 1843 and 1879. He also taught and undertook portrait commissions at Mason's gallery and is the artist of a watercolour of a cricket match presently hanging in the Pavilion at Lord's[25]. In a *Brighton Guardian* advertisement Mason advised his clients that he had an agent in Lewes, Mr Baxter, and one in Worthing, Mrs Carter. The Lewes agent would have been John Baxter (1781–1858) bookseller, printer and father of George Baxter, the inventor of the famous oil-coloured 'Baxter Prints'. These contacts were undoubtedly courtesy of the Ackermann family. In common with Mason, the father John Baxter was a great lover of cricket and author and publisher of a book of rules for that sport under the title *Lambert's Cricketers' Guide*, named after the well-known professional cricketer William Lambert. Mason must have valued this association greatly, as *John Baxter's Cricketers' Guide*, published in 1828, ran to 12 editions and 'produced a sale of more than three hundred thousand copies'[26]. Mason himself published a concise list of the laws of the game in Lillywhite's *Hand-Book of Cricket*, one of his last publications with Ackermann & Co, in 1844.

These business practices of offering art lessons in his gallery and having agents in other towns were typical of the Ackermann business model employed in London for the previous 30 years. Rudolph Ackermann's other successful marketing method was to cater particularly for his women customers: his monthly *Repository of Arts Magazine* was aimed at this female market, and similarly Mason emphasised his stock of ladies' fancy articles, white wood boxes for transfer decorations, colours, pencils, attractive papers and instructive drawing books, as had his father in Cambridge.

Mason had four different addresses in Brighton during his career. According to his imprints, 1 Ship Street was between 1833 and 1839 (although we know from the *Brighton Guardian* advertisement that he opened in March 1832), then 81 King's Road from May 1839 until the summer of 1848. In the spring of 1848 Mason advertised in the Brighton Herald: 'Wanted in the course of a few months, a shop or house and shop—for an old established and respectable business'. He found what he needed next door, at 80 King's Road, his first publication from this new address being in June 1848, the six lithographs after Alfred Crowquill entitled 'A Peep at Brighton'.

The freeholder of 81 King's Road was Robert Ackerson and on his death in 1846 the property passed to Mr & Mrs Henry Verall, who had both died by October 1847. Ackerson's will then required that the property be sold and the proceeds shared between the Verall children. In the end Mason and Drummond's combined struggle to stay at number 81 was for the sake of just a few years. By the time Mason had repurchased the lease from his friend William Drummond late in September 1847, following the court case with Wisden three years earlier, the new freeholders, the Verall husband and wife, both died the next month and Mason had to find his third premises. Like many traders of the period Mason never seemed to be in a position to buy property, although at this time it is possible he was still the owner of his father's original shop in Cambridge[27].

It was from this new address at number 80 that he published his print of 'The Cricket Match between Sussex and Kent' in May 1849. His final publication with the '80 King's Road' imprint was in August 1850. His last trading premises were 108 King's Road (just a couple of hundred yards further west), from which gallery his first publication was in 1852. He and his family lived above the premises in Ship Street and at 81 and 80 King's Road, but this final address at 108 did not include residential accommodation, so in the 1851 census the family home was 22 Norfolk Road and it was from here that he declared himself bankrupt in 1855. This date of 1852 for the new premises at 108 is three years into the 'Cricket Match' publication, which was not going as well as hoped and which in the end caused Mason's bankruptcy in 1855, so it is possible the move was in response to an increasingly difficult financial situation.

After the bankruptcy he published a pair of seafront scenes in

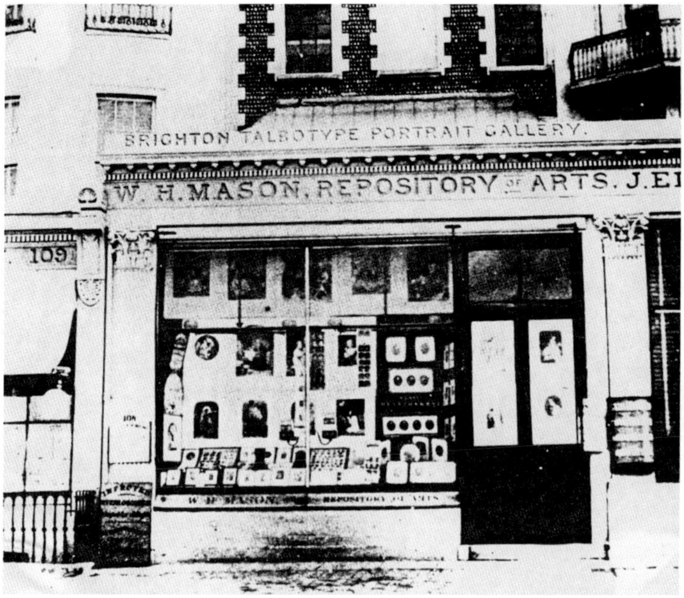

51
In Philippe Garner's *A Seaside Album* (p25) this photograph is credited to either William Mason Sr or Jr. In the Post Office Directory of Sussex for 1851 there is the entry for King's Road '106A Mason, Henry, printseller and repository of arts', but this seems to be transitional until it is fixed at 108, just west of Cannon Place. These premises were finally demolished to make way for the enlargement of the Hotel Metropole

October 1860 and a print of Emmanuel Church, c1870, both coming from Mason's Repository, but these appear to be the only actual Brighton views published after 1855. Moving from Norfolk Road, by 1861 the family was living at 3 Lansdowne Terrace and then in 1871 they were at 4 Westfield Gardens, just off King's Road. The gallery was still at 108 King's Road, with the photographers Hennah & Kent in the upstairs rooms from 1852, but by 1883 the whole premises had been taken over by Hawkins, the world-renowned photographers of Preston Street, Brighton. This fate of succumbing to the advancing photographic industry also happened to his younger brother. John B Mason had taken over their father's print publishing business in Cambridge in 1842 but by 1864 the shop was occupied by Nicholls' photographic studio. Regarding W H Mason's bankruptcy, there was another hearing in 1873, when he is described as 'being of 45 (late 108) King's Road and 21 George Street, Croydon'.

He seems to have moved out of 108 King's Road [**51**] early in 1873, and into number 45, which in 1873 was listed as a wine merchant but a year later was a Fine Arts Repository and artists' colourman, run by Henry H Stewart. In previous years maybe Stewart had worked for Mason, and was offering his old employer some shared retail space.

The process of moving premises for a print publisher involved considerable upheaval and time spent in moving stock, workroom contents, paper, heavy printing presses and lithographic stones, and of course Mason was always moving home at the same time. The first print from 108 King's Road appeared in July 1852, 'The New Race Stand, Brighton, preparing to start for the Brighton Stakes, August 6th 1851', after the sporting artist Samuel Alken.

Jill Seddon in *The Georgian Group Journal* (2003) mentioned that print-shops facilitated the meeting of professional and amateur artists and wrote: 'The most distinguished of the many in Brighton was owned by W H Mason, who had worked for the famous Rudolph Ackermann in London; he bought Ackermann's Brighton branch in 1832, and advertised himself as "Carver, Guilder, Print Seller and Publisher".' Apart from artists' materials, he provided an important service to the amateur artist, the loan of prints to copy. As previously mentioned, Mason did not take over a branch of Ackermann's in Brighton (see page 79), rather he opened his own gallery with their support.

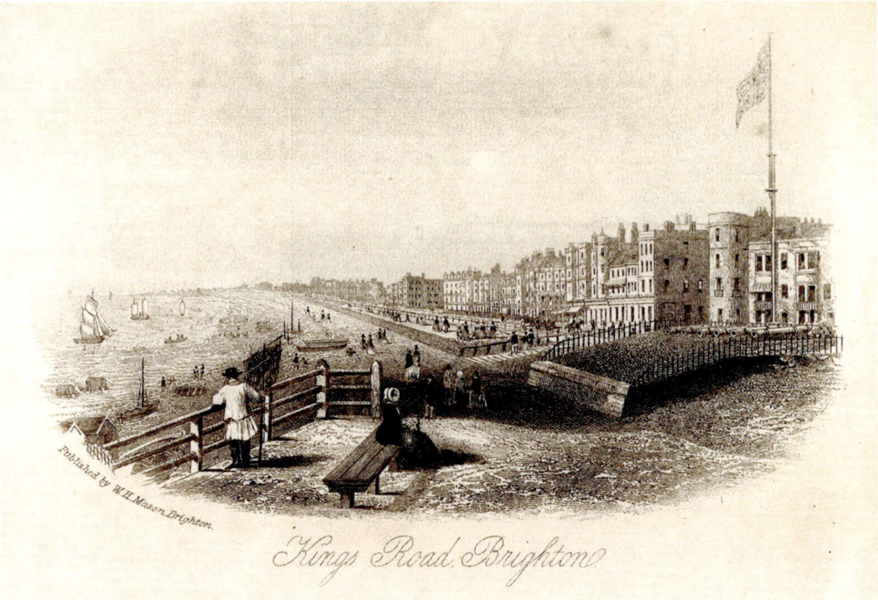

52
'King's Road, Brighton'. One of the very few steel engravings published by Mason c1845, no artist or engraver named

Royal warrants

Within a year of his move to Brighton, Mason's first publication from his new gallery in Ship Street was the aquatint engraving of the 'Panorama of Brighton'. This bore the Royal Coat of Arms on its boxwood drum and on the card wrappers for the folded edition. In Mason's newspaper advertisement in the *Brighton Guardian* on 11 December 1833, Mason announced this print as 'Under the Immediate Patronage of Her Most Gracious Majesty, Queen Adelaide'.

Following on from this 'Panorama' being 'Under the Patronage of', in the mid-1830s he published 'The Norfolk Suspension Bridge, Shoreham'. The bridge was opened in 1833 and while the print is not dated the paper of a known example has a watermark of 1836. The publication line reads: 'W.H. Mason, Printseller to Her Majesty at his Repository of Arts, Ship Street'. The bridge was a favourite destination for William IV's drives during his long periods of residence at the Pavilion.

Four examples of Mason's prints claiming that he was specifically 'by Royal Appointment' have been found to date. His 1838 publication of 'Illustrations of Brighton', featuring three prints, carried the claim of 'Printseller by Appointment to Her Majesty', and the same claim appeared on the publication line of his study of Robert Henderson of 1843. A rarely seen c1836 sheet of five aquatints entitled 'Mason's Views of Brighton' also carried the claim 'by Appointment to Her Most Gracious Majesty'. Lastly, his print of 'The Rev. James Anderson' engraved by H Dawe after C J Basebe was published on 30 March 1840 and claimed 'Printseller & Publisher, by Appointment to the Queen, Repository of Arts, 81 King's Road, Brighton'.

Unfortunately claims to some sort of Royal Appointment were common in the first half of the 19th century, often with little foundation, and the problem with establishing their accuracy is a lack of formal records. The Royal Archives at Windsor Castle has limited information relating to Royal Warrants for the reigns of William IV and Queen Adelaide, or for the first few years of Queen Victoria's reign. As far as is known, apart from being poorly recorded, the actual arrangements around the granting of anything like Royal Warrants to individual shop-keepers was haphazard. Specific arrangements, with severe sanctions for false claims, did not take shape until a little later in the Victorian era, and the 'Royal Warrant Holders Association' did not become active in pursuing false claims until the early 1900s. As with many traders, Mason's claims are difficult to prove or disprove.

Mason seldom repeated these specific 'by Appointment' claims, and 19 further prints (some in guides) were issued from 1839 up to 1848 with only the above two portraits, the 'Rev. James Anderson' 1840 and 'Robert Henderson' of 1843, claiming 'Printseller by Appointment'.

Apart from these two, three other prints were published with slightly less bold declarations. First was 'The Exterior and Interior of the Royal Chapel, St James's' [**53**]. This was a single plate, showing a view of the outer doors of the Chapel, with guards in attendance, and the doors were represented by flaps on the print, which fold back to reveal The Queen and Prince Albert kneeling at the altar-rail, with the Archbishop of Canterbury presiding over their marriage.

53
'The Exterior and Interior of the Royal Chapel', St. James's Palace, 1840

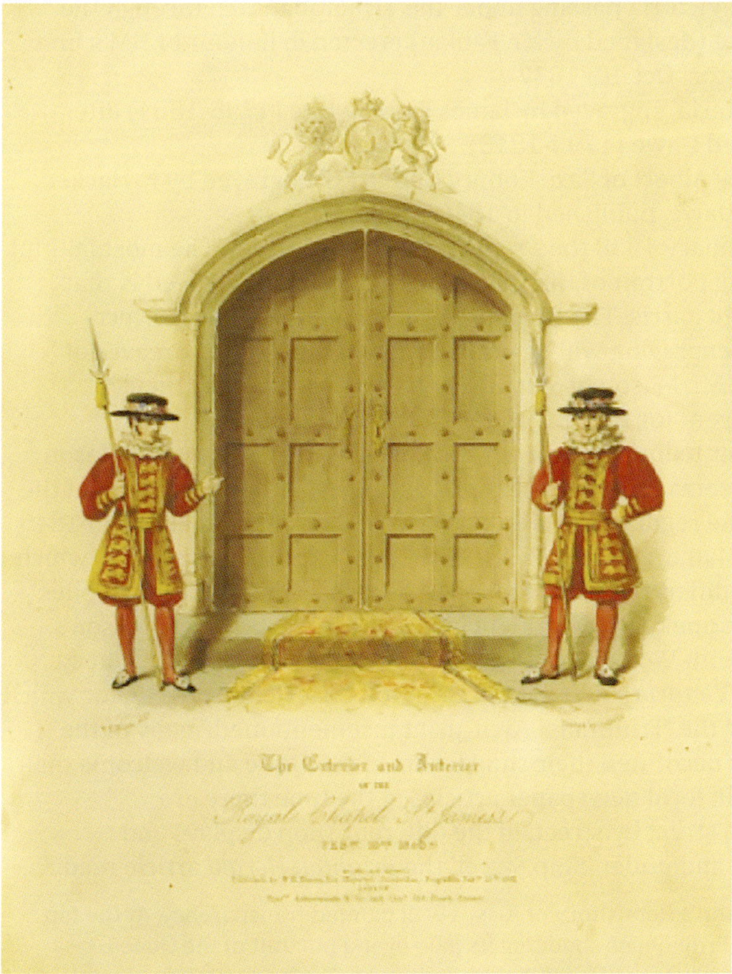

The imprint is 'Published by W.H. Mason, Her Majesty's Printseller, Feb 10th 1840, Messrs Ackermann & Co. London, and Charles Tilt, Fleet Street'. In the title line of this print, Mason finishes the date thus—'Feb 10th 1840!!'—with two exclamation marks, something of a celebratory flourish in honour of the occasion, and emphasising the fact that the print is 'on the day!'

The second example was an 1844 print 'Captain Warner's Experiment' that had the line 'Printseller and publisher to the Queen'. Then two years later he published 'The Pavilion, Brighton', a lithograph by Bachelier after George Earp Jr, which read 'W.H. Mason, Her Majesty's Printseller and Publisher, 81 King's Road, May 1846'. With the lack of formal records it is impossible to ascertain whether this terminology, rather than using the specific phrase 'by Appointment', was sanctioned or dictated by the Royal Household, or just at the whim of the individual trader.

Mason then claims royal association on his 1849 publication of the 'Sussex v Kent Cricket Match', where the separate descriptive key-plate noted that the print was 'Dedicated by Express Permission to His Royal Highness Prince Albert, etc etc', and this dedication appeared on the engraving itself. But his final claim, just before he left 108 King's Road, was found on the two 1872 letter-headings[28] where he clearly claimed 'By Appointment to Her Majesty'.

Apart from these specific claims, Mason published various prints with connections to Queen Victoria:

- 'HM Queen Victoria passing under the Triumphal Arch through the Amphitheatre (designed by Mr. Fabian) erected in honour of HM's first visit to Brighton, Oct 4th 1837'
- 'Queen Victoria' engraved by James Posselwhite (1798-1884) after Henry Edward Dawe (1790-1848)
- 'HRH Prince Albert of Saxe Coburg Gotha, KG' engraved by E. Hacker after Henry Dawe, published in 1840

On 23 January 1838 the *Brighton Patriot* reported: 'The most faithful and charming portrait of Her Majesty the Queen yet executed is that painted by Mr. Parris. The Duke of Sussex pronounced it a perfect likeness. An engraving will be published by Hodgson and Greaves of London, and Mr. Mason of Ship Street has been appointed their publishing agent for this town.'

It is rather telling that the practice of claiming Warrants by Mason and others seems to have gone into a decline from the late 1840s, at the time when the regulation of Royal Warrants was strengthening. In 1849 his 'Cricket Match' was merely 'Dedicated by Express Permission', which seems quite different from claiming to be an appointed Royal supplier.

However, one other fact might give some indication as to Mason's connection with Victoria, and enable his claims to be taken seriously. With Queen Victoria's first visit to Brighton on 4 October 1837, for which he published the 'Triumphal Arch' print just mentioned, many of the local traders decorated their shop fronts to celebrate and welcome their new queen. In local newspaper articles of the time there are descriptions, street by street, of the different shop displays and decorations, and under 'Ship Street' the *Brighton Herald* article read:

> 'At Mr. Mason's Repository of Arts, a well painted transparency. At the top the eye of Providence shedding its halo over a portrait of the Queen, beneath a part of the Chain Pier, shipping etc. The bottom of the picture

represents Church and State, with the flags of the Army and Navy on each side, and the rose, thistle and shamrock entwined—the whole encircled in a wreath of laurels: the corners filled up with an appropriate verse from the National Anthem. The transparency was much admired'.

This was a typical Rudolph Ackermann practice, who illuminated his shop front at 101 Strand with back-lit transparencies to celebrate important national events. Nine other traders' displays in Ship Street were briefly mentioned in this article, but Mason's Repository display took up most of the text. The various displays remained in place for some time and in the *Brighton Patriot* eight months later, on 26 June 1838, under the heading 'Queen Victoria's visit to Brighton' was the comment that Mr Mason's shop front transparency is 'not exceeded, indeed not equalled, by anything in this town'. Mason seemed to have a loyal and patriotic admiration for Queen Victoria.

Local and national press advertisements and press

Following any plans that Rudolph Ackermann cancelled due to failing health, Mason opened his new gallery at 1 Ship Street in March 1832, having spent several months in Preston Street. The following advertisement first appeared in the *Brighton Guardian* on 28 March, in the *Brighton Gazette* on 29 March and 12 April, then in the *Brighton Herald* on 31 March and 7 and 14 April 1832:

> 'W. MASON From R. Ackermann's London, Carver, Gilder, Printseller and Publisher. Most respectfully informs the Nobility, Gentry and Inhabitants of Brighton and its vicinity, that he has opened a shop in the above line, at No. 1, SHIP STREET, KING'S ROAD, Brighton, where all who may favour him with their commands may depend on their being executed with attention. William Mason has on sale a very extensive assortment of ancient, and the most modern prints, drawings and paintings of merit: likewise colours, pencils, drawing papers, and every article requisite for drawing and painting. A choice assortment of Ladies' fancy articles, circulating folios kept for hire by the evening, or to copy: consisting of drawings, prints, etc, of various subjects. Transfer varnish, with very explicit directions for use; various white wood articles, and prints suitable for ditto. Specimens may be seen. Prints, drawings, etc, framed, chimney frames, etc, made and re-gilt on the shortest notice, by workmen on the premises. Schools supplied on liberal terms'.

The wording of his advertisement is reminiscent of his father's entry in the local Cambridge press in 1821.

On pages 25 and 26 of his 1841 *Hand-Book for Visitors to Brighton* there were more details of his business and stock-in-trade at the 81 King's Road premises, with family living accommodation above:

> 'The leading features of this establishment are the constant supply of every work of art upon the day of publication. Periodicals, H.B. sketches (caricatures by John Doyle) etc., drawings and paintings by eminent masters, lent to copy; portfolios of amusing prints lent for the evening; a

large assortment of albums, scrap books, elegant bound books, stationery, card plate engraving; and every article in general request connected with the arts. Mr. William Drummond, portrait and miniature painter resides here. Mr. Earp, teacher of painting in oil and water colours, pencil drawing, perspective etc., also exhibits his specimens. The art of lithography taught on the premises. Picture frame manufactory. Publisher of Brighton views and other local subjects in great variety. Drawings lent to copy. W.H. Mason's circulating portfolios of water colour and pencil drawings, (also oil pictures,) are extensively supplied with drawings by the principal artists of the day, amongst many others are those by Copley Fielding, Prout, De Wint, Cattermole, Nash, Earp, Scott, G.B. Campion, Poole, Taylor, Leatham, Nibbs, Cox, Varley, Hunt, George Smith etc. etc.'

As explained, for Mason to concentrate part of his business on satisfying the artistic ambitions of wives and daughters from monied families was a strategy copied directly from Rudolph Ackermann. Ackermann had published his first drawing book *Lessons for Beginners in Fine Art* in 1796, to cash in on what was by then a polite recreation[29]. With regard to the note about lithography being taught, Mason himself had obviously learnt this skill in London, but the artist William Drummond was also a lithographer.

From Mason's advertised list of artists, six of them had close publishing connections with Ackermann's Strand Repository. On the final page of his *Hand-Book* he continued describing his stock-in-trade: 'Albums, Scrap Books, Blotting Cases and Hand Screens – Colour Boxes in great variety'. Mason's 'Terms of Subscription' for his circulating portfolios were advertised as follows: 'Annually £3.13s.6d.; Half Yearly £2.2s.0d.; Quarterly £1.1s.0d.; Monthly 8s.0d.; Weekly 2s.6d.; Or by the single drawing according to its value. Subscribers may change their drawings or prints as often as they wish. Subscribers residing away from Brighton, are supplied with as many changes at a time as is desirable, to avoid the expense of frequent carriage, and a constant supply ready for changing. Terms of subscription for non-residents, to be paid in advance: Yearly £3.15s.6d.; Half-yearly £3.3s.0d.; Quarterly £1.11s.6d.; Monthly 10s.6d. The expense of carriage to be divided. Portfolios of prints, suitable for the drawing room, lent for the evening's amusement, consisting of all modern publications, H.B. and other humorous sketches'.

In a little over a year from opening his new gallery, and in partnership with his father and Ackermann's, Mason published what has become one of the iconic printed scenes of Brighton (see page 83); an advertisement in the *Brighton Guardian* on 11 December 1833 read:

'Mason's Panorama of Brighton under the immediate patronage of Her Most Gracious Majesty Queen Adelaide published.
On Monday last, December 2nd by Mr. Mason (from Ackermann's) at his Repository of Arts, No. 1 Ship Street, a Panoramic engraving of the entire West Cliff – The Work is handsomely made up in a portable case for a

> guinea and a half and in neat Album folio at thirty shillings. The heavy expenses the publication has been at, in order to produce a correct and amusing picture of Brighton, emboldens him with confidence to appeal to the patrons of the art for encouragement. A copy is always ready to forward for inspection, either in town or country'.

The advertisement continued: 'Agents: for Lewes, Mr. Baxter, for Worthing, Mrs. Carter – the Trade supplied – W.M. has received a fresh supply of excellent drawings and prints for the Albums Etc., or for hire, to copy. Portfolios of prints lent for the evening's amusement – Every necessary material for Painting or Drawing may be had at this Repository. In a few weeks will be published a very superior Engraving by Dawe (from a sketch by Hardy) of the Rev. Mr. Sortain.' Joseph Sortain (1809-1860) was the non-conformist minister for the Countess of Huntingdon's Chapel in North Street. Of Mr Sortain's ministry Cyrus Jay[30] wrote 'very few persons of any note ever visit Brighton without hearing him'.

In the *Brighton Patriot* on 8 January 1839, the editor wrote:

> 'Mr. Mason's Portrait of the Queen.
> 'We have sometimes read and heard of . . . portraits that have stolen quietly and unostentatiously upon the world without parade, and yet in the end have given greater satisfaction and have obtained more real and lasting reputation than works about which there was originally immense puffing. This was possibly the case with Mr. Mason's portrait of the Queen. It was not painted, we understand, to order, but as an essay, by Mr. Dawe, the father-in-law of Mr. Mason. The likeness is . . . excellent. Mr. Mason's gratuitous exhibition has been crowded on Saturday and yesterday. We hope Mr. Mason will meet with the encouragement that his enterprise and taste merit'.

This was the engraving by J Posselwhite after Henry Dawe's drawing.

Two years before this study of Queen Victoria, Mason had brought out a mezzotint study of the Earl of Egremont, and while it was on exhibition in his gallery, still in its unfinished proof stage, it fell foul of the art critic on the *Brighton Patriot*. In its edition of 14 February 1837 the *Patriot* published an article on this new 'Portrait of the Earl', by 'Criticus', who started by saying he is 'not in the slightest degree hostile to Mr. Mason, to whom I wish the greatest success'. From the time of Van Dyke, however, he wrote, 'we have had very few good portraitists', then went on to dismiss the works of Kneller and Lely, and included George Clint (1770-1854), Mason's portraitist of the Earl, in that same dismissive vein. Mason took an advertisement in the *Brighton Guardian*, calling the *Patriot* criticism 'premature and uncalled for'. Mason had two proofs of the mezzotint in his shop, one by the door and another on the chimney-piece, and assured his public that 'in two or three weeks I hope to be able to submit a finished proof to the public'. 'Good,' wrote Criticus in his second article in the Patriot, 'but will a finished proof give us an altered outline? Will the labour of three weeks change the figure of the noble Earl, bend down his body to that feeble inclination suitable to his age, reduce the protuberance of his calves, attenuate his arms, enfeeble his form, and give to his countenance that appearance of decline and decay which belong to his advanced age? I fear not'.

Criticus was none too kind to Mason or the Earl, although maybe he deliberately ignored the point that the print was taken from the oil painting of the Earl hanging in the Town Hall, which did not show him in quite such a decrepit state. If the engraver had taken the unlikely course of following the advice given by Criticus, it would not have born much resemblance to the original oil by Clint, which was quite flattering to the Earl's age (The painting is in the Brighton & Hove Art Gallery collection.) However, from various press articles in the following months Mason's sales seemed unaffected.

In the *Brighton Patriot* (4 April 1837) Mason took the following advertisement:

> 'The Earl of Egremont
> 'Just published by W.H. Mason at his Repository of Arts, a fine whole length portrait of His Lordship, engraved by Lupton, from a painting in the Town Hall by Clint. W.H. Mason in soliciting subscriptions to this publication, respectfully assures the public that he has spared no expense necessary in order to produce as excellent an engraving as could be obtained. W.H. Mason avails himself of this opportunity to acknowledge his gratitude to the inhabitants of Brighton for entrusting him with the loan of their portrait of the Earl of Egremont, for the purpose to which it has been applied. To secure the best impressions an early application is necessary. The price to subscribers will be prints one guinea, proofs two guineas. A great variety of neat and appropriate frames. Repository of Arts, Ship Street, Brighton.'

Then on 18 April 1837 the *Patriot* wrote that 'Mason's engraving from Mr. Clint's portrait of the Earl of Egremont has found that patronage which the merit of the work deserves. It has already had an extensive sale, and the demand for it is on the increase. Few mansions in Sussex will be without this specimen of the fine arts.'

The following week the virtues of the print were expressed differently, but no less enthusiastically, in the Sussex Advertiser of 10th April 1837: 'Mr. Mason of Ship Street has just published a print, engraved from the portrait of the Rt. Hon the Earl of Egremont, painted by Clint and lately presented to the Town Hall. The engraving is highly finished and reflects great credit on the talents of the engraver, Mr. Lupton. The likeness of the venerable and Noble Earl is admirably kept, and this print altogether will, we doubt not, meet with public approbation'.

Prior to this public discussion on the merits of the engraving, on 2 August 1836, when the original oil painting was presented to the town, the *Brighton Patriot* announced that a 'Public Dinner will be on Thursday 4th August at the Town Hall in honour of the Rt. Hon The Earl of Egremont to celebrate the placing of His Lordship's portrait in the Town

Hall'. Among the guests included were James Cordy, Henry Faithfull and W H Mason.

The *Brighton Patriot* of 2 October 1838 contained the following:

> 'On Saturday next, October 6th will be published W.H. Mason's Illustrations of Brighton, consisting of three very highly finished engravings, coloured in imitation of the original drawings by G.B. Campion taken expressly for this work. Size of plates 21 by 14 inches. Price to subscribers 15s the set, in an appropriate wrapper, adapted either for the scrap book, framing or the drawing-room table. W.H. Mason earnestly solicits the support of the inhabitants to this undertaking, respectfully assuring them every exertion has been used regardless of great expense, to produce a work superior to anything of a local nature before attempted. Repository of Arts, Ship Street, Brighton.'

The three engravings in the *Illustrations of Brighton* were 'The Chain Pier, Brighton', 'St Peter's Church, Brighton' and 'Kemp Town, Brighton' [**54**[31]]. All were engraved by the London-based aquatint engraver Charles Hunt, and carried the imprint 'W.H. Mason, Printseller by Appointment to Her Majesty'. With his usual sense of self-promotion coming to the fore, Mason was trying to put himself a cut above all the local publishers. He used an established Ackermann artist, and could hardly have chosen a better aquatint engraver than Charles Hunt, hence his claim to have produced a work 'superior to anything of a local nature'. With his Ackermann pedigree, Mason viewed himself on a par with the London publishers, which he probably thought necessary as so many of his customers were not just from London but specifically from the Ackermann son's Strand Repository. This insistence on quality would have been instilled in him during his time with Ackermann's, quality being a watchword of Rudolph Ackermann's business.

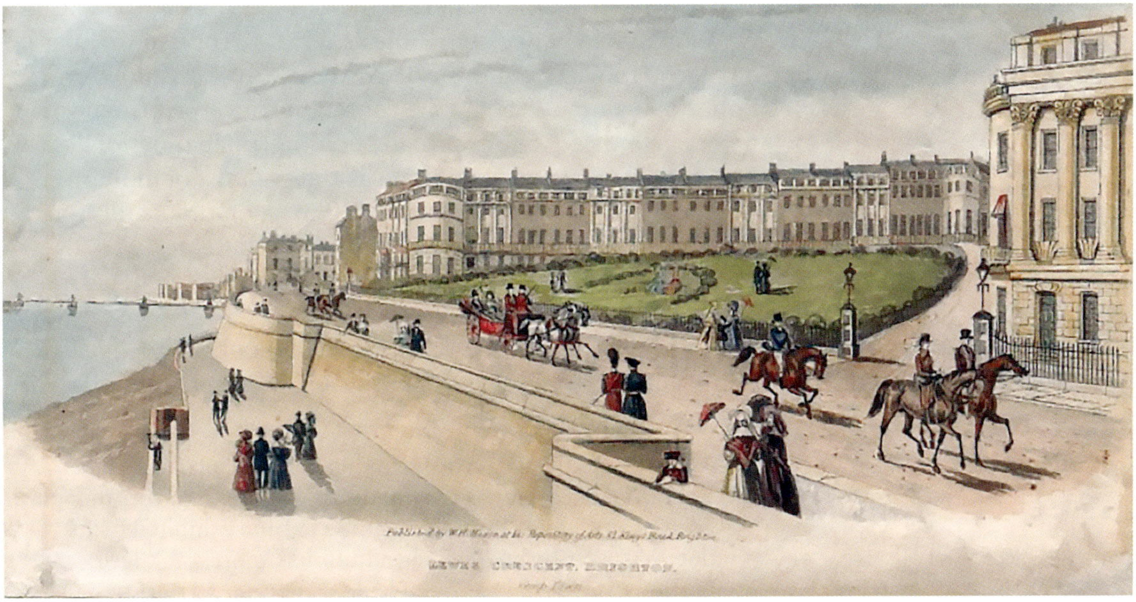

54
'Lewes Crescent, Brighton – Kemp Town'. Hand-coloured aquatint published by W H Mason at his Repository of Arts, 81 King's Road, from his *Fashionable Hand-Book for Visitors to Brighton* 1841-1842

The *Brighton Herald* of 13 July 1839 reported: 'MR. DERBY'S PANORAMA OF BRIGHTON, executed for the benefit of the Sussex County Hospital is now to be seen at W.H. Mason's 81, King's Road, where copies to original subscribers may be had next week'.

The following appeared as a Cricket & Cricketers' advertisement in the *The Times* on 4 January 1849:

> 'W.H. Mason announces to those connected with cricket and others that the Descriptive Book and Key which will accompany his National Print of a "Cricket Match" (which has been four years engraving, and is now preparing for immediate publication) will remain OPEN for ADVERTISEMENTS to be inserted til Jan 10th 1849 upon the usual terms. As there must be upwards of 20,000 of the book circulated it will be found an excellent medium for advertisements, particularly those relating to cricket. Applications to be forwarded to W. H. Mason, Repository of Arts, Brighton'.

This rare Descriptive Book and Key starts: 'Dedicated by Express Permission to His Royal Highness Prince Albert, etc etc Descriptive Key of W. H. Mason's National Print of "A CRICKET MATCH".' It goes on to mention the portraits, the engravers and subscribers. A circulation of 20,000 copies of an early Victorian booklet by a provincial publisher is an impressive claim. (For more on this print, see the following chapter.)

The Times, 5 and 7 September 1853: 'The late Rev. F.W. Robertson MA., Incumbent of Trinity Chapel. W.H. Mason begs to announce to friends of the late Rev. F.W. Robertson that he is preparing for immediate publication an authentic likeness (the only one extant) painted in June last by Mr. Chas. J. Basebe, etc etc'. **[55]**

55
'The Late F.W. Robertson MA'. Lithograph after C J Basebe, published September 1853

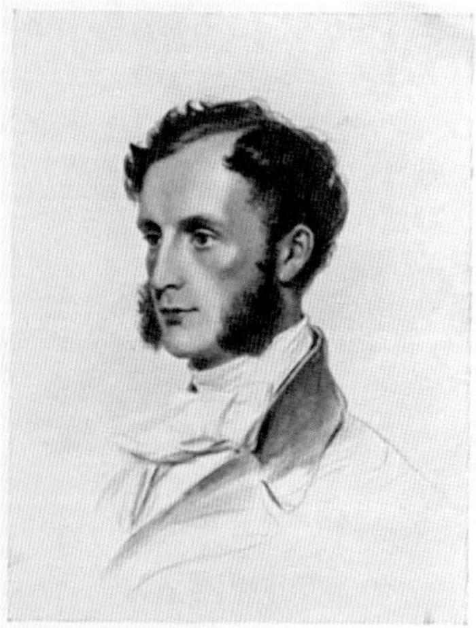

Robertson was involved in this period's soul-searching battle within the Church of England, to believe the Bible as it stands, or a more liberal view encompassing the new scientific discoveries. Owen Chadwick[32] describes Robertson as 'battered by the contending forces, introspective and . . . agonising' but eventually holding 'the banner of liberal Christianity'. Regarded by some as the greatest of modern preachers, he died on 15 August 1853, when thousands lined the route from his home to the Extra-Mural Cemetery and, being part of Robertson's congregation at Trinity Chapel, no doubt Mason was among them.

The *Brighton Gazette* of 31 May 1855 published an editorial describing a 'Stereoscopic Cosmorama' exhibition of pictures of the war in the Crimea:

> 'Mr. W.H. Mason, the enterprising publisher of prints, has, since the war commenced, attracted hundreds of anxious gazers to view the prints, which he has from time to time exhibited in his window. ... By way of affording additional interest to these illustrations Mr. Mason has opened a Cosmorama of the Russian

> War, by which the scenes enacted in the Crimea and elsewhere are more vividly portrayed, and many of them have really a life-like interest ... The exhibition is open daily at a reasonable charge; and we trust that Mr. Mason will reap a benefit from his exertions. Hitherto attendance has been numerous'.

This exhibition may well have been in memory of his younger brother, Goodburn, who had died of fever there earlier in the year. Mason obviously had for sale a variety of prints and drawings from the Crimea, a selection of which he set up to be viewed in this 'stereoscopic cosmorama', a binocular viewing system that he rather disingenuously claimed as his own invention. The writer in the *Brighton Gazette* obviously thought that the wonder of the exhibition was to the detriment of the print-selling business: 'We question, with all his desire to furnish the public with a graphic illustration of the various scenes at the seat of war, whether he has not in the end been a loser. Passers-by view and admire, but their admiration rarely extends beyond their own personal gratification at the sight of the pictures, and the interest of the print seller is too frequently overlooked'.

The Times of 24 October 1856 reported:

> 'To Exhibitors and others. For disposal or hire, an entirely novel Exhibition, being a stereoscopic cosmorama, with all highly interesting subjects by first class artists, now exhibiting at the Royal Pavilion, Brighton, and has never been exhibited elsewhere. It is portable, light, well worthy attention as the inventor and proprietor is unable to devote the necessary time to it from other business engagements. Apply personally, or by letter, to W. H. Mason, Repository of Arts, Brighton'.

The Pavilion archives have no record of this exhibition but Mason's use of the words 'stereoscopic cosmorama' is sufficient explanation. There had been an exhibition in the 'Cosmorama Rooms' at 209 Regent Street, London. According to the *Gentleman's Magazine*[33], it was composed of 14 pictures of interesting views and objects from around the world. The article described it thus: 'The nature of the place is neither panoramic or dioramic, but a little upon the plan of both'. This exhibition (which was not a stereoscopic show) was originally planned for Somerset House but because of insufficient room it was moved to the venue in Regent Street. By 1835 it was discussed in *The Spectator* (Vol 8) and had progressed into an exhibition of people and faces from around the world by the artist E V Riffingille. Orrin Wang[34] gives an illustration of the 'Cosmorama Room' and describes it as a venue where 'pictures are viewed through optical lenses'. He gives an explanation in two diagrams showing each picture being viewed through a single lens, which, with careful illumination, gives the image greater realism.

Mason, by making the Pavilion exhibition, and his show of The Crimea the year before, both stereoscopic cosmoramas, attempted to create a new level of experience, presumably with his eldest son's photographs. Stereoscopy was a technique for creating the illusion of depth in photographs by means of viewing two almost identical photographic prints through binocular vision. The object was first photographed from two positions corresponding to the positions of the viewer's left and right eyes. The effect, when viewing these two photographs through binocular lenses, was to make the image three dimensional, an exciting experience in Victorian times. The principle had been discovered by Charles Wheatstone in 1833 and became a practical everyday proposition when Sir David Brewster invented his Stereoscope in 1849, which became a considerable industry that flourished for the rest of the century.

Philippe Garner[35] quotes the *Art Journal* of 1857 describing Hennah & Kent's apprentice, W H Mason Jr, as producing 'a series of stereoscopic views of very conspicuous merit . . . issued by Mr. Mason, the well-known and much respected print seller—they are the production of his son, a young and promising artist . . .' The article goes on to describe the young Mason as 'producing photographs of various subjects cleverly grouped and arranged and that they "tell" with good effect in the stereoscope'. Garner illustrates a number of stereoscopic pairs of albumen prints, and The Keep at Falmer has several examples[36]. This archive contains 11 stereoscopic photographs. Five are attributed to W H Mason, one to Fox, one to T Rowley, optician, 12 St James's Street, Brighton, one a joint venture between Mason and Rowley, and three to F S Mann, 13 Wellington Place, Hastings. The subjects include the 'Chain Pier', 'Brighton West Pier', interior views of 'The Aquarium', the 'Grand Hotel', 'Old Steyne Gardens', the beach, 'Old Roar Hastings' and 'St Andrew's Spa, Hastings'.

That these are photographs points to them being by Mason's son, William Henry Jr. The photographs of the 'West Pier', 'Grand Hotel' and 'Aquarium' could not have been included in W H Mason's 1856 advertisement in *The Times* but possibly three or four of the others were remnants of, or similar to, this Pavilion exhibition that the father had arranged for his photographer son. The note of Mason's time constraints due to 'other business engagements' might refer to him having to deal with his bankruptcy proceedings the previous year.

In the original cosmorama exhibition in London the article refers to there not being enough room at Somerset House, which implies a fairly bulky exhibit. This would be the case if visitors were viewing original framed oil or watercolour paintings, with some distance required between the picture and the viewing lens. With this exhibit not being described as 'stereoscopic', it does imply the use of original paintings rather than the smaller double photographs. Mason, in *The Times* advertisement, describes his exhibition as 'light and portable', obviously through the use of his son's smaller stereoscopic photographs.

For Mason to claim his exhibition at the Royal Pavilion was a 'cosmorama' it needed views of various people and locations around the world, and these photographs probably came from a foreign trip that

Mason Jr made. The Victoria & Albert Museum has a stereoscopic photograph by him of the statue of Augustus in the Villa Albani, Rome. To augment these, if necessary Mason Jr could have taken double photographs of some of the paintings or prints of foreign views that his father had on exhibition and for hire at the Repository.

However he did it, this was undoubtedly an exhibition of international people and views, in stereoscopically produced photographs, viewed through binocular lenses to give the three-dimensional effect. For the visual experience of visitors, this was one step up from the London Cosmorama exhibitions. Of this show at the Pavilion, Mason claimed he was the 'inventor and proprietor'. Mason's interest in this kind of enterprise may have stemmed from his experience of Ackermann's stock in London, where the public were offered such objects as 'celestial and terrestrial globes' and 'three-dimensional maps'. Brighton museum has one other pair of stereoscopic photographs by William Mason Jr, a view of 'The Brighton Fancy Basket Shop'[37]. The Museum's website comment is that this scene was one of a series of views of Brighton's working classes that Mason Jr produced in the late 1850s. The Victoria & Albert Museum has a Mason Jr *carte-de-visite* of Lord Byron's wife, Lady Noel, which it dates to c1860, and two other photographs—'William Henry Hunt displaying one of his paintings', and a cartoon which has no descriptive text.

The following appeared in *The Times* on 3 October 1860: 'Portrait of Henry Harrap, Esq of Brighton. Just published a first class authentic portrait of Henry Harrap of Brighton. Proofs 10s 6d, prints 7s 6d. W.H. Mason, Brighton'. Henry Harrap, born in Cornwall in 1794, was an extraordinary Brighton character on the fringes of medical science. His early trade was as a boot and shoe maker with his brother Richard in Ivory Place, just off Grand Parade. But he developed a massage procedure, which he referred to as 'rubbing', to which Sake Dean Mahomed acknowledged great indebtedness for many cures effected at his Indian Vapour Baths, opposite the Star & Garter Hotel, King's Road. John Ackerson Erredge personally credits Harrap with saving a leg that he was in danger of losing by amputation, but for Henry Harrap's 'rubbing' intervention[38].

The photographic business and bankruptcy

Charles Basebe undertook portrait commissions at Mason's gallery and possibly this established service made renting the upstairs of the Repository as a photographic portrait business such a logical step, in addition to the immediate financial considerations. (Mason and his eldest son embraced the new art form of photography with enthusiasm, as did some of Basebe's children.) In 1852 Mason made an agreement for Thomas Henry Hennah's photographic business to have the first floor of the premises at 108 King's Road[39]. Hennah, from London, and William Henry Kent from the Isle of Wight[40] purchased a licence from William

Fox Talbot to produce calotype photographs. The two businesses complimented each other and from Hennah & Kent's point of view they gained access to Mason's valuable client-list of visitors. William Lane (1818-1889), the early Brighton photographer, had been working as an assistant in the Repository at the time of the 1841 census and by the mid-1840s had set up his own photographic and print publishing business in Castle Square and later at 213 Western Road, which was the corner premises where Western Road meets Dyke Road (then part of North Street)[41]. Lane had previously been living with the Mason family, together with the portraitist William Drummond.

The *Brighton Gazette* of 12 October 1854 ran an article about Mason's new-look premises:

> 'Those who have visited the gallery of Messrs Hennah and Kent at Mr. Mason's Repository, 108 King's Road, need not be told that here portraits are taken in the very highest style of photographic art. Some who have not yet had the pleasure may be inclined to give themselves the gratification, by the enumeration of a few of the distinguished persons who have recently honoured these eminently skilful artists with a sitting. Among these are the Duke of Devonshire, Countess Grenville, Lord Carnworth, Lady Keats, Hon A. Kerr, Sir Joseph Paxton, Messrs. Bodkin, Ballantyne and Parry (Old Bailey Bar), Dr. Pickford, the Revs. H.M. Wagner and A. Wagner, W. Greasley, C.D. Maitland, S.R. Drummond and also several of the County Magistrates resident in the town and neighbourhood. The pictures are truly inimitable'.

Although having the photographers upstairs did not solve his financial problems in the end, this must have been a good move on Mason's part, bringing such important names into his gallery, with the possibility of more framing work if nothing else. Garner's *A Seaside Album* notes that Hennah & Kent quickly established themselves as the 'pre-eminent artistic studio in the town'. The Photohistory website actually credits Mason with playing an important role in the early history of photography in Brighton by allowing Hennah & Kent to establish themselves in his premises; they enlisted the services of William Mason Jr (1839–1888) as principal assistant to one of the partners, Mr Hennah.

While sharing the Repository premises with Mason, Hennah & Kent issued the following advertisement in *The Times* on 23 November 1859:

> 'England's Twelve Champion Cricketers – on the 13th inst will be published to subscribers only, the photograph of "England's Twelve Champion Cricketers"—on board ship the morning of their departure for America, by J.H. Hennah (Hennah & Kent, Brighton). The subscribers' proofs will be the choicest impressions upon India paper, and as it is impossible to produce more than a limited number, early application is necessary, they will be delivered in the order they are subscribed for. Prices to subscribers—one Guinea. W.H. Mason, Repository of Arts, Brighton. A proof copy is now on view at John Wisden's cricketing establishment, 3 New Coventry Street, Leicester Square, London'.

This was the first overseas tour of an English team, and the story is told in a rare book by Frederick Lillywhite, *The English Cricketers Trip to Canada and the United States in 1859*. These must have been strange times for Mason, hoping for the success of a second picture of cricketing personalities, but in a different medium from his own ill-fated engraving of the 'Cricket Match between Sussex & Kent' a decade earlier.

Unfortunately the Hennah & Kent relationship with William Mason Jr soured with the opening of a rival studio. In 1872 W H Mason Jr and William Edgley Hennah (son of Thomas Henry) opened their own photographic studio[42] at 88 King's Road, in competition with Hennah & Kent.

On Friday 5th April 1873, the original business issued a notice in the *Brighton Herald*: 'Messrs. Hennah & Kent, artists and photographers, 108 King's Road, Brighton, Regret that they are compelled to CAUTION their Friends and the Public that they have NOT REMOVED THEIR STUDIO from the premises they have occupied for the last twenty years. It continues to be personally superintended by Mr. T.H. Hennah, who with Mr. W.H. Kent, are, and have been the only members of their Firm. They have no connection with the entirely new firm of Hennah & Mason of 88 King's Road, and they beg to caution their Friends against mistakes which may arise from similarity of name'.

This brought the sons' business to a quick end. The *London Gazette* (26 August 1873) reported: 'A special resolution for Liquidation by Arrangement of the affairs of William Edgley Hennah and William Henry Mason the younger, of 88 King's Road, Brighton—photographers and co-partners—dated this 22nd day of August 1873'.

This arrangement with Hennah & Kent upstairs in the Repository flourished until the closing of the sons' business during the spring/summer of 1873, at which date W H Mason greatly reduced his Brighton activities and moved to his son's new home at 21 George Street, Croydon, where he died in 1879. With the closing of the young Mason's short-lived photographic studio, the Mason family's association with Brighton came close to its end.

It is too much of a coincidence that Hennah & Kent effectively closed down Mason Jr's photographic studio in King's Road mid-1873, and at the same time Mason senior moved out of his premises at 108. So this dispute over rival photographic businesses, together with the continuing effort of paying rent for home and gallery, paying off his debts and curtailing his publishing, may have been the final event that moved W H Mason out of his own well-established premises and ended his relationship with Hennah & Kent. By August 1873, Mason shared a gallery for a short time with Henry Stewart, who that year took over a wine merchant's shop and changed it to his own 'Repository of Arts' at 45 King's Road. These premises obviously did not have suitable accommodation for Mason and his wife Mary, hence their move to their son's home in

Croydon. With the rise in photography's popularity, this was not a good time to open another 'Repository of Arts' and Stewart's business appears not to have lasted beyond 1876. Until he moved his home and business to Croydon in 1873, Mason Jr was active as a photographer in Brighton from the late 1850s and issued photos of Brighton landmarks in his *carte-de-visite* format. By the 1860s these small photographic local views or personal calling cards were very popular and the Brighton photographer John Mayall was reportedly selling half a million cards a year.

The referenced date, on the previous page, of 1872 for the joint studio venture between the Mason and Hennah sons may be a year early, according to two *pro forma* invoices in the Keep archives[43]. These are on W H Mason's headed notepaper from 108 King's Road, but they are from William Mason Jr to the Aquarium Company, dated November and December 1872, the year the Aquarium opened. They cover the supply of photographs, 24 Cabinet Views for 11s 0d in November, and seven dozen views for £1 12s 0d in December. If William Jr was still working from 108 King's Road in December 1872, it seems more likely that the two sons opened their new studio at 88 King's Road and closed down, all in the first eight months of 1873. Supplying photographs to the Aquarium might have been quite a prestigious commission. *The Graphic* (22 November 1873) described the new venue as 'a meeting place for ladies and gentlemen . . . where you can look in and read the papers . . . have some luncheon and listen to a little good music'.

After the sons' photographic business closed in Brighton, W H Mason Jr continued his career as a professional photographer from his new home in Croydon. William E Hennah seems to have emigrated.

Taking the story back 17 years, in his book *The Story of a Cricket Picture* A D Taylor hints that Mason's publication of 'The Cricket Match between Sussex and Kent' almost caused Mason's bankruptcy. Mason did indeed go bankrupt just six years after its publication and, as can be seen from the transcripts below, he attributed his problems to this print. Papers were filed by Mason himself in October 1855, where he was described as 'Printseller of 108 King's Road, Brighton'.

The *Brighton Herald* of Saturday 20 October 1855 carried a notice of Mason's bankruptcy, declared on Tuesday 16 October. Notices also appeared in the *Bristol Mercury* (22 October 1855) and the London *Morning Chronicle* (1 December 1855 and 18 February 1857). The other Brighton paper, the *Brighton Gazette*, carried an extensive article on Mason's bankruptcy proceedings at the court in Basinghall Street, London, in its issue of 1 November 1855:

> 'Court of Bankruptcy Re: Mason
> 'This was the first meeting for the proof of debts and choice of assignees in the matter of William Henry Goodburn Mason, of King's Road, Brighton, printseller. Mr. Dupleix of Lincoln's Inn Fields attended for the bankrupt, who came to this court of his own petition of 13th October last,

> and Mr. Linklater represented several creditors. The preliminary statement of Messrs. Paul & Turner shows the debts unsecured to amount to £1,036. Creditors secured £285, holding works of art etc., among them "Views in Brighton" and "The Cricket Match" of the value of £391. The remaining assets are stock £400, furniture (after deducting excepted articles) £40, book debts £100, and legacy expected to be received by the assignee £100 to £150. The bankruptcy is attributed to "inadequacy of the profit of The Cricket Match", an engraving produced by the bankrupt, with the portraits of the best players in England, to meet the expenses incurred in its production. The bankrupt's protection having been enlarged until the examination meeting, which is fixed to be held on 27th Nov next at 12 o'clock, the proceedings concluded'.

After the admission of several proofs of debts between £200 and £300 in amount, the creditors nominated Mr William Winsor of the firm Winsor & Newton of Rathbone Place, London (who would have supplied Mason's gallery with paints and brushes), a creditor for £90, to act as trade assignee, and 'that gentleman having accepted the trust, the Learned Commissioner confirmed him as appointed'.

Mason applied for an allowance. It was stated he had a wife and seven children living at home; the court allowed £2 per week, with liberty to apply to have it increased in the future. With a large family, this bankruptcy might explain why, by the 1871 census, none of his four daughters, ranging in age from 23 to 29, had married. The year 1855 turned out to be hard for Mason. Apart from the bankruptcy problems, his father had died in January (that might have been the legacy of £100-£150 he was expecting) and one of his brothers, Goodburn Mason, died in the Crimea in February.

The points of interest in this report are that Mason himself filed for bankruptcy, the charge was not brought by others, and he attributed his financial failure to the 'inadequacy of the profit of The Cricket Match'. Given the range of articles for sale, the print publishing and the loan activities from the gallery, it is indicative of the amount of money spent on this print that he attributed his difficulties to this one engraving. Its publication seems to have been extremely time-consuming for Mason over several years. The first advertisement in 1843 announced 50 portraits and that number again in 1844 in *Lillywhite's Hand-Book of Cricket*, then in 1845 100 portraits were promised and finally it was published in 1849 with a key-plate of 72, including topographical locations.

Mason's in-house artists had been very busy on this venture but with no income to show for their work for nearly six years. When it finally appeared in May 1849, within six months of what must have been an intensely busy period trying to gain a return on this investment, Mason was involved in the added complication of being charged with indecently assaulting a child, and on 2 November 1849 was briefly committed to the Lewes House of Correction (see page 114). With this awful accusation hanging over him, for which he was quickly acquitted, it is possible that Mason took his eye off the ball, so to speak, in marketing this ambitious engraving, with the publication being further compromised by the bad local publicity possibly keeping people away from the gallery.

At another Court of Bankruptcy meeting on 27 November 1855 his creditors presented evidence of their debts and, as a result, on 21 December a second-class certificate was awarded. This meant that the commission found his losses were not entirely his fault. From the reported text of the court case it does appear that there were amicable relations between Mason and his creditors. None of them had called in their accounts with him and the provision of £2 per week, with the option of an increase later, indicated that he was managing to earn enough income to pay his business rent, the few staff he had left, and begin to pay off his debts.

Prior to 1869 an 'insolvent debtor' could be sent to prison and remain there until creditors were paid. By contrast, if a 'bankrupt debtor', which category particularly applied to traders and shopkeepers, agreed a repayment plan, they would avoid the threat of imprisonment. Mason's application for bankruptcy was a sensible move and this category was thankfully confirmed by the court, finding that his situation was not wholly unavoidable[44]. By contrast the losses of the insolvent debtor were generally deemed to be a result of their own extravagance or misjudgement.

To give Mason some credit for his hopes for this enterprise, from an article in *The Era* (9 July 1848) he might be forgiven for expecting a good return from his print. *The Era* was advertising *The Cricketers' Manual* for that year, which included enthusiastic praise for the 'Manly and Noble Game' and was for 'all those who patronise this truly national pastime'. The *Manual* was published by William Brittain of Paternoster Row and sold by Ackermann and Mason and 'all booksellers and dealers in cricketing paraphernalia throughout the United Kingdom'.

Unfortunately, the public's love for this 'national pastime' did not extend to what was probably the most expensive Brighton publication of the 19th century and further financial problems followed. The *Brighton Gazette* (20 August 1858) reported that William Murrell took Mason to court claiming £9 17s 0d for eggs and milk supplied, while just £2 15s 0d had been paid into court. Murrell had supplied the Mason household for years and had let the account run on after Mason's 1855 bankruptcy. The court allowed Mason to plead his initial bankruptcy and the verdict for the plaintiff was just for the £2 15s 0d that Mason had already paid in.

The *Brighton Gazette* then recorded, on 23 July 1863, an action brought by Edwin Wright to recover £10 5s 2d owed in commission. Wright had formerly carried on business as a bookseller at Esplanade House, King's Road. He had described himself as 'a very great friend to Mr. Mason', when called as a character witness in Mason's trial several years earlier. He had asked Mason to employ him in some way and it was suggested that he collected some long-standing debts owed to the Repository, for a commission of 10 per cent, but he was not to approach more recent customers or the trade. The newspaper reported that unfortunately he had approached Mason's customers indiscriminately, occasionally with 'insulting letters. His Honour said it appeared that Mr Wright had recovered no more than £20, and had kept back £3 16s 8d which was more than he was entitled to for commission. He did not see what claim the plaintiff had'.

Interestingly, for an insight into the Repository staff, a Mr James Tassell was named as Mason's 'principal shopman' who had gone through the ledgers with Edwin Wright, and John Meldrum (see page 110) is named as 'assistant print-seller'. Wright's Library had been one of the establishments that issued tickets to view the 'Cricket Match' print at the Newburgh Rooms in February 1849.

On 31 May 1866 the *Brighton Gazette* reported that the bankruptcy ruling was still in place and at a dividend meeting Mason's debts were £1,030—not much changed from the original £1,036 figure of October 1855. His assets in-hand amounted to £204 9s 10d. After his initial bankruptcy, the same paper noted on 12 February 1857 that creditors were offered a first dividend of 1s 0d in the pound, with a second dividend of 3s 7d in the pound being paid in October 1866. During this time and into the early 1870s Mason was still listed as 'Print-seller & Repository', with Hennah & Kent, at 108 King's Road, but on the two 1872 *pro forma* invoices (see page 106) Mason's letter-heading described him as 'Printseller & Publisher—Photograph Artist', which gives the impression of 'Mason & Son' running the gallery by this time, with the son's photographic work being an important part of their income.

As noted, he had moved the business out of 108 King's Road by the summer of 1873 and into shared premises at number 45, which became the 'Fine Arts Repository' run by Henry Stewart, while Mason Jr moved to a new home in Croydon, taking his mother and father and his two eldest sisters with him. Bearing in mind the few prints published by him after the initial bankruptcy, it seems that Mason and his creditors felt the most likely policy to ensure maximum dividends was to curtail print publishing and concentrate on the retail business of artists' materials, fancy goods, framing photographs for Hennah & Kent's clients, and the print-lending library. Apart from the difficulty of getting an engraver or printer to work for a bankrupt publisher, it must have been an obvious decision for his creditors that copper-plate prints were suffering decline through topographical and portrait photography.

Moving out of 108 and into shared premises probably meant that Mason lost a fair amount of his own stock due to lack of space, and it seems likely that as Croydon is given as his home address, he spent a couple of years commuting to Brighton, until Henry Stewart's business closed in 1876. Mason's financial problems continued and a further bankruptcy hearing was held 18 years after the original ruling. By a newspaper notice of 17 July 1873[45] advice of the First General Meeting of creditors was given, to be held at 33 Gutter Lane, London at 12 noon on 6 August 1873. Mason's attorney at this time was Charles Lamb of 14 Ship Street, Brighton, and Mason is described as of '45 (late 108) King's Road, Brighton and of 21 George Street, Croydon—printseller and publisher'.

Family life

W H G Mason married Mary Dawe at St Pancras Parish Chapel, Camden, on 10 February 1838 and during their 41 years together they had eight children. In the 1841 census Mary's younger sister Emma Dawe, aged 20, was living with them at the Repository of Arts, 81 King's Road. Mary and Emma's father was Henry Edward Dawe, who was born in Kentish Town, just north of Camden. He was an important artist and engraver who was working for Ackermann's before the couple married. There are 60 examples of his work in the National Portrait Gallery collection, and many in Russia. He had spent several years working with his elder brother, the portraitist George Dawe RA (1781-1829), at the Imperial Academy of Arts in St Petersburg, before returning to London in 1827. William could have met his future wife in 1833, when she was 18, at the time of Mason's first published engraving from Mary's father, the portrait plate of Mr Joseph Sortain.

The 1841 census entry for 81 King's Road, Brighton has William Mason print-seller, aged 30; Mary Mason wife, aged 26; William Mason, aged 1. Their first-born was noted in the *Brighton Herald* of 2 November 1839: 'Birth on Tuesday, at 81 King's Road, W.H. Mason, of a son'. Also included as living with the Masons, apart from Mary's sister Emma, was William Lane, described as 'man-servant' born 1818; William Drummond, portrait painter, born 1811; George Yates, 'man-servant' aged 14; James Martin, 'man-servant', aged 45; and Elizabeth Burrows, aged 19, 'servant'. Presumably these five individuals all worked in the gallery.

By 1851 the repository was at 108 King's Road, with no family accommodation, so the census entry was for 22 Norfolk Road. It lists the much increased Mason family: William Mason print-seller aged 40, born Shoreditch, Middlesex; Mary Mason wife aged 36, born Middlesex; William H Mason son aged 11, scholar; Mary Elizabeth daughter, aged 8; Annie, daughter, aged 5; Florence Sarah, daughter, twin aged 3; Rachel Emma, daughter, twin aged 3; Charles Walter, son aged 1. All the children were born in Brighton. The employees and servants in the household were John Mildrum, assistant print-seller, aged 25, born Middlesex; Ann Boyde, housemaid, aged 22, born Brighton; and Elizabeth Simmonds, housemaid, aged 18, born Brighton.

Also in this 1851 census William Mason senior, aged 64, is described as a retired print-seller living at 74 Newmarket Road, in the Barnwell Abbey ward to the north of Cambridge, with his wife Elizabeth, aged 62. His household still included two daughters, Caroline Mason, aged 24, dressmaker, born in Cambridge, and Emma Kelly, aged 23, born in Cambridge, together with John Kelly, son-in-law, aged 25, a cook. William Mason senior died on 22 January 1855—thankfully 10 months before he would have had to witness his eldest son declare himself bankrupt. The Barnwell area of Cambridge suffered from considerable poverty in the mid-century and a local mission was opened there in 1875 to alleviate the social problems.

In the 1861 census W H G Mason's home at 3 Lansdowne Terrace shows a further increase to the family. The progress of the first six children from the previous census is noted; William H, 21, photographic artist; Mary, aged 19, dependent; Annie, aged 15, dependent; then the next three are listed as scholars—Florence Sarah, aged 13; Rachel Emma, aged 13; Charles Walter, aged 10 and by now the last two members of the family had been born: Henry Dawe, aged eight and Frederick George, aged four. Then finally there are Ann Pengelly, aged 30, servant-nurse; Mary Burton aged 20, servant-cook; and Margaret Scott, aged 19, general servant. This address, part of the early development of the present Lansdowne Road, features in the Regency Society's James Gray Collection[46]. Gray's annotation describes 'two houses to the west of Farm Road, owned by the successful trader W.H. Mason' who 'had domestic servants to do household chores at his home'.

The two photographs show 'the charwoman washing the steps leading to the house [**56**] and inside a maid laundering some clothes' [**57**]. The suggested date for these photographs is 'during the 1860s'. Mason still managed to have three servants in his household, no doubt

56
Below left
The charwoman washing the steps leading to the house

57
Below right
Maid laundering some clothes

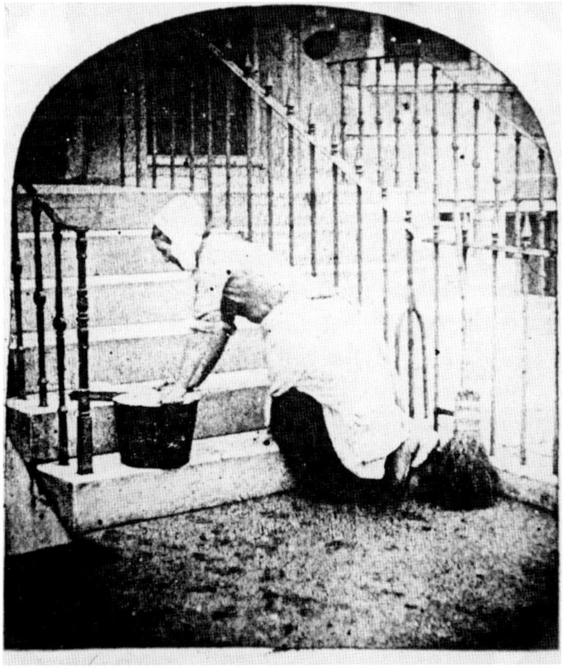

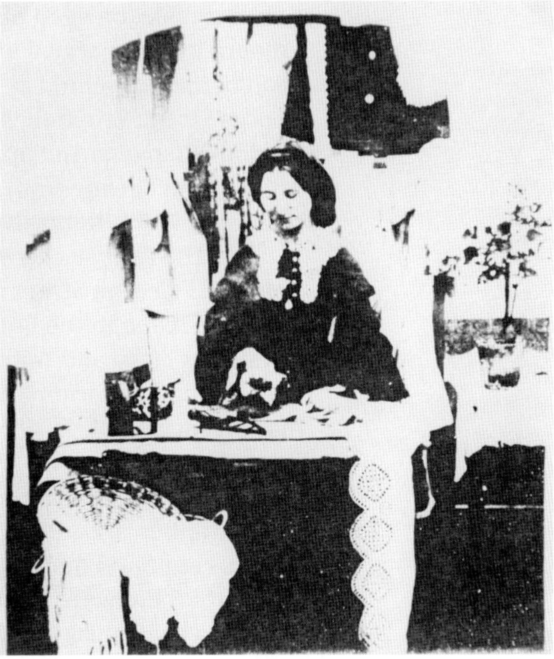

with help from his eldest son's business and the rent from Hennah & Kent. In the photograph, it would be the general servant Margaret Scott washing the front steps.

In the 1871 census the family lived at 4 Westfield Gardens, off King's Road and very close to the gallery at number 108. (*Folthorps Directory* describes the address as 'turns out of the King's Road at 109'.) The eldest son William H was still listed as a photographer, and the other seven sons and daughters, ranging in age from 29 down to 14, were all still living at home. No occupations are listed apart from William Jr, who at this stage was working with Hennah & Kent upstairs in the Repository. None of the daughters, Rachel being the youngest at 23, was married, although one or more would surely have been involved in their father's gallery, and in earlier years would most likely have helped with colouring lithographs printed on the premises. They had a 17-year-old general servant, Elizabeth Ridgway, living in the house. Giving some insight into family relationships, Mason's surgeon, who had known him since he first arrived in Brighton, is quoted as testifying (see page 115) that he had never known a man more attached to his family.

William Henry Goodburn Mason died aged 68 on 14 May 1879 at 21 George Street, Croydon, the home of his eldest son. On the death certificate his youngest son, Frederick George Mason, of 10 Baker Street, Oxford Street, London, wrote his occupation as 'artist' rather than printer and publisher. The cause of death was noted as 'disease of prostate gland'. His death was announced in both the Croydon papers on 17 May 1879[47]: 'Mason. May 14th at 21 George Street. Mr. William Henry Goodburn Mason aged 68 years'. In the 1881 census this youngest son Frederick is unmarried and working as a photographer's assistant to the head of the household at 10 Baker Street. The site of the Mason home in George Street, Croydon, is now part of The George, a popular restaurant. Having taken over the upper floor of Mason's repository at 108 in the 1850s, for a decade from 1873 the photographers Hennah & Kent had the premises to themselves as the King's Road Art Studio.

The 1881 census records Mason's eldest son as head of the household at 21 George Street and his widowed mother, aged 66, living with him. Also listed in the house are the two eldest daughters, William Henry Jr's sisters Mary and Annie. Mary was an artist but Annie, by this time aged 35, had 'no occupation'. William Henry Jr was a bachelor and had made a success of his photographic business. He employed assistants, Edgar Burton, aged 27, and Benjamin Welch, aged 16, who both lived with the family. Henry Dawe Mason, the second youngest son, was also a photographer, aged 28 by this time, and had a wife called Nell. They lived with his aunt and her husband, John and Henrietta Meldrum, at their home at 86 Edgware Road, Willesden. This John Meldrum was the alternatively transcribed John Mildrum, the 25-year-old assistant printseller to the Mason business in the 1841 census, who married one of

Mary Mason's younger sisters. One of the twins, Florence, married a William Baker in 1874 and they lived at 11 Prestonville Road, near the Seven Dials in Brighton.

Four of Mason's children became photographers: William Henry Jr, Henry Dawe, Frederick George, and finally Mary is listed in the final section as having some of her photographs published.

The court case

The Dyke House Hotel [**58**] was owned by William and Mary Thacker, who took frequent adverts in the local papers. Typical was that of May 1849 in the *Brighton Gazette*, where William Thacker wrote: 'In no part of England can a spot be found which shall excel the summit of the Dyke Hill, from whence a view is obtained of scenery the most enchanting . . . the spectator being able to distinguish . . . six counties'.

Mason had become friends with William Thacker and his family, frequenting the Dyke House on his many walks over the Downs on painting trips. The *Brighton Gazette* (16 July 1846) reported Mason taking a coach up to the Dyke with two of his children and a friend, when the coach overturned. Of the six other passengers, Dennis Sullivan, a porter at the Clarence Hotel, suffered a broken leg and died in hospital

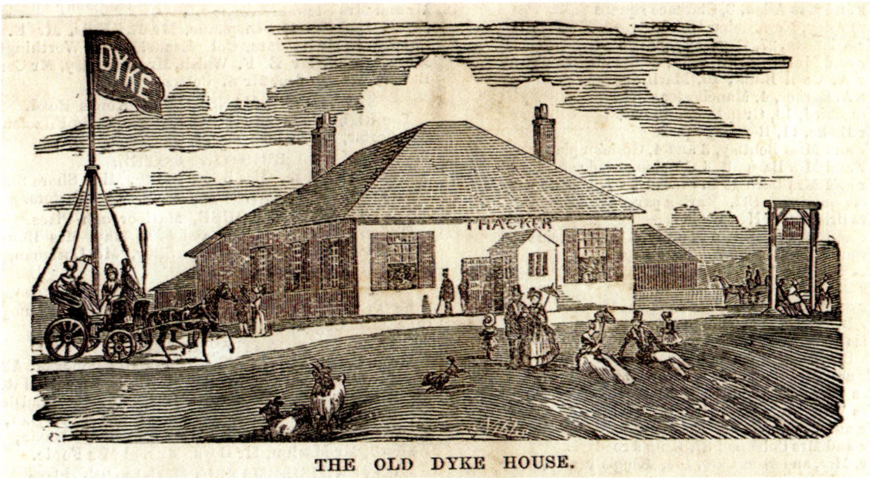

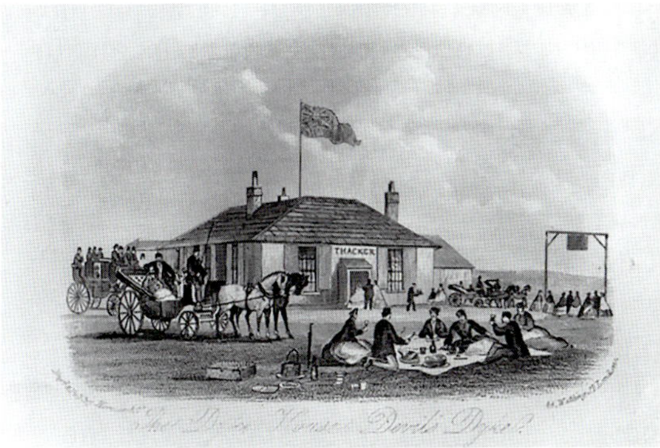

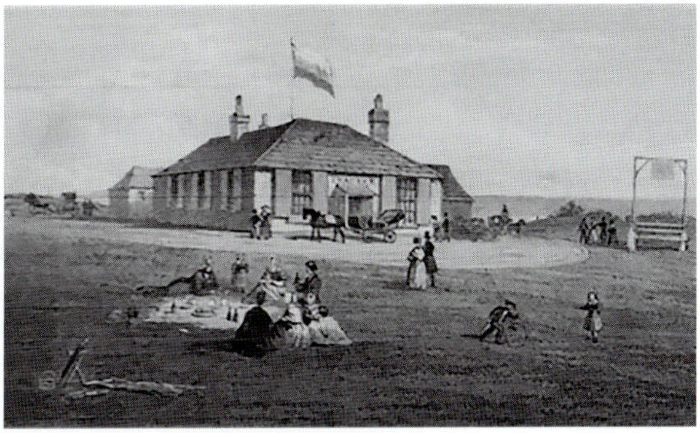

58
The three known c19th views of William and Mary Thacker's Dyke Hotel.
right 'The Old Dyke House' Wood engraving by Richard Henry Nibbs, 25 May 1846; plate 1 of his set of four views from the Devil's Dyke.
below left 'The Dyke House, Devil's Dyke'. Steel engraving by Newman & Co., Watling Street, London c1850.
below right 'The Dyke House' Lithograph by W Walton after F Earp, published by W H Mason

the next day, but there were no other injuries. Mason's two children were William, who was six, and the three-year-old Mary, both of whom would have been friends with the Thacker children, Mary aged eight and the three-year-old Alice.

Some years later, on a day in September 1849, Mason and George Earp Jr went off for a day's sketching over the Downs, taking with them Mary Thacker and her young six-year-old sister Alice; the children were carrying the refreshments supplied by Mrs Thacker. During the course of the afternoon Mason went off gathering blackberries with the two children[48].

Many weeks later, towards the end of October, Mary made accusations against Mason to members of her family and finally to her mother, who called the police. Mason was brought before Brighton Magistrates and committed to the Lewes House of Correction by Mr C Carpenter on 2 November 1849; he was bailed on committal. Being brought to Lewes Crown Court he was prisoner number 32 in the list of adjourned cases for 28 November of the Michaelmas Sessions, and the case was heard the next day. Mason's plea was entered as 'not guilty'.

In the Sussex Register of Indictable Offences 1849, Mason was charged with sexual abuse of a child. While the *Brighton Herald* reported that the incident was thought to have taken place on 8 September, the trial papers confirmed this date in the four counts against Mason. The crime was noted as 'assault with intent to commit rape'. The four counts read out in court vary slightly in their wording, but the first count is sufficient to quote: 'William Henry Mason, printseller, on the 8th September 1849, at the parish of Poynings, did make an assault on Mary Elizabeth Carr Thacker, then and there did beat, wound and ill-treat with intent, violently and against her will then and there feloniously to ravish and carnally know, and other wrongs to the said Mary Thacker then and there did to the great damage of the said Mary Thacker'. Mary is described as an infant, 'above the age of 10 and under the age of 12, to wit eleven years'. At the trial Mason 'firmly' pleaded, 'I am not guilty'.

His defence counsel described Mason as 'in the very respectable business of print-seller. He was in the habit of going up on the Downs to take views of the countryside, and on this occasion was with the artist George Earp Jr'. Mason employed two other members of the Earp family for a couple of publications but George Jr was his favoured artist and in the 1830s gave Mason's Repository as his working address[49]. Mason's counsel described Mason as of high position, a respectable and exemplary man. He resided in Brighton but had previously 'carried on business in Windsor'. The character witnesses that were called included Henry Reeves, print-seller of Cheapside, who had been acquainted with Mason for 25 years and his firm had the highest opinion of him. Mr Heddings (with Messrs Ackermann) had known him for 12 years and held him in the highest respect. Mr Goodburn, a pawnbroker of Islington, was Mason's uncle and had known Mason from birth, stayed with the family occasionally and never heard a charge of immorality against him. Mr William Frederick Taylor, bookseller of Windsor, had often been at Mason's home and had known him for seven years as a respectable, moral and religious man. Mr John Rogers, of the company Holtham & Rogers, had been doing business with him for 15 years and added he was 'incapable of committing the charge against him'. Mr E Burn, a bookseller of Brighton, had known him for 17 years and testified that his conduct was irreproachable. Mr Bowdidge of Brighton had known Mason for 16 years as a highly respectable member of the chapel of which Mr Bowdidge was the warden.

Mr Wilcox of the Sea House Hotel had been a friend to Mason for 17 years and testified to his character being irreproachable. Mr Wilcox had seven children and, notwithstanding all the accusations he had heard during the trial, he would trust Mason with any of them. Mr E Wright of the Esplanade Library was the father of a large family and would have no hesitation in trusting any of them to Mason. Mr Rugg, a surgeon, had attended Mason for 18 years and said he was irreproachable, a pattern to society, and had never known a man more attached to his wife and family. For Mr Wilcox of the Sea House Hotel to have known Mason for 17 years, they had obviously struck up a relationship as soon as the Repository was opened in 1832, and it seems his surgeon, Mr Rugg, must have been introduced to Mason when he was first in Brighton making arrangements to open the gallery.

The witnesses called for the prosecution were Mary Thacker herself, Harriet Payne, Francis Tate, Susannah Strivens and William Thacker, the child's father. The total expenses allowed to prosecutors and witnesses came to £13 12s 10d. The jury was made up of William Attwood, George Bates, James Davies, William Avery, Richard Corner, John Goldsmith, John Bassett, Michael Cornwall, Henry Cullis, Trayton Dapp, William Daniels and Edward Cutress.

The proceedings lasted that one day, the verdict was 'not guilty' and Mason was acquitted and discharged in the order of court papers[50]. During the case it was reported that the child Mary had previously made a similar accusation against a member of her own family.

This whole episode came at a critical time for Mason. Earlier in the year he had published his large engraving of 'The Cricket Match between Sussex and Kent' (see Chapter 6), which had been nearly six years in preparation. During this time there had been no return on considerable expense and effort and successful marketing was important for the financial well-being of the Repository. The publication was available from May 1849, so for Mason to face arrest for these dreadful accusations just six months later and spend the whole of November establishing his defence and arranging character witnesses must have been such a difficult distraction.

The episode may have had another effect on Mason. During 1846 he had published a set of four prints of the Devil's Dyke landscape, including the print of Mr & Mrs Thacker's 'Dyke House Hotel'. By 1850 he seems to have sold these plates, or given up the lease on them, to William Grant. It is possible Mason could no longer bring himself to sell these images in the Repository, and with the likelihood of a soured relationship between himself and the Thackers, these images as 'Mason publications' would no longer have been offered for sale at the Dyke House Hotel.

Thankfully, within a decade, Mason's reputation seems to have been restored. The 1857 *Art Journal*, in a report on his son's photographic work, referred to Mason senior as 'the well-known and much respected print seller'.

Interests: painting, politics, cricket, the theatre

With Mason described by his youngest son as an 'artist' on the death certificate, this may have been how he liked to think of himself in his retirement. From his trial papers of 1849 we know that he loved to go sketching on the Downs, frequently with the local artist George Earp Jr (1818–1888), whom he used for 19 of his publications. In addition the trial papers tell us something of Mason's social circle in Brighton and people he counted as friends. Mr Taylor, the son of the Windsor bookseller with whom he had served an apprenticeship, had often visited his home and he was well-known by Mr Bowdidge, his local churchwarden, by Mr Wilcox of the Sea House Hotel and Mr Wright of the Esplanade Library, together with various print publishers in London with whom he had long associations.

Viewing Mason as an artist, little of his work can be identified today. So to judge his talent is not easy. Despite his painting days on the Downs with George Earp Jr, there is only one printed image credited to Mason as the original artist, 'The Exterior and Interior of the Royal Chapel, St James's' [**60**]. The exterior view shows two guards standing either side of the chapel doors, and the lettering reads 'W.H. Mason delt., printed by Lefevre, published by W.H. Mason, Her Majesty's print-seller, Brighton, Ackermann & Co., and Chas. Tilt, Fleet Street'. The interior view shows Victoria and Albert kneeling at the altar. The print is dated 10 February 1840, thus while the title does not indicate so, it is depicting the royal wedding, issued on the actual day.

In the exterior scene the figures of the two guards are well-formed, if a little naive, but their faces are rather simply depicted. The stonework and wooden doors to the chapel are well drawn. From the evidence of Mason's hand in this 'Royal Chapel' print, there are six other scenes that we can reasonably attribute to Mason: the set of six beach scenes engraved on steel by R Forse ([**70**] and catalogued as WM14 in Appendix 2, page 188). From the depiction of the eyes, nose and lips of the male faces in these prints they could all be judged to be by the same hand as the faces of the guards in the 'Royal Chapel'. Another particular similarity is the way Mason drew the woodwork on the chapel doors and then in the beach groynes on the set of six.

The other scenes from Mason's hand are the pair of 'Brighton Hurdle Race' engravings, published in 1833, the year after he opened his Brighton gallery, and most likely his second publication after the Panorama. However, these racing prints are described as 'drawn by George Earp after sketches by W.H. Mason', so they might show more of Mason's work of composition than detail. The various members of the Earp family were respected local artists, and these racing scenes were then engraved by Charles Hunt, which takes us another step away from Mason's original hand. Mason's association with the engraver Charles Hunt would have been through Ackermann's, who used both the Hunt brothers for many publications. This pair of engravings indicate Mason's ability and willingness to portray horses—something he would have familiarised himself with through the various sporting artists and engravers he met at Ackermann's, and a skill he used effectively with the two well-drawn riding figures in the Roe Park lithograph. This print of 'Roe Park, Withdean' [**48**] , after the architect A H Wilds and lithographed by Mason, is a very competent copy onto the stone of Wilds' original drawing. The second known example of his lithographic skills, three of which are in the Royal Collection at Windsor, is a set of four 'Illustrations of Arundel Castle', which are after original drawings by three of George Earp senior's sons.

At the close of his career, while Mason was living with his son in Croydon, an announcement in *The Times* on 7 July 1877 tells us that 'Messrs. Bonhams are instructed to sell paintings and watercolours . . . ', then follows a list of some of the artists included: 'A. Hulk, Pether, E.J. Niemann, W.H. Mason . . . and others'. The fact that we have no record of the W H Mason from Chichester being an artist adds weight to this being our man. The other artists listed were all mid-Victorian landscape painters, contemporaries of Mason, and, like him, not blessed with much money at the end of their careers.

From a witness in Mason's trial we know that he was described as a highly respectable member of his local chapel for 16 years, as this was the length of time the chapel warden had known him, indicating that Mason joined the chapel as a young bachelor within a year of his arrival in Brighton. This was Trinity Chapel in Ship Street [**59**], just a few yards from his gallery and home. Trinity, built by Thomas Read Kemp in 1817, was a non-conformist chapel led by George Faithfull for a while. It was the first building commission in Brighton for the Wilds father and son[51]. The Rev. Robert Anderson purchased the chapel in 1825 with his brother James, and they commissioned Charles Barry to adapt it for Anglican worship[52]. By an Act of Parliament it joined the Anglican communion the following year and became a chapel of ease to St Peter's.

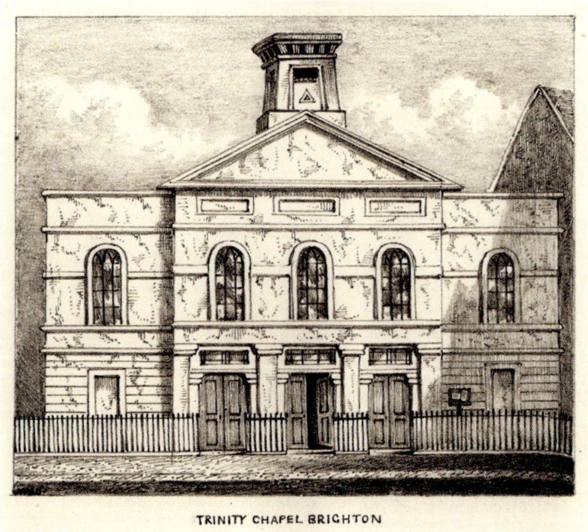

59
'Trinity Chapel, Brighton'. This shows the Wilds' original neo-classical façade, which was replaced by Somers Clarke & Micklethwaite, who designed the present flint Gothic design in 1885-87. Lithograph, published by Harry Hawkins, 35 West

Mason published a mezzotint of Anderson in 1840 and had to re-engrave it in 1843 due to demand. It was then later produced as a lithograph after Charles Baugniet, a copy of which is in the Royal Collection. The next incumbent was the renowned preacher F W Robertson, who came to Trinity in 1847 but died in August 1853. In September that year Mason published 'The late Rev. F.W. Robertson MA., Incumbent of Trinity Chapel', a lithograph after Charles J Basebe [**55**]. Known as 'Robertson of Brighton'. he was one of the most exciting and charismatic preachers of his day.

With regard to his politics, Mason makes a couple of statements in illustrative form. An article in the *Brighton Patriot* on 20 February 1838 was headed 'A Serious and Profound Examination of Mr. Mason's Political Sketch, the Brighton Omnibus Legislator'. The editor was seeking to discover 'the hidden satire and delicate humour designed to be insinuated in the sketch', which included caricatures of Captain George Pechell MP and Major Allen. A copy of this sketch, the 'Brighton Omnibus Legislator', has not been found. However, it seems reasonable to infer from the comments in the *Brighton Patriot* article that Mason's publication was in support of the Tory Party. We know that he was a keen admirer of the Royal Family and the gentry, an important part of his clientele.

He was sufficiently interested in politics to publish this 'Omnibus' print in criticism of the Whig Party and would not have been sympathetic to the Whig ideas of the supremacy of parliament over the monarchy and landowners. In fact, Mason would have been just as unsympathetic to the views of George Faithfull, the Liberal MP who owned the *Patriot* newspaper. Mason's 'Omnibus' print seems to have come from a comment made in the Commons debate in July 1831, discussing the proposed Reform Bill[53]. One of the arguments against the status quo and in favour of voting reform was that a wealthy Tory landowner could get his candidate and constituents, 'which amounted to eight including his cook and gardener', all together on the Brighton Omnibus and 'was this not a mockery, a caricature upon Representation, and calculated to throw ridicule upon the House of Commons?'

Mason's point in his print seems to be that to him it was reasonable a rich landowner should be able to choose his own man for parliament. The *Patriot* describes the print as an 'extreme and burlesque delineation of the persons represented. ... Capt. Pechell ... sits on the box, neither like a coachman nor a gentleman ... and appears as if the least jerk would unship him'. From the caricature the two horses pulling

60
'A Wick'd Subject'

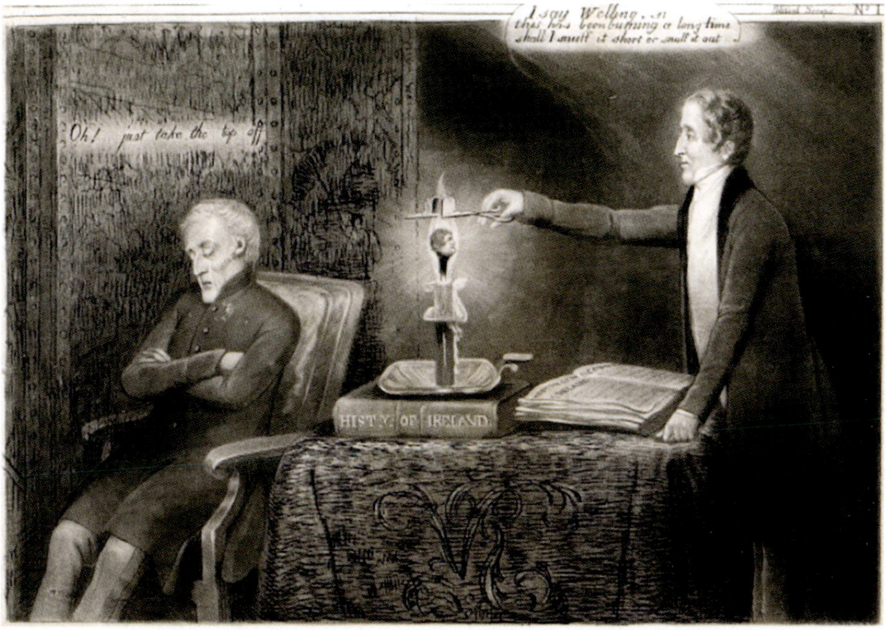

the coach could be taken for the editor of the *Brighton Guardian* and the editor of the *Brighton Herald*. Within the picture are the words 'Parcels left at the Shades will be called for daily' and the Patriot thinks this phrase 'may have a double meaning. We shall take the occult and sarcastic meaning, intimating that the Whigs will descend to anything'.

A further political publication, listed earlier in the text, comes under the heading of 'Political Scraps No: 1'. The title of this mezzotint engraving [**60**] is 'A Wick'ed Subject'. Mason is making a play on words with the central image of the print being a candle. It was published by Mason, 81 King's Road and Ackermann & Co. Strand, on 10 November 1843 but with no artist or engraver named. With the Duke of Wellington asleep in a chair, the scene is portrayed as if it is the Duke's dream. On the table beside him is a candle, standing on a large volume of the History of Ireland. On the other side of the table the figure of Daniel O'Connell appears in the dream and is asking the question 'I say Welling**n this has been burning a long time, shall I snuff it short or snuff it out?' O'Connell is holding a pair of snuffers to the flame, in which is drawn a small face, probably that of John Mitchell, who wanted social and political revolution in defiance of British law. O'Connell's stand for peaceful change in Ireland was appreciated by the Duke, and the speech-bubble from the Duke's dream reads 'Oh! Just take the top off'. In this he is suggesting to O'Connell, in military terms, that the best way for him to deal with Mitchell's movement would be to neutralise its leadership, leaving the rank and file membership free to join O'Connell and the Catholic Relief Agitation.

At the time of the print's publication the Duke was Minister without Portfolio and Leader of the House of Lords in Peel's government;

O'Connell had been working to establish universal suffrage in Ireland by non-violent means. A note on the top right corner of the plate of 'Political Scraps No: 1' indicates that other political cartoons were at least intended, although to date none has been found.

Through a mutual interest in cricket, A D Taylor, the author of a book about Mason's cricket print (see next chapter), developed a close friendship with Joseph Colbron. Colbron was born in Brighton in 1827, and died in late 1915 while living in Osborne Street, Hove (now Osborne Villas). He became surveyor for Hove and Clerk to the Hove Commissioners, and when the cricket ground on the Level closed, Colbron laid the first brick of the Park Crescent development. For our purposes, the friendship between these two Brightonians is interesting because Colbron described himself to Taylor as an 'intimate acquaintance' of William Henry Mason and during their many conversations an aspect of our gallery owner's personality emerges.

Taylor wrote that Colbron described Mason as 'of a very retiring disposition—so modest indeed that while he induced many to sit for their portraits he could never himself be persuaded to sit—his shyness was painful'. Also enabling us to know Mason a little better we have the complimentary testimonies of the trial witnesses who were called in his defence. From these friends and business associates we have the comments that, over many years, 'his conduct was irreproachable'; he was 'a highly respectable member of the chapel' and 'a pattern to society'.

Despite the painful shyness described by Colbron, on 2 May 1837 the *Brighton Patriot* recorded the following cricketing dinner: 'Mr. Brown of the Hanover Arms held his annual dinner yesterday—50 supporters and players sat to a splendid dinner. Mr. Mason of Ship Street was in the Chair, supported by W. Pickett as deputy. The evening was spent with glee and good humour.' And in the previous month, on 4 April 1837, the same newspaper reported that '7 men, including . . . Mr. T. Wisden of Hampden Place and Mr. W.H. Mason of Ship Street . . . were sworn in as Headboroughs for the present year'.

Another civic duty was mentioned in the *Brighton Gazette* on 1 April 1852: 'A notice was published giving the 150 names of people all summoned to attend as Jurymen at the Court Leet for the Hundred of Whalesbone, held at the Town Hall, April 13th to elect a High Constable for the forthcoming year.' Among the names was 'William Henry Mason, printseller, King's Road'.

From Taylor's book we learn that Mason was an 'excellent amateur actor, making more than one appearance at the Theatre, yet privately would do anything to hide from the possibility of being asked to propose or respond to a toast, or render a song'.

Apparently, like many people with a degree of shyness, Mason seemed happy on stage behind a theatrical character. Apart from his first appearance, all his other roles were after he had declared himself bankrupt, and this hobby was obviously a pleasant diversion from his business problems.

Henry C. Porter[54] listed his few stage appearances:

1844 from theatre poster (in the Erredge Collection, Brighton Museum Rare Books Department) for *The Hunchback* at the Theatre Royal on **Tuesday 14 October** performed by Her Majesty's servants—Waiter: Mr. Mason

1862 February 27 The Garrick ADC produced Victims in which Mason played Butterby and then they staged *The Slave* with Mason as Fogrum.

1862 March 26 *The Bachelor of Arts* was staged with Mason playing Andrew Wylie.

1862 April 4 he was Silver Jack in *The Rent Day*.

1863 February 9 Mason sang 'Tippity Witchet' at a benefit show for the clown Allano.

1863 June 7 saw the Brighton Regatta amateur performance of *Aladdin* (burlesque) in which Mason was Sultan.

1864 March 23 he was Snaffle in *The Four Sisters*.

1865 August 8 saw a Grand Amateur performance, in aid of the Regatta funds, of *Plat and Passion*, in which the men's chorus, including Mason, 'was assisted by the ladies of the company'.

1866 March 12 Mason gave another performance of Butterby in *Victims*,

1866 May 14 Mason was Jacob Earwig in *Boots at the Swan*, then on the 15th he played Moss in *The Ticket-of-Leave Man*.

Then the last show in this original New Road theatre was on 21 May 1866 for the Regatta fund—a performance of *Lady of Lyons* in which Mason played Clopin.

The new theatre that was built on the site of the old had its inauguration on Monday 15 October 1866. Mason's first appearance here was on 5 December in *The Rent Day*, appearing with W Hogarth, J K Nye and D H Greening.

1867 July 9 saw the annual amateur performance in aid of the Regatta fund of *Still Waters Run Deep* and *Esmeralda*, a burlesque with Mason in the role of Clopin.

1868 March 16 he appeared in *The Ticket-of-Leave Man* and *Black Ey'd Susan* burlesque.

1868 May 6 Mason took the role of Flipper in the drama *No. 1 One Round the Corner*.

1869 May 3 saw a special amateur entertainment including *Mason's Burlesque—Macbeth Mystified* with Mason and C W Mason in the cast. C W Mason was William Henry's 19-year-old son, Charles Walter.

1869 July 18 Mason and Roe's burlesque *The Corsican Brothers* was performed, with Mason as Renard and C W Mason as Martelli.

1871 May 2 *Aladdin* (burlesque) was second on the bill, with Mason in the role of the Magician and this seems to be his last appearance on the stage—an amateur career that spanned nine years, and two Brighton theatres.

[1] Sue McKechnie: *British Silhouette Artists and their work 1760–1860*. London & New York: Sotheby Parke Bernet, 1978
[2] Fitzwilliam Museum Collections Explorer, accessed June 2012
[3] NPG.org.uk lists 11 portrait plates by William Mason, line engravings and mezzotints
[4] DNB Vol. 54. Contributed by F M O'Donoghue
[5] *Cambridge News,* 18 November 2014, p17, 'Memories' with Mike Petty
[6] There is no artist, lithographer or publisher noted on this unrecorded print, but it is likely to be a Mason publication. There are only four publications listed in 'Images of Brighton' that are printed by Lefevre, and three of these are published by Mason. The fourth is too early for Mason in Brighton. To this must be added the fact that Mason was the major producer of lithographs in Brighton, 30 in all. The composition of the plate also points to Mason. In the complete print (illustrated in full in Appendix 2) there is a Royal Mail Coach outside the hotel to the right, but the building line is going away from us, so Mason's gallery, with its very clear wording, is closest to the viewer.
[7] Brighton Museum & Art Gallery FA203236
[8] This would have been the view out of Mason's Ship Street windows, although by the time he moved The Repository to 81 King's Road in 1839, the hotel had undergone much re-orientation and rebuilding work. W Saunder's *Stranger's Guide in Brighton* (1839) records: 'The Old Ship Hotel is one of the oldest and most respectable concerns in the town . . . its situation commands the finest prospect of the road, beach and vast expanse of ocean . . . a portion of it has lately been rebuilt'. Regarding the hotel's lovely view, the same could be said of the prospect from Mason's own home above the Repository
[9] J G Bishop: *Peep into the Past*, 1880, p360
[10] Jill Seddon: 'The Visual Arts in Regency Brighton & Hove' in *Georgian Group Journal*, Vol XIII, 2003, p277
[11] Charles Fleet: *An Illustrated Hand–Book of Brighton and Its Environs*. Brighton: W & C Fleet, 1847, p45
[12] Harold P Clunn: *The Capital By-The-Sea*. Brighton: The Southern Publishing Co. Ltd, 1953, p43
[13] W H Attwick: *Jubilee of the Brighton Corporation*, 1904, p36
[14] John Bruce: *The History of Brighton with the Latest Improvements*. 1833, p2
[15] Charles Fleet: *An Illustrated Hand-Book of Brighton*. Brighton: W & C Fleet, Herald Office, 1847, p55
[16] The Keep (East Sussex Records Office): HOW/88/4 Manor of Attlingworth, copy of grant by the Lord of the Manor to Charles Scrase Dickins the elder and the younger, 4 September 1818.
[17] John Ford: *Ackermann 1783-1983 the Business of Art*. London: Ackermann, 1983, p105
[18] John & Jill Ford: *Images of Brighton*. Richmond-upon-Thames: Saint Helena Press, 1981, p139
[19] The Keep (East Sussex Records Office): HOW/75/9: 81 King's Road leases and assignments. Ackerson, Mutton etc
[20] Edmund Gilbert: *Brighton Old Ocean's Bauble*. London: Methuen & Co, 1954, p182
[21] Harold H Clunn: *The Capital By-The-Sea'*. Brighton: The Southern Publishing Co, 1953, p32
[22] *Brighton Herald*, 9 November 1851
[23] The Keep (East Sussex Records Office): BH/B/4/35/2 and /36B/2
[24] The Keep (East Sussex Records Office): DAP/269/1 Court records.
[25] Eric Parker: *The History of Cricket'*. London: The Lonsdale Press, plate 29 opposite p257
[26] George Holman: *Some Lewes Men of Note*. Printed by E Baxter, 1911
[27] Hundred of Cambridge Poll Books, 1832 and 1835.
[28] The Keep (East Sussex Records Office): BH/B/4/35/2 and 36/B
[29] Ford: *op.cit.* 1983, p21.
[30] Cyrus Jay: *Recollections of William Jay*. London: Hamilton Adams & Co, 1869, p32. Cyrus was William Jay's son.

[31] Neither the print nor the hand-book itself credit an artist or engraver, but it is certainly from the original drawing by George Campion. He was the artist of a similar but larger view, differing just in the figures, published in Mason's 1838 *Illustrations of Brighton*

[32] Owen Chadwick: *The Victorian Church.* London: A & C Black, 1970

[33] *Gentleman's Magazine*, May 1828. p449

[34] Orrin Wang: *Romantic Sobriety.* Baltimore: John Hopkins University Press, 2011

[35] Philippe Garner: *A Seaside Album*. Brighton: The Royal Pavilion, Libraries & Museums, Brighton & Hove in association with Philip Wilson, 2003, p27.

[36] The Keep (East Sussex Records Office): ACC8742/1 up to /11.

[37] Brighton Museum Local History Collection HA930066.

[38] *History of Brighthelmstone*. Reprint by John Farrant. Forest Row: Brambletye Books, 2005, pA6

[39] photohistory-sussex.co.uk, accessed April 2014

[40] Spartacus-educational.com

[41] Laurie Keen: 'Close Up' in *Argus* Magazine 15 February 2014

[42] photohistory-sussex.co.uk, accessed April 2014

[43] The Keep (East Sussex Records Office): AMS6432/2/54 and AMS/6432/2/55

[44] V Markham Lester: *Victorian Insolvency: Bankruptcy, Imprisonment for Debt, and Company Winding-up in Nineteenth-century England*. Clarendon Press, 1995

[45] *The Times* website: newspaper.bl.uk, accessed October 2011.

[46] James Grey Collection, volume 11, image 44

[47] *The Croydon Advertiser* and *The Croydon Times.* Croydon Local Studies Library

[48] The Keep (East Sussex Records Office): QR/E1849/944

[49] Ford and Ford: *Op.cit*, 1981, p365

[50] *Brighton Herald*, 1 December 1849

[51] Raymond Flower: *The Old Ship—A Prospect of Brighton*. London: Croom Helm, 1986, p88

[52] Berys Shipley: *The Lost Churches of Brighton and Hove.* Worthing: Optimus Books, 2001, p16.

[53] HC debate, 6 July 1831, vol 4, pp804-906

[54] Henry C. Porter: *The History of the Theatres of Brighton 1774-1885*. Brighton: King & Thorne, 1886

61
'Cricket Match played between Sussex and Kent 1849, painted by W H Mason. Published for the Brighton & Hove Gas Company' (see page 128). A hand-coloured chromo-lithograph

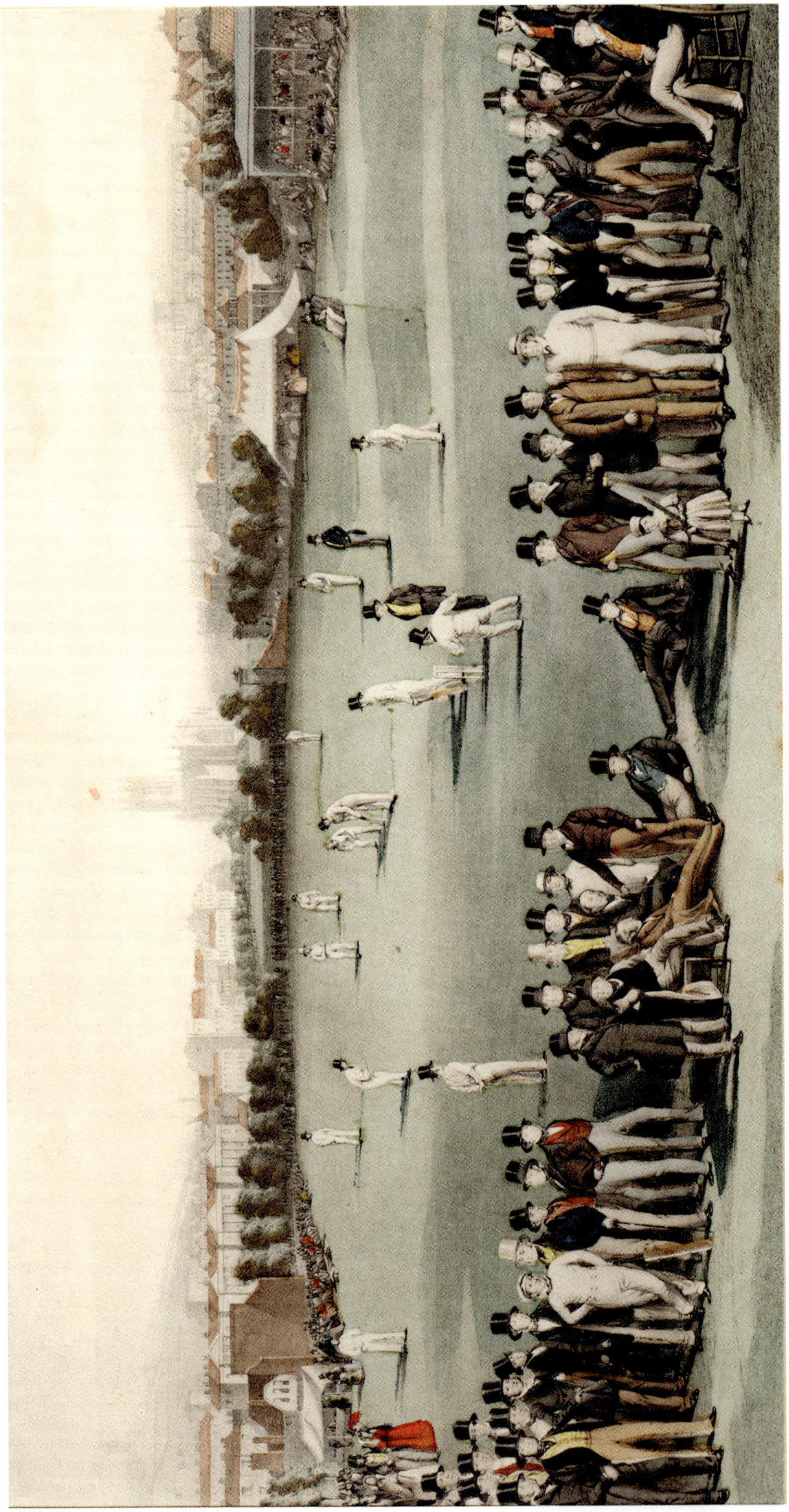

6 The Cricket Print

In his leisure time, apart from being a chapel member, a devoted family man and sketching on the Downs, William Mason pursued his other great love: the game of cricket. Mason played for Sussex, his highest score was in a match against Kent on 7-8 June 1841 at Brighton, he scored 38 runs, then two in the second innings. He was bowled out by W Hillyer in both innings[1]. He included cricket in his publishing output, the most important result of which was the large engraving of 'The Cricket Match between Sussex and Kent, at Brighton' of 1849. With Mason's love for the game it seemed right that this engraving should be given its own chapter.

Mason took a particularly keen interest in this sport, always having himself listed as a professional player rather than an amateur, but nevertheless paying his own expenses[2]. Apart from the enjoyment of playing, he surely valued the social and business contacts it gave him. But this love of the game may have blinded him to the economic realities of the 1850s. With a plate size of nearly 60cm by 90cm, 'The Cricket Match between Sussex and Kent' was one of the largest engravings published in Brighton, and at the time by far the most expensive, with customers being asked six guineas a print and eight guineas for an artist's proof (approximately £900 in present values). At much the same time, the local publisher William Grant was offering a small booklet of 'Six Views of Brighton' at a price of 'sixpence plain' and 'one shilling coloured'.

The commercial appeal of the cricket match scene, at the right price, was demonstrated by the success of the slightly smaller and no doubt much cheaper lithographic imitations which followed a few years later. The trading conditions at this time were such that the middle/merchant-class visitors to the town (very much the new collectors of prints) were buying small steel engravings, for a few pence or shillings, which they carried back home on the trains, while the gentry were developing a taste for the new art of portrait and topographical photography, which was celebrated in the 1851 Great Exhibition.

Mason's two artists, William Drummond and Charles Basebe, spent over five years producing the necessary sketches, which would have meant travelling to London and around southern England, but generating no income. In the sporting art genre there are engravings showing a range of important portraits (in some of the Hunt Meet scenes and a dozen in the 'Melton Hunt Breakfast', after Sir Francis Grant) but nothing on the scale of this venture; at one stage in the print's development Mason was planning 100 portraits.

It was an extraordinary undertaking for a provincial publisher, even with a London-based partner. So at a time when the Brighton print market was generally being taken over by more modest and smaller steel engravings, and just before engraved plates virtually disappeared

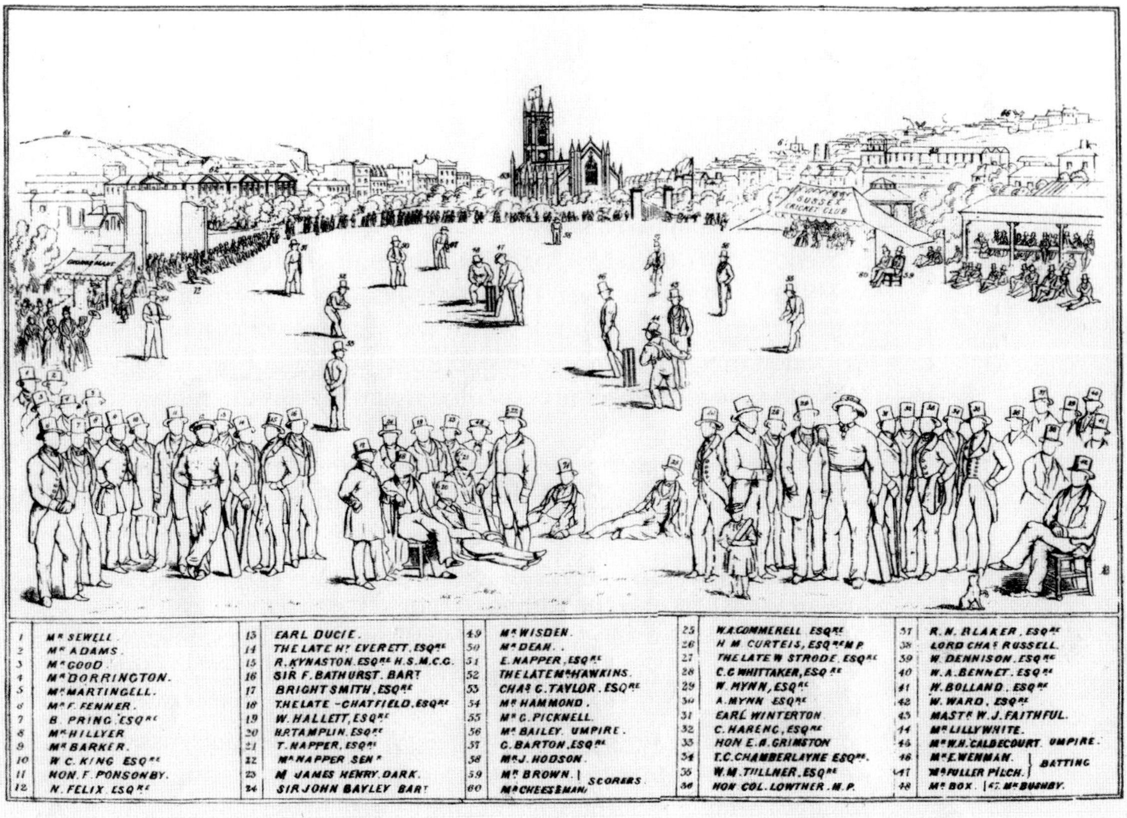

62
Key plate to the Cricket Match print

under the popularity of photography, Mason was harking back to the days when the Brighton publishers could successfully market large and expensive copper-plate engravings. He was no doubt expecting sales throughout Kent, Sussex and London, and remembered *John Baxter's Cricketers' Guide* of 1828, which sold more than 300,000 copies. But with his reluctance to produce smaller steel plates, Mason's methods of production and his understanding of the market were stuck in the past and within six years he was blaming this publication for his bankruptcy.

Apart from the problems arising from Mason's trial, which also came a few months later in 1849, another reason for the poor sales of this large print was probably the popularity of the much cheaper key-plate **[62]**, which portrayed the scene in outline, as an alternative purchase. The key-plate gave a complete list of everyone portrayed, obviously the large original print did not do this and, being much smaller, the key-plate was easier to find hanging space at home. Mason's co-publisher in London for the actual print was E Gambart & Co, but on the key plate, Rudolph Ackermann's sons at 96 Strand were co-publishers with Gambart and Mason.

In Lillywhite's 1844 *Illustrated Hand-Book of Cricket* from Mason and Ackermann, a notice at the back announces 'A very large Engraving of A Cricket Match is now preparing for publication', with Mason and

Ackermann listed as the publishers, no mention of Gambarts, but listing G B Campion as the artist of the townscape behind. However, perhaps due to the long delay in getting the plate ready, Ackermann's pulled out and was not involved in the large print, but might have thought the key-plate would sell well, making participation in that worthwhile.

The plans to produce the 'Cricket Match' were started in September 1843, and it was the following year that saw the last of the Mason/Ackermann joint publications. Ackermann's non-involvement coincided with the parting of the ways (for reasons unknown) and Gambart became Mason's co-publisher. This was another remarkable partnership, although only for this print, for Ernest Gambart became one of the top Victorian fine art publishers and art dealers in London's West End, going on to publish Holman Hunt's 'Light of the World' and Frith's 'Derby Day'.

An additional reason for Ackermann's to pull out could have been a problem they had with a similarly large copper-plate engraving of 'The Derby 1847'. This was the first plate in a proposed series of 'National Races', but few were sold and the series was abandoned[3]. The market for large and expensive copper-plate engravings was already showing signs of decline. With his print of 'Derby Day' Ernest Gambart bucked this trend but of course this was a steel engraving, so its printing and commercial life were greater and the costs per print were less.

For the present-day collector, one unique aspect of Mason's important Victorian cricket print is that there is no other single engraving, of any subject from the nineteenth century, ever to be made the subject of a book, *The Story of a Cricket Picture* by A D Taylor, first published in Hove in 1923[2]. Taylor was a famous collector and authority on the game, who owned the largest known cricketing library.

Three years before the 'Cricket Match' print appeared, in his 1846 *Fashionable Hand-Book* Mason described the Hanover Arms (the land-lord being Thomas Box, the celebrated wicket-keeper) together with the Royal Cricket Ground (also called the Prince of Wales' Ground—where Park Crescent now stands) and mentioned that portrait studies of several leading players had been published, which he dedicated to Benjamin Aislabie, 'the zealous supporter of the Noble Game of Cricket'. His portrait print of Aislabie himself was mentioned in the *Brighton Gazette* editorial of 6 June 1839, where it was described as 'an excellent likeness of the veteran cricketer: and the engraving is beautifully executed'. The *Dictionary of National Biography* makes the point that Aislabie truly loved the game but didn't play it very well. His portrait by Henry Dawe is in the National Portrait Gallery.

In this 1846 *Fashionable Hand-Book* Mason continued:

> 'W. H. Mason has also in the engraver's hands, a very large picture of a Cricket Match, containing upwards of sixty portraits of the leading noblemen and gentlemen connected with, or patrons of the game, as well

as players engaged in the match, and the principal players in England, all of whom are painted from the life, by Mr. William Drummond and Mr. Charles J. Basebe: the attention of all lovers of art, as well as admirers of cricket, is respectfully directed to this important undertaking'.

It seems most likely that the original picture was a watercolour, this being the preferred medium of both artists, and on its key-plate the original is described as a 'drawing'. According to Taylor the original was destroyed by accident. In *Images of Brighton* the Fords write: 'G B Campion . . . was chosen by Mason to prepare the background with the architecture and landscape, although his contribution was not recorded on the print'[4]. Taylor quotes this fact of Campion's involvement from Mason's advertisement in the *Brighton Herald* of September 1843, where Mason named just William Drummond, so presumably Basebe was a later addition to the artistic team.

Looking south, this scene takes the view of the artist standing on the upper floor of the Pavilion building on the northern edge of the Royal Cricket Ground. Brighton Cricket Club was the forerunner of Sussex County Cricket Club and with this continuing history Sussex has a claim to be the oldest county club in England. There was a much earlier and smaller engraving of a cricket match being played on this ground, by George Hunt after H Jones, c1827 [**63**], but the cricket is in the middle distance of Ireland's Royal Brighton Gardens, and there is no watching crowd.

Mason's 'Cricket Match' [**64**] was a copper-plate mixed-method engraving by George Henry Phillips, one of London's most accomplished

63
'Ireland's Royal Brighton Gardens'. Aquatint engraving by George Hunt after H Jones

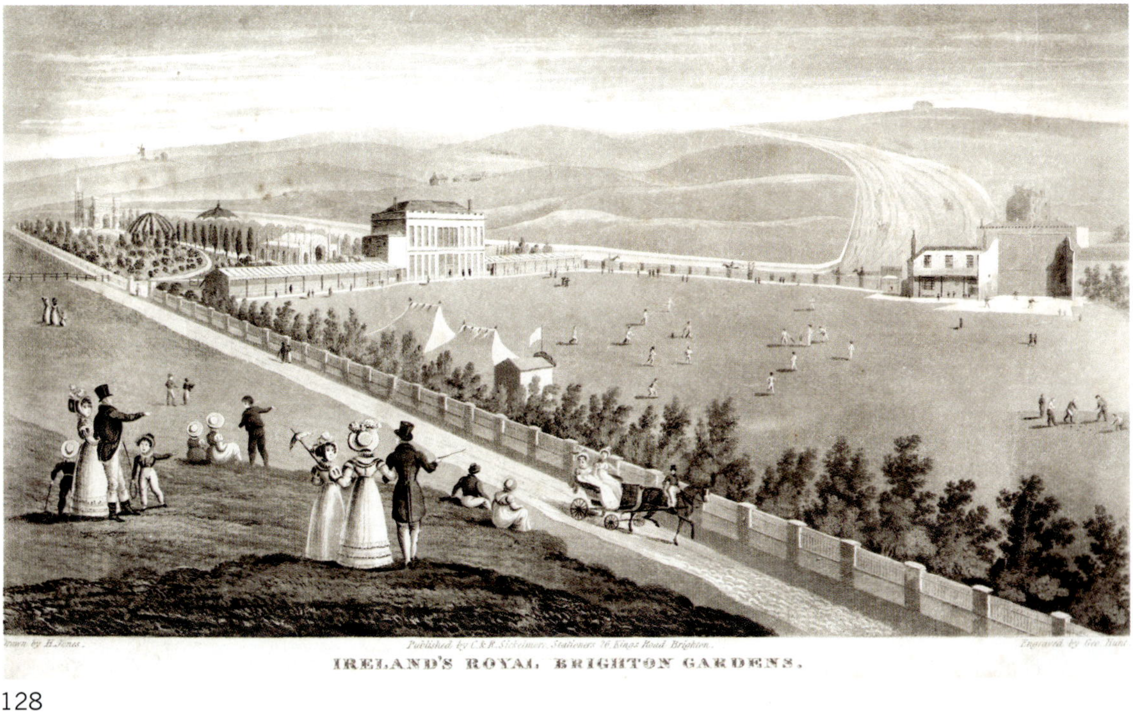

mezzotint portraitists. Today this print can be found in black and white, with early impressions printed on India paper, occasionally with early colouring but often with later colouring, in later impressions with about three inches missing from the left margin, and in still later lithographic form, often with incorrect titles. Taylor describes the print thus: 'Mason's masterpiece—was ever a more popular print engraved? Not only at Lord's, the Oval, Nottingham or Manchester is the picture to be seen, but in every clubhouse in the kingdom. Whether hunting for cricket treasure in the remotest village, or indulging in modern pleasure in a West End hotel, we are faced with the old familiar plate. It haunts us in the wilds of northern Canada, it follows us to the wastes of Western Australia'. Taylor's list of where we might find the print is interesting, in 'hotels and clubhouses', but nothing about the homes of his many cricketing friends he must have visited.

Taylor's mention of Australia is worthy of note, as a few years after Mason's print, similar publications appeared in Australia. J Fowles of Sydney published the 'Grand National Cricket Match' c1857, showing one of the many inter-colonial matches, and having a similar composition to Mason, with an array of spectators in the foreground. Then in 1864 a small woodcut was published in Melbourne—the 'Grand Inter-colonial Cricket Match'—again with the same composition as Mason.

Mason's marketing was quite energetic, sending an early example of the drawing, or possibly more than one, to various cricketing counties to gain public interest and reaction. The *Leicester Journal* (1 August 1845) carried a long editorial: 'Novel Cricket Picture. By courtesy of Mr. W. Mason, of the Repository of Arts, Brighton, we were shown, on Monday, at Lord's . . . a painting on the eve of completion, to depict this, the very finest and the most peculiar of our English pastimes . . . of a tip-top eleven in the field . . . with an infinity of likenesses of aristocratic supporters . . . and players from all quarters of England, collected on the spacious and picturesque ground of the celebrated Sussex specimen. Mr. Mason has selected a match between the two crack counties of Kent and Sussex.' The article also explains that the 'landscape scenery is from the easel of Mr. Hine, and exquisitely painted it is'. Henry George Hine (1811-1895) was a Brighton-born watercolourist and wood engraver, who worked for *Punch* and the *Illustrated London News*, although as explained below, he was not the final background artist.

On 23 May 1846 the *Cambridge Press* ran an advertisement from J Dimmock, Repository of Arts, Sydney Street, Cambridge, inviting 'all lovers of Cricket and the Fine Arts to inspect Mr. H. Mason's National Picture of a Cricket Match, which we will have the honour to exhibit for this day only. The picture contains nearly one hundred portraits'. Mason family relationships are unknown and we can only wonder why it was not shown in his younger brother's gallery in Cambridge—John B Mason had taken over their father's business just four years earlier. On

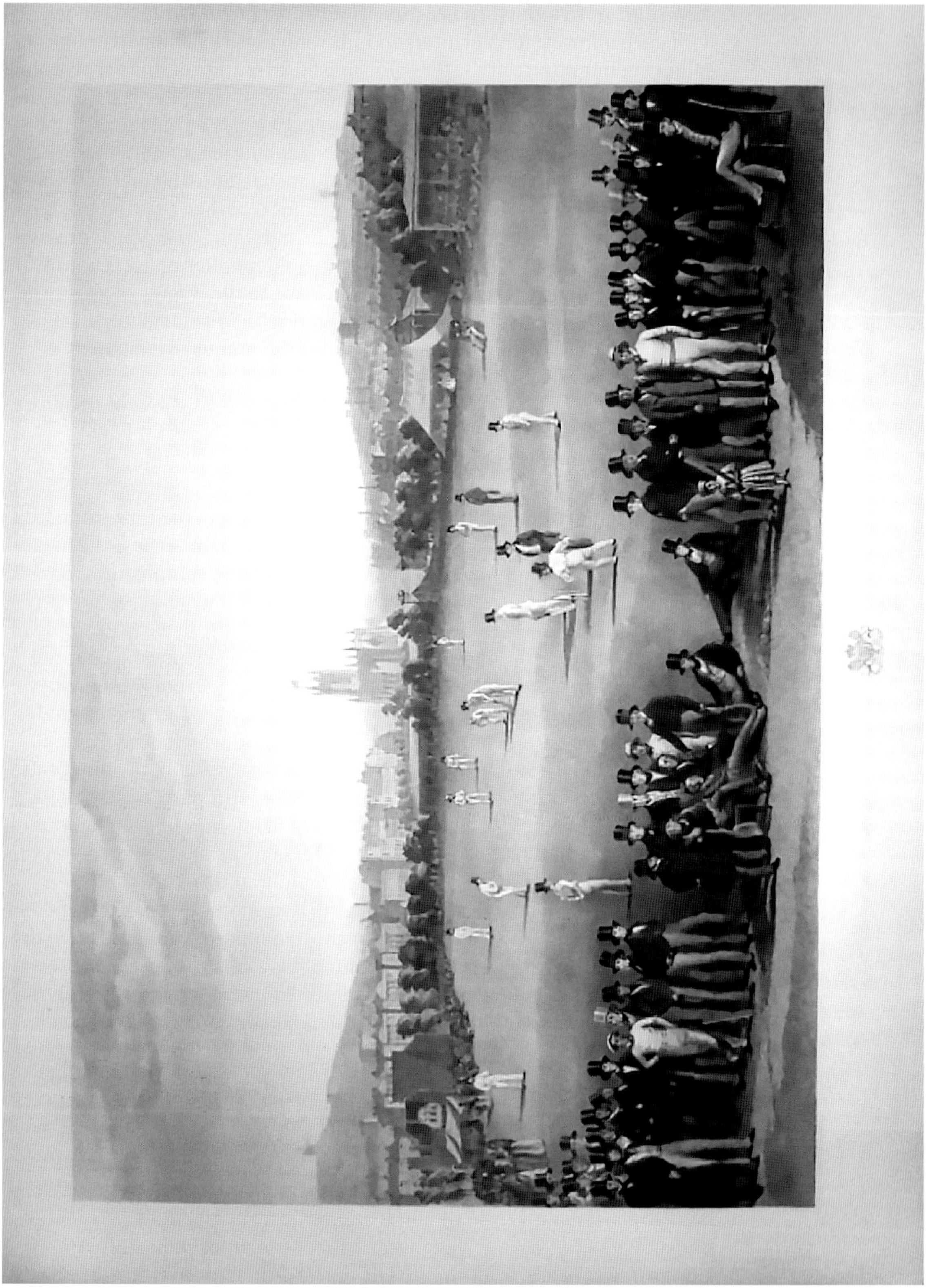

30 May 1846 the *Bristol Mercury* announced: 'To Cricketers. Mason's National Picture of a Cricket-Match between the counties of Kent and Sussex, will be On View, until 6th June, at Mr. Mitchell's Royal Albert Rooms, 37 College Green, Bristol.'

Taylor reports that after the first impressions for subscribers and early sales, the plate was rested for about 30 years, but gave no reason. During this time the other slightly smaller lithographic plates were published, sometimes with spurious dates prior to the original 1849 and sometimes misrepresented as 'Hants v. England' or as a 'Match at Lord's'. In *Images of Brighton* Ford also mentions the 30-year gap after the initial printing, adding that the copper plate was eventually sold by the photographer Hawkins, who had taken over Mason's gallery in 1883, four years after Mason's death. This implies that in bankruptcy Mason had retained the original plate but as neither he nor his creditors saw any profit in using it, when he moved out of 108 King's Road he left it behind. And the suggested 30-year lapse in any printing from the plate takes us from the original publication date of 1849 to the year of Mason's death, 1879.

Today the original plate is owned and still used for sales of the print by Thomas Ross and Co, a London-based printing company with the world's largest collection of 18th and 19th century plates. Its safe journey from Hawkins the photographer to Ross the printer is unknown.

In addition to the copper-plate engraving a small chromolithograph edition was published [**61**], about five by nine inches, which was finished by hand in watercolour with the publication line saying, incorrectly, that it was 'painted by W.H. Mason', noting it was 'reproduced from a print in the Brighton Museum and published for the Brighton & Hove Gas Co'.

Taylor writes: 'as a matter of history the publication of the print all but resulted in the bankruptcy of Mason's repository'. He gives no further explanation but from the bankruptcy papers we now know that this print was cited by Mason as the cause of his financial problems. Despite quoting several claims to the contrary, Taylor insisted the match depicted was never played, and this seems reasonable. Mason may well have thought that depicting one particular match would limit the print's appeal. While it is titled as a 'Match between Sussex and Kent', a number of the foreground portraits in the crowd are not directly connected with either county, no actual playing date is given and in advertising at the time Mason referred to it as his 'National Print of a Cricket Match'.

The crowd in the foreground included Sir Frederick Bathurst, who played for Hampshire and was president of the MCC in 1857, Sir John Bayley, who lived in London was a member of the Inner Temple and MCC President in 1844, and Lord Charles Russell who played for the MCC from 1833 to 1846. Four players in the print died before the publication date. To these objections to it being an actual match must be

64
'The Cricket Match between Sussex and Kent, at Brighton'. Copper-plate mixed method engraving by George Henry Phillips after William Drummond and Charles Basebe. Published May 1849 by W H Mason, Repository of Arts, King's Road, Brighton and E Gambart, Berners Street, London

added the fact that the construction of Park Crescent, designed by Amon Henry Wilds, was commenced in 1848, the year prior to the print's publication, and by this date the Royal Brunswick Ground, near Adelaide Crescent, was already in use[5]. George Washer, in his *Complete Record of Sussex County Cricket 1728-1957*, states that the last match played on the Royal Brighton Ground was between Sussex and All England in September 1847, which Sussex won by 27 runs. Bishop[6] noted that the ground was said to be 'the finest piece of turf in England'. It is interesting to see players in top hats. Taylor noted, 'there used to be a special law embedded in the code—Hat knocked on wicket'.

To summarise the changing plans for the print, Taylor cites an announcement that Mason first put in the local press[7] in September 1843 that it was to contain 'about 50 portraits of the most celebrated players of the present day, also many of the Nobility and Gentry amateur supporters of this noble and scientific game . . . the landscape incidents etc., etc., by G.B. Campion'. This announcement did not appear in the *Brighton Gazette* of September 1843, neither in the available copies of the *Brighton Herald*. Unfortunately that year is not available on the British Newspaper Archive website and The Keep's collection omits the weeks of 9 and 30 September, so it is assumed Taylor found the text in one of those. He describes his discovery of it in one of these September issues in enthusiastic language.

An announcement then appeared in *Lillywhite's Hand-Book* in 1844, again promising 'about fifty portraits'. A second subscription was advertised in 1845, when 100 portraits were suggested, then in Mason's 1846 *Hand-Book* 60 or more were promised. In June 1847 he announced the print was 'in a very forward state, contains upwards of 100 portraits, and will be published at the latter end of the season'. The year 1848 passed with no print. Finally, in February 1849, Mason sent each of the eight-guinea subscribers a 24-page pamphlet announcing the details of the print, and in May of that year delivery commenced of the artist's proofs, printed on India paper at eight guineas each and featuring 66 portraits, plus six named topographical features of the town.

The reasons for the delays are now clear. Mason was guided by public reaction to the initial watercolour—or versions of it—as they toured around southern England. The landscape artist was Hine in an 1845 advertisement while the watercolour was on tour, but noted as Campion in 1843 and 1844 announcements. There may have been trial watercolours by both artists.

Mason appears to have been torn between the two during the six years leading up to publication, Campion being his final choice. Mason added Basebe's hand to Drummond's work on the portraits and made several changes to the number of characters to be included. All these alterations would have necessitated different watercolours, which were taken to various counties for exhibition and promotion. The final choice of Campion as the landscape artist might have been because Hine was rather a rustic and 'pretty' watercolourist, whereas Campion would have given a more robust portrayal of the townscape setting. One wonders if Mason destroyed all preliminary drawings or watercolours or if some remain undiscovered, although Taylor's suggestion that the original was destroyed by accident hints that the destruction of all the versions was a bit too efficient.

In February 1849 the final watercolour painting for the print was put on exhibition by Mason in the Newburgh Rooms. The *Brighton Gazette* of 15 February carried an advertisement by Mason:

'Under the Patronage of His Royal Highness Prince Albert. Free Exhibition (by ticket) of W. H. Mason's National Picture of a Cricket Match at Brighton, between Sussex and Kent, containing upwards of sixty portraits . . . on Wednesday next, February 21st and during the week – Tickets upon application at W. H. Mason's Repository of Arts, or at Mr. Edwin Wright's Library.'

The Royal Newburgh Assembly Rooms were in St Margaret's Place, off Cannon Place. William IV is said to have attended their opening in 1833 and they were a popular social venue for many years. Today they form part of the Metropole Exhibition Halls. In the quote below it's interesting to read the comment of regret regarding the development of Park Crescent on the old ground.

The *Brighton Gazette* (22 February 1849) carried the following editorial:

> MASON'S CRICKET PICTURE.
> This picture is at length completed and is now being exhibited at the Newburgh Rooms. As a work of art it surpasses everything we have seen before, both as regards the fidelity of the numerous portraits with which the foreground is studied, and the beauty of the painting; and on looking at this picture we regret that so picturesque a spot as the Royal Brighton Cricket Ground should have been converted to other purposes than the manly game of cricket. There are nearly 70 portraits all taken from life. Among the most conspicuous are Earl Winterton, Mr. Bright Smith, the late Mr. Strode, Mr. W.A. Commerell, the late Mr. Chatfield (of Wick), the late Mr. Everett, Mr. R. Kynaston, Mr. W. Hallett, Mr. W. Ward, Mr. H. P. Tamplin, Sir John Brayley, Bart., Mr. A. Mynn, Mr. W. Mynn, Adams, Hillyer, Mr. N. Felix, and the Kent cricketers generally; and amidst the throng is our own "Little Wisden", who cannot be mistaken. To account for his not being in the field with the Sussex cricketers, we may mention that the eleven was formed before he "came out". Upwards of three years have been consumed in the completion of this picture; and we have no doubt that all supporters of the game will enrol their names as subscribers.

Finally, in May 1849, five years and eight months from its original announcement, impressions of the most famous cricket engraving ever published became available. In the *Brighton Gazette* (16 August 1849) Mason again advertised under the heading 'Mr. Mason's National Print of a Cricket Match' and 'respectfully announces that his Cricket

Engraving is now ready, and offers the following prices: Prints 3 Guineas. Proofs 6 Guineas. Artist's Proofs 8 Guineas'. 'Should any subscriber not have received his copy, Mr. Mason will feel obliged by informing him'. Presumably an 'artist's proof', apart from being among the early pulls from the plate and printed on India paper, was a copy actually coloured by Drummond or Basebe.

The Era newspaper, which by 1856 was claiming to be 'the largest newspaper in the world' and was known for its features on sport and the theatre, carried a glowing report in its issue of 19 August 1849:

> W.H. Mason's National Print of a Cricket Match (Between the Counties of Sussex and Kent) at Brighton. Introducing characteristic portraits of the players engaged in the match, as well as many noblemen and other gentlemen, patrons of the Noble Art of Cricket. Mason's Repository of Arts, Brighton, and Gambert & Co., Berners Street, London'.
>
> The above are the particulars of a print, just now published, dedicated, by express permission, to Prince Albert, and possessing extraordinary claims to the notice of the public, particularly the large portion of it who take an interest in, or simply admire, the manly game of Cricket. It is long since a print of so much peculiar interest has come before us. In the first place, it is, as a work of art, no common production. The above title is, of itself, no ordinary recommendation; but appropriate as it is, the merits of the work are not to be told in a few lines. We have given the description in question as a perfectly truthful one so far as it goes; but it remains for us to say, that a prettier and more spirited picture, independently of its value in regard to the likenesses it sets forth, could not be easily conceived. There is an artistic arrangement of the figures, so admirably contrived that nothing is sacrificed to it, and the scene, of course, represents that game as it is played, introducing, altogether, no fewer than sixty individuals, whose features can be recognised, besides others who complete the background. The field itself is made more picturesque by the view that flanks it, and the church, the houses, and the foliage are drawn with care and effect, and finished with great skill. The fidelity of the likenesses is striking, but there is one equally remarkable feature in the entire engraving, and that is the similarity of the stature of the cricketers. They are evidently all of one genus – "all of one kidney". Here and there one is conspicuously more athletic or tall than his fellows; such as A. Mynn, whose athletic proportions are exhibited by the absence of his coat, and the same may be said of N. Felix, both of whom front a crowd of admirers in everyday apparel. In the play Messrs. E. Wenham and Fuller Pilch are batting, and the former is about to strike, while Lillywhite is in the act of bowling, and the picture is complete to the minutest particular. You look upon a meeting of well-knit frames, ranging mostly below the common height, but displaying an expansion of chest and width of shoulders calculated for strength, activity and endurance. All this is remarkable even among the veterans, and there are many. The general effect of the picture is pleasant in the extreme, but we have not space to particularise all its attractions. Indeed the print is fit to hang beside the choicest engravings, and is a gem of itself; but cricket is a national sport, and

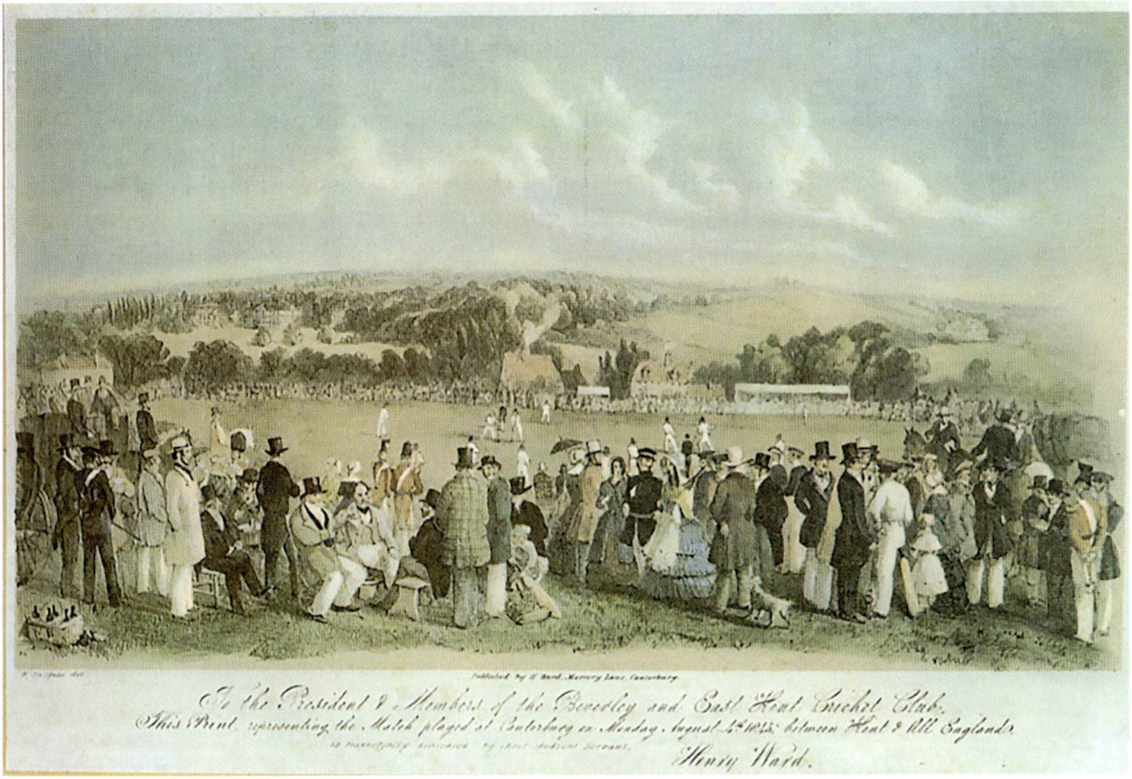

65
H Ward of Canterbury: 'The Match Played at Canterbury on Monday August 4th 1845 between Kent and All England'

> those who would see a charming representation of the game, exhibiting forms and faces of those whose achievements when the performers shall have passed away, and have an additional reason for desiring to possess so interesting a souvenir and so beautiful a plate' [8]

Despite this glowing praise, the story behind the origins of the idea and innovative composition of this print is complicated. There had been a similar lithograph by W Burgess, published nearly four years earlier by H Ward of Canterbury, 'The Match Played at Canterbury on Monday August 4th 1845 between Kent and All England' [**65**].

Although it is less than half the size of Mason's, being just 30cm by 49cm, it is a similar composition. There are about 30 spectators dominating the foreground, seven of them facing the artist as direct portraits, and the match going on in the middle distance. The print is dedicated to the president and members of the Beverley and East Kent Cricket Club. At the time of this Canterbury print, Mason's idea for his publication had been advertised for nearly two years, when he had promised 50 portraits, and some of the players in this match at Canterbury would have already been approached by Mason.

Ward, the Canterbury publisher, undoubtedly stole a march on Mason but it is not known if he came to this composition independently or if he conceived the idea of this previously untried arrangement of identified spectators in front of the match itself from talking to some of the Kent players. Alternatively he saw Mason's newspaper advertisements or the watercolour itself on exhibition at Lord's (it does not appear to have been sent for exhibition in Canterbury). However, despite the fact that Kent had been the most successful county side during the 1840s, the impact of this very local image in Canterbury, at the time and certainly when Taylor was writing, was as nothing compared with Mason's 'National Cricket Match'. It is also worth remembering that Taylor was writing over seventy years after its publication and yet was still describing it as 'Mason's masterpiece—was ever a more popular print engraved?'

The point here is that prior to this 1845 Canterbury print, none of the known cricket engravings had ever featured the spectators—they all just showed the match itself. This is true of such publishers as John Bowles in the 1740s, the John Wallis *Laws of the Noble Game* of the 1780s, the few Francis Hayman prints, and the H Jones Brighton print [**63**]. The 1827 Robert Cruickshank print of the Darnall Ground in Yorkshire had a sketchy view of the crowd on the far side of the pitch, and the established Victorian sporting artist James Pollard had no spectators in his 1824 cricket print.

Ward's 1845 Canterbury engraving showing the large crowd of spectators in the foreground, with some portraits facing us, was a major development in the portrayal of cricket, probably inspired by Mason's advertisements. But Mason's unique and revolutionary composition four years later, was to have every man on the field, and in the watching crowd, facing the artist rather than the game. Every Mason portrait, in the crowd and playing, was a known cricketing personality, which was not the case in Canterbury.

Never before nor since has there been a single composition putting together so many well-known cricketing faces, or indeed faces from any 19th century sport. Considering Mason's idea for his publication had been in the public eye, and certainly in the social circle surrounding cricket, for nearly two years before Ward's print appeared, it does seem reasonable to think that Mason was responsible for this transformation in the portrayal of cricket, even if he was not the first to publish it. In the 19th century sporting art genre, cricket is one of the rarest subjects and Mason's print is the largest. Within this context, his publication is the only engraving to portray so many cricketing personalities of the period. No other 19th century sporting print had such accolades in the local and national press and, as mentioned, no other single 19th century engraving has been made the sole subject of a book.

The Sickelmore engraving [**63**], issued about 20 years earlier than Mason's, is viewing the same Brighton cricket ground from the south, with a match in progress, the artist viewing from the hill that will later carry the Ditching Road out of the town centre. Left of centre is the pavilion building from which Mason's artists portrayed 'The Cricket Match' of 1849. The carriage road in the foreground later became Park Crescent Terrace. On the far right of the scene is the wide track-way, the

Race Hill Road, that became Elm Grove, going up the hill away from the Hanover Arms. James Taylor in his 1827 *Royal Brighton Guide* describes the pavilion as a 'spacious building, with awnings right and left, containing on the lower story a commodious bar, reading-rooms, and various other apartments, over which is a saloon and promenade room, measuring 80 feet in length, and 30 in breadth'. Sickelmore expands on this description: 'on the ground floor are various parlours or sitting rooms, reading rooms, a well-constructed bar, with other tavern requisites, upon the best scale of comfortable accommodation.'[9]

Prior to this 'Cricket Match' print, Mason was involved with *Lillywhite's Illustrated Hand-Book of Cricket*, which he co-published with Ackermann & Co in 1844, having previously published in 1841, as single portraits, the four plates of professionals **[66]** and four of gentlemen

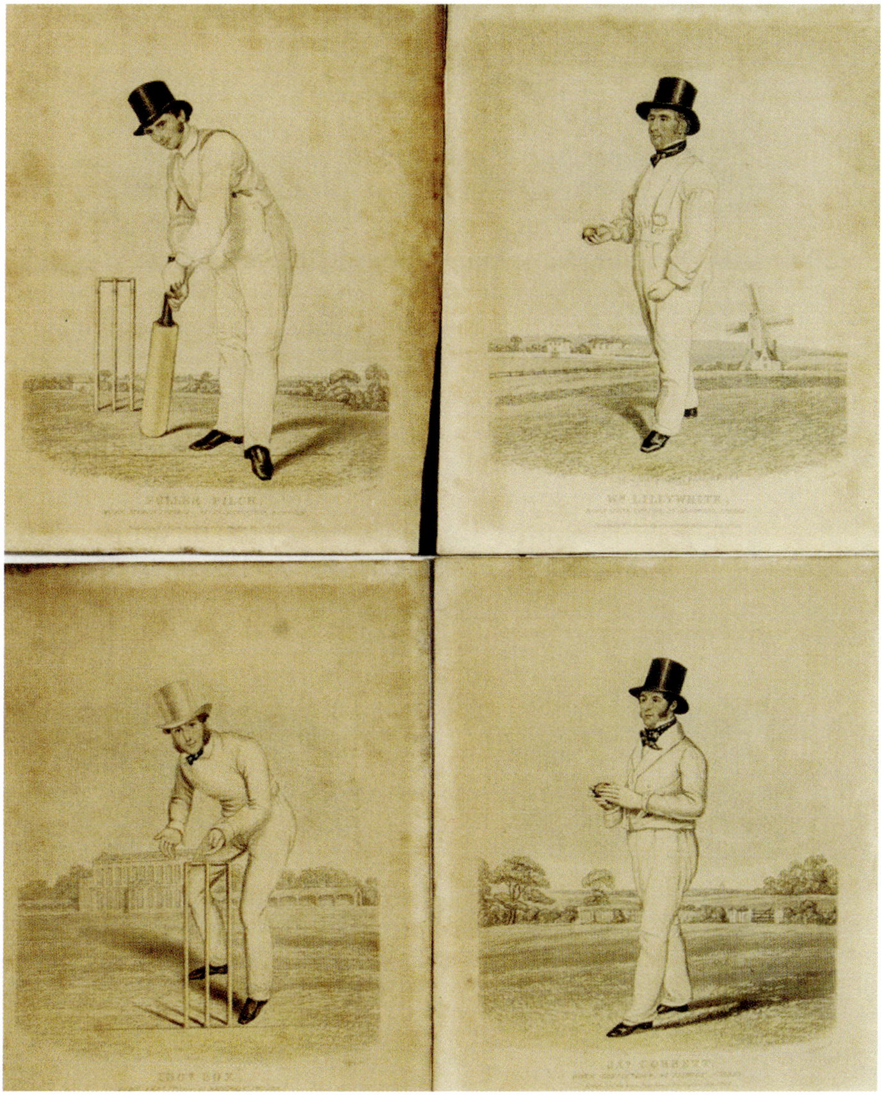

66
The four plates of professional players: Fuller Pilch, William Lillywhite, Thomas Box and James Corbett. Copper plate line and aquatint engravings by Charles Hunt after Charles Basebe, in *Lillywhite's Illustrated Hand-Book of Cricket*, published by Mason & Ackermann, October 1841 to 1844

players that are included in the *Hand-Book*. This small book reproduced the 'Laws of Cricket' as confirmed by the Marylebone Cricket Club and included words of advice to players. One note of guidance to bowlers was 'Do not make a point of appealing to the umpire, unless you feel confident the reply will be favourable, it becomes unpleasant to all parties if the appeal is made frivolously'.

It was in 1844 that F William Lillywhite retired from playing, started selling cricket equipment, set up a scoring tent at Lord's from where he sold score-sheets, and began independently publishing his own *Hand-Book of Cricket*. He relinquished his lease on the Temple Fields Ground, where Montpelier Crescent now stands near the Seven Dials in Brighton, and moved to Islington. In Palm Coast, Florida, there is the Lillywhite Family Museum, owned by his great-great-grandson, John W Lillywhite. FW's son, James Lillywhite (1825-1882), together with other family members, founded the famous London sporting goods store in 1863.

Following on from Mason's many cricket publications, around 1850 it was realised that something more convenient than sealing-wax was necessary to firms with a reasonable amount of correspondence to seal and post every day. It is not known if this was Mason's original idea but he certainly produced the solution with his 'Cricketer's Adhesive Envelope Wafers'. Mason had all of his cricket publications re-engraved in miniature, presumably on steel plates, onto small adhesive wafers with which to seal envelopes. They were retailed in boxes of 50 for one shilling, until gummed envelopes came to the market. Taylor noted that to his knowledge there is just one box still in existence.

Taylor also mentioned Mason's proposed *Illustrated Cricketers Journal*, extensively advertised in 1849 and 'devoted expressly to the game and produced in a style of art fully equal to the best of the illustrated journals of the period'. Unfortunately the venture failed to bear fruit, possibly because of the time and effort being put into selling the 'Cricket Match', together with Mason defending himself in court.

[1] H F & A P Squire: *Pre-Victorian Sussex Cricket*. Ditchling: Ditchling Press, 1951
[2] Alfred D Taylor: *The Story of a Cricket Picture*. Hove: Emery & Son, 1923, republished Wakefield: S R Publishers, 1972, p31
[3] Ford: *op.cit.* 1983, p115
[4] John & Jill Ford: *Images of Brighton*. Richmond-upon-Thames: Saint Helena Press, 1981, p89
[5] *Brighton Gazette*, 12 July 1849. Advertisement for the Royal Brunswick Ground
[6] Bishop: *op.cit*, 1880, p102
[7] Taylor: *op.cit*,1923, p27
[8] *The Era*, 19 August 1849, p10
[9] Richard Sickelmore: *Sickelmore's Descriptive Views of Brighton*. Brighton: R Sickelmore Jr, 1824, p67

7 W H Mason's contribution

Mason's historic contribution: some important publications

Mason's advertisement in the *Brighton Guardian* of 11 December 1833 announced his first Brighton publication, the aquatint engraving of the 'Panorama of Brighton', which he described as 'Under the Immediate Patronage of Her Most Gracious Majesty, Queen Adelaide'. In fact, from the frontispiece illustration of the 'Panorama' [**45**] it can be seen that the 'Royal Patronage' was simply that he 'most humbly dedicated' the print to Queen Adelaide. Apart from being Mason's first Brighton publication it was also the first of many joint ventures between Rudolph Ackermann's sons and Mason[1].

According to maps of the period[2], Ship Street's entrance onto the seafront was the dividing line between the East Cliff and the West Cliff. Suiting Mason's sense of self-promotion, this 'Panorama' publication portrayed just the West Cliff, so as you unfolded it from its covers, the first building you saw was his gallery on the corner of Ship Street, and the scene went westwards from there. This meant that the oldest hotel in Brighton, The Old Ship on the opposite corner, was not included in the scene.

This engraving was a bold undertaking for a first publication. There had been an earlier Brighton panorama published in 1824 by Robert Havell, with a length of 330cm, but Mason had outstripped this with a length of 462cm. Strictly speaking the title 'panorama' referred to the original 18th century 360-degree visual extravaganzas, of which the painting of London in the 'Regent's Park Colosseum', published in aquatint by Ackermann in 1829, was a fine example. However, the meaning of the word changed to include a simple 'full-width view' and such is the importance of Mason's 'Panorama' in Brighton's print-publishing history that Brighton Museum has produced a complete facsimile of it, although the explanatory notes mistakenly date Mason's business as 'from the 1820s onwards'.

By 1839 he was involved in the publication of C Derby's panorama entitled 'Brighton, 1839'—a coloured lithograph that Mason sold in aid of the Sussex County Hospital. This print did show the East and West Cliff sections of the seafront but as viewed from the seaward end of the Chain Pier, so unlike Mason's first version, the architectural details are indistinct. Mason's next two publications were the portrait of 'The Rev. Sortain' in late 1833, and the pair 'Brighton Hurdle Race, Dec 20th 1833 – The Start – Coming In', presumably issued in January 1834. The pair were drawn by George Earp, taken from sketches by W H Mason himself and engraved in aquatint by Charles Hunt. These scenes represent one of only three examples of Mason's own artwork in his publications. They were also the first of the very few sporting prints featuring Brighton.

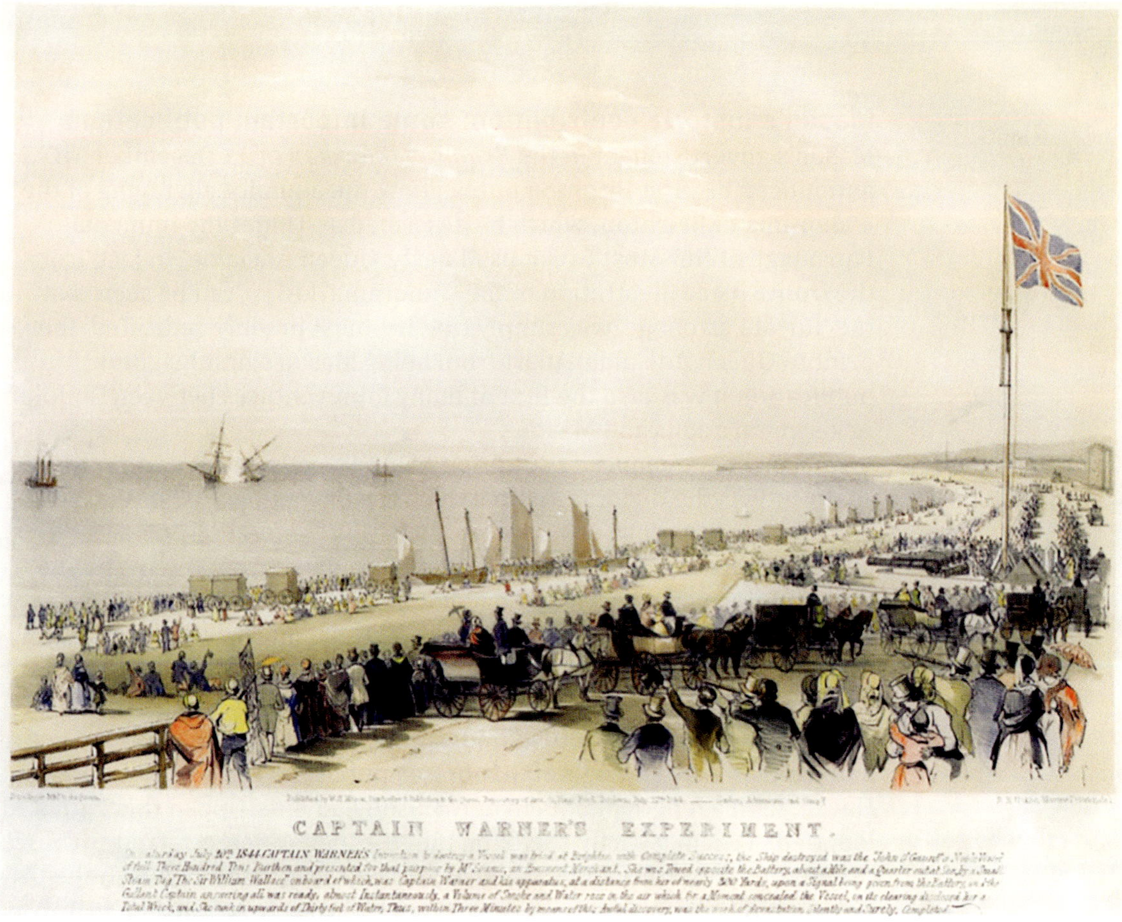

67
'Captain Warner's Experiment'. Lithograph by Day & Haghe after Richard Henry Nibbs. Published by W H Mason, 81 King's Road and Ackermann & Co, London, 27 July 1844

In addition to the panorama there are six other known joint Ackermann/Mason publications of Brighton. Among them was one of the 'Interior of the Royal Chapel, Brighton', aquatinted by Hunt, with the c1835 publication line reading 'W.H. Mason (Printseller to the Queen) Repository of Arts, Ship Street, Ackermann & Co., London, and Mason, Cambridge', and then this 'Captain Warner' lithograph [**67**]. This was published by the two galleries in 1844. Previously they had published the 'Swiss Cottage, Chalybgate', (sic), a lithograph of c1837. This is a rare unrecorded print of the cottage that stood at the entrance to the Chalybeate, now St Ann's Well Gardens. The remaining three joint publications were the 'View of Brighton's New Parochial Burial Ground', an aquatint after George Earp Jr, showing a proposed but never executed development, 'The Beach, Brighton', published in 1842, showing a lady with her back to us gazing at the Chain Pier, and 'The Esplanade, Brighton', both lithographs by Charles Basebe and each published with Ackermann & Co, London.

The 'Captain Warner' lithograph detailed one of the most exciting spectacles seen on Brighton seafront in the 19th century. Captain Warner, on board his own boat, destroyed the 300-ton vessel the John o'Gaunt from a distance of 300 yards, by what the Captain claimed was an 'invisible shell'. The text on the engraving reads: '. . . the signal being given from the battery, and the gallant Captain answering all was ready, almost instantaneously a volume of smoke and water rose in the air which for the moment concealed the vessel, on its clearing disclosed her a total wreck, and she sunk in upwards of thirty feet of water'.

When the delight and amazement of the crowd, many of whom had come down from London to watch, had passed, some suspicions surfaced. Correctly as it turned out. Warner was a charlatan trying to sell his military 'inventions' to the British government. Mason published this print within seven days of the event, and as he ends the text with the words: 'thus within three minutes by means of this awful discovery, was the work of devastation silently and surely completed,' he, together with the Ackermann sons as his publishing partners, obviously believed Captain Warner's claims, as indeed did the government at the time.

Two years before the print's publication *Hansard* records that Warner was the subject of a House of Commons debate on 21 June 1842, when Sir Robert Peel reported that he had privately seen the 'extraordinary effects produced by Captain Warner's invention'. At the time he suggested the matter be referred to the Admiralty or the Board of Ordinance for investigation by experiment 'on a large scale and under adverse circumstances'. Two days after the Brighton display, during the House of Commons debate of 22 July, Lord Ingestre read out a letter he had signed, together with C B T Dickenson RN and W H Henderson RN, trying to diffuse the developing suspicions. They wrote that the operation against the John o'Gaunt had been under 'their management and control and that the explosion did not take place from any combustible matter either on board or alongside the ship, but was caused by Captain Warner . . . at a distance of about 300 yards'.

However, articles appeared in local papers nationwide. One typical example was as far away as the *Dundee Courier* on 6 August 1844. The paper quoted an examination of the John o'Gaunt by four pilots from Shoreham Port who found new 'warp ropes' (a rope about three inches diameter) in an unusual configuration around the ship—'the ropes could be traced under the bottom of the vessel'—and which would 'appear to all nautical men as unusual and extraordinary'.

The Captain was still being debated 10 years later, during which decade Warner had avoided all attempts to get him to divulge his secret, all the while trying to sell it to the government. In the Hansard record of the House of Lords debate on 14 May 1852, Lord Vivian referred to scientific investigations but that 'it appeared to him that Captain Warner, at the eleventh hour, had always shelved such an inquiry'. There were five separate prints published on this Brighton beach event, including one in the *Illustrated London News* and one in the *Pictorial Times*. Like Mason's offering, four of them showed the large animated crowd on the shoreline.

Mason's 'Capt. Warner' print was published in July 1844, but in May of the previous year his publishing partners, Ackermann & Co., had been forced to announce in The Times (5 May 1843), 'we find ourselves compelled to suspend our payments'. The *London Standard* (27 June 1843) stated Ackermann's liabilities to be £30,664 and their assets £28,314. The creditors meeting seemed an amicable affair and the company continued until 1856. This did not have any impact on Mason's supply of prints or his output but the year of 1844 was the last for their joint publications until the key-plate for 'The Cricket Match between Sussex and Kent' in 1849.

As explained earlier, the Ackermann sons were involved in the key-plate but not with the cricket print itself. But this virtual end to the joint publications did not affect Mason's activities. From 1846 through to 1852 he produced many fine prints including the large lithograph of 'Pool Valley during the Storm' [**50**], the 'Cricket Match' print itself, and eight prints in parts one and two of 'Brighton Illustrated'.

On 9 May 1844 the *Brighton Gazette* carried a notice of the trial of one Charles Gill, who was charged with robbing Mason of £70 cash while he was in the Exeter Coffee House, Strand. If the report is accurate, with that amount of money, almost £8,000 today, Mason was no doubt on a stock-buying visit and, being just a year after Ackermann's announcement, could have been bringing his account with them up to date and intending to buy some discounted goods to help their cashflow. This amount of money would indicate that, while Mason started off in business with goods on consignment from Ackermann's in the 1830s, by this time he was buying stock outright. If not all of that stolen money was recovered, the loss may have been instrumental in Mason not paying Thomas Wisden's claim of £450 just three months later, with the resulting court case (see page 85).

Returning to their joint publications, in addition to local Brighton subjects, Mason and Ackermann produced 'A Wick'ed Subject' [**60**] from a series of 'Irish Political Satire' engravings in 1843; 'The Exterior and Interior of the Royal Chapel, St. James's' published by Mason, Brighton, Ackermann & Co, and Charles Tilt, 86 Fleet Street, London; 'The New Windsor Pear (or Magnum Bonum)' published by L M Lefevre, Newman Street, London, Mason in Brighton and Ackermann & Co., London; 'Queen Victoria' after Henry Dawe, published by Mason in Brighton, Ackermann & Co, London, J B Brown in Windsor and Dawe himself from 6 Bartholomew Place, Kentish Town (Henry Dawe, Mason's father-in-law, had a house just three miles from Mason's early childhood home in Shoreditch). More joint publications included 'The Rt. Hon the Earl of Egremont', a mezzotint after Thomas Lupton (1791-1873) published by Ackermann & Co, 96 Strand and Mason in Brighton, and a lithograph with W F Taylor of Windsor showing 'Eton from the North Terrace'.

Another couple of trio publications by Mason, Ackermann and Charles Tilt again, included the stipple engraving of 'HRH Prince Albert of Saxe Coburg Gotha, KG', engraved by E Hacker after Henry Dawe, issued in 1840, and the poem 'Flora and Pomona's Fete'. This last piece was dedicated to the 'Floral and Horticultural Societies of England' by Elizabeth Steele Perkins and was successful enough to run to six editions by 1838. In 1844 Mason and Ackermann published *Lillywhite's Illustrated Hand-Book of Cricket*, which included various portraits and 'The Laws as confirmed by the Mary-le-bone Club'.

With the end of their publishing partnership in sight, there is one strange print that sounds as though it was collaboration but without mentioning Ackermann by name. It is the portrait of the cricketer John Wisden, a lithograph by Thomas Fairland after Mason's company artist C J Basebe. The imprint reads 'W. H. Mason, Repository of Arts, Brighton & London, May 5th 1849', just four days after the 'Cricket Match' engraving.

Mason was the largest local publisher of what could be termed 'fine art' Brighton views in aquatint and lithographic form. Some of them were quite large prints, obviously to hang in important positions in wealthy homes. But the commercial aspect of some of his smaller prints was four-fold. They might be printed as illustrations within a guide-book, sold singly for the customer to keep with other prints in a folio for an evening's entertainment, or to be framed for hanging. Finally, many were sold as letter-headings.

68
Letter-heading illustrating 'Marine Parade Brighton', published by W H Mason, undated with no artist/engraver named. This shows the central fold with page four and page one. Overall size eight by 10 inches

Such Victorian letter-headings were typically on a sheet of paper folded to give four pages, with the illustration at the top of page one [**68**]. They varied in size from eight by five inches folded (eight by 10 inches unfolded) up to nine by seven-and-a-half inches (nine by 15 inches unfolded) and could be purchased coloured or uncoloured; they can been found as aquatints, lithographs and steel engravings, and a number of the illustrations in this text are from letter-headings. Steel engraved letter-headings from William Grant were a few pence to buy; from Mason they were a shilling or more.

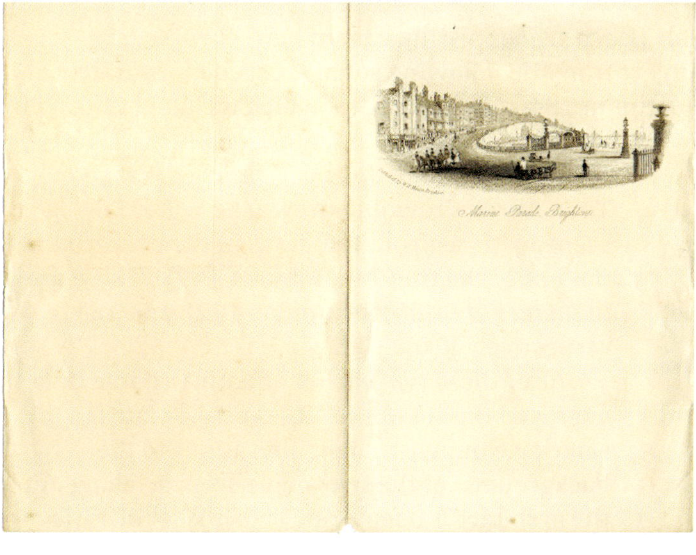

Mason's most favoured artist was the local George Earp Jr with 19 publications, Basebe was involved with 10 prints either as artist or lithographer, then George Bryant Campion (1795-1870), drawing master at the Royal Military Academy, Woolwich[3], with Mason producing six publications after his work.

The Repository's subject matter found so far includes numerous cricketing, clerical and political figures, and one legal portrait. There are various royal portraits and Queen Victoria's visit to the town, views of the seafront townscape and residential terraces, many seaside/beach scenes and fishing boats, seven views of the two piers and 15 views of churches or related subjects. Mason published six views of the Pavilion, three horse-racing scenes, the local transport infrastructure and two stations, views of the Downs, Arundel, Hurstpierpoint, Seaford, Eton and a series of views of China, India and South Africa.

Mason's portrait publications are worth looking at in detail, as he exhibits a wide range of contacts with locally important figures, and some national personalities, as did his father. His clerical publications include Dr Edward Pusey; Charles Kennaway, the canon of Gloucester Cathedral; Robert Henderson; the Rev. James Anderson; Robertson of Brighton; Joseph Sortain, the Countess of Huntingdon's minister in North Street; Dr Martin Luther and a print in tribute to Hugh Latimer, the Reformation martyr. He produced portrait plates of Sir David Scott, a local magistrate and director of the East India Company, the London lawyer William Seymour, George Richard Pechell, Brighton's MP for 35 years and the Astronomer Royal, G B Airy. The cricketing subjects were numerous, including plates of William Lillywhite, Benjamin Aislabie, John Wisden and, of course, the 66 portraits in the 'Cricket Match' print.

The list of artists, authors and actors portrayed, some published from photographs by Mason Jr, includes the caricaturist John Doyle, the artist William Henry Hunt, the actors Charles Keen and W H Chippendale, and the author William Harrison Ainsworth. There were several publications of Queen Victoria and Prince Albert and one of the Earl of Egremont. Also among his photographic prints was one of Abraham Lincoln. This range of sitters gives Mason a unique position in Brighton's publishing history, and for the plates of Robert Henderson and James Anderson he was 'Printseller By Appointment to Her Majesty'.

Two sets of his beach scenes are illustrated here. R Forse first engraved one subject from the following set of six scenes separately as a copper-plate aquatint in 1846, 'The First Dip', which included the Chain Pier in the distance and appeared in his *Fashionable Handbook for Visitors* of that year. Then Alfred Crowquill drew 'The Water Lily' scene, with seafront buildings in the background, but under the title 'Amphibious' [**69**][4]. These are in *Images of Brighton*, numbers 128 and 131 respectively [**70**].

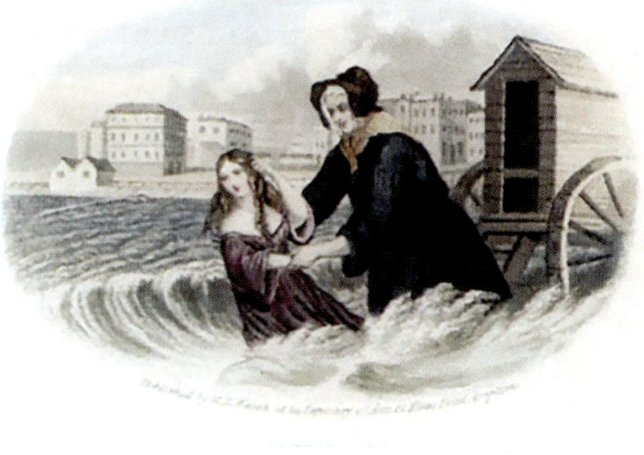

69
'Amphibious'. Single aquatint plate after Alfred Crowquill, published by Mason, also in his *Fashionable Hand-Book for Visitors to Brighton*, 1846

After these two earlier aquatints, Forse then engraved the set of six [**70**] on steel plates in the same size but with slight alterations to the backgrounds of the two single scenes, taking out the architectural features. This full set of six is

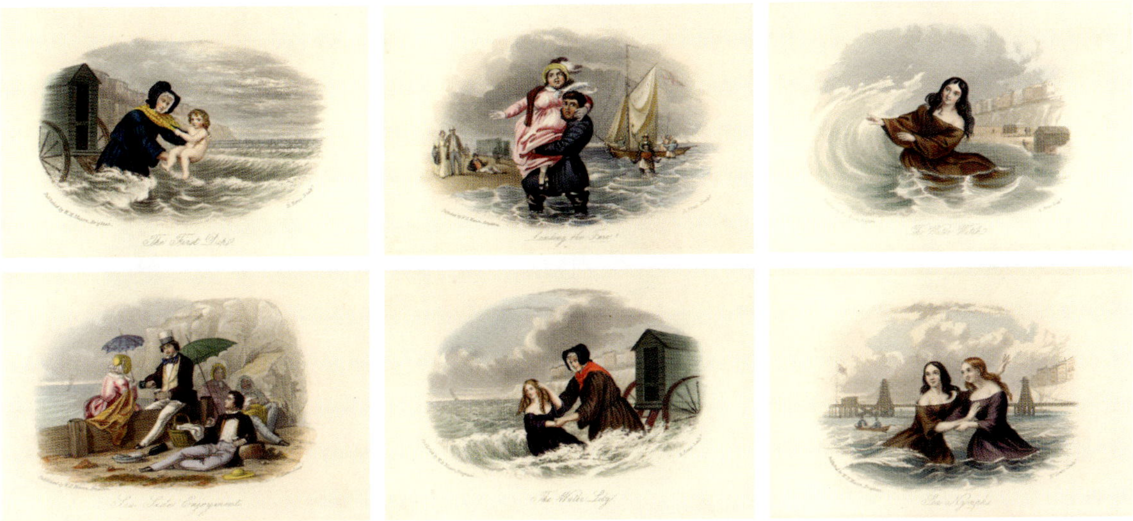

70
The complete set of six steel engravings by R Forse, published by W H Mason, Brighton, no artist named, an unrecorded set, c1850

'The First Dip' 'Landing the Fare!' 'The Water Witch'
'Sea Side Enjoyment' 'The Water Lily' 'Sea Nymphs'

rarely seen, although one of the set is listed in *Images of Brighton* number 132. It is the 'Sea Nymphs' scene from the set but published under the title 'Beauties of Brighton'—obviously its designation as a single publication before the set was produced.

The publication line of the set is 'W. H. Mason, Brighton' and it was something of an experimental publication for Mason's rare excursion into steel plate printing. Four of the set were produced in the typical line engraving method of steel plates but two, 'Landing the Fare!' and 'Sea Side Enjoyment' were engraved in aquatint. Using aquatint on steel is very unusual. Having given in to the new printing material, it was almost as if Mason could not completely abandon his traditional engraving method. Engraving in aquatint on steel was a logical experiment but is seldom seen, simple line engraving being a much quicker process.

A similar set of six beach scenes by Mason, but probably issued before the Forse set, were after Alfred Crowquill shown overpage [**71**]. They were larger lithographs by C J Basebe, although his name is spelt 'Basebi' on the prints. Having been published between 19 June and 23 June 1848, they were obviously sold separately, but also published bound under the title *A Peep at Brighton*, where Basebe's name is correct on the title page.

These lithographs have an image size of 20cm by 15cm, the set of six by Forse are 8cm by 11cm each. Four of the smaller Forse prints are close copies of the Crowquills, with just minor differences. Forse's 'Water Witch' is Crowquill's 'The Impudent Wave', then 'Landing the Fare' is taken from 'The Heavy Squall' and 'Sea Nymphs' is Crowquill's 'Don't be Frightened Dear!' (which has a suggestive subtitle worthy of the later postcard artist Donald McGill: 'It's only a little swell from the pier.') Finally Forse copied Crowquill's single aquatint plate of

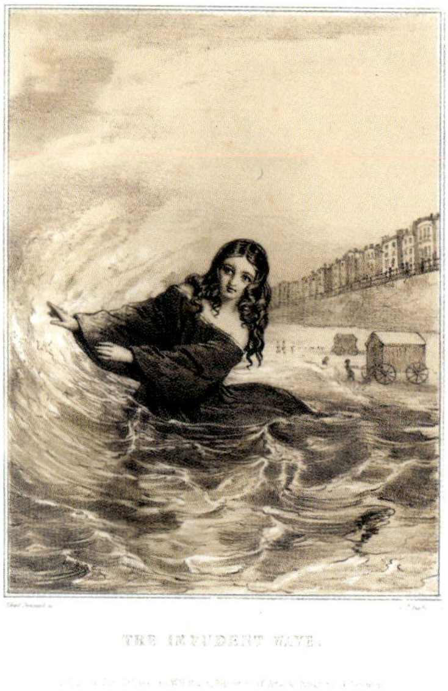

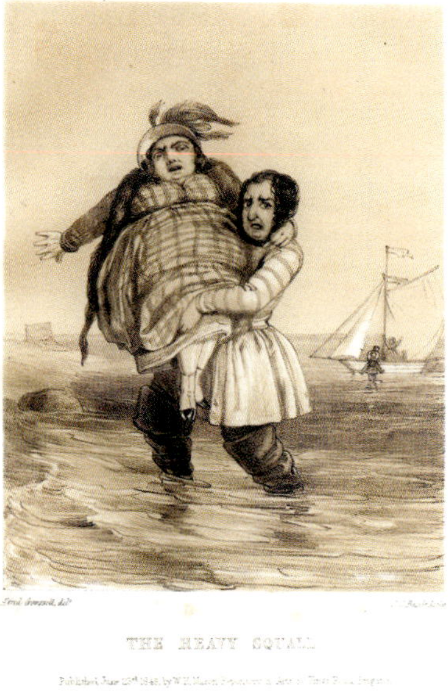

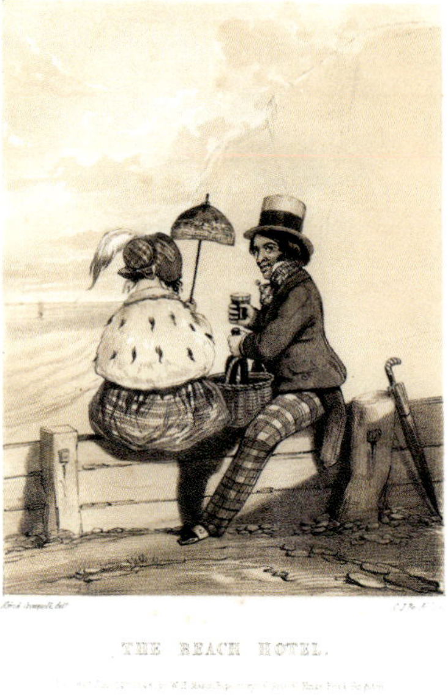

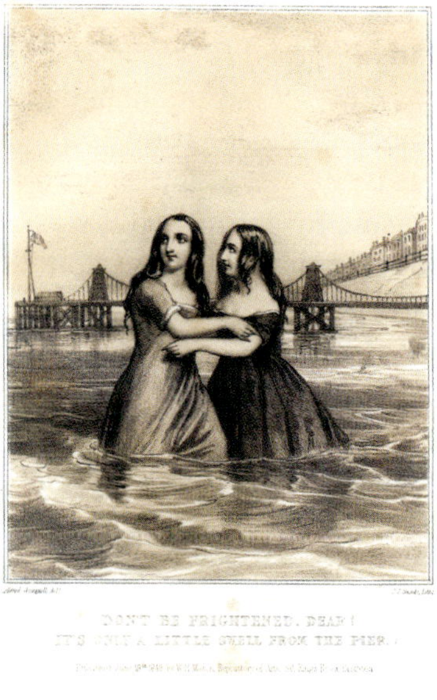

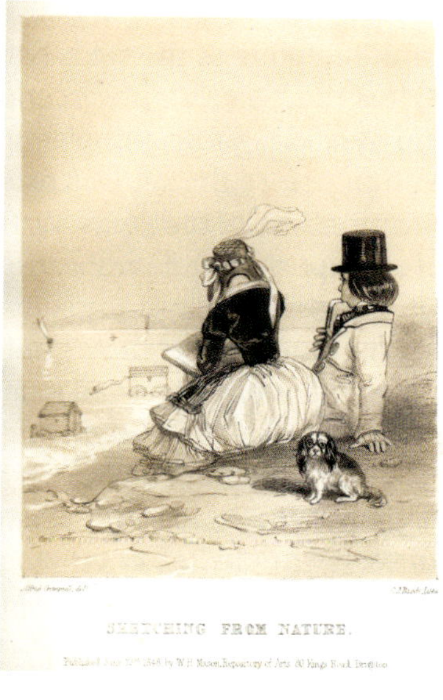

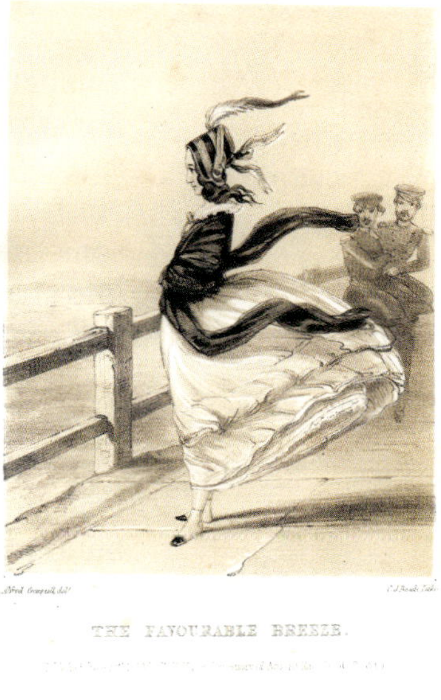

71
The set of six engravings by Alfred Crowquill

'The Impudent Wave' 'The Heavy Squall' 'The Beach Hotel'
'Don't be Frightened, Dear!' 'Sketching from Nature' 'The Favourable Breeze'

'Amphibious', entitling it 'The Water Lilly'. This set of six by Crowquill is listed in *Images of Brighton* but not illustrated, and their individual titles are recorded in Appendix 2.

Here the six smaller R Forse engravings are another example of Mason using other artists' work as a source of inspiration, taking designs from George Earp Jr and Alfred Crowquill, and as explained with aspects of the drawing in the 'Exterior and Interior of the Royal Chapel' (see page 93), it seems reasonable to claim the Forse set as being from original drawings by Mason himself.

Bearing in mind the attraction of the seafront to Brighton's many visitors, it is surprising that Mason was unique among the local print publishers in producing two such sets of people enjoying themselves on the beach or in the sea, showing scenes of a couple sketching, having a picnic, bathing, and a couple sitting on a groyne enjoying a drink. Many typical sea-front prints were of the bathing machines or the Chain Pier, which do feature in Mason's smaller set, or they depicted the beach as a place of marine industry, with the fish-market, the fishermen and their boats. But it was not until 1859/60 that the *Illustrated London News* followed Mason's lead and produced some woodcuts of crowds of day-trippers having fun by the seaside.

The final aspect of these prints worth noting is that Mason was the only publisher to produce 19th century scenes of Brighton as sets of six (the two sets illustrated here). In *Images of Brighton* there is just one other set listed, the 18th century four by Eleanor Lay of 'The Steine at Brighthelmstone'. Townscapes were frequently published in series but the subject does not lend itself to being portrayed in sets with a particular theme. Mason's time at Ackermann's, where many sets of four and six sporting prints were produced, may have been behind his inspiration in seeing Brighton beach as a good vehicle for sets. In Brighton Art Gallery there are five lithographs of 'Characters from Brighton Beach', of which it seems likely that one is missing that would make up the series. Being lithographs from c1850 these could well be Mason's, or from his apprentice William Lane, but unfortunately the publication lines are missing.

Finally, William Grant published his small booklet *Six Views of Brighton* but this is the more typical 'series' of townscapes, rather than what could be termed a 'themed set'. The known booklet has three scenes of the Pavilion buildings, two of St Peter's and one of Park Crescent, a combination probably chosen by the purchaser. W J Taylor similarly published a series of six small lithographs of various views around the town, all on one sheet. Grant did publish one 'themed set' of six, not views of Brighton as such but six interior scenes in the Pavilion, once it had been purchased by the Town Commissioners in 1850.

Returning to the original Repository of Arts business, Mason and his eldest son embraced the new artistic science of photography. But when the method of steel engraving became commonplace in the mid-nineteenth century, he did not follow the new process but continued to publish mostly aquatints and lithographs. His few steel plates consisted of his publication of the above set of six by Forse, then a view of 'The King's Road', one of 'The Pavilion' and one of 'Marine Parade' [**72**]. These last two were published in the mid-1850s, around the time of his bankruptcy. 'The Pavilion' engraving has a watermark of 1855.

Several of the established Brighton publishers like Bruce, Sickelmore and Joseph Cordwell similarly stayed with the traditional

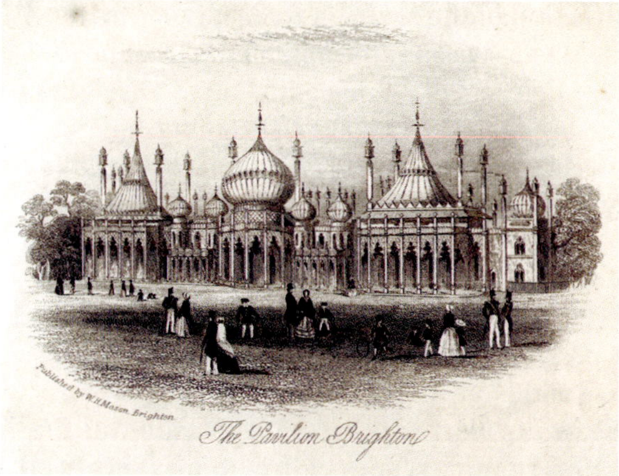

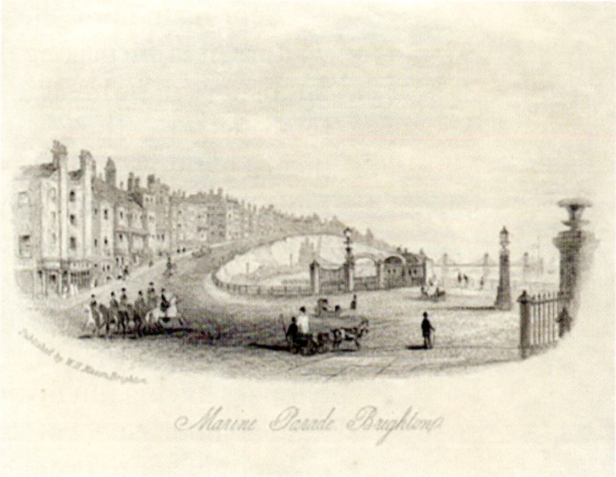

72
'The Pavilion Brighton' and 'Marine Parade, Brighton'. Among the few steel engravings published by Mason, both published as small letter-headings and are rare unrecorded scenes. The Pavilion view shows the townsfolk enjoying the grounds once the Town Commissioners had bought the palace in 1850

printing methods, whereas other local print-makers—William Grant, Saunders and William Leppard—did embrace this innovation of engraving on steel, keeping up with the London publishers, Rock & Co, the Newmans, and JS & Co, who all produced small topographical views around the country in considerable numbers.

In addition to teaching the art of lithography at the Repository, and portraiture instruction by C J Basebe, other art lessons were offered at 81 King's Road. Advertisements in the *Brighton Gazette* in 1846 featured Mr Friend from Somerset House, who gave instruction in 'his peculiar style of Drawing, the advantages of which are facility of execution, as well as depth and clearness of effect'. Miss Louisa Corbaux from Portland Place in London also visited every week, 'to give instruction in Figure Drawing and Water Colour Painting'.

As seen from Mason's bankruptcy proceedings, the years following the 1849 'Cricket Match' publication must have been a disappointing time. Income from this expensive print was not meeting expectations and it is possible that Mason's 1852 offer to sub-let his first floor rooms of his new gallery at 108 King's Road to Hennah & Kent was an attempt to solve developing financial difficulties. It might have been a clever combination of services—drawn portraits by Basebe on the ground floor, photographic portraits on the first floor, together with the Repository's mounting and framing service. But by October 1855 bankruptcy had caught up with him, and apart from seven photographic portraits, there are just four print publications after that date. They were the portrait of 'Henry Harrap Esq., of Brighton', the pair of black & white woodcuts of 'Brighton Excursion Day' and 'Brighton Morning Promenade' in October 1860, a lithograph of 'Dr Pusey' in 1867 and finally 'Emmanuel Church' of c1870.

The pair of woodcuts [**73**] were out of the ordinary for Mason, first by being woodcuts, and second being scenes of the working/middle-classes enjoying the seafront promenade, so trying to tap the new market of the day-trippers. They represent Mason's only work with the artist/illustrator Edward Hull.

74
opposite
'The Victoria Fountain, Brighton'. Lithograph by W L Walton after T Earp, with attractive views of the Albion Hotel and the Royal York Hotel. Published from 81 King's Road

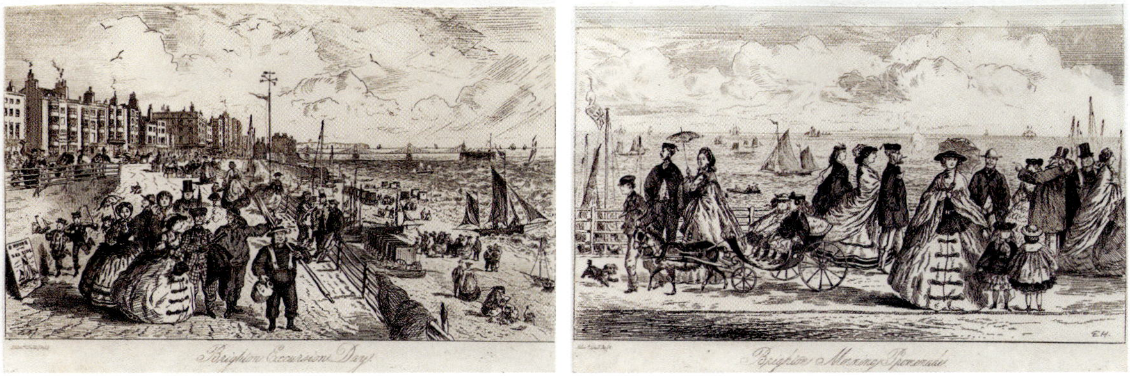

73
'Brighton Excursion Day' and 'Brighton Morning Promennde'. Pair of woodcuts by Edward Hull, published by W H Mason, 10 October 1860

Mason's varied print production included six subjects celebrating interesting events included within a view of Brighton. Of these six he managed to publish two of them on the actual day, one just a week later and one a month later. One of the same-day publications was 'The Victoria Fountain, Brighton' [**74**]. The fountain was unveiled and the print published on 26 May 1846.

'Captain Warner's Experiment', described above, was carried out on 20th July and the print was published on 27th July 1844. Then 'Pool Valley during the storm of July 17th 1850' [**57**] was published a month after the event, on 19 August 1850. 'The London and Brighton Railway Terminus, Brighton' was published in June, three months before the 21 September 1841 official opening ceremony of the London to Brighton

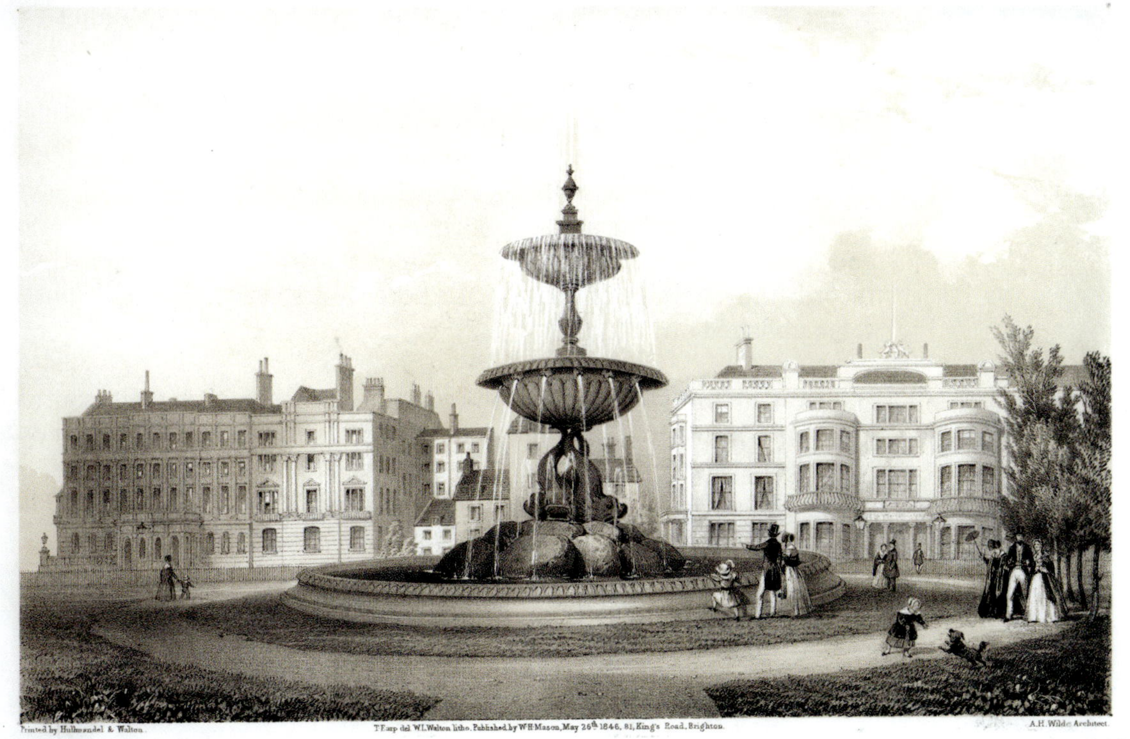

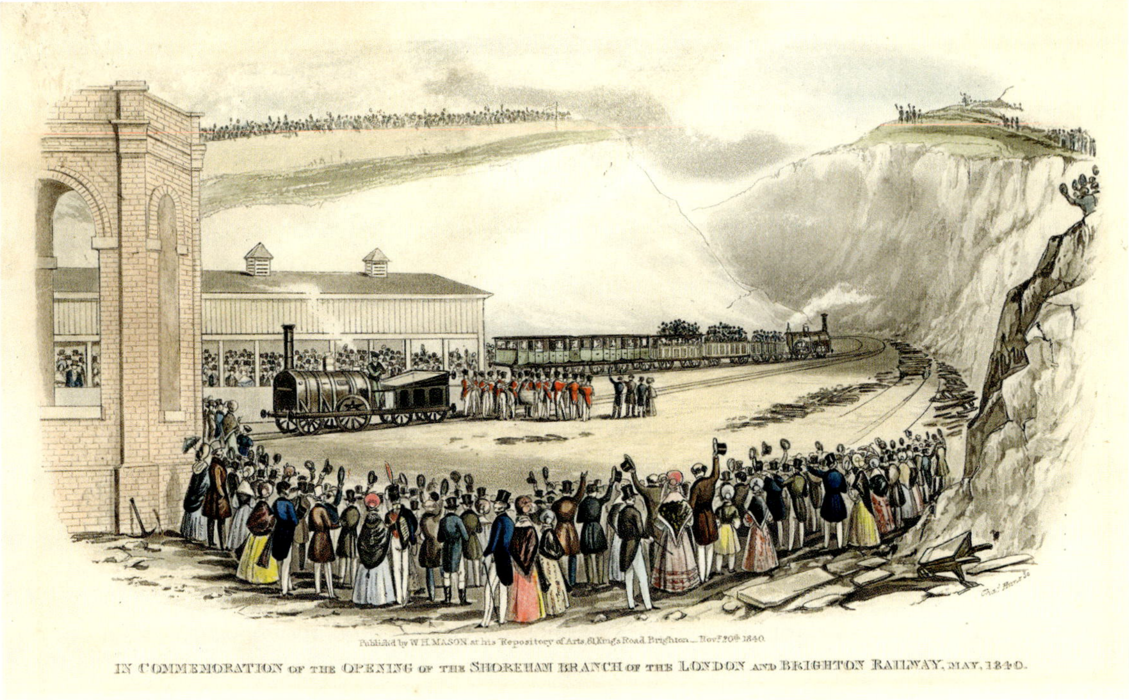

75
'In Commemoration of the Opening of the Shoreham Branch of the London and Brighton Railway, May 1840'. Aquatint engraving by Charles Hunt, no artist is named. Published by W H Mason, 81 King's Road, Brighton, 20 November 1840

line and the station itself. The year before this Mason had published the first of his three Brighton railway prints, 'In Commemoration of the Opening of the Shoreham Branch of the London and Brighton Railway, May 1840' [**75**], but this came out six months after the event. However, in time with the official opening day of the Brighton line, Mason did issue an aquatint engraving titled 'This print of The Viaduct, in commemoration of the opening throughout of the Brighton & London Railway, Sept 21st 1841' [**76**] (now known as the Ouse Valley or Balcombe Viaduct). While not a Brighton view, this was the second publication to coincide with the actual event.

Another same-day publication, but not of Brighton, was his 'Exterior and Interior of the Royal Chapel, St. James's' [**60**]. This lithograph records the marriage of Victoria and Albert on 10 February 1840 and was published on that day.

William Cobbett (1763-1835), the social reformer, pamphleteer, journalist and MP, was complimentary about Brighton's beauty yet deplored the fact that the town had virtually no trade or commerce. The once busy fishing industry was important but beyond catering for the needs of its fashionable visitors, Cobbett felt that not much was 'made in Brighton' in the 18th and early 19th centuries. However, in common with other fashionable towns of the period, one of its successful commercial activities was the making and publication of local topographical engravings, many of which made their way to London and across the Channel.

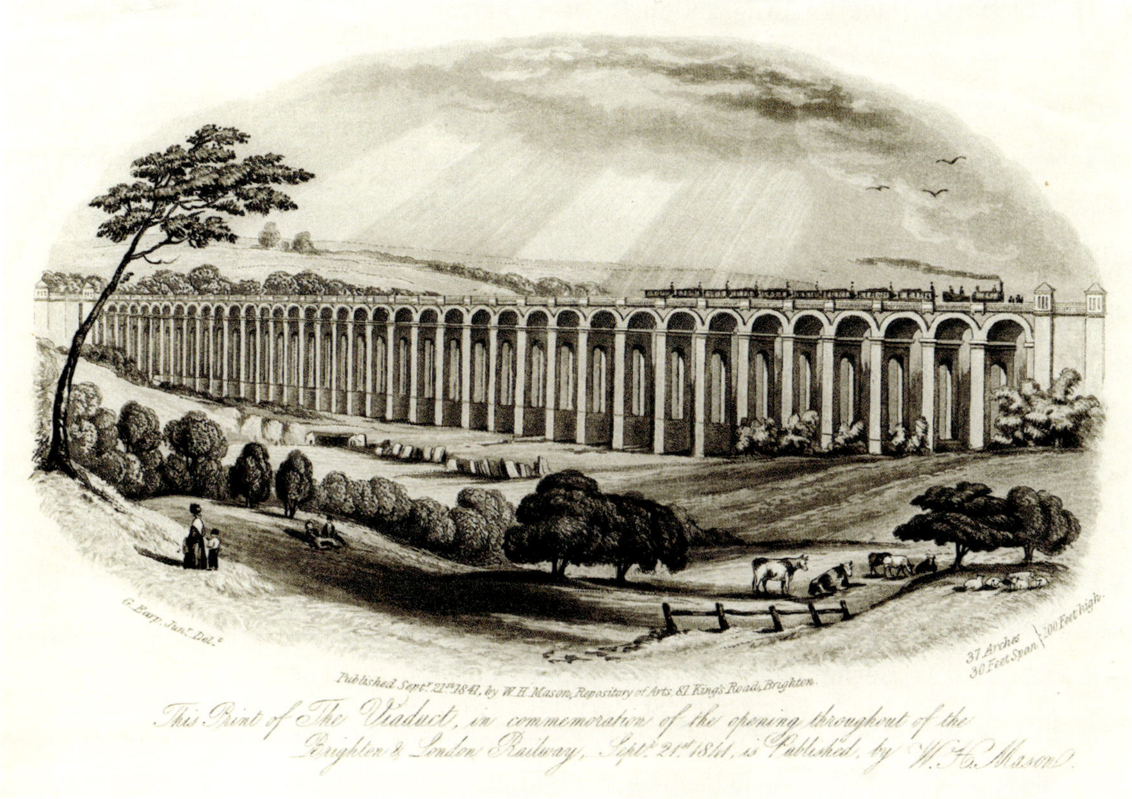

76
'This print of The Viaduct, in commemoration of the opening throughout of the Brighton & London Railway, Sept 21st 1841'. An aquatint after George Earp Jr, published 21 September 1841 by W H Mason, Repository of Arts, 81 King's Road, Brighton. Mason adds the technical details: '37 Arches, 30 feet span, 100 feet high'. The example shown is in the form of a letter-heading on folded paper, overall size: 16 by 10 inches

Mason and William Grant of Castle Square were at the forefront of this success story, and together with other local and London publishers produced more engravings of Brighton and Hove than were made of any other town or city in the UK outside the capital. Such print publishing then laid the ground for Brighton's successful and pioneering photographic businesses, with the already established mounting and framing services to support it, and film-making enterprises followed at the end of the century and early 20th century. But in line with Cobbett, R H Green[5] also wrote: 'I could never discover that anything whatever is manufactured in Brighton, the town imports both its goods and its customers. And judging from the articles displayed in most of the shop windows, the wares that are most in request seem to be gold watches, chains, rings, pebble brooches and bracelets, riding whips, leather leggings, pork pie hats, old china, pianos, lace, gauntlet gloves and saddles and bridles.'

The local guide-books and topographical prints, produced in abundance, obviously give the lie to Green's idea about 'anything whatever . . .', as do the Tunbridge ware manufactories, bookbinding services, the local tailors and boot and shoe makers, rope-makers etc. Then in the second half of the 19th century there were many foundries producing the cast-iron ornamentation for the new Victorian terraced houses, and the Brighton & South Coast Railway company's locomotive works at the station. However, Mason seemed happy with this perceived imbalance of trade. In his 1841 *Fashionable Hand-Book for Visitors to Brighton*, in the introduction he remarked:

> 'It is not desirable that Brighton should be converted into a trading town, but it is to be wished that it should possess every advantage and improvement necessary to render it a place of constant resort for the nobility and gentry of the land; and to insure their patronage ought to be the undeviating study of the inhabitants, whether possessors of property or engaged in business'.

Sentiments that were very much in line with Sir Henry Cole's observation that Brighton's industries were 'health, recreation, education and pleasure'[6]. As if to confirm his commitment to 'fashionable Brighton', Mason issued no prints specifically illustrating the market or trade subjects. In the above-quoted 1841 hand-book he included a short paragraph on the variety of shops in the town but didn't name one of them. However, he did list 21 names under 'book-sellers and stationers', including Andrews, Leppard, Wallis, Booty and Cordwell—but noting only the last two as selling prints—and he just listed himself as the sole 'publisher', where in fact all of the above were print publishers. He published a print of just one hotel, 'The Old Ship', and two schools, 'St Mary's Hall' and 'Belvedere' in Montpelier Road.

He had a good deal of competition, not just from other print-sellers and publishers, many who set up in business within a decade of Mason's opening in Ship Street. Most of the circulating libraries sold books, pamphlets, plays, musical instruments to hire, stationary wares, book binding services and articles of Tunbridge ware. As also mentioned, William Lane, the early Brighton photographer, worked in the Repository as a young man, learning the framing business. But by the late 1840s he owned his own publishing, photographic and framing establishment at 3 Market Street, near Castle Square, advertising that he framed pictures '30% cheaper than anywhere else in the country'. In 1846 Lane published a series of local 'Brighton Characters' (street vendors) in lithographic form, as most of his prints were, a skill no doubt learnt while he worked for Mason.

Regarding guides and hand-books, one way to increase sales and profits was to publish the booklet undated and as long as there were not too many noticeable changes in the fashionable centre of town, one publication would serve two or three years, as did some of the 18th century guides to Brighton published by the libraries on the Steine. With dated publications occasionally one can find Victorian guide-books with a sticker for the next year over the original publication date. Another way a publisher extended the life of his guide-book was to have nothing dated within the text of the book but on the outside front cover to stick a decorated piece of dated letterpress with the title and description of the contents, which was easy to change for the next year.

In one privately-held undated copy of W H Mason's *Fashionable Hand-Book*, the title page has a handwritten note by the purchaser of the guide: 'At Brighton, Saturday 24th September 1842, purchased this book at No 81 Kings Road, and I was assured that it was published within the past fortnight, NB there is no date to it', signed 'Wm. Lowe', presumably a visitor to the town. The purchaser then wrote 'Sept 1842' by the inscription on the title page where Mason had printed 'For the Present Year'. This 'present year' printed statement is on the example in The Keep (BH64868). According to John & Jill Ford's *Images of Brighton* Mason had originally published this guide in 1841. The reason for Mr. Lowe's rather suspicious tone could be that he belatedly remembered purchasing it last year, or he noticed things that were out of date in the text. The assurance from Mason's shop that it was published 'within the past fortnight' was a strange claim, it being September, whereas publication dates were usually at the start of the year or in April, to coincide with updates to civil, ecclesiastical and fiscal arrangements. However, in Mason's defence, it is fair to say that he was not always the well-organised businessman that his teacher and mentor in the Repository of Arts in London had been. It had taken him well over five years to arrange the publication of his engraving of 'The Cricket Match', and this particular edition of his *Hand-Book* might not have been published until quite late in 1841.

Many of the other local publishers' guide-books varied little between some years but most did put the relevant date each year. Mr Lowe certainly had grounds for suspecting that he had bought an out-of-date guide. Ironically, in the back of this guide, Mason advertises 'Prayer Books and Bibles for sale', and claims 'By Special Appointment to Her Majesty'. In the list of contents Mason goes through all the usual attractions, mentioning 'Musical Parties, Soirees etc', that will be held at particular venues, either weekly or monthly, but without giving days or dates. Alternative town guides produced by some of the rival publishers were in the format of an indexed series of articles on different areas and features of the town, giving a comprehensive overview of all that Brighton offered the visitor. Apart from Sickelmore and Bruce, who frequently used uncoloured aquatints printed to the page size, others were mostly illustrated with small black and white steel engravings or lithographs, together with smaller quarter-page vignettes, usually wood-engravings.

As far as we know Mason produced five guide-books, one titled *Illustrations of Brighton* in 1838. In 1841 he produced his *Fashionable Hand-Book for Visitors* that was still selling several years later, the same title issued again in 1846, and then parts 1 and 2 of his lithographic publication *Brighton Illustrated* in 1851. These publications had a similar quantity of explanatory notes to his competitors but no small vignette wood engravings, and were far more ambitious in their engraved illustrations. In true Ackermann tradition, most of the illustrations were hand-coloured copper-plate aquatint engravings or fine hand-coloured tinted lithographs, being twice the size of the majority of guide-book prints, and folded twice to fit the typical guide size of about seven by five inches. Of the *Brighton Illustrated* publications, just parts one and two have been found but, according to the cover of part two, Mason claimed: 'It is proposed to complete this work in about twelve parts . . . published monthly '

A seen copy of the *Fashionable Hand-Book for Visitors* of 1841 includes 'The Chain Pier, Brighton', 'The London and Brighton Railway Terminus, Brighton', 'Brunswick Terrace, Brighton', 'Lewes Crescent, Brighton, Kemp Town' and 'The Pavilion'. The copy at The Keep just has 'The Chain Pier, Brighton' and 'The Pavilion'. Apart from being able to buy these prints separately, for framing and wall display, Mason obviously allowed customers to choose a varying number of prints in a guide, therefore offering a variety of prices. From his *Fashionable Hand-Book* of 1846 just two illustrations are listed in Images of Brighton, both seaside scenes: 'The First Dip' and 'Amphibious'. Variations of these two scenes were later included in Mason's set of six beach scenes by R. Forse [**69**]. In his 'Illustrations of Brighton' he published 'St Peter's Church, Brighton', 'Kemp Town, Brighton' and 'Chain Pier, Brighton'. Examples of these prints can be found today in their unfolded state, having been sold outside the guide-book format. For *Brighton Illustrated* Mason placed the following advertisement in the *Brighton Gazette* (17 April 1851):

> 'BRIGHTON ILLUSTRATED, Part 2 now ready, the second number of W.H. Mason's Brighton Illustrated. Price 4s proof, 2s 6d prints. Contents William Seymour Esq with biography and a copy of the Bust in the Pavilion, lately placed there to his honour by the inhabitants, also a view of the Town Hall'.

The 'copy of the Bust' was a lithograph after Charles Basebe, showing the head and shoulders sculpture of Seymour [**77**][7], standing on its black column, with a crest of two dolphins above his name. According to the imprint in most of these handbooks, Mason had the text printed in London by B Clarke of Falcon Square, and if he didn't print the lithographs himself, he occasionally used L M Lefevre but mostly either W Walton working on his own, or Hullmandel and Walton. Charles Joseph Hullmandel was one of the finest London-based Victorian lithographic printers, much favoured by Ackermann, a very considerable compliment from one lithographic printer to another.

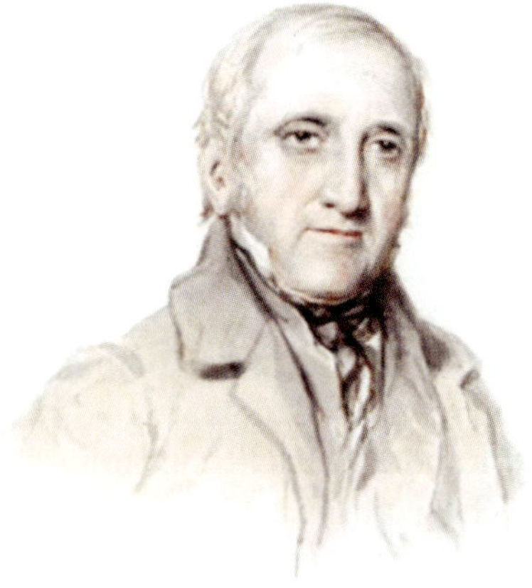

77
'William Seymour'. The original pencil and wash drawing by Charles Basebe, for Mason's lithograph

Returning to the range of engraved subjects Mason produced, the series of 14 church or ecclesiastical subjects mentioned included the only known views published of 'Emmanuel Church', the 'Royal Chapel' and 'St. Mark's, Kemp Town'. He also produced 14 small tinted lithographs of boats on Brighton beach, these last can all be found in volume eight of the Erredge Collection in Brighton Rare Books department. From other Brighton and London publishers there were also many views produced of the main line Brighton Station, but Mason's was the first, published in June 1841, about three months before the London line was actually declared open on 21 September that year, at which time the station was the largest public building in Brighton. Then Ackermann's published a much larger but similar view (they were both from the architect David Mocatta's drawing, who was a frequently used architect by the London, Brighton and South Coast Railway Company). Mason's was in aquatint and the Ackermann print was a lithograph. Coming from the same drawing by Mocatta, and with the Ackermann print coming out three months later, on the actual day of the opening in September, they would seem to be produced in collaboration rather than in competition – in line with the known Mason/Ackermann relationship.

With his abiding interest in cricket, in addition to his large 1849 print, Mason produced *Lillywhite's Illustrated Handbook of Cricket*, published with Ackermann & Co, in 1844. Offered in a variety of editions, the most expensive had large folded portraits of four players engraved in aquatint by Charles Hunt, including Lillywhite himself [**65**] then four smaller plates of gentlemen cricketers. All these portraits had been previously published as single plates by Mason in 1841, and the whole book was republished by J W McKenzie in 1988.

Other known political/society publications by Mason include 'Capt George Richard Pechell, Royal Navy, as he received the several deputations with addresses at Brighton on the evening of the 4th Oct., 1836'. This is a lithograph by Thomas Charles Wageman after Edward Morton, published at the Repository of Arts, Ship Street and printed by J Graf. George Pechell became an Admiral, was MP for Brighton for 25 years, and was the subject of Mason's satirical 'Brighton Omnibus' print. Another is a portrait plate of the novelist William Harrison Ainsworth. This was one of Mason's few albumen photo-prints that he published for Hennah & Kent in the 1850s. Ainsworth published his story of Charles II's escape, *Ovingdean Grange*, in 1860 while living at 5 Arundel Terrace in Kemp Town.

In the Erredge Collection of Brighton's Rare Books department, Vol 4 page 116, is an untitled black and white aquatint by Charles Hunt 'From a Sketch by H.B.' It is a self-portrait of Mr Doyle on horseback, published from the Repository of Arts at 1 Ship Street, which dates it before 1839. In his early life in Dublin John Doyle (1797–1868) was an accomplished horse painter but in moving to London he failed to establish himself in the thriving early 19th century school of sporting art. He found his forte as a political caricaturist and with the print publisher Thomas McLean, of 26 Haymarket, produced a successful series of lithographs known as the 'HB Caricatures'. Doyle's only known

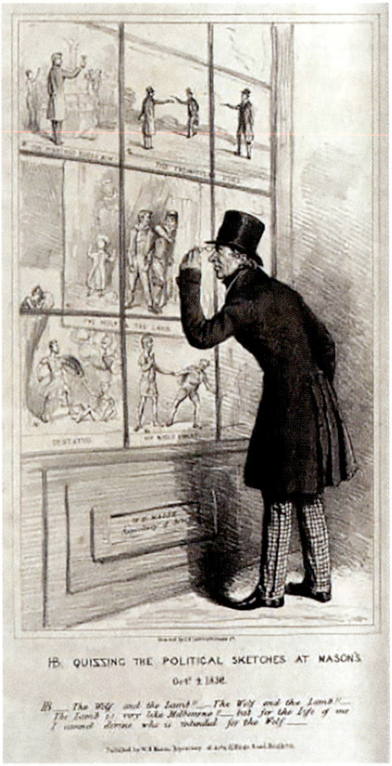

78
'HB Quizzing the Political Sketches at Mason's'

sporting prints were a set of four, published in 1835, of 'A Celebrated Stag Hunt'[8].

Mason featured Doyle's work again in October 1839, in a print titled 'HB Quizzing the Political Sketches at Mason's' [**78**]. This lithograph shows the front of Mason's gallery at 81 King's Road. He had moved into these premises from Ship Street in the spring of that year. The 'HB' is Henry Brougham, who is pictured looking into Mason's window where there are exhibited a variety of political prints including 'The Duke! God Bless Him', 'The Triangular Duel' and 'My Noble Friend'. The text underneath the print, taken from the title of one of the window prints, the Aesop's Fable of 'The Wolf and the Lamb', reads: 'The lamb is very like Melbourne, but for the life of me I cannot divine who is intended for the wolf'.

In a letter to the authors, John Ford explains: 'Brougham was one of John Doyle's favourite "villains". Brougham does not recognise that it is he himself who is the wolf pictured as threatening the Lamb (Lord Melbourne). Brougham was Melbourne's Lord Chancellor in his first Ministry, but Melbourne believed it was Brougham's actions which had led to the downfall of that administration. When he was re-elected he refused to re-appoint Brougham as Chancellor and Brougham engaged in a series of running battles against his former associates.'

The *Brighton Patriot* (20 February 1838) was scathing about Doyle. 'The works of this artist are characterised by flimsiness and haste which

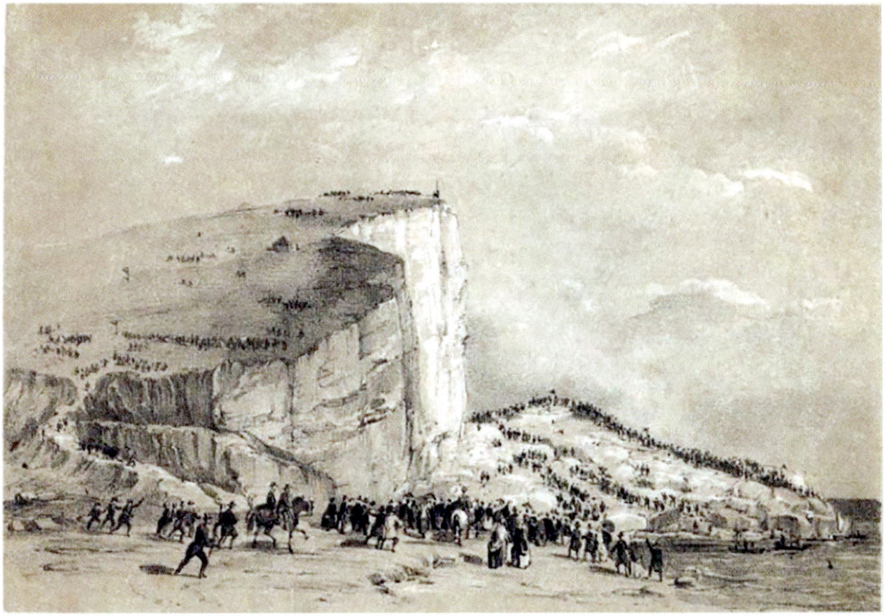

79
'Seaford Cliff'

are disgraceful. Perhaps out of 600 sketches which H.B. may have made, there are not 50 that are worth looking at; the rest have neither good drawing nor humour—mere waste paper'. Comments no doubt politically motivated.

One print has been found with the imprint of Mason's address but without his name being mentioned: 'Seaford Cliff as it appeared immediately after the explosion (by voltaic battery) Sept 19th 1850'. It is a sepia lithograph drawn by 'Miss Nanny' and was 'Published for the Proprietor at 80 King's Road, Brighton'. Mason published a second version of this scene, taken from out at sea [**79**]. The intention of the exercise depicted here was to halt encroachment of the sea into Seaford town, but the large amount of chalk rubble that ended up on the beach was soon washed away by the tide, and the problem was not solved.

This chapter started with Mason's first publication of 1833. His contribution to Brighton's print publishing history ended 40 years later. With Hennah & Kent having brought the sons' rival photographic studio to an end in 1873, this was the year Mason left his fourth gallery, 108 King's Road, where he had been trading since 1851, and had what was probably his final bankruptcy hearing. During these last 18 years at 108, while paying off his debts, his publishing was very limited and there were no copper-plate aquatints produced.

His pair of Edward Hull woodcuts and the three lithographs of this period were mentioned earlier but he did produce several photographic publications for his son during this time. These included the portrait of Albert Edward, a photographic-process hand coloured print of 1860, and the portrait of the artist William Henry Hunt, published in the early 1860s from a *carte-de-visite* photograph. Two portrait photographs of the English actor William Henry Chippendale were also produced at this time, one oval and one oblong, and all were taken by Mason Jr. He also published a portrait of Abraham Lincoln, a photograph by Mathew Brady, in 1860.

In 1862 Mason also published the two photographic prints by his daughter Mary—'The Late Prince Consort' and 'Queen Victoria'—which she had produced from photographing earlier lithographs by C J Basebe. Mason's last recorded print is 'Emmanuel Church', a lithograph after M Hall c1870. After his first and only experiment with wood engraving, his publishing during bankruptcy was constrained to lithographs and photographs. Having been taught lithographic printing during his apprenticeship days at Ackermann's, he undoubtedly produced these final prints himself. All these publications are listed in Appendix 2.

[1] Ford and Ford: *op.cit.* 1981, p135
[2] *Brighton As It Is 1836*, Wallis's Royal Edition. Brighton: The Booksellers
[3] Michael Bryan: *Dictionary of Painters and Engravers*, Volume 1. London: George Bell & Sons, 1886

[4] A similar composition and size to the Forse plate of 'The Water Lilly' but depicting the Albion and Royal York Hotels in the background. Before this, Mason also published an unrecorded Basebe lithograph after George Earp Jr in 1844 titled 'Young Amphibious'. It was another image very similar to Forse's 'The First Dip' but larger and included a backdrop of the Chain Pier

[5] R H Green: *Brighton: The Road, The Place, The People.* London: J H Thomson, 1862, p123

[6] Elizabeth Bonython and Anthony Burton: *The Life and Work of Henry Cole.* London: V & A Museum Catalogues, 2003

[7] The Keep (East Sussex Records Office) QCV/2/32: Letters between Seymour and the Earl of Chichester. Seymour was a successful London lawyer who became chairman of the Brighton Bench. This publication looks as if it coincided with his retirement as a county magistrate. In replying to his resignation letter, the Earl of Chichester wrote of his appreciation of the constant support of 'my own kind friend' and how 'abundantly thankful' he was for Seymour's work in prison reform and 'the manifest improvement in the House of Correction at Lewes'

[8] Dudley Snelgrove: *British Sporting and Animal Prints—The Paul Mellon Collection.* New Haven: Yale Center for British Art, 1981, p69

Appendix 1
Grant's publications

The following list details the known prints published by William Grant. It is not considered to be exhaustive, as further prints are still uncovered from time to time. The numbered prints comprise those catalogued by John & Jill Ford in their book *Images of Brighton* (their catalogue number precedes the title in **bold**). Uncatalogued prints have been given a new number preceded by a prefix WG. References to illustrations in the main text are placed in square brackets, eg [**23**].

Where publication dates have been given, the source has generally been from local newspaper advertisements. Where a single estimated date is given, such as c1854, it has been based on known factors and similarly, where a date range is given, known factors indicate the publication could have been anywhere within that range. Where no date is given it is because there is nothing conclusive to indicate when it was published but it will nevertheless be somewhere between 1845 and 1855, the period that Grant was known to be publishing prints.

Where prints were acquired by Grant from other publishers, the approximate date of acquisition has been given. In such instances the scene depicted may pre-date the acquisition by a considerable time.

Catalogued prints (that can be dated)

17 *Fish Market on the Beach, Brighton (From the sea)*. Drawn: G Attwick.

203 *East View of the Chain Pier from the Beach Brighton (Bathing Season)*. Drawn: G Attwick.

260 *View of the Marine Parade & Chain Pier, Brighton*. Unnamed artist (embossed greeting card shown).

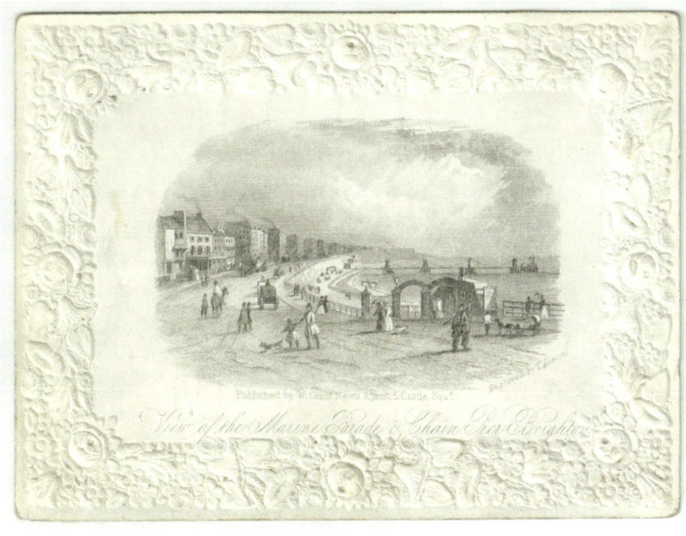

260

275 *Chain Pier & Bazaar from the Beach, Brighton (Looking West).* Drawn: G Attwick.

357

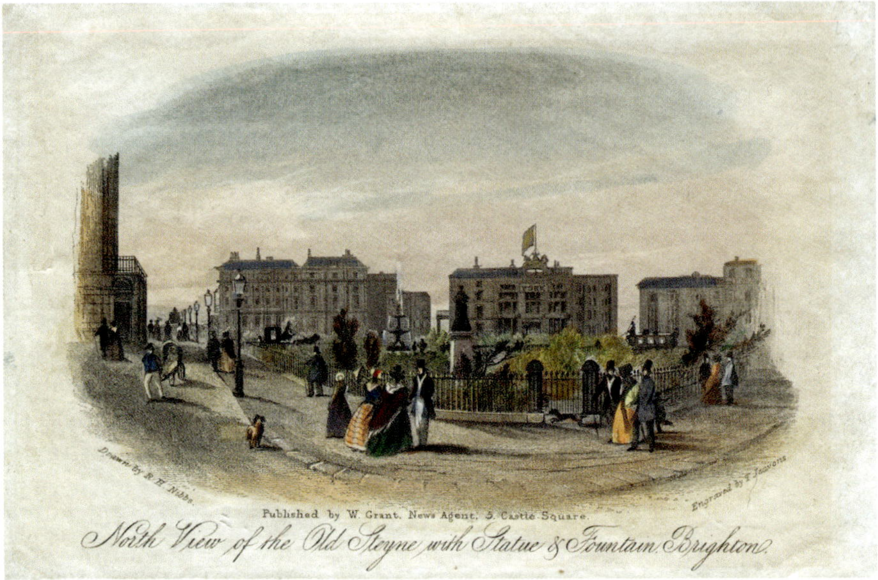

357 *North View of the Old Steyne with Statue and Fountain, Brighton.* Drawn: R H Nibbs.

361 *South View of the Old Steyne with Fountain & Pavilion, Brighton.* Drawn: R H Nibbs.

524 *NE View of the Pavilion & Royal Stables, Brighton.* Drawn: G Attwick.

546

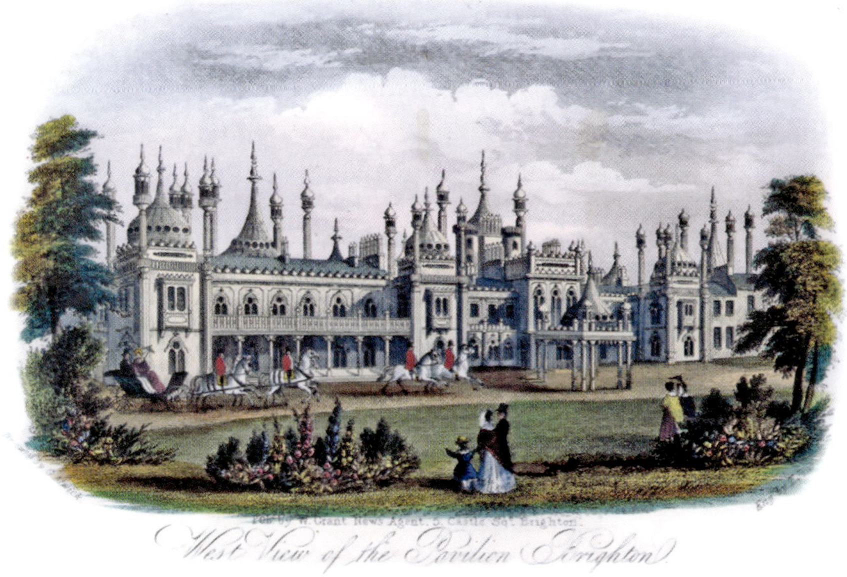

546 *West View of the Pavilion, Brighton.* Drawn: G Attwick.

838 *View of the Railway Terminus, Brighton.* Drawn: R H Nibbs.

860 *Brighton from Preston*. Drawn R H Nibbs (note: some smaller type (ii) versions of this print have a different title: *Viaduct and Brighton from Preston Hill*. The original title seems to have been *View of Brighton from Preston Hill*[1], so there may have been numerous variants).
869 *Bedford Hotel and Esplanade, Brighton*. Unnamed artist.
877 *Bristol Hotel & Sussex County Hospital, Brighton*. Unnamed artist.
896 *Norfolk Hotel & Esplanade (Looking West)*. Unnamed artist.
901 *View of the Old Ship Hotel & King's Road*. Drawn: R H Nibbs.
1031 *View of Brunswick Square & Terrace from the Sea*. Drawn: R H Nibbs.

1146 *View of Kemp Town from the Sea*. Drawn: R H Nibbs (embossed greeting card shown, right).
1164 *Marine Parade & Chain Pier from Kemp Town Esplanade*. Drawn: R H Nibbs.

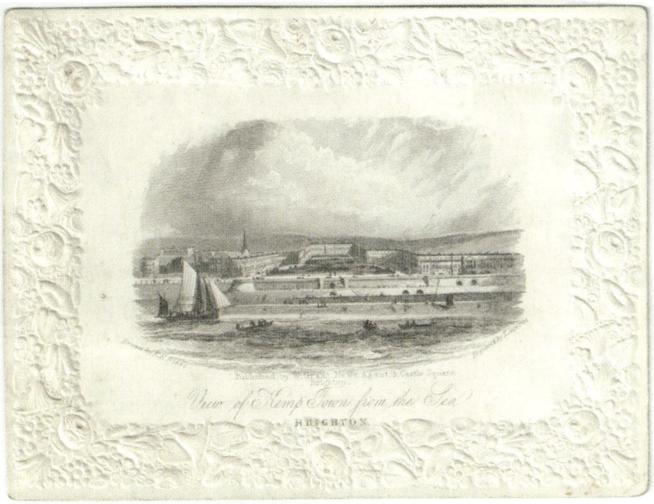

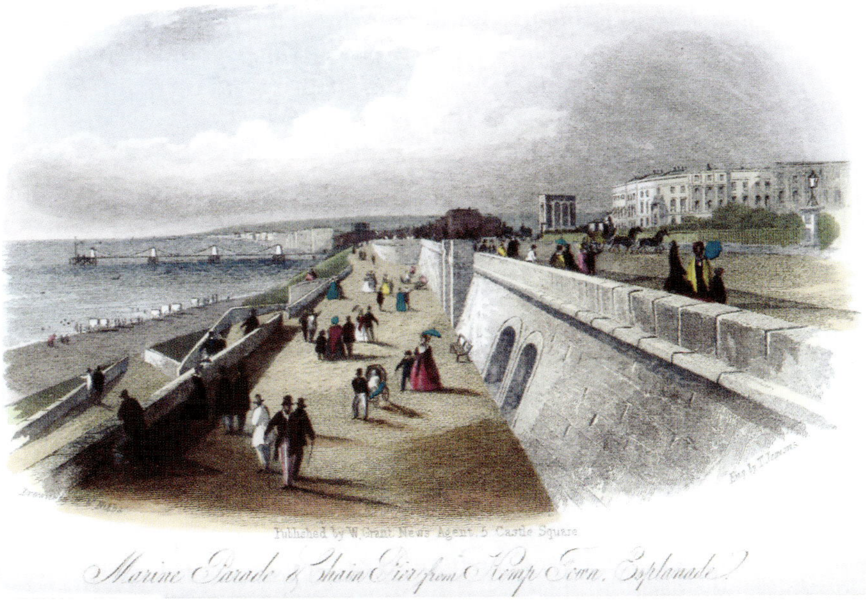

1164

> Lately published by W.G.,
> SEVENTEEN VIEWS IN BRIGHTON
> of the most popular attractions of the town, from drawings by R.H. NIBBS and G. ATWICK, and engraved in the first style by T. JEAVONS, of London, and beautifully Coloured by G. ROTHERHAM. Sold as prints, and on letter and note papers, plain and coloured.
> Books cheaply and firmly bound to any pattern.
> Orders received also at W. Grant's Branch Offices:—27, EDWARD STREET (top of George-street, St. James's-street), and 19, Queen's Road (close to the Railway Terminus).
> Books lent to read, at each of the Branch Offices, at One Penny per volume.

All of the original series of 17 prints were engraved by Thomas Jeavons and published simultaneously around the end of 1847. Grant (identified as 'W.G.') placed this advertisement in the *Brighton Herald* of 8 January 1848 .

These prints are probably the ones that are most commonly found nowadays, owing to the very large quantity produced. An analysis of the known examples, indicate that they were from steel plates produced in three sizes: (i) 95mm by 160mm; (ii) 60mm by 90mm and (iii) 95mm by 150mm (all plus or minus 10mm).

Type (i) prints were generally sold for framing or display purposes and can be found both coloured and uncoloured. Type (ii) prints were generally sold as notelets, letter headed notepaper and later as greetings cards. Both type (i) and (ii) prints were engraved by Jeavons, but it is worthy of note that numerous later examples are known of that were engraved by Newman, both for Grant and after his bankruptcy in 1855-56, under their own name. Type (iii) prints were probably new Newman plates published under their own name. A number of these later issues by Newman appear to be new lithographic prints.

Almost all of the known examples of embossed greetings cards (except for catalogue no **715** by Newman) were produced from the type (ii) plates for the above series of 17 prints. These prints, together with others from his extensive range could be bought singly, or more often as a booklet containing six prints, at 6d plain, or 1s 0d coloured.

> GRAND BALL AT THE PAVILION.—
> Purchasers of the BRIGHTON GAZETTE of Thursday, January 23, at GRANT'S NEWSPAPER OFFICE, 5, Castle Square, will receive GRATIS a beautiful STEEL ENGRAVING of the WEST VIEW and GRAND ENTRANCE to the PAVILION.
> The BRIGHTON GAZETTE will contain a full and accurate description of the Rooms and Decorations, Names of Fashionables Present, &c. &c.

On 23 January 1851, in commemoration of the Grand Ball at the Pavilion, Grant's advert in the *Brighton Gazette* offered his print *West View and Grand Entrance to the Pavilion* [sic] (**546**), free to all purchasing the newspaper from his Castle Square news office.

1085 *View of Pool Valley during the Storm, July 17th 1850*. Drawn: G Ruff, engraved: T Jeavons.

On 17 August 1850 Grant published a print of flooding in Pool Valley following a tumultuous storm that had occurred during the previous

1085

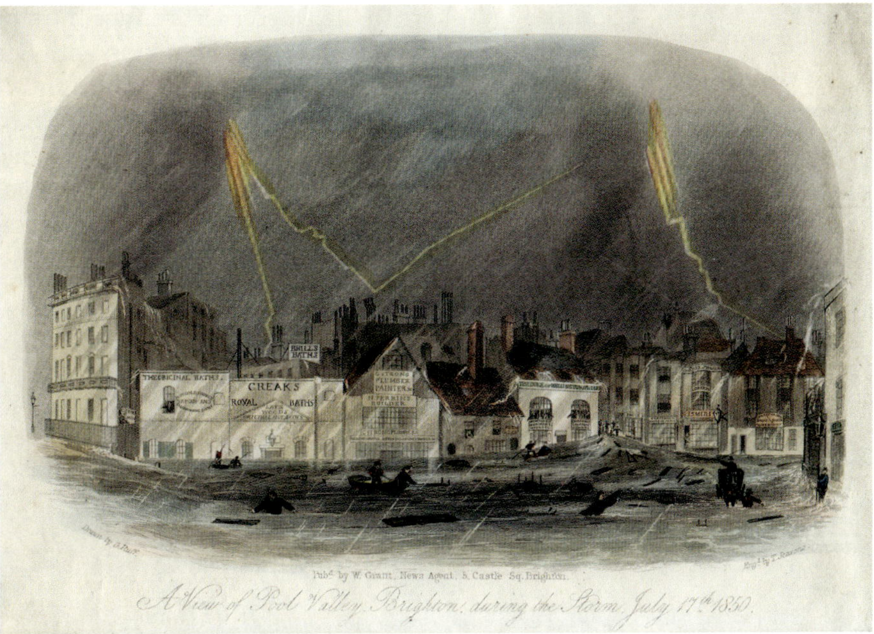

THE LATE STORM AT BRIGHTON.
Will be ready on Saturday,
A HANDSOME STEEL ENGRAVING by JEVOUS, of London, of THE LATE STORM AND INUNDATION OF POOL VALLEY.
Prints, 3d each; on letter paper 2d; coloured impressions, 6d.
To be had of the Publisher, W. GRANT, 5, Castle Square, Queen's Road, and Edward Street, and of all Booksellers.

month. This was a popular subject, also published by three of his competitors: J Smith, W H Mason [**50**] and J Watkins. Whereas his competitors offered lithographic prints of the event, Grant offered a steel engraving of 115mm x 180mm by Jeavons, also being the smallest of the depictions. The print could be purchased for framing uncoloured for 3d, coloured for 6d, or as a headed letter for 2d.

1200 *View of the intended Harbour*. Drawn: T Picken, lithograph: Day & Son.
In 1850, Grant had a pivotal role in the promotion of a scheme for a new breakwater in Brighton, using a radical new design by chartered engineer William Henry Smith. Since the 1830s numerous schemes had been proposed, perhaps the most significant of them being a harbour promoted by George Adolphus Wigney in early 1842[2] and a floating timber breakwater proposed by Captain J N Tayler in 1845[3]. Although a trial of three sections of Tayler's breakwater was undertaken off the coast of Brighton, it was not considered a success and both schemes ultimately failed to reach fruition. The new scheme proposed by Smith was presented to a meeting at the Town Hall on 27 September 1850 and received unanimous support. Further meetings urged the adoption of the scheme.

Grant was enlisted to publish a View of the Intended Harbour at Brighton, on the Recoil Principle, drawn by T Picken and using Day &

Son, lithographers to the Queen, to produce the stone plates. He was also the Brighton publisher, in conjunction with Longman & Co. of London, of an accompanying paper by Smith, entitled *Harbours of Refuge; or, the Sea Wall Question Analysed and Practically Resolved, by a Principle applicable to all Marine Structures*. It would appear that, despite the Vestry urging for the adoption of proposed scheme, the necessary funding by central government was not forthcoming and consequently the breakwater failed to be built.

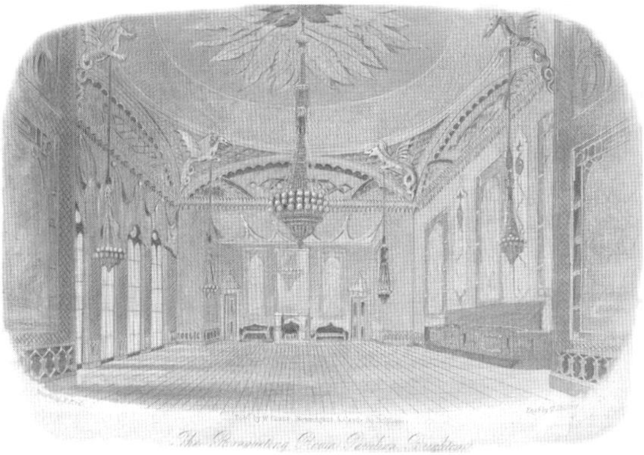

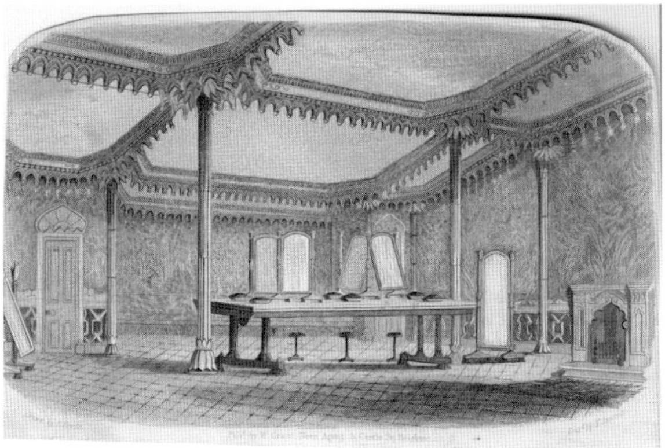

561 *left*, **575** *right*

561 *The Banqueting Room, Pavilion, Brighton.*
565 *The Saloon, Pavilion, Brighton.*
567 *The Music Gallery, Pavilion, Brighton.*
572 *The Music Room, Pavilion, Brighton.*
575 *The Ladies Retiring Room, Pavilion, Brighton.*
576 *Grand Entrance to the Chinese Gallery, Pavilion, Brighton.*
All drawn: F Forde, engraved: T Jeavons.

In March 1851, Grant announced that he would be publishing a series of six prints depicting rooms at the Pavilion newly opened to the public. Following the purchase of the Pavilion in 1850 by the Town Commissioners and its subsequent refurbishment, a grand opening ball was held on 21 January 1851. In the following week a further ball was held for the inhabitants and this became an annual event. The *Brighton Gazette* of 20 March 1851 carried an article about the intended publication of the prints: 'Mr. Grant, of Castle Square, is publishing a series of views of the principal suite of rooms at the Pavilion. The pictures are from the pencil of the clever local artist, Mr. Ford, whose name is an ample guarantee for their correctness; and they are lithographed by Mr. Jeavons, of London, at a great cost to the spirited publisher. These beautiful views are offered at a charge so low that it must ensure a great sale'. It should be noted that the newspaper reportage was inaccurate in that the prints were published as steel plates and not lithographs.

The six steel engravings of the Pavilion were ultimately not published until the following year. They were incorporated into a booklet published by Grant, to coincide with the Grand Inauguration

Now Ready,
SIX SPLENDID VIEWS
OF THE
ROOMS IN THE BRIGHTON PAVILION,
One Shilling and Sixpence Plain, Two Shillings and Sixpence Coloured.
Together with an account and the names of all persons present at the GRAND INAUGURATION BALL.
PUBLISHED BY
W. GRANT, NEWS AGENT,
5, CASTLE SQUARE AND 19, QUEEN'S ROAD,
Brighton.

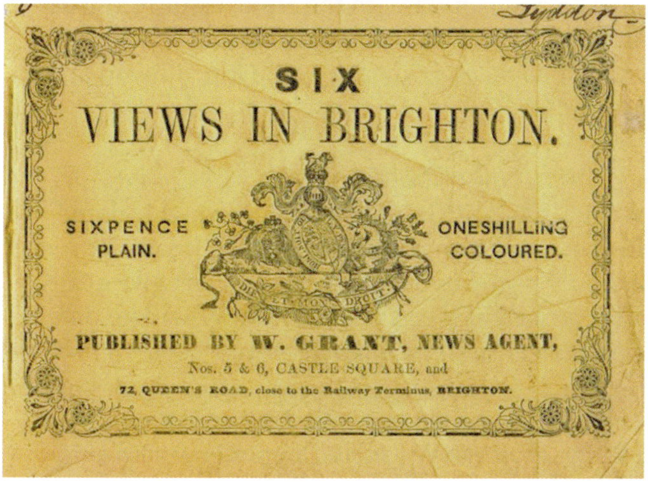

Ball at the Pavilion of that year. The booklet was entitled *Six Splendid Views of the Rooms in the Brighton Pavilion*[4] and carried a list of the attendees, descriptions of the rooms and an account of the ball. On 29 January 1852, the *Brighton Gazette* announced: 'Our fashionable readers (many who were present at the Grand Ball last evening) will be pleased to learn (see advertisement) that Mr. Grant of Castle Square, has lately published a little work, carefully compiled, and containing a description of the rooms, the inauguration ball, with a list of company, and six views of the interior of the Pavilion, very accurate and striking. The work, we doubt not, will find its way to the drawing room table of our resident and visiting gentry'.

The prints were approximately 110mm by 165mm and the booklet was sold at 1s 6d plain, 2s 6d coloured. It is probable that individual prints continued to be offered, after the initial release, as part of Grant's stock selection of prints.

Panoramic Views of Brighton

JUST PUBLISHED, A GRAND PANORAMIC VIEW OF BRIGHTON FROM THE SEA, embracing the whole extent of the town from East to West, with the Magnificent Rides and Drives, not to be surpassed by any town in the kingdom. The whole range of Splendid Buildings, Squares, Full View of the Chain Pier, &c. &c. In cloth case, plain, 3s. 6d., coloured 5s.; or in a cover as Four Separate Prints for Framing, plain, 2s. 6d., coloured 4s.—Published by W. GRANT, News Agent, Circulating Library and Reading Rooms, 5 and 6, Castle Square, Brighton; and sold by all the Booksellers.

6 *West no 2.*
7 *West no 1.*
8 *East no 1.*
9 *East no 2.*

These four prints were published around June 1852 as a continuous strip, entitled *W. Grant's Panoramic View of Brighton from the Sea*. The artist was unnamed and they were lithographic prints, being offered as either coloured or uncoloured. A review by the *Brighton Gazette* (17 June 1852) states: 'Mr. Grant of Castle Square has just brought out in cheap form, a lithographed panorama of Brighton, taken from the sea. It represents the whole line of frontage, from Kemp Town to Brunswick Terrace, with such minuteness that every house in our magnificent marine promenade of three miles is individualised. It will, we anticipate, become a favourite souvenir with the Brighton visitors'. They were sold as either a continuous view (uncoloured in a cloth case at 3s 6d; coloured in a cloth case at 5s 0d) or as a series of four separate prints titled *Panoramic Views of Brighton*, approximately 160mm by 320mm, for framing, at 2s 6d uncoloured, 4s.0d coloured.

1078 *Odd Fellows Hall, M.U. Queen's Road, Brighton*. Drawn: J Harris, engraved: W J Alais. Steel engraving, 75mm by 100mm; 1854
In June 1853 the cornerstone of the Odd Fellows Hall in Queen's Road was laid and the building opened in 1854. Although no adverts have been found for Grant's print of the hall, it must have been published around 1854. Grant had an association with the Manchester Unity of the Oddfellows and in 1853 was vice-chairman to the Loyal Brunswick Lodge, no. 118, which held its meetings at the Globe Inn, Edward Street, before the new hall was built.

Catalogued prints (with no identifiable date)

The majority of prints published by Grant can be only roughly dated, there being no specific date noted on the prints nor any known adverts for them. In some instances, features depicted on the print give a fair idea of the date of publication and this is given below. Where no date is stated, the print was published sometime between 1845 and 1855.

46 *Gloucester Hotel, Railway Terminus and St. Peter's Church, Brighton*. Drawn: G Ruff, engraved: W J Alais. Copper engraving, 175mm by 295mm, c1852.

48

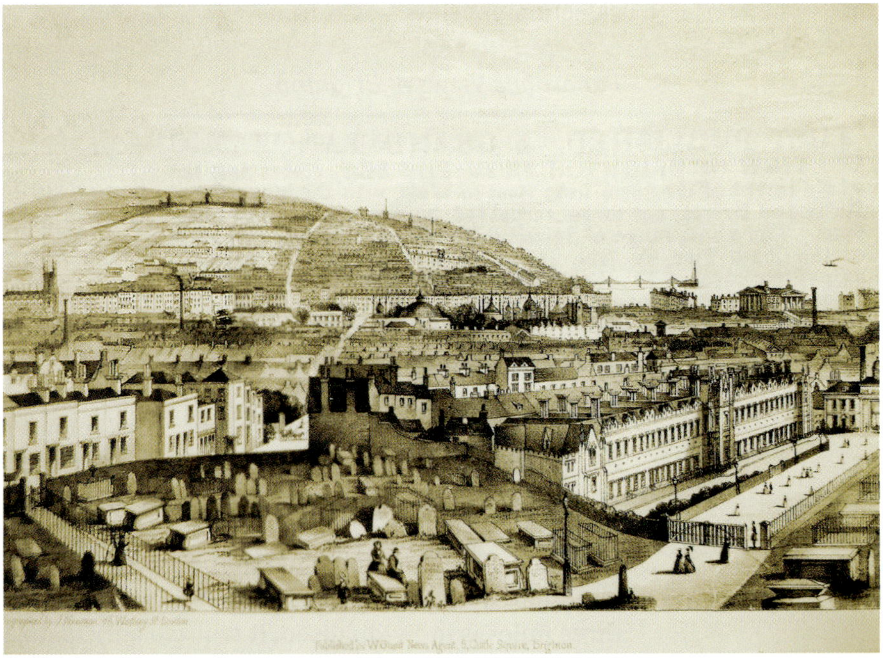

48 *North East View of Brighton from the top of the Old Church.*

49 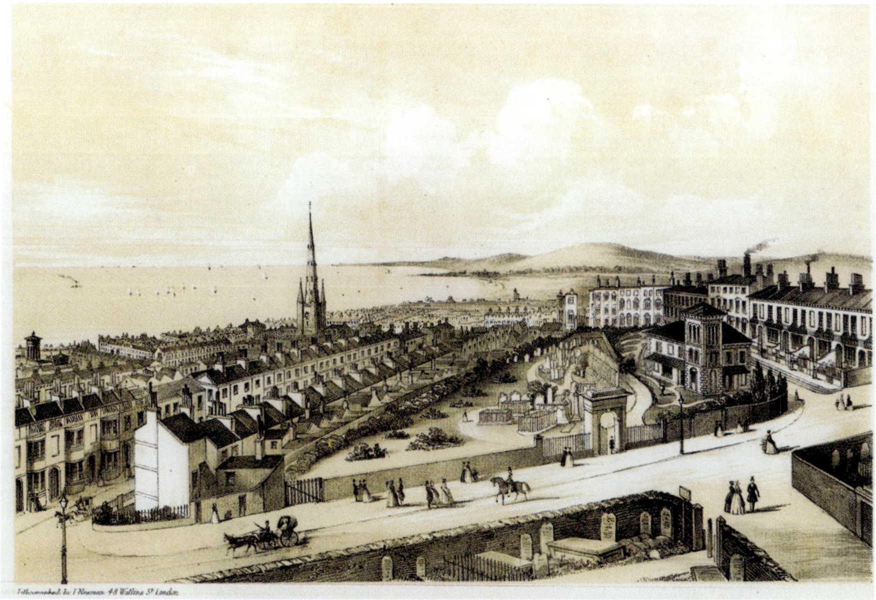

49 *West View of Brighton from the top of the Old Church.*
A pair of lithographs by J Newman, 220mm by 325mm, c1850. Sold at 1s.0d each.
The original drawings are in the British Museum.

372 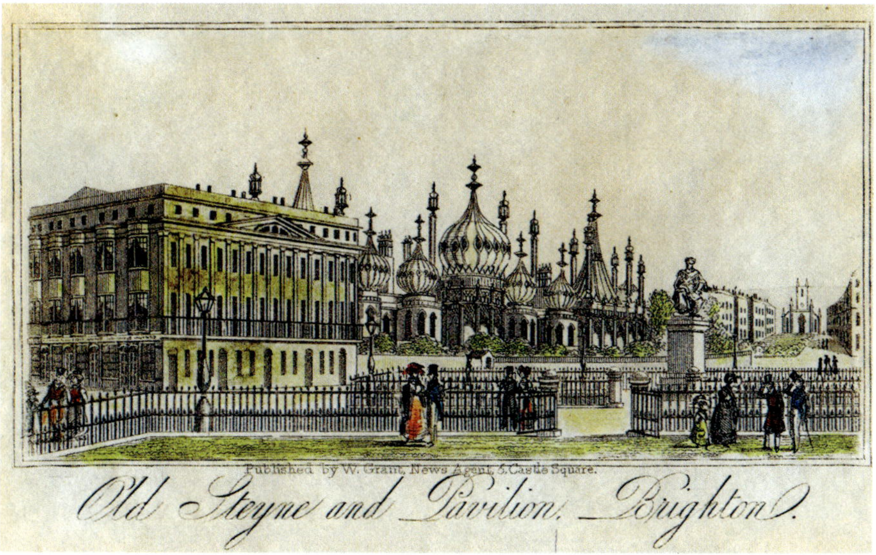

372 *Old Steyne and Pavilion, Brighton.*
Images of Brighton catalogues this print as *Part of Steyne and Palace* and describes it as a copper engraving 50mm by 100mm. However, the Grant version is a steel engraving 53mm by 103mm.

This print is possibly an acquisition by Grant, but as the other version carries no accreditation it is not possible to ascertain this for certain.

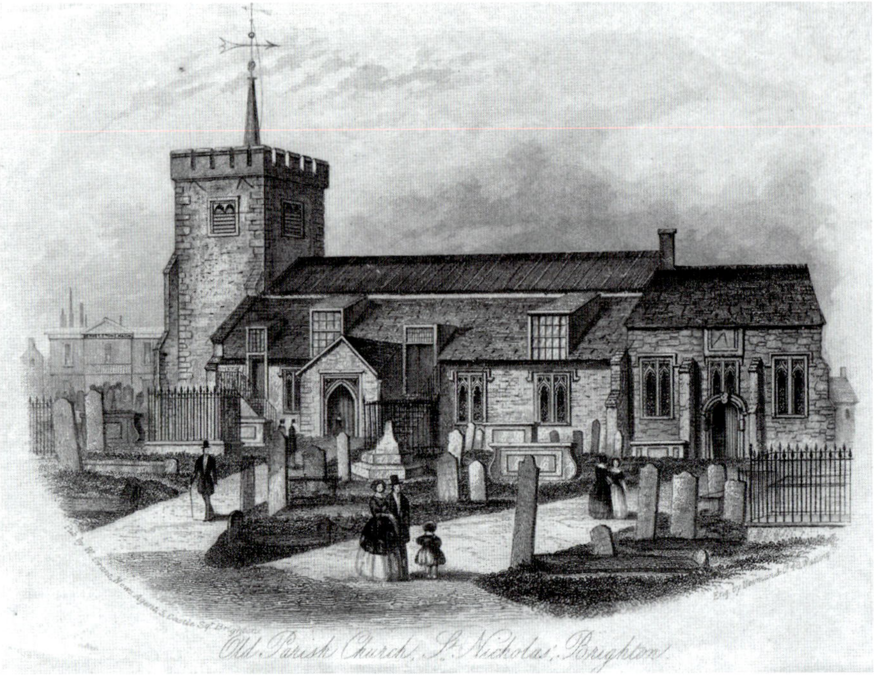

695

695 *Old Parish Church, St. Nicholas, Brighton*. Unnamed artist, engraved: J Newman. Steel engraving, (i) 115mm by 160mm or (ii) 60mm by 90mm, 1848-53.

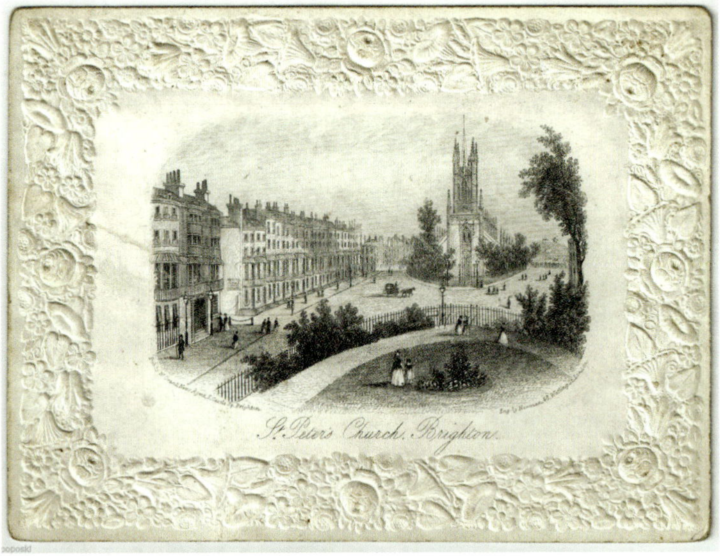

715

715 *New Church, St Peter's, Brighton*. Unnamed artist, engraved: J Newman. Steel engraving, (i) 110mm by 155mm. Another version, with the title *St Peter's, Brighto*n. Unnamed artist, engraved J Newman. Steel engraving, (ii) 65mm by 95mm (embossed greeting card shown, left).

802 *Entrance to the New Cemetery, Lewes Road, Brighton* and
803 *New Cemetery Ground, Lewes Road, Brighton*. Drawn: F Forde, engraved: J Newman. Pair of steel engravings, approximately 60mm by 100mm, 1852-54

817 *Sussex County Hospital, Female Orphan Asylum & St. George's Church, Brighton*. Drawn: W H Delamotte, engraved: W J Alais. Steel engraving, 60mm by 100mm, c1854.

865 *Albion Hotel and Marine Parade, Brighton*. Unattributed to artist and engraver in catalogue. Copper engraving, 50mm by 100mm.

918 *View of the College, Brighton*. Drawn: G Ruff, engraved: T Jeavons. Steel engraving, 60mm by 105mm, c1850.

998 *German Spa, Queen's Park*. Drawn: F Forde, engraved: J Newman. Steel engraving, 95mm by 175mm.

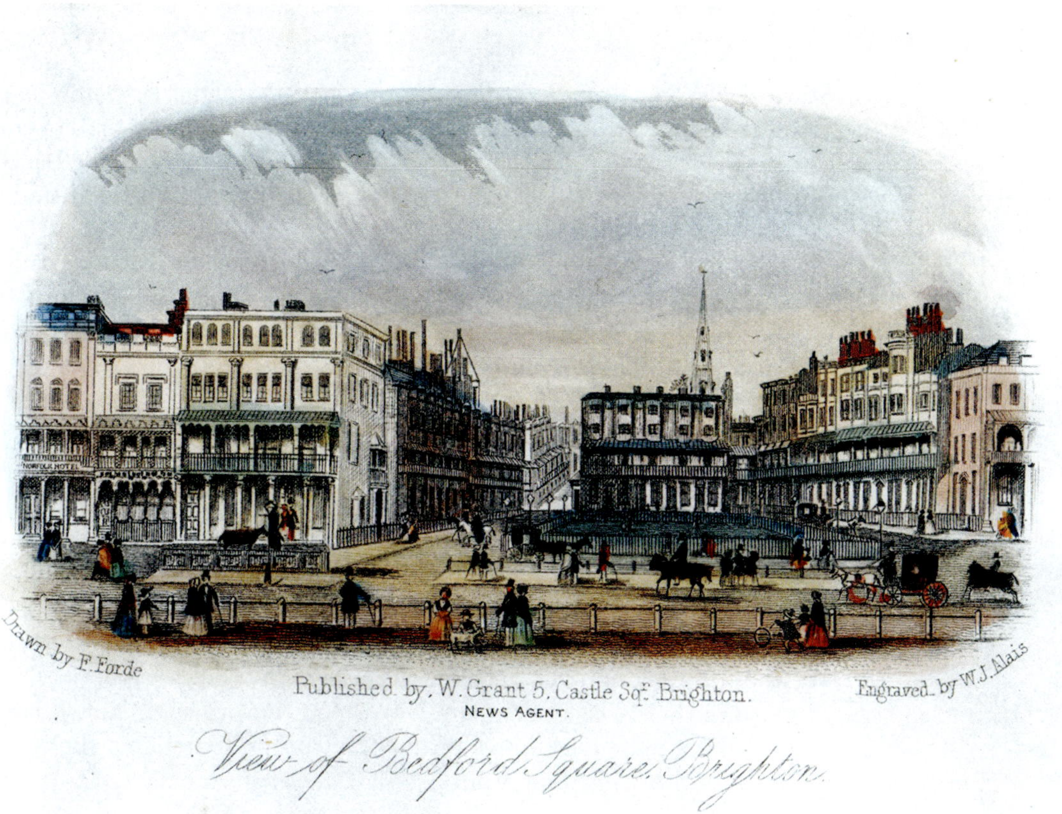

1036

1036 *View of Bedford Square, Brighton*. Drawn: F Forde, engraved: W J Alais c1854. Steel engraving, 55mm by 100mm as letter-headed notepaper.

The above numbered print was attributed to Newman c1865 as publisher and engraver in the *Images of Brighton* catalogue, but a copy of the original by Grant is shown above. The Newman version has been re-engraved with a different façade to the Norfolk Hotel on the left-hand side of the scene, which was rebuilt in 1865.

1039 *Montpelier Crescent, Brighton*. Unnamed artist, engraved: J Newman. Steel engraving, (i) 90mm by 160mm or (ii) 60mm by 90mm.

1064 *View of the Battery, King's Road Brighton from the Sea.* Drawn: W H Delamotte, engraved W J Alais. Steel engraving, 70mm by 100mm, c1854.

1119 *View of Portland Place, Marine Parade, Brighton*. Drawn: F Forde, engraved: W J Alais. Steel engraving, 100mm by 150mm, c1854.

1168 *New Steyne & Devonshire Place from the Chain Pier, Brighton.* Drawn: F Forde, engraved W J Alais. Steel engraving, 95mm x 150mm, c1854.

Acquisitions from other publishers

From George Wise of Tunbridge

600 *The Riding School, Pavilion, Brighton.* Unnamed artist and engraver.

Grant's print of the riding school was evidently originally made by Wise's manufactory for use on their Tunbridge Ware boxes, entitled *The Royal Mews.* Although Ford catalogues the earlier version used by George Wise as a copper plate image of 55mm by 95mm, dating it to around 1805, there is no reference by him to the Grant publication. It will be readily seen that the Grant plate has some minor differences to the original, but it is beyond doubt that it is essentially the same print.

From Samuel Ballard, c1847

290 *Chain Pier, Brighton.* Unnamed artist, engraved J Newman. Steel engraving, 95mm by 155mm.

The original print by Samuel Ballard was published circa 1845 and the address of J Newman, the engraver, is given as 30 Budge Row, London. Those published by Grant, probably from around 1847 onwards, initially continued to carry the same address for the engraver but a later version has the engraver's address as Newman & Co., 48 Watling Street. After 1855 the rights to the print were acquired by Newman, who re-engraved the plate with the addition of a woman seated in a shelter to the right of the scene and republished it under his name.

From W J Taylor, c1854-5

29 *Brighton from the Race Hill.* Unnamed artist. Tinted lithograph by C Graf, 160mm by 265mm.

1008 *West Cliff & Esplanade, Brighton.* After John Baker Pyne. Tinted lithograph by C Graf, 160mm by 270mm.

1071 *Marine Parade, Brighton.* Unnamed artist. Tinted lithograph by C Graf, 170mm by 280mm.

1159 *The East Cliff, Brighton.* Unnamed artist. Tinted lithograph by C Graf, 170mm by 260mm.

W J Taylor's lithographic prints were published between 1850 and 1854, probably originally being released separately as large lithographs of around 170mm by 280mm. Taylor also published an identical set of six scenes, each of around 70mm by 115mm, on a single sheet, which were then usually cut into single small prints. It was probably shortly before Taylor went out of business in April 1855 that Grant acquired the rights to the above four prints (and very likely the other two in the series as well). It is also likely that Grant also acquired the set of six scenes on a single sheet. Although Ford attributes one of these smaller sized prints to Grant, there is no positive method of ascertaining who the publisher was after a sheet was cut up due to the absence of any publisher's markings. It is reasonable to suppose that Taylor had rented the lithographic plates from Charles Graf and that amended stone plates were subsequently commissioned from Graf bearing Grant's own name. These must have been amongst the last prints that Grant published, as his stock-in-trade was seized on 7 June 1855 and bankruptcy was declared a month later. After his bankruptcy these prints were acquired by Saunders and subsequently published in *The Stranger's Guide in Brighton* (1855) in a smaller size of around 65mm by 105mm.

Uncatalogued prints (that can be dated)

WG1-4 *Panorama of the Dyke*. Drawn by F Forde. A series of four views, tinted lithographs by Vizetelly.
View of the Dyke No 1.
View of the Dyke No 2.
View of the Dyke No 3.
View of the Dyke No 4.

These four prints were published on 21 April 1851 and saw a move away from the cheap, mass-produced steel engravings Grant usually offered. It is worth speculating upon how these prints might have been conceived, as ultimately Grant published more different views of the Dyke than any other publisher. The known facts are that on 25 May 1846, W H Mason had previously produced Views on the Downs, a set of four lithographs by Day & Haghe, drawn by Frederick Earp. The individual prints were entitled *The Dyke House, Poynings &c. from the Dyke, The Devil's Dyke* and *Fulking, Edburton, &c. from the Dyke*. All four of these prints were later published by Grant under his own name (see **WG11-14** below). It may have been that the acquisition of these prints was the catalyst for Grant to commission his own panorama. Like his later Panoramic View of Brighton from the Sea, the four lithographic prints could be joined to form one long vista.

It is known that Frederick Forde had come to Brighton to teach watercolour painting in late 1850 at Harriett Shelly's Repository and that he undoubtedly started undertaking work for Grant not long afterwards. By the spring of 1851 Forde was lodging in Borough Street, Brighton and was stated in the press to be a local artist. James Vizetelly (Vizetelly & Co. of 135 Fleet Street, London) was given Forde's artworks to create the lithographic plates for the series of prints. The move to 'collectable artistic prints' encroached into the market sector that Mason excelled at and the complete panorama, nearly five feet in length, was offered at 7s 6d for plain copies, 10s 6d for coloured. The 'Fine Arts' column in the *Brighton Gazette* (24 April 1851) gives a glowing review of the panorama.

PANORAMA FROM THE DYKE.—W. GRANT, NEWS AGENT, of 5, Castle Square, having just completed a beautiful Panorama of that magnificent expanse of country viewed from the Dyke, near Brighton, splendidly lithographed in tints, by Vizetelly, of London, from a very fine drawing by F. Forde, most respectfully informs the Gentry and Inhabitants of Brighton, that it will be published on MONDAY, the 21st inst. Plain Prints, 7s. 6d.; Coloured, 10s. 6d. Subscribers will be supplied with Proof Prints.

'Our enterprising townsman, Mr Grant, of Castle Square, has just published a panoramic view of the beautiful scenery of the Weald of Sussex, as seen from the Dyke hill, the most picturesque spot, perhaps, along the whole range of the South Downs. The drawing is from the well-known pencil of Mr Frederick Ford; and the prints are in the first style of tinted lithography from the equally celebrated presses of Vizetelly. The station of the artist must have been just northward of host Thacker's front door; and the picture embraces the whole of the scenery now adorning what the geologists tell us was once the delta of a European Mississippi, the "everlasting" Chanctonbury ring showing itself on the left, and Poynings Hill appearing on the right, while the Surrey Hills bound the view in the distance, and the foreground gives a portion of the Dyke Hill itself, with appropriate picnic groups, such as may be every day seen about the place in the holiday season, that is, in fine weather. The delineation is most accurate and the arrangement of light and shade skilful and artistic. The size of the panorama, which is nearly five feet in length, gives ample room of the detail; and while the villages of Fulking and Poynings, the latter with its interesting and ancient cruciform parish church, stand boldly out to view at either end of the picture, the intervening fields, buildings, roads, nay even single trees, are shown with an accuracy which renders each spot and object recognizable. Many of the more distant objects are also shown, among the most interesting being Barry's beautiful church at Hurstpierpoint. The panorama is just such a remembrance as the delighted visitor will gladly purchase in order to assist his description of the spot to his friends on his return home; and the price is sufficiently low to command for it, what it so richly deserves, a sale extensive enough to remunerate the publisher'.

WG5 *The Russian Prisoners in Lewes Gaol.* Drawn: W Delamotte, steel engraving by W J Alais, 120mm by 190mm, from a pencil drawing by William Alfred Delamotte—a 125mm by 190mm steel engraving by William John Alais.

Perhaps one of the most unusual prints, published in December 1854 by Grant. Only plain examples are known of this print, which were sold at 6d. The *Brighton Gazette* of 21 and 28 December 1854 announced: 'Mr. Grant, the enterprising newsagent of Castle Square, has just published, from

Just Published.

A SPLENDID STEEL ENGRAVING OF THE RUSSIAN PRISONERS, as seen at Lewes Gaol. Price Sixpence.

Published at W. Grant's Library and News Rooms, 5, Castle Square, and Sold at all Print and Booksellers in Brighton.

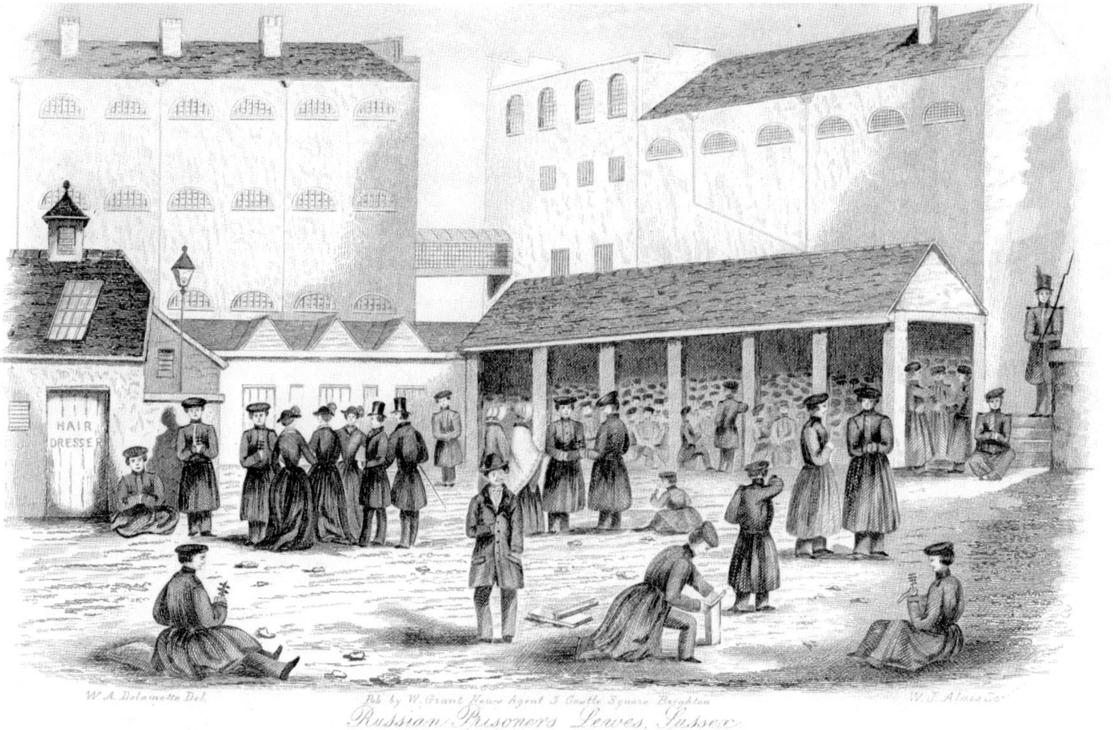

Russian Prisoners Lewes, Sussex.

WG5 the pencil of Mr. W.A. Delamotte, an engraving, representing the airing yard of the government prison at Lewes, with the Russian prisoners, some under cover of a shed, others scattered about the yard engaged in their occupation of toy-making, and still others engaged in conversation with visitors. The print gives an excellent idea of the place and the prisoners'.

Grant was also known to have stocked maps and views of the seat of war with Russia and whether the plight of the Russian prisoners struck a chord with his own encounter at Lewes Gaol, or was in response to the public sympathy shown towards the unfortunate captives, is unknown. Around 350 prisoners captured in August 1854 at Bomarsund, Finland were incarcerated in Lewes Gaol, but they had been afforded an extra-ordinary degree of freedom. Visitors were permitted to enter the prison, where the inmates fabricated toys and other items and were allowed to sell them. These proved to be very fashionable and the income generated allowed the prisoners to have quite a luxurious lifestyle in the circumstances.

Uncatalogued prints (with no identifiable date)

WG6 *St Peter's Church from the Level, Brighton*. Drawn: G Ruff, steel engraving by T Jeavons, 65mm by 95mm, c1852 (overleaf).

WG7 *View of Park Crescent, Brighton*. Drawn W Delamotte, steel engraving by W J Alais, c1854 (overleaf).

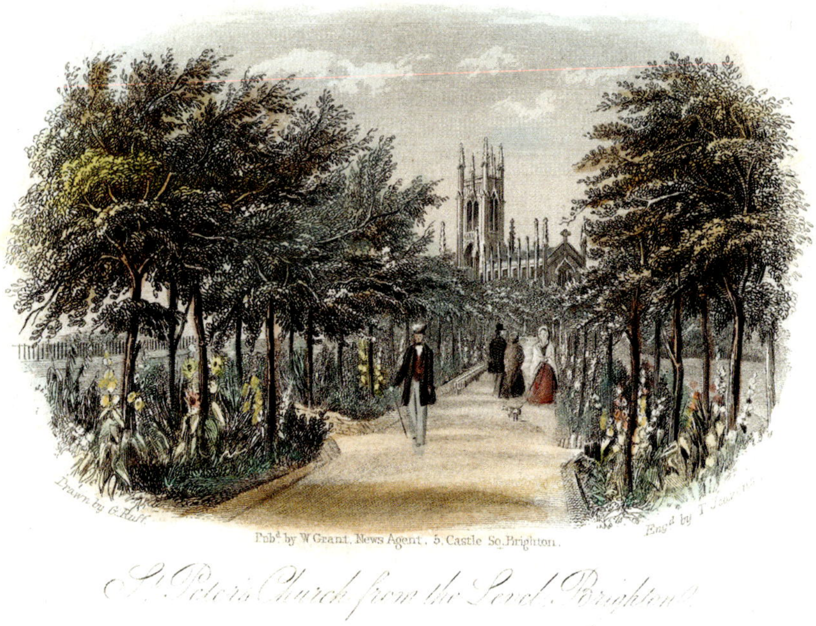

WG6

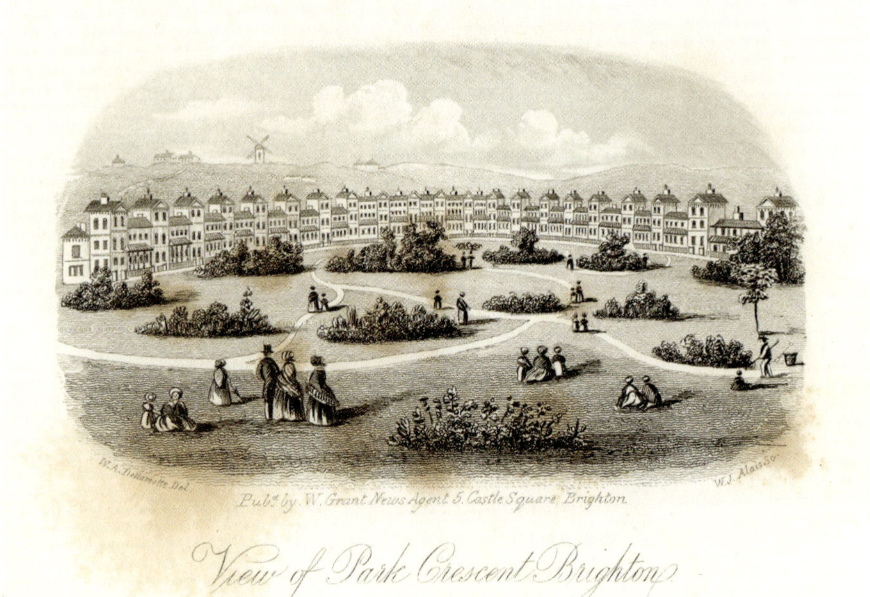

WG7

WG8 *The Pavilion and Observatory, Swiss Gardens, Shoreham.* Engraved: Newman & Co

WG9 *The Lake and Temple, Swiss Gardens, Shoreham*. Engraved: Newman & Co.

WG10 *View from the Castle of Falkenstein, Swiss Gardens, Shoreham.* Engraved: Newman & Co.

It is probably from his association with the Oddfellows that Grant published the set of prints of the Swiss Gardens at Shoreham. The Oddfellows held an annual fête at the Swiss Gardens throughout the 1850s.

WG11 *Fulking from the Dyke Hill*. Drawn F Forde.
WG12 General view from Dyke Hill. Drawn F Forde.
WG13 *The Devil's Dyke*. Drawn F Forde.
WG14 *Poynings Church*. Drawn F Forde.
Coloured lithographs, 65mm by 110mm, c1851.
These four small coloured lithographic views are rather crudely executed depictions of the scenery around the Devil's Dyke, drawn by Frederick Forde, by an unknown lithographer. They may have either been hastily executed precursors to the panorama published by Grant or more likely a cheaper alternative set of small prints for those unable to afford the panorama.

Almost certainly, all of his views of the Devil's Dyke would have been offered locally at the Dyke Hotel. At least one (but probably all) of this small series of prints was later published by Charles Moody of London under his own name.

Acquisitions from other publishers

From W H Mason, published by Grant c1850-52
Four Views of the Devil's Dyke, near Brighton. A booklet of four views after Frederick Earp; W L Walton, Lithographer; printed by Day & Haghe.
WG15 *The Dyke House.*
WG16 *Poynings &c. from the Dyke.*
WG17 *The Devil's Dyke.*
WG18 *Fulking, Edburton, &c. from the Dyke.*
It is unlikely that Mason would have conferred the right to publish these prints to Grant in normal circumstances. However, during the latter half of 1849, Mason was charged with a very serious crime against the daughter of William Thacker, the proprietor of the Dyke Hotel (see page 113). This distressing situation, or perhaps the subsequent compromisation of Mason's ability to sell these prints, most likely led to him divesting himself of them around 1850. It should be borne in mind that host Thacker would have been the primary outlet for the sale of prints at the Devil's Dyke and would hardly have been favourably disposed towards Mason after the trial.

It might reasonably be assumed that Grant's contact with Day & Son, the printers of his *View of the intended Harbour*, led to the acquisition of the Mason prints around 1850. Grant published these prints sometime later and might have delighted in having the 'up-market' prints to sell under his own name, but in reality the sales could have been equally poor.

Serious collectors would already have the identical earlier prints, whilst the association of the print with the Mason trial may well have deterred some buyers. The 255mm x190mm booklets of prints were offered for sale at 1s 6d for tinted lithographs and 3s 0d for coloured—remarkably cheap in consideration of their originally intended market.

[1] W Grant: *W. Grant's Illustrations of the Dyke*. c1850-52, A list of Grant's other publications is given on the rear cover of the booklet.
[2] *Mechanic's Magazine*, no. 970, 12 March 1842
[3] *Illustrated London News*, 3 March 1845, p245
[4] *Brighton Gazette*, 29 January 1852

Appendix 2
Mason's publications

The known prints of Brighton published by W H Mason

This first section contains those prints listed in John & Jill Ford's *Images of Brighton* (*IoB*) the first numeral in bold text is the *IoB* entry. When Mason is a co-publisher he is named with the other companies involved in the print, or if he claims royal patronage, otherwise just the address he gives on the publication line is noted. Occasionally he gives no address.

10 *Brighton 1839*, a long panorama from the sea, also issued in three parts. Lithographed by Day & Haghe, drawn by F C Derby. Published by W H Mason and sold for the benefit of the Sussex County Hospital.
Ford puts c1839 for the publication date, and mentions a label seen with 'W.C. Mason 81 King's Road, Brighton' (the 'C' might be a mistake by the London lithographers). In the *Brighton Herald* of Saturday 13 July 1839 Mason placed an advert for this print saying that 'it was now to be seen' and 'copies to original subscribers may be had next week'.

22 *Panorama of Brighton*, aquatint by A. Edington after H. Wilds. Published by W.H. Mason, Repository of Arts, 1 Ship Street, W. Mason, print-seller, St. Mary's Place, Cambridge and Ackermann & Co., London 1833.
In Mason's newspaper advertisement (*Brighton Guardian*, 11 December 1833), he announces this print as 'Under the Immediate Patronage of Her Most Gracious Majesty, Queen Adelaide'. This is the earliest dated Mason publication.

128 *The First Dip*, aquatint engraved by R Forse, in his *Fashionable Hand-Book for Visitors* 1846, from 81 King's Road.
Apart from the inclusion of the Chain Pier in the background, this image is similar to the same title in the set of six beach scenes engraved by R Forse at **WM14** below. For this and the next two see [**69**] on page 145.
131 *Amphibious*, aquatint from the *Fashionable Hand-Book for Visitors* 1846.
Differs in the inclusion of seafront buildings in the background and its title.
132 *Beauties of Brighton*, steel engraving by R Forse, published c1845.
Differs only in its title.

142 A scene of fishing boats on the beach, lithograph published 1840.
148 A scene of fishing boats and the beach fish market, lithograph published 1840.
149 A scene with a boat and passengers on the beach, lithograph published 1840.

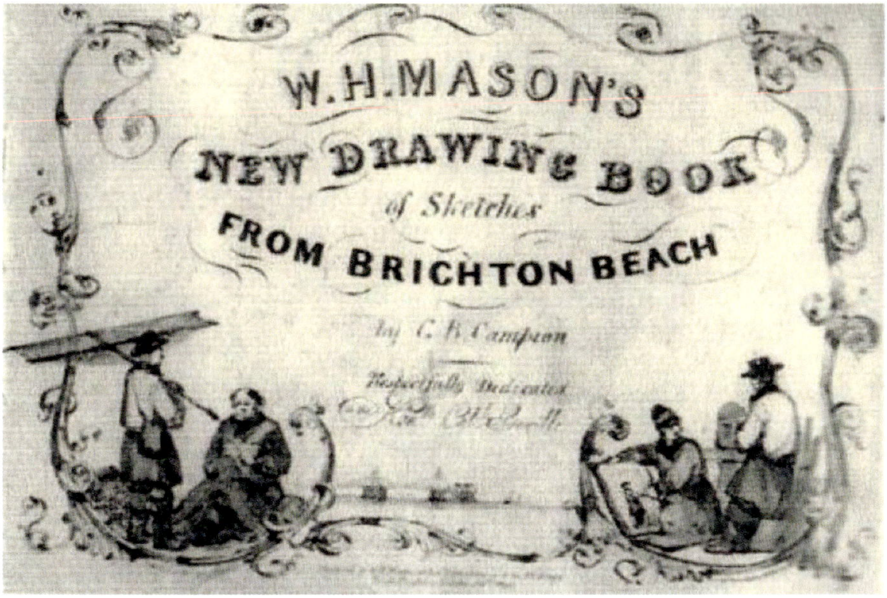

142, 148, 149
Title page of
W H Mason's New Drawing Book

These last three untitled prints are probably from G B Campion's *New Drawing book of Sketches from Brighton Beach*. Listed in *Ackermann—The Business of Art 1783-1983* (Ford, p222) as published by Ackermann & Co., London and W H Mason, 81 King's Road, Brighton, 29 October 1840. A copy of this booklet, in wrappers, was listed in a trade catalogue as having just '3 lithographic plates—stitched as issued in highly decorative printed wrappers'.

158 *Captain Warner's Experiment*, lithograph by Day & Haghe. Drawn by R H Nibbs, published by W.H. Mason, Printseller and publisher to the Queen, 81 King's Road, and Ackermann & Co. London, 27 July 1844.

168 *The Chain Pier*, aquatint by Charles Hunt after J M W Turner. A copy, with many alterations, of the original George Cooke line engraving of this scene. Re-published by Mason under the collective title *W. H. Mason's Views of Brighton* with five prints on one sheet, including numbers 520, 580, 676 and WM13.

233 *The Chain Pier*, aquatint, W H Mason, Brighton. (listed with a date of c1830 but must be later).

280 *Chain Pier, Brighton*, aquatint by Charles Hunt after G B Campion, from 1 Ship Street, 1 September 1838, included in Mason's *Illustrations of Brighton*, 1838. The original watercolour is in Brighton Museum & Art Gallery.

281 *The Chain Pier, Brighton*, aquatint from 81 King's Road. Included in his *Fashionable Hand-Book for Visitors to Brighton*, 1841, also in subsequent undated editions where the title page reads 'For the Present Year'.

283 *The Chain Pier, Brighton*, aquatint after George Earp Jr. From 81 King's Road, c1845.

292 *The Chain Pier Promenade, Brighton*, aquatint after George Earp Jr. From 81 King's Road, c1829. This listed date is too early for Mason in Brighton, or for the artist George Earp, who worked for Mason during the 1840s.

293 *The Chain Pier, Brighton*, lithograph by Jules Arnout after George Earp Jr. From 81 King's Road, 5 May 1846.

520 *The Pavilion*, aquatint. Unattributed, but this is an early Mason publication re-engraved by Charles Hunt from the image in J D Parry's 1833 book *An Historical and Descriptive Account of the Coast of Sussex*, and re-published by Mason under the collective title *W.H. Mason's Views of Brighton* with five prints on one sheet, including numbers 168, 580, 676 and WM13.

525 *The Pavilion, Brighton*, lithograph by Bachelier after George Earp Jr. From Her Majesty's Printseller and Publisher, 81 King's Road, 5 May 1846.

526 *The Pavilion*, aquatint (listed with a date of c1830 but must be later).

527 *The Pavilion*, aquatint from 81 King's Road, included in the *Fashionable Hand-Book for Visitors to Brighton 1841*, and in subsequent undated editions.

580 *New Entrance*, aquatint. Unattributed, but this is an early Mason publication re-engraved by Charles Hunt from the image in J D Parry's 1833 book *An Historical and Descriptive Account of the Coast of Sussex*, re-published by Mason under the collective title *W.H. Mason's Views of Brighton* with five prints on one sheet , including 168, 580, 676 and WM13. The Parry steel engraving, which Mason copied, is listed 581.

625 *The Pavilion, Brighton*, aquatint after George Earp Jr. From 81 King's Road, 1 January 1842.

640 *The Victoria Fountain, Brighton, erected May 26th 1846*, lithograph by W L Walton after T Earp. From 81 King's Road, 26 May 1846.

654 *The Rural Arch. Designed by Mr. G. Cheesman, Junr., and Erected in Honour of Her Majesty's first visit to Brighton*, lithograph after G B Campion, printed by L M Lefevre, c1837. This print is not recorded as being published by Mason but undoubtedly is. The artist Campion, from Ackermanns, worked for no other Brighton publisher and of the four prints recorded from Lefevre's presses, two are for Mason, this one is unattributed and the fourth is too early for Mason.

664 *HM Queen Victoria passing under the Triumphal Arch through the Amphitheatre (designed by Mr. Fabian) erected in honour of HM's first visit to Brighton, October 4th 1837...*, lithograph by G B Campion. No publishing address given.

676 *The Old Church*, aquatint by Charles Hunt c1833. No publication line given but this is one of the five scenes on one sheet (see page 184), together with entries 168, 580, 676 and WM13.

679 *St Nicholas Church, Brighton*, lithograph by Bachelier after George Earp Jr. From Her Majesty's Printseller and Publisher, 81 King's Road, 5 May 1846.

629 *St Nicholas' Church, Brighton, the Revd H.M. Wagner, Vicar*, lithograph by W L Walton, after F Forde. Included in *Brighton Illustrated*,1851.

728 *St Peter's Church, Brighton*, aquatint by Charles Hunt after George Earp Jr. From 81 King's Road, 20 November 1840.

731 *St Peter's Church, Brighton, the Revd Thos. Cooke, Curate*, included in *Brighton Illustrated*, 1851.

742 *St Peter's Church, Brighton*, lithograph, sketched by ECJ and printed by Hullmandel & Walton, 14 December 1850. Included in *Brighton Illustrated*, 1851.

745 *St Peter's Church, Brighton, and view of E. Hildyard's family hotel, The Richmond*, aquatint after George Earp Jr, from 81 King's Road, 1 January 1842.

747 *St Peter's Church, Brighton*, aquatint by Charles Hunt after G B Campion. Print-seller by Appointment to Her Majesty, 1 Ship Street, Brighton, 1 September 1838. Included in *Illustrations of Brighton*, 1838.

762 *Hove Church*, lithograph by W Gauci after George Earp Jr, 29 June 1848, no address given.

774 *Christ Church, Brighton (The Revd. James Vaughan, incumbent)*, lithograph by W L Walton. Included in Brighton Illustrated, 1851.

775 *Emmanuel Church, Brighton*, lithograph after M Hall, c1870. The church building was completed in 1868.

781 *Interior of the Royal Chapel, Brighton, with members of the Royal Family at a service, including Princess Augusta, H.R.H. William IV and Queen Adelaide, Prince George of Cambridge*, aquatint by Charles Hunt. Published by W H Mason, Printseller to the Queen, Repository of Arts, Ship Street, Ackermann & Co., London, and Mason, Cambridge c1835. This is the only known engraving of the chapel interior. Mason dedicated this print 'By Permission to His Serene Highness the Prince Ernest of Hesse-Philippsthal' by 'His Most Obd^{t} Servt'. Below the publication line, Mason took the opportunity to advertise other features of his Repository, a move presumably sanctioned by the Royal Family, so after his Ship Street address he wrote: 'Where may be had his Panorama of Brighton, drawings and paintings for sale or to copy, Elegant Albums, etc., and every material for drawing and painting'.

782 *St George's Chapel and the Sussex County Hospital*, aquatint, from 81 King's Road, 1 December 1841.

787 *St Mark's Church and St. Mary's Hall, Kemp Town, Brighton*, lithograph by C Moody after Page. From 108 King's Road, 28 April 1854.

791 *St Paul's Church, Brighton*, lithograph by W L Walton. Included in Brighton Illustrated, 1851.

825 *The Town Hall, Brighton (Erected 1827—T. Cooper, arch)*, lithograph after F Earp. Included in Brighton Illustrated, 1851.

836 *The Opening of the Shoreham Branch of the London and Brighton Railway, May 1840*, aquatint by Charles Hunt. From 81 King's Road, 20 November 1840. Re-published under this title as a lithograph, drawn by H G Hine.

and Charles, the engraver of this sheet would certainly be Charles. None of Mason's nine Hunt publications was engraved by George.

So three of the four surrounding aquatints detailed above are clearly taken from earlier steel engravings. There are minor alterations to the foreground figures and trees, but apart from this the images are the same.

However, the large central view of the *Chain Pier* can be viewed in a different light. It is listed as **168**[iii] in *IoB* as the fifth, slightly smaller edition of the J M W Turner image and described as 'a copy of Turner's view', but again without the publisher's imprint. Four of the editions of this famous view of Turner's *Chain Pier* were line engravings, either on steel or copper, by George Cooke, taken from Turner's original watercolour that included the prominent rainbow. This 'rainbow' picture, of which Brighton Museum & Art Gallery purchased the original watercolour in 2012, was first published in September 1825 and went through these four different states. The first was the copper-plate line engraving by George Cooke. Cooke then engraved the scene on steel for Turner's *Antiquarian and Picturesque Tour* publication of 1849, and Virtue & Co. of London republished this steel plate c1878. The original copper-plate was then re-engraved to strengthen the worn parts and printed again by Huish in 1892 (the sky on this plate is dark).

But long before the steel edition and the re-engraved copper plate were published, Mason produced this, the only aquatint version, in the mid-1830s. The image of the *Chain Pier* on W H Mason's sheet has many differences from the 'rainbow' image, which was a feature of Turner's original watercolour (see contrasting illustrations below). In Mason's aquatint the view to the left of the Albion Hotel is considerably shortened (right-hand image below) and it misses out Lamprell's Baths and the beginning of King's Road. There are different figures in the two fishing boats, a different portrayal of the crowd on the pier head, there is no buoy floating to the left of the pier and the large water-wheel/treadmill near the pier entrance is not in place (having been blown down a few years earlier).

It could be said that Mason's aquatint is the more dramatic of the two compositions: the engraver has set the horizon line differently, so

Turner's *Chain Pier*:
Below left
Cooke's line engraving (1825)
Below right
Mason's aquatint (1833/37)

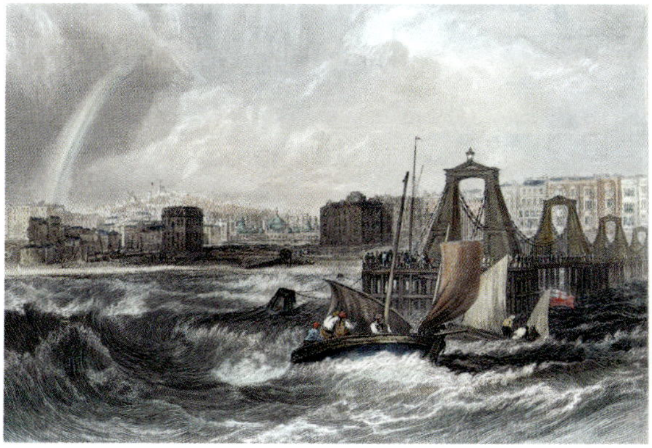

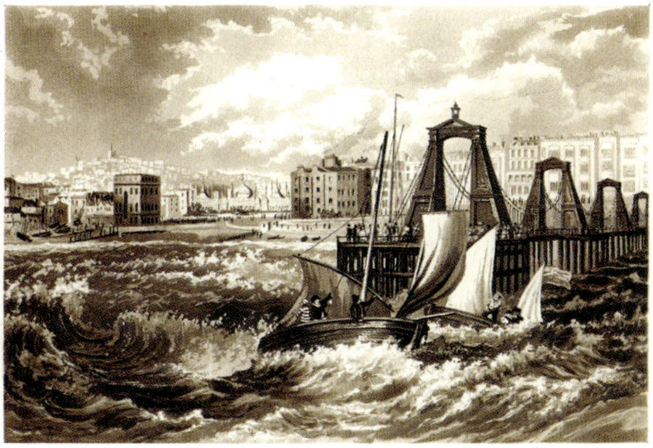

portraying more of the turbulent sea. Also the pier arches have a more imposing feel to them, the foremost arch is much closer to the top of the paper in Mason's view, and of course there is no rainbow. Because of the rarity in finding this sheet uncut, this aquatint edition of Turner's *Chain Pier*, engraved by Charles Hunt, is not recorded in any Brighton reference books as being published by Mason.

In a private letter to the authors, Ian Warrell (international expert on Turner and Constable) puts this Mason aquatint into context. Turner's work had been the subject of much plagiarism for years, until the artist finally brought a court case against the London publisher Charles Tilt (who later co-published a number of plates with Mason). The case caused much public interest in October 1833 but Turner represented himself sufficiently badly that the case went against him. Warrell writes 'as a result there was a further free-for-all in adapted uses of Turner's images by others during the 1830s'. So it is into this category of artistic plagiarism that Mason and Charles Hunt's print of the five scenes on one sheet must fall.

In three of the smaller surrounding scenes on Mason's publication the copying from other lesser-known artists is blatant, with little effort made to differentiate from the originals. But in the use of Turner's Chain Pier Mason and Hunt made these numerous alterations, presumably in an attempt to distance themselves from any complaints. Warrell's letter continues 'If Mason was prepared to borrow designs so readily, without giving any credit to the other artists, he would obviously not have felt any qualms about taking on Turner at a time when the Lord Mayor of London (who had presided over the Charles Tilt case) had effectively sanctioned the re-use of Turner's images for commercial gain'.

From the point of view of Turner's original scene of 1825, it must be remembered that a year earlier, in September 1824, Robert Havell, the artist of *The Coasting View of Brighton*, published a small aquatint titled 'Brighton from the Sea'. It was included in Brayley's *Topographical Sketches of Brighthelmstone*. Exactly like Turner, Havell's view was from out at sea, a little south-east from the Chain Pier Head, with a distant view of the Pavilion domes in the centre of the townscape on the shoreline. Turner created drama out of the scene, but Havell is rather 'matter-of-fact' in his composition (see page 82-83).

Unrecorded Brighton publications by Mason

For ease of future reference these have been given numbers. The full publication line has been given where Mason was the co-publisher.

WM1 *Parish Church*, aquatint included in *Brighton Illustrated*, Part one.

WM2 *Young Amphibious*, lithograph by Charles J Basebe after George Earp Jr,printed by Day & Haghe lithographers to the Queen. Published 1 July 1844, by W H Mason, Repository of Arts, Brighton. London, Ackermann & Co. Strand, Reeves & Son, Cheapside. A very rare lithograph.

The print shows a view at Brighton, with the pier behind; a woman holding her naked child over the water, with a traditional bathing machine to the left. It is a similar scene to *The First Dip* in the set of six steel engravings by Forse, but much larger, being 10 ins x 14 ins.

WM3 *The Brighton Pavilion*, black & white letter-heading, steel engraving with a watermark 'Towgood 1855' [**71**]. (Mason declared himself bankrupt 13 October 1855.)

WM4 *Marine Parade Brighton*, black & white letter-heading, steel engraving [**71**].

WM5 *Roe Park, Withdean, Near Brighton*, lithograph drawn by A H Wilds, Archt., W H Mason lithograph. Printed by Hullmandel and Walton. Published from 81 King's Road, Brighton. This plate shows the suggested (but never built) Roe Park development at Withdean [**48**]. William Roe owned extensive lands contiguous with the northern boundary of Brighton. The print is 18 ins by 11 ins and, with the 1833 *Panorama of Brighton*, is the only other venture between Amon Henry Wilds and Mason.

WM6 *Brighton Excursion Day* and *Brighton Morning Promenade*, pair of woodcuts from drawings by Edward Hull. Engraved by Hull and published 10 October 1860.

WM7 In Vol 8 of the Erredge Collection in Brighton's Jubilee Library Rare Books Department there are 14 small uncoloured lithographic vignettes of fishing boats on the beach, no titles, but several have the publication line 'W.H. Mason—Brighton'.

WM8 & **WM9** The *Brighton Companion* 1841 (a very brief existence) and the Illustrated Cricketers' Journal. In *The Story of a Cricket Picture* (p31) Taylor notes these had very limited success and examples of either publication have not been seen.

WM10 *Swiss Cottage, Chalybgate*, lithograph published by Mason and Ackermann c1837. This is a rare print of the cottage that stood at the entrance to the Chalybeate, now St Ann's Well Gardens, Hove. The word 'chalybeate' is incorrectly spelt in the title.

WM11 *Capt George Richard Pechell, Royal Navy, as he received the several deputations with addresses at Brighton on the evening of the 4th Oct., 1836*, lithograph by T. Wageman after Edward Morton. Published from Ship Street. Printed by J Graf. Pechell was MP for Brighton from 1835 to 1860, becoming a vice-admiral and baronet.

WM12 *HB Quizzing the Political Sketches at Mason's*, lithograph published in October 1839 from 81 King's Road. This is the earliest King's Road publication found [**77**].

WM13 *The New Church*, aquatint engraved by Charles Hunt and published between 1833 and 1839 under the collective title *W.H. Mason's Views of Brighton* with five prints on one sheet, together with entries 168, 520, 580 and 676 from *IoB*. This same view is listed in *IoB* as number 730 with the title *St Peter's Church, Brighton*, which is the steel engraving found in Thomas Allen's 1829 book *A History of the*

Counties of Surrey and Sussex, from which this view by W H Mason was copied. This aquatint version is not listed in *IoB*.

WM14 The set of six beach scenes: steel plates published by W H Mason, Brighton. Undated, no artist or engraver named, but thought to be after drawings by Mason himself: *The First Dip, Landing the Fare, The Water Witch, Sea Side Enjoyment, Sea Nymphs, The Water Lily* [**69**]. R Forse first engraved two of these scenes on copper c1840 (they are listed as aquatints in *IoB*, numbers 128 & 131). He then engraved the this set of six on steel in much the same size but with alterations to the backgrounds of the two previous aquatint scenes. It is not known if the two listed in *IoB* as 128 and 131 are part of a set of six; if they are, then a full set of aquatint plates has not been found.

WM15 *Key Plate to W.H. Mason's Drawing of a Cricket Match at Brighton between the Counties of Sussex and Kent*, line engraving published by Mason in Brighton, Ackermann at 96 Strand and E Gambarts, Berners Street, London, 1849. Whilst it is listed in *IoB*, it is worth noting that on the key plate Ackermann was named as Mason's co-publisher but was not involved in the print itself, and it was Dedicated by Express Permission to HRH Prince Albert, as was the print itself.

WM16 *Sir David Scott*, lithograph by T Wageman after Edward Morton, undated but published from Ship Street c1836. Sir David was a local magistrate, director of the East India Company and the developer of Oriental Place.

WM17 *The late Rev. F.W. Robertson MA., Incumbent of Trinity Chapel.* After C J Basebe, published September 1853 [**55**]. Robertson succeeded Rev. Anderson at Trinity in 1847.

WM18 *The Rev. Robert Anderson*, mezzotint engraving by Henry Dawe after C J Basebe. The British Museum has a copy dated March 1840 and the National Portrait Gallery has a copy dated 25 March 1843. In 1842 Mason placed an advertisement the *Brighton Herald* saying that due to demand the print had been re-engraved and copies were ready for inspection, with proofs printed on India paper priced at £1 11s 6d. There is also a lithograph of Rev. Anderson in the Royal Collection. Rev. Anderson purchased Trinity Chapel [**59**] from T R Kemp and brought it into the Anglican Church in 1825.

WM19 *The Rev. Thomas Cooke*, lithograph published January 1851. The copy in Brighton Museum was presented by Rev. Cooke's widow in August 1893. Cooke, the Curate at St Peter's from 1824 to 1873, was one of Rev. Henry Wagner's closest associates and on retirement was presented with a silver model of St Peter's, which is in the Brighton Museum collection.

WM20 *William Seymour*, lithograph after Charles J Basebe, published 1851 [**76**]. Seymour was a successful London lawyer who became chairman of the Brighton Bench. Included in Part 2 of *Brighton Illustrated*, with biography and a lithograph of Seymour's bust in the Pavilion.

WM21 *Portrait of Henry Harrap, Esq of Brighton*, probably a lithograph, published October 1860.

Non-Brighton publications

WM22 *Dr Martin Luther*, mezzotint book illustration after Henry Dawe, engraved from an authentic portrait. Published 1840 from 81 King's Road.
WM23 *Robert Henderson*, clerical portrait engraved by H Dawe after C J Basebe, published 25 March 1843. On the publication line Mason described himself as 'by Appointment to the Queen'.
WM24 *Latimer*, mezzotint engraving after Henry Dawe, published c1840 from 81 King's Road. On the British Museum copy is the lettering 'Born 1480. Burnt alive and died a martyr to the Reformation October 1554'.
WM25 *Dr Pusey*, lithograph by J H Lynch after J Watkins. Published 21 January 1867. Edward Bouverie Pusey (1800-1882) was one of the leaders of the Oxford Movement and Professor of Hebrew at Christ Church, Oxford. He was of significant influence in all the major controversies affecting the Church of England in the mid-19th century.
WM26 *H.R.H. The Late Prince Consort*, photographic print, photographed by M Mason from a print after C J Basebe. Published 12 January 1862. The title line continues 'Born Augt 26th 1819. Died Decr 14th 1861'.

WM30
Frontispiece of the 1846 edition of his *Fashionable Hand-Book for Visitors to Brighton* is a portrait of The Queen and Prince Albert, printed by L M Lefevre, Newman Street, London. The version below shows the variation resulting from hand colouring

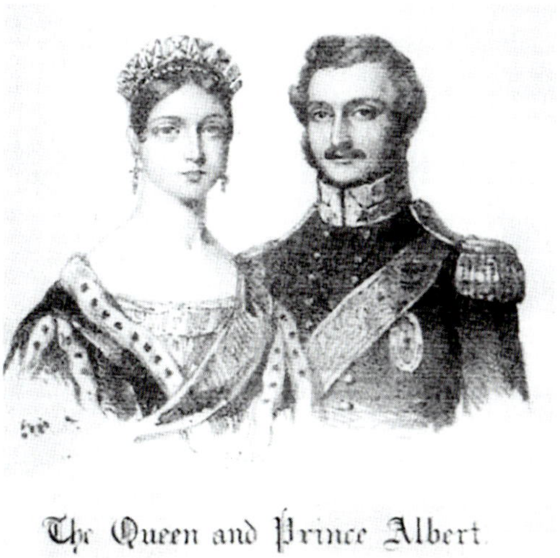

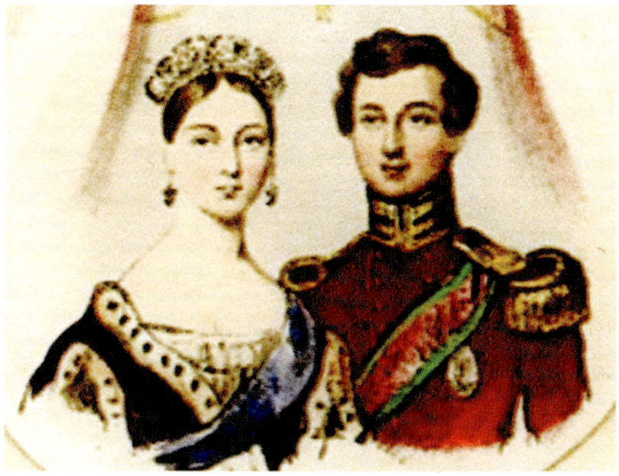

WM27 *Her Majesty The Queen Victoria*, photographic print by M Mason from a print after C J Basebe. Published 1862 as a companion piece to *The Late Prince Consort*. This 'M. Mason' is the eldest Mason daughter, Mary. The whole family was living together at this date, so the 20-year-old Mary was still with her older brother, the 22-year-old photographer, William.
WM28 Two portrait photographs of the English actor William Henry Chippendale, in the V & A collection. One is oval, one oblong, both taken by W H Mason junior, no publication line but presumed to be published by his father.
WM29 *Her Most Gracious Majesty Victoria in the Royal Closet St George's*, stipple engraving by J Posselwhite after Henry Dawe. Published by Mason, 81 King's Road, H E Dawe of Kentish Town, Ackermann, Strand and J B Brown of Windsor.
WM30 *The Queen and Prince Albert*, lithograph printed by L M Lefevre, London 1846.
WM31 *Mr. Chas. Kean as Claude Melnotte*, published by W H Mason and Lefevre & Kohler, c1845. A copy is in the V&A collection.
WM32 *Albert Edward*, photographic process, hand coloured print. Photograph by John & Charles Watkins, published 1860.

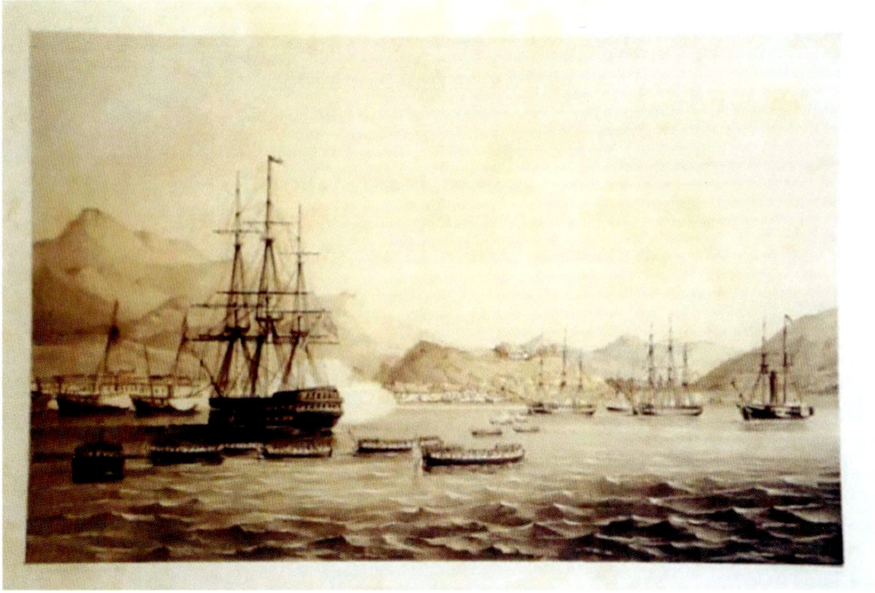

WM35
'Taking of the Island of Chusan by the British, July 5th 1840'

WM33 *HRH Prince Albert of Saxe Coburg Gotha, KG*, stipple engraving by E Hacker after Henry Dawe, published 1840 by R Ackermann, London, Mason of 81 King's Road and Charles Tilt.

WM34 *Panorama of the Fort of Multan*, from the British Library India Office Select Materials, lithographs, one of a pair after William Vincent, Ensign 49th BNI. Published 1850.

WM35 *China, India, Cape of Good Hope and Vicinity*, a volume of 13 lithographic views after sketches by Lieut-Col Sir Harry Francis Colville Darell, Bt, (1814-1853) 7th Dragoon Guards. Published by Day & Sons, London and W H Mason, King's Road, Brighton 1852. The titles include *Small Indian Temple, Parell*; *The Government House, Bombay*; *The Interior of the Caves of Elephanta*; *Caves of Elephanta, exterior*; *Taking of the Island of Chusan by the British, July 5th 1840* and *Colonel Hare, Lieut-Governor with the Caffir Chiefs at Blockdrift Run*. Four of these are in the India Office Select Materials section of the British Library.

WM36 *A Wick'd Subject—Political Scraps No: 1*, mezzotint published by Mason 81 King's Road and Ackermann & Co. Strand, 10 November 1843 [**60**].

WM37 *The Rev. Mr Joseph Sortain*, mezzotint engraving by Henry Dawe after a sketch by Hardy. Sortain was highly regarded as a preacher in his day, and noted for his sermons rarely exceeding half an hour. He wrote novels as well as theological and philosophical texts. A copy of this engraving is also in the National Portrait Gallery.

WM38 *The Norfolk Suspension Bridge, Shoreham. From a Sketch in the Possession of the Revd. Robt. Fennell*, aquatint by Charles Hunt after E W Woledge. Printseller to Her Majesty from his Repository of Arts, Ship Street. Known watermark 1836. The bridge was opened in 1833.

On the publication line Mason advertises his 'Panorama and other Views of Brighton—paintings and drawings for sale or to copy, with every necessary material for drawing or painting—elegant albums, scrap books etc.'

WM39 *Political Sketch, the Brighton Omnibus Legislator*, includes caricatures of Captain George Pechell MP and Major Allen. Published c1838.

WM40 *This print of The Viaduct, in commemoration of the opening throughout of the Brighton & London Railway, Sept 21st 1841*, aquatint after George Earp Jr, published 21 September 1841. The scene shows what is known as the Balcombe Viaduct today.

WM41 In the Erredge Collection in Brighton Jubilee Library Rare Books Department, Vol 4 page 116 is an untitled black & white aquatint by Charles Hunt 'from a sketch by H.B', a self-portrait of John Doyle on Horseback, published from 1 Ship Street.

WM42 *Lillywhite's Illustrated Handbook of Cricket*, published by Ackermann & Co. Strand, Moore, corner of West Street & St. Martin's Lane, and W H Mason, Repository of Arts, 1844. Published in a variety of editions, the most expensive with portraits of four players, four gentlemen and Lillywhite himself.

WM43 *Seaford Cliff—as it appeared immediately after the explosion (by voltaic battery) Sept 19th 1850*, lithograph drawn by 'Miss Nanny', printed by Chape & Lefevre, 99 Guildford Street, Russell Square, London and 'Published for the Proprietor at 80 King's Road, Brighton'. The imprint has Mason's address, but not his name.

WM44 *The Explosion of Seaford Cliff, Sepr. 19th 1850*, lithograph by Day & Son, Lithrs to the Queen after F Forde, published by W H Mason, 80 Kings Road, Brighton, 2 October 1850. The text reads: 'By Means of two Mines of Twelve Thousand Pounds of powder each, fired by two of the Groves Voltaic Batteries, at the same instant / one by Captain Frome, R.E., the other by Lieutenant Ward, R.E / to whom this plate is respectfully dedicated / by their most obedient Servant, W. H. Mason'. Unlike the Seaford Cliff print above, in this one the view of the cliff is taken from out at sea.

WM45 *W.H. Mason's Illustrations of Arundel Castle*, a set of four lithographs by Mason after members of the Earp family—two are after George Earp Jr, one after F Earp and one after H Earp. Published by Frederick Mason, High Street, Arundel and W H Mason, Brighton, 1 December 1846. The titles are: *Triumphal Arch* after George Earp Jr; *Distant View of Arundel Castle* after F Earp; *The Dairy, Arundel Castle* after H Earp and *Arundel Castle from the Meadow* after George Earp Jr. The Royal Collection at Windsor has three of the four, but the complete set does not appear to be in a public collection. Not having been seen by the authors, the complete set is only known by virtue of a copy of an invoice from a print dealer in Arundel who sold a set 30 years ago.

The Van Earps were originally from Holland, but the father of the Earp family involved with Brighton was George Earp Snr (1795-1854) and the artists involved in this set are his three sons; his first son George Jr (1818-1888), his second son Frederick (1827-1898), who taught art at St Mary's Hall and Lancing College, then Henry Earp (1831-1914), his third son who taught Aubrey Beardsley at the Grammar School. Of George Earp Jr's family, three of his sons were artists. (See Appendix 3 for the Earp family tree.)

WM46 *The Plan of the Village of Hurstpierpoint in the County of Sussex*, copper-plate line engraving, a coloured map by the land surveyor and accountant James Fisher, published 1841. This was a large publication, 48 ins by 20 ins, printed in sections, then lain upon linen and presented in a cloth slipcase. The map was published with a separate explanation, dedicated by permission to the Rev. Carey Hampton Borrer MA, listing the names and addresses of the 142 residents of the village.

WM47 *Views on the Downs*, a set of four lithographs by W L Walton, printed by Day & Haghe after Frederick Earp. Published 25 May 1846 from 81 Kings' Road. Three are in Brighton Museum, without lettering, but one has the hand-written note 'Poynings etc from the Dyke' and 'Day & Haghe, litho to the Queen'. The full set of titles are I: The Dyke House; II: Fulking, Edburton etc from the Dyke; III: Poynings etc from the Dyke; IV: The Devil's Dyke. The set was taken over by William Grant (see page 175).

WM48 *The Generous Enemy—Russian Prisoners at Lewes, (from life)*, lithograph after Alfred Crowquill. Printed by McLure, McDonald and McGregor c1855. Publication line just reads 'Repository of Arts', but no address.

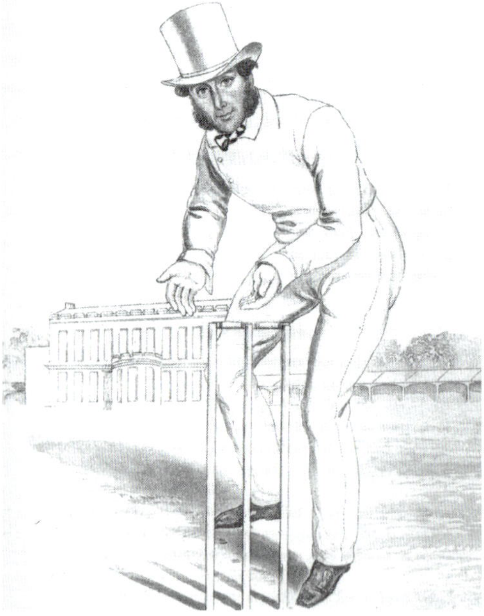

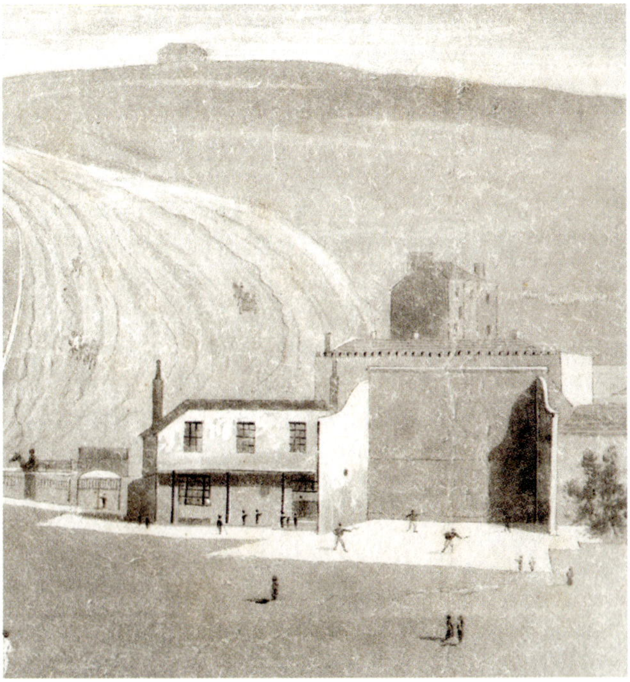

WM51
Left The portrait of Thomas Box from the *Hand-Book of Cricke*t showing the Pavilion of the Royal Cricket Ground with awnings right and left.
Right Thomas Box's Hanover Arms with the fives court beside it. This image is a detail from Ireland's Royal Gardens [**63**]

WM49 *The Cricketer Benjamin Aislabie*, 1839.

WM50 *Cricketer's Adhesive Envelope Wafers.* Most of Mason's cricket publications, re-engraved in miniature and printed on small adhesive wafers to seal envelopes, c1850. They retailed in boxes of 50 for 1s.

WM51 Eight portraits from *Lillywhite's Hand-Book of Cricket.* The book was published by Mason and Ackermann in 1844 but the portraits were published individually by Mason between May and October 1841. They are aquatint and line engravings by Charles Hunt after Charles Basebe: *William Lillywhite—born June 13th 1792 at Goodwod, Sussex; Fuller Pilch—born March 17th 1803 at Horningtoft, Norfolk; Thos Box—born Feb 7th 1809 at Ardingly, Sussex; Roger Kynaston, jun^{r} Esq; Ja^{s} Cobbett—born Jan 12th 1804 at Frimley, Surrey, George Leopold Langton, Esq; Charles George Taylor, Esq; Alfred Mynn, Esq*

Of these personalities, James Cobbett and George Langton are not in Mason's 1849 *Cricket Match* print. Box's public house was on the eastern edge of the Royal Cricket Ground, the Lewes Road running behind it and the unmade track of Race Hill Road (later Elm Grove) going up the hill. It was in the Hanover Arms that Mr Brown held his annual cricketing dinner, chaired by Mason in 1837. Sickelmore in *Descriptive Views of Brighton* (1824), explains that behind the inn there was 'extensive stabling . . . desirably obscured from the cricket ground by a racket and fives court'.

Additional non-Brighton prints in the Royal Collection, Windsor

These have been included in the WM numbering.

WM52 *The Exterior and Interior of the Royal Chapel, St James's*, lithograph drawn and published by W.H. Mason, Brighton, Ackermann & Co, London and Charles Tilt, 86 Fleet Street, London, 10th February 1840.

WM53 *Queen Victoria's Visit to the City of London, 9th November 1837*, coloured lithograph. The pair to this print: 'Queen Victoria's coronation procession to Westminster Abbey' is in Brown University Library, USA. The pair is after G B Campion and printed by J Graf.

WM54 *Eton from the North Terrace*, lithograph by W Walton after George Earp, printed by F Dangerfield and published by W H Mason, Brighton and W F Taylor, Windsor.

WM55 *The New Windsor Pear (or Magnum Bonum)*, published by I M Lefevre, Newman Street, London, W H Mason, Brighton and Ackermann & Co., London.

WM56 *Rev. James Anderson (1800-1869)*, lithograph by Day & Hague after Charles Baugniet (1814-1886), published by J Hogarth, 60 Portland Street, and W H Mason, Brighton.

WM57 *The Rt Hon the Earl of Egremont*, mezzotint by Thomas Lupton (1791-1873) after George Clint (1770-1854). Published by Ackermann & Co. 96 Strand and W H Mason, Brighton.

Non-Brighton prints and photographs from the National Portrait Gallery website

WM58 *William Harrison Ainsworth*, oval albumen photo print from the 1850s for Hennah & Kent. A *carte-de-visite*.

WM59 *William Henry Hunt—displaying one of his paintings*, published in the 1860s from a photograph probably by W H Mason Jr. A carte-de-visite.

WM60 *Edward Bouverie Pusey*, photograph published in the 1860s. A carte-de-visite. Mason also published a lithograph of the Rev. Pusey (WM25).

WM61 *Sir George Biddell Airy*, lithograph by Thomas Wagemen and printed by Graf & Soret. Sir George was the Astronomer Royal 1835-1881. Co-published with W Mason, Cambridge.

WM62 *Charles Edward Kennaway*, stipple engraving by William Drummond after Thomas Wright, published 1 September 1848. The Rev. Kennaway was Canon of Gloucester Cathedral.

WM63 *Abraham Lincoln*, photograph by Mathew Brady, published 1860. A *carte-de-visite*.

Regarding this photographic portrait of Abraham Lincoln, the photographer Mathew B Brady (1822-1896) was one of the most important of the 19th century American photographers, who was a favourite with Abraham Lincoln. It seems unlikely that Brady visited Brighton but during his 1851 tour of Europe he visited the Great Exhibition of that year, where he was awarded a medal, having exhibited 20 photographs there. It is very likely that Mason father and son visited the Exhibition, for the photographic display if nothing else, and clearly at some stage contact was made between the Masons and Brady, and agreement was reached to publish this portrait a few years later. The Great Exhibition had over six million visits by the time it closed in the October of that year, and covering the opening, an edition of The Times reported that 'it was the first morning since the creation of the world that all peoples have assembled from all parts'.

Non-Brighton prints in Brown University, USA

WM64 *The Eleventh or Prince Albert's Own Hussars*. Aquatint engraving by Charles Hunt after J Earp. Published by W H Mason & Ackermann & Co, 1840.

WM65 *Inniskilling Dragoons, 25th Octr. 1854* Lithograph by E Walker after A F De Prades. Published by W H Mason and Lloyd Brothers, 1858. Printed by Day & Co.

There are a total of 178 known engraved plates and photographs published by W H Mason, counting each individual plate included in pairs or sets. He produced a known total of 125 publications, counting pairs and sets as one unit publication.

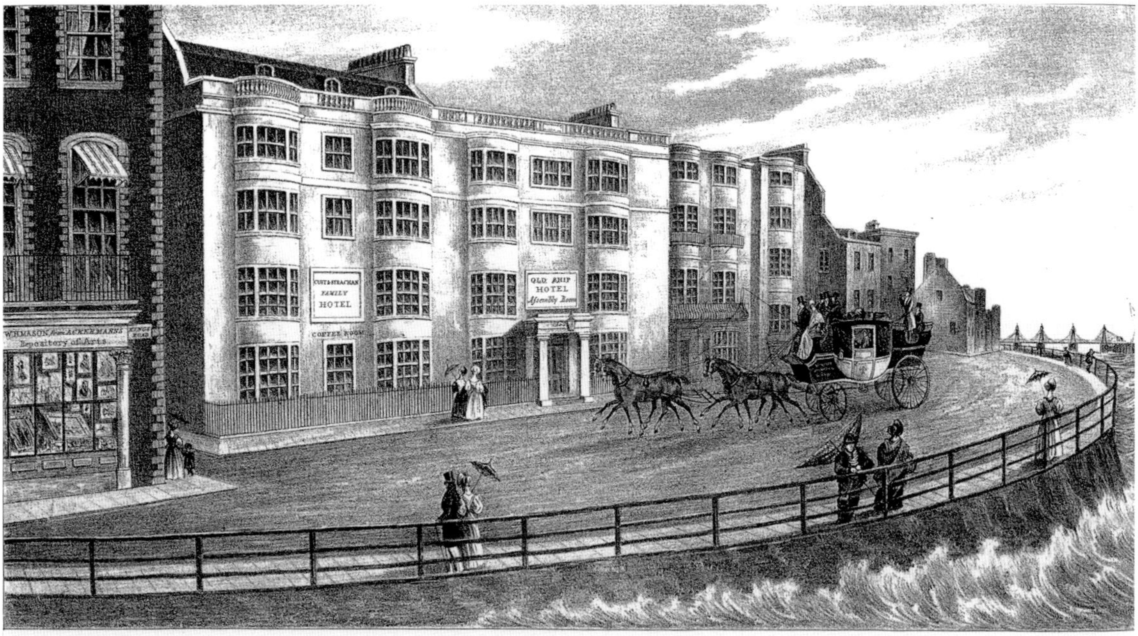

CUFF & STRACHAN.
OLD SHIP HOTEL BRIGHTON

WM64 *Cuff & Strachen, Old Ship Hotel, Brighton*, c1837
One final print is a lithograph that has no identified artists or publication line, the left-hand detail of which is shown at [**43**], and which could well be a Mason publication (see page 122 *n*6).

The curve in the road, going eastwards past the Old Ship towards Pool Valley, is a little accentuated in the print, and the oak railings lasted until the 1880s, when the replacement cast iron ones were installed. This first part of the original sea wall was started in 1825. Thomas Attree, the freeholder of Mason's premises, also owned the hotel, which he leased to Edward Cuff and John Strachan from 1834 for £604 a year.[1]

1 Flower: *Op.cit.*, 1986. p106

Appendix 3
Artists from the Earp family

Described as 'Brighton's most distinguished family of artists', the Earps were William Mason's most used artists. Their ancestors were the Van Earps from the Netherlands. Artists' names in **bold**.

- **George John Earp** (London 1795-Brighton 1854) *Self-taught artist*
  - **George Earp Jr** (London 1818-Brighton 1888)
    - Georgianna Earp (1842-1920)
    - **Charles (William) Earp** (1844-1880)
    - **Edwin John Earp** (Brighton 1848-Lewes 1931)
      - **Clarence Alfred Earp** (Brighton 1872-Lewes 1938)
        - Stella Earp (1906-1929)
        - **St John Clarence Earp** (Lewes 1909-Brighton 1955)
          - **St John William George Drinkwater Earp** (1937-1990)
      - Ida Clara Earp (1878-1891)
    - Herbert George Earp (1849-1851)
    - **Jesse Inson Earp** (Brighton 1852-Barnet 1915) *Known as Inson, also a composer*
    - **William H Earp** (1854-) *Moved to London*
    - Emily Elizabeth Earp (1858-) *musician*
  - Elizabeth A Earp (London 1825-Brighton 1901)
  - **Frederick Earp** (London 1827-Brighton 1898) *Taught art at St Mary's Hall and Lancing College*
    - **Willie Arthur Earp** (1867-1927)
    - Lilian M R Earp (1877-1948)
  - **Henry Earp** (London 1831-Brighton 1914) *Taught Aubrey Beardsley at the Grammar School*
    - **Edith Mary Earp** (1873-1953)
    - Henry Edward Earp
    - Mabel Blanche Earp
    - Mabel Blanche Earp

Index

Principal references are in **bold**.
References to images are in *italics*.